SYSTEMS DRAFTING

SYSTEMS DRAFTING

CREATIVE REPROGRAPHICS FOR ARCHITECTS AND ENGINEERS

FRED A. STITT

McGRAW-HILL BOOK COMPANY

New York   St. Louis   San Francisco   Auckland
Bogotá   Hamburg   Johannesburg   London
Madrid   Mexico   Montreal   New Delhi
Panama   Paris   São Paulo   Singapore
Sidney   Tokyo   Toronto

TO MY PARENTS: JACK AND LEONE STITT

TO TWO GLENDALE TEACHERS, MR. A. I. SMITH AND
MR. TAYLOR, WHO KNEW HOW TO ENCOURAGE INNOVATION

AND TO THE MEMORY OF FRANK LLOYD WRIGHT, WHO USED TO
WALK INTO HIS DRAFTING ROOM SHOUTING, "SIMPLIFY! SIMPLIFY!"

Library of Congress Cataloging in Publication Data
Stitt, Fred A
    Systems drafting.

    Includes index.
    1. Structural drawing. 2. Architectural drawing
3. Mechanical drawing. 4. Copying processes.
I. Title.
T355-S75   604'.2   79-20128
ISBN 0-07-061550-0

The editors for this book were Jeremy Robinson and Christine M. Ulwick, the designer was Mark E. Safran, and the
production supervisor was Thomas G. Kowalczyk. It was
set in Melior by Waldman Graphics, Inc.

Printed and bound by Halliday Lithograph.

On the Cover: Multicolor working drawing floor plan courtesy of Bill
Smith, Jarvis Putty Jarvis, Architects, Dallas, Texas

CONTENTS

PREFACE

Architects and engineers already have a pretty good idea of what Systems Drafting and reprographics are all about. Almost all have used some kind of photoreproduction or appliques or paste-up at one time or another. Most of that experience has been very limited, however, and frequently disappointing. Limited experience has led to some pretty widespread misconceptions and misunderstandings. I've personally been experimenting with new production systems since 1960, and the reservations and considerations I heard then are the same ones I hear now. There's nothing wrong with some reasonable caution and skepticism, but most of the fears or concerns are groundless.

For example, if you mention new drafting systems and reprographics, architects and engineers start talking about big equipment and big repro costs. It isn't necessarily so. Not that you can't spend lots of money if you want to. But high costs and high technology machines are *not* a necessary part of new systems. They're just options.

Smaller-office designers say systems are OK for the large firms, but too complex and costly for *them*. This is not so. Many one-person offices get full benefit from systems, as do medium-sized firms and the largest interdisciplinary, international companies.

Creative, design-conscious people say the systems are OK for hack work, but *their* stuff is too original to be standardized. They're half right. "Hack work," that is, highly standardized construction with many repetitive elements, is ideal for integrated drafting systems. So job shops that adopt systems become even more like job shops. The systems, however, are also a boon for the most design-conscious office. They give designers new power to manipulate design elements, to rearrange them, revise them, refine them, and vary them with far more speed and control than

are available with pen or pencil and paper. Sometimes the designers in an office use the new techniques long before production people can be persuaded to.

In terms of construction-drawing production, the integrated systems have a clear-cut selling point: They save time and money. You can do more with less. Saving time and money means accelerating the design and production process. That meshes better with client and financing needs and especially with phased and fast-track construction.

There is another advantage: enhanced direct control over your work. There are fewer people on a project, and the time span is shorter. That means fewer conflicts, fewer arbitrary revisions and counterrevisions, less confusion, and greater clarity.

If you're a designer, you'll find your original design intent surviving the design development, production, and construction processes with greater integrity than you might be used to—and with fewer hassles along the way.

Every office that has adopted systems has a story to tell. Spencer Jue of Stone Marraccini and Patterson in San Francisco reported the firm doing the same amount of work as 10 years earlier, with only half the production staff.

Jerry Quebe of Hansen Lind Meyer (HLM) in Iowa City says they've reduced their budget for production from 40% of gross fee to 32%—a good 8% savings. HLM reported doing one aspect of their work—using symbols and titles on appliques—in one-tenth the time required for hand drawing and lettering.

Cynthia Phifer of the Princeton office of Geddes Brecher Qualls Cunningham says a restoration project that would normally take 80 to 150 person-hours per detail sheet took 24 hours through the use of photodrafting.

Bob Stauder of Hellmuth, Obata, and Kassabaum wrote that they had gained a 20% savings in construction-drawing cost by switching to a sophisticated freehand detail-drawing system.

Ray James of James-Childers in Oklahoma estimates they started saving 10 to 15% of drawing time and cost just by switching to a typewritten notation system.

A Phoenix design office tells us they're getting 85% reusability of construction details from their unusually well-conceived and organized standard detail system. A partner of that firm tells of a colleague who's now getting 80 to 90% reusability of final design drawings using overlay drafting and photocopying.

And so it goes. The most common story (I've heard it dozens of times now) is the one about the typical job that used to take 12 people and 6 months now taking 6 people and 3 months. The figures vary, but the net gain is about the same each time I hear it.

Naturally not all firms have done well with systems, and I'll report why in this book. And not all are rigorous in measuring their successes—they just say there's more money left over in the drawer after a project than there used to be, and that's convincing enough. One such architect approached me at the 1977 American Institute of Architects (AIA) convention and said, while jingling change in his pocket, "Fred, we've started using those systems you talk about, and now we're making so much money, why, it's almost indecent!"

Here are some of the specific advantages of using new techniques—all reported by offices that are well into systems:

Lower bids because of greater clarity and finer coordination within the construction documents.

Greater accuracy and fewer interferences in the work of various disciplines and construction trades.

Fewer construction claims for extras.

Reduced liability risk because of readability and accuracy of the drawings.

Less conflict with contractors because the "booklike" printed quality of the prints conveys more credibility and authority.

Faster construction phase. Drawings can be fast-tracked to match fast-track construction.

Impressive appearance of final prints. Many offices use them as brochures to demonstrate high standards of quality.

Improved and simplified coordination and control of the various consultants' work and greatly reduced lag time between delivery of architectural data and return of consultants' data.

It goes on and on. *I can't imagine where you'd ever find so many benefits from just one single fundamental change in office practice.* And that includes the computer-aided design (CAD) and automated drafting (AD) coming down the line. Computer drafting, when fully developed, will still require all the same basic revisions of procedure required by the systems described in this book. And the computer changeover won't work without those changes in procedure. Consequently, the offices that are most eagerly looking forward to computer drafting are those that are already most deeply committed to reprographic systems. If you want to go computer later, these systems will make it possible.

That list of benefits will grow and grow as people find new uses for their new tools. There's one benefit in particular to look at. It's subtle but potentially the most important of all. I'll describe it from a personal viewpoint:

My main interest in life is studying the mental processes of creative problem solving. I chose architecture as a career because, at its best, it's specifically a problem-solving profession. Architecture deals with the widest spectrum of problems of any profession, encompassing, as it does, the arts, the social sciences, and technology.

As I moved into my chosen profession, I discovered, with much enthusiastic interest, that the design professions themselves had problems. Everyone in the profession was hurt by them to some degree. The most hurt of all were the most sensitive young designers and the most creative young innovators. They'd come out of school (if they survived school), go into practice, and get swatted like flys.

Since first observing all that, I've given most of my working life to studying and experimenting, talking and writing about problem-solving processes and about problems and solutions within the design professions.

The sources of the problems are deeply rooted and broadly intertwined. The philosophies that govern the schools are part of it—as are the building and zoning codes, and the professional licensing system, and the constraints of the professional societies on their members. Those and other factors add up to a diffused but weighty repression throughout the design profession. It's far harder than it should properly be to step out and do something truly adventurous, innovative, or beautiful. The tools seem to be missing—or locked up somewhere.

The traditional tools of the design professions are, most charitably, hopelessly archaic (grinding graphite on paper—instruments that are actually centuries old!). The habits of thought that go with the old tools are equally archaic.

Design opportunities of unparalleled scope and complexity are opening up: from undersea communities and orbiting space colonies on one hand to aesthetically, psychologically, and environmentally integrated, small, personal habitats on the other. And there are plenty of other new opportunities and problems in between those extremes. The opportunities and problems are too important, too elaborate for traditional methods and tools. The laborious seat-of-the-pants techniques are no match for the scope, intensity, complexity, and pace of design in the remaining years of this century.

ACKNOWLEDGMENTS

Creating a book of this scope is a long and rather hellish endeavor. I owe a great debt of thanks to those who so capably stuck it out with me: my partner in *Guidelines*, Marjorie Stitt; editorial assistant, Christine Dorffi; and for typing and additional editorial assistance, Cynthia Hilton.

And special thanks to all the innovative people who also helped to make this book possible: Ned H. Abrams, AIA, Design Production Techniques, Los Altos, CA; Philip Bennett, University of Wisconsin, Madison, WI; George Borkovich, Editor, *The Paper Plane*, Philadelphia, PA; Ernest Burden, New York, NY; E. L. (Chris) Christopher, DuPont, Los Altos, CA; Robert Allan Class, Director, Practice Division, American Institute of Architects; Jack Cushing and Catheleen Cushing Calcott, Mini-Max, Chicago, IL; Louis DiPaolo, Reprostat, New York, NY; Michael Goodwin, Michael and Kemper Goodwin, Tempe, AZ; Richard C. Hein, AIA, Anshen and Allen, San Francisco, CA; C. Page Highfill, Highfill-Smith Associates, Richmond, VA; Donald Jarvis, FAIA, William Smith, and William Workman, Jarvis Putty Jarvis, Dallas, TX; Spencer Jue, Stone Marraccini and Patterson, San Francisco, CA; Paul Koze, Blue Print Service, San Francisco, CA; E. Russell Molpus, Aeck Associates, Atlanta, GA; Edgar Powers, Jr., Gresham and Smith, Nashville, TN; Jerry Quebe, AIA, Hansen Lind Meyer, Iowa City, IA and Chicago, IL; Stuart Rose and John Simons, Professional Development Resources, Inc., Washington, DC; Terry Schilling, Schilling and Arnold, Oakland, CA; Brian Smith, AIA, RIBA, New York, NY; August K. Strotz, AIA, Tiburon, CA; Roland D. Thompson, FAIA, Design and Construction Procedures, New York, NY; Jack Wally, Opti-Copy, North Kansas City, MO; and C. Herbert Wheeler, Jr., FAIA, Department of Architectural Engineering, Pennsylvania State University, University Park, PA.

FRED A. STITT

SYSTEMS DRAFTING
WHAT IS IT AND WHY BOTHER?

The easiest way to grasp the essence of Systems Drafting is to think of recycling. "Systems Drafting" is the application of the recycling principle to the drafting room.

A staggering amount of perfectly reusable drawing has been thrown away over the years. It's been tossed out, forgotten, then recreated and redrawn when needed for a new job. Similarly, an immense amount of project data is drawn, then drawn again for the same project, and then drawn again and again. Sometimes the same basic floor plan appears dozens of times in a set of drawings—drawn from scratch each time. In addition, there are repetitions within the floor plans; for example, the same stairs may appear a half dozen times on the same plan, each stair drawn as if it were the first one ever invented.

There's lots of other information that's repeated over and over. It's always illuminating to take a set of prints and red-mark just how many repetitions there are. Even the most unique buildings are full of them.

There are details that repeat both in architectural and structural drawings: general notes; schedule forms; portions of exterior elevations; symbols; titles; and so on.

Many times a repeat isn't obvious as a repeat because it's not 100% identical. A suite of rooms that's reversed in plan from another suite is a repeat, for example, even if it is a mirror image. A symmetrical half of an auditorium plan or office building floor plan is a repeat. So are the ¼"-,⅛"-, and ¹⁄₁₆"-scale drawings of the same plans that often appear in a set of construction drawings. There are always a multitude of partial repeats, as when wall sections are created showing one common basic wall construction with variations in through-wall openings: spandrels, headers, etc.

Architects and engineers have noted these repetitions for years, and many have done their best to cut out the waste. But it's almost always been a partial and piecemeal effort. One draftsperson creates an elaborate set of rubber stamps to take care of common titles and symbols—with limited success. Another has small repeat elements printed onto stickyback applique—again with partial success. Others go to the typewriter, the camera, office copiers—and most often are stymied by unexpected limitations of equipment and materials.

Now, at last, enough people have gone through the trial-and-error experiments that we have some good information for avoiding the old limitations and unexpected problems. That's why this book was created. People are recycling their drawing and other graphic information now as never before.

After passing through the slowdown of the learning period, the innovators are saving impressive amounts of time and money. They're also discovering many more opportunities for reusing repetitive elements than anyone initially suspected.

That's one of the most exciting aspects of this whole field. First you try some new techniques to solve a mundane production problem. As you use the techniques, new uses come to mind. After a while, you discover new applications far beyond the original intention.

Thus designers find out they design faster and with more assurance using new tricks with photo, composite, and overlay systems. The principals of a firm discover their working drawings are suddenly in demand—documents so sharp in appearance that they're impressing prospective clients more than the office brochures are. People on the job site find the new drawings are uniquely valuable in coordinating trades and subcontractors. Everyone discovers a new kind of continuum: more ways to reuse drawings from design development, through construction, through graphics for the finished building.

I cited recycling, or reusability, as the essence of Systems Drafting. Sometimes that idea causes confusion in people's minds and requires some clarification. For example, it doesn't mean that building designs become mass-produced.

People will argue that their buildings, their designs are too original to be "standardized." No one needs to argue that. The point is, there are going to be repetitions no matter how unique the project. I've studied and written about Frank Lloyd Wright for many years. I've spent time with Paolo Soleri in Arizona and Bruce Goff in Oklahoma. You can't find more original designers than those men. Yet even they didn't invent whole new structural and construction and mechanical systems—at least not for every single job. Nor did they create whole new symbols, titles, drawing conventions, general notes, details, schedules, and all the rest of the graphic nuts and bolts of construction drawings. There are repetitions—no matter how unique or how high-quality the design.

Another source of confusion is: There are different kinds of repetitions, and some of them shouldn't exist at all. There's no point in using the finest new systems to clutter up drawings with extraneous redundancies. Frank Lloyd Wright sometimes entered his drafting room saying loudly: "Simplify! Simplify!" And he and his people did simplify their drawings considerably by eliminating unnecessary information. He used modular design grids as a built-in measuring grid for the contractor, so many working drawing floor plans out of the Taliesin drafting room required virtually no dimensioning.

I deal with problems of overdrawing and simplification further on in this book. That subject leads to another source of confusion. Drawings can be *underdrawn*, as well as overdrawn, to the point of unreadability. The trick is to eliminate the extreme excesses but keep *some* redundancy. Then use the easiest ways possible to create that redundancy, without drawing and redrawing.

The purpose of Systems Drafting is to eliminate waste in producing production drawings. The purpose of the drawings is to convey design and construction data to contractors so that they can make the design into a real object.

One of the main problems that drafting staff have when being introduced to new systems is that they've never learned what their drawings are for. They think their role is to *draw*. They believe drawings are the means *and* the end.

The misunderstanding starts in school. Students are graded on their *drawing*. Later, when looking for work, the prospective employer wants to see their *drawings*. At the drafting board, virtually all the draftsperson can look for in job satisfaction is to do high-quality drawing. Quality in drafting isn't necessarily the same as producing quality construction documents. In fact, they may be mutually exclusive. I remember having a small knot of draftspeople crowd around and admire an elaborately drawn and lettered set of details I had done. It was a beautiful document to someone who admires drafting, but it was highly repetitive in its parts, useless to the contractor, and needlessly expensive for the boss and the client.

Drafting staff have to revise their perceptions a bit. Their job is *not* to draw. Their job is to *produce graphic construction information*. Drawing is only *one* of the ways to do that.

"Producing graphic construction information" is a far more complex beast than laying down a sheet of paper and drawing on it. The phrase contains far more options than that. There are very limited ways of drawing on paper. There are virtually unlimited ways of "producing graphic construction information." And the key to all of them is *reusability*. You find the reusable or partly reusable data and then manipulate it. There's no limit to your options:

You can enlarge or reduce an element, move it anywhere you want in the drawings. You can turn it upside down or sideways, reverse it, make a mirror image of it.

You can multiply an element, make as many copies as you want. You can combine and recombine them any way you want, in any size you want.

You can reproduce any part of a drawing that's reusable and leave the rest.

You can combine drawings, photos, diazo prints, office-copier prints. You can use originals, elements from old drawings, photos from the job site, or items from catalogs or technical books. You can use them, modify them, and adapt them any way you want to.

You can alter the lightness or darkness of a drawing element. You can make a common repeat part as a gray "shadow print" background for the unique information to be added. When you really get into it, you can add and manipulate color as a clarifier for the documents.

I've just listed your primary areas of control: size, location, position, quantity of repetitions, selectivity, darkness or lightness, color, and reuse from outside sources. All of these options are made comparatively easy with reprographics and Systems Drafting. You can do the same things with traditional drafting, that is, with pencil and eraser. It just takes infinitely longer, and there are more steps, errors, and ambiguities along the way.

Some of the traditional pencil pushers in the trade like to call Systems Drafting "assembly-line stuff." "How are things at the factory?" they ask their faster-moving colleagues. It's a little galling to hear that, even if it's partly true. The lead pencil and paper users all do the same "assembly-line stuff" themselves. They just do it ever so slowly.

The word "assembly" has unfortunate connotations for people, but in Systems Drafting it's a fact of life—a very positive fact. If you want to understand systems in a nutshell, just think about what has to happen in any recycling or reuse process. You must first sort out and *separate* certain elements: the reusable from the nonreusable. Then you assemble the reusable materials into something new.

Separation means preparing graphic information with all its potential uses in mind. For example, traditionally, a final design drawing might be prepared with special titles, shadows, planting—various graphic and illustrative devices suitable for presentation to a client. Then, once approved, a production person would redraw or perhaps trace some or all of the presentation drawing for reuse as a production drawing. Nothing else could be done because the original was covered with shadings, textures, and so on, that do not go on working drawings.

Now, however, a designer can bring final design drawings up to the point of reusability, then stop, and, through one means or another, provide a reproducible original for production staff to start on. The designer then proceeds with elements that specifically should go on a presentation drawing. Thus we have a separation process.

Here is another familiar example: Floor plans are used as background by the consultants. To be useful, the floor plans shouldn't be completely cluttered with architectural data. To avoid having the consultant completely redraw or trace the floor plan, you should stop the design of the floor plan at the right time, make reproducibles of it, and then continue the design.

Separation means isolating the reusable and copying it as appropriate for the later assembly process.

Assembly is the next big step after separation. You'll stop drawing so much and start assembling instead, just as the traditionalists say—except there's no actual assembly line. "Paste-up" drafting is an obvious and well-known form of assembling drawings. It's a form of what I call "horizontal assembly."

Systems Drafting consists mainly of horizontal separation and assembly and vertical separation and assembly. I often use the concepts of horizontal and vertical when teaching the relationships of the main divisions of Systems Drafting. They're very useful concepts for getting the idea across.

Visualize yourself at a drafting board, preparing a site-plan drawing sheet. You're not drawing it, you're assembling it. You have a vicinity map copied from a road map. You have some sitework details cut from 8½" × 11" standard sheets. There's a group of photographs that identify important site features, and there's a small map that keys where the photos were taken. There's a copy of the surveyor's plot, altered in size and touched up. There are also some patterned tapes that represent utility and other lines; a print of the building floor plan; a cut-and-fill profile on an 8½" × 11" sheet; a legend of symbols, conventions, and abbreviations; a strip of typewritten general notes and keynotes; landscaping indications on dry-transfer "instant-letter"–type applique sheets; and titles and scales for the various drawings that will be assembed on the drawing sheet. You have all those components and you pull them together, horizontally, to make a collage. That's the way you do applique drafting and composite drafting. Various separate elements are assembled together on a carrying sheet. Later that sheet will be photoprocessed as a reproducible on drafting medium.

Now imagine a different kind of separation and assembly. Suppose you're doing a floor plan. You have a full sheet showing the exterior wall construction, another sheet that shows interior partitions, and still a third sheet that shows notes and dimensions for the previous two drawings. They are created, separated, and will later be assembled into a single composite *vertically*, as a stack of overlays. (The value of doing this kind of separation and assembly will be explained in Chapter 13.)

Or imagine a smaller version of vertical assembly. Suppose you're doing design development drawings. You know your basic building configuration—the mass—is as it should be. You're just refining details of fenestration, mullions, and exterior panel patterns. You want to test different options; so you use a base sheet of the building outline, lay translucent drafting media over the base sheet, and one by one create variations and refinements of the original design. That's vertical separation and assembly. Later you might create a reprographic composite of the building outline and the final exterior components as one "drawing." Use that as a new base sheet. To create a presentation drawing, lay translucent media atop the base and create shadows, textures, planting, human figures, etc. Later combine the entourage overlay with the base sheet reprographically while preserving the original base for later revisions and direct reuse when starting working drawings.

Vertical separation and assembly, or overlay drafting, is also called "pin-register drafting." It's been a mainstay in the mapping industry and in film animation for many years. It's also part of the graphic arts, used mainly to create what they call "color separations" in preparation for offset printing.

Virtually all the techniques, materials, and equipment described in this book provide the means for horizontal or vertical separation and assembly of graphic information. Much of what's said in the chapters ahead will make more sense when viewed from the perspective of the recycling principle and the horizontal or vertical applications of that principle.

ELEMENTS OFTEN REPEATED ON A SINGLE DRAWING

Material identifications and sizes

Room names, space identifications

Dimensions

Rooms or bays

Exterior bays, windows, doors

Elevation repeats from bay to bay

Exterior elevation repeats from floor to floor

Symmetrical sections

Common backgrounds, such as wall sections that vary only in specific sill and header details

ELEMENTS OFTEN REPEATED FROM DRAWING TO DRAWING IN THE SAME PROJECT

All the above plus:

Title block data

Floor plans: portions at large scale, others at small scale

Floor plans: backgrounds for engineers, consultants

Structural grids, planning modules, ceiling grids, paving patterns, parking patterns

Symbols

Key or reference plan

Schedule formats

Drawing titles, titles of components on drawing sheets

ELEMENTS OFTEN REPEATED FROM DISCIPLINE TO DISCIPLINE (STRUCTURAL, MECHANICAL, PLUMBING, ELECTRICAL, ETC.)

All the above plus:

Site plan

Floor plans

Building sections for riser diagrams

Equipment and fixture connection details

ELEMENTS OFTEN REPEATED FROM PROJECT TO PROJECT AND OFFICE TO OFFICE

All the above plus:

Drawing border and title block design

Schedule forms

Nomenclature lists, symbols, legends, abbreviations list

Construction details (see the list in Chapter 9)

Wall sections

General notes

Materials indications, walls, partition materials

Titles

Fig. 1-1. **Commonly repeated elements in construction drawings.**

The book is laid out according to what I call the "five stages of transition" to Systems Drafting. The stages are outlined in the next chapter. The stages are a logical sequence for moving into Systems with a minimum of disruption and a maximum of success.

Each major chapter closes with a Synthesis section that relates the technique(s) in the chapter with those described just before and those coming in the next chapter. These sections integrate part to part and parts to the whole idea. Later, you'll find these sections and chapter summaries of main points to be valuable refresher reading.

You can also profit by reading the Synthesis sections in a string before reading the main body of the book. They provide the larger picture and convey the truth of this whole subject: mainly, that all the systems, subsystems, techniques, and so on, in this book are integral parts of one *big system*. When you grasp the parts and how they relate, you'll gain tremendous control and flexibility. You'll be able to pick and choose, almost automatically, what techniques and materials are just right for each job situation. You'll know how to convey the information efficiently to other people. And, most provocatively, you'll have a whole new way of thinking about construction, about design, about the documents, and about the nature of the design professions in general and your role within them.

FIVE STAGES OF TRANSITION TO SYSTEMS DRAFTING

2.1 INTRODUCTION

Design firms have lost countless hours by plunging into aspects of Systems Drafting prematurely. People get excited about the promise of some material or technique and run off with it—into side tracks and dead ends.

It's easy to get excited when you see a way to reduce drafting time from hours to minutes, weeks to days, or months to weeks. But it's a time-waster when a system isn't chosen, tested, and introduced in a coordinated fashion.

New systems and subsystems have to complement one another. They have to fit in with the office's overall production system and the kinds of projects the office does. They have to work with other equipment and materials that the office is already accustomed to. Production systems should be coordinated with designers' needs, or a large part of their value will never appear. Systems have to be chosen and implemented in a way that complements the staff. If they aren't, there will be trouble galore.

There is a great variety of usable materials, equipment, and techniques for Systems Drafting now, and many more are coming down the line. That's great, except for one problem. Many of them don't work well together. So, besides getting systems that mesh with everything else in your practice, you have to be very selective to be sure they mesh with one another.

It may all seem like a bit much. And it is. But it's worth it and it's manageable. It's manageable if you adopt a system for introducing systems. If you follow a plan, get people used to one technique and material at a time, get techniques adjusted gradually to your project needs, get all the pieces adjusted to one another, and do all this in simple, clear-cut steps and stages, you'll end up with a priceless, productive office asset. If you don't, you'll end up with an endless series of experiments, false starts, and backtrackings.

This book is designed as a guide through a logical step-by-step transition to Systems Drafting. It's laid out according to what I call the "five stages." These stages introduce techniques, equipment, and materials in an integrated progression. Each stage is preparation for the stage to follow. Each stage is reinforcement and elaboration of the stages already implemented.

The stages have many flexible components. No one is going to start right from the first of Stage 1 as I describe it in this book and proceed one-two-three all the way through. For one thing, most offices are already in a mixture of stages. For another, most offices will adopt a combination of techniques and stages and push them through simultaneously rather than consecutively. That's OK so long as it is done with finesse.

When I train management and staff in systems, I always urge them to do some backtracking—to exploit what they've accomplished, but at the same time, to get back to Stage 1 and other earlier stages and fill in the gaps. Filling in the gaps will prevent lots of time and energy wastage.

One of the most glaring problems among offices well into a mixture of systems is that they use advanced methods to produce graphics that shouldn't be done at all. Their finish and door schedules cover acres of drawing space. Details are oversized and otherwise deficient. Lettering isn't consistent and is too small to reproduce properly.

There is another problem: Offices that suffer management and supervision difficulties sometimes resort to systems to make up the difference. They try to move ahead of their problems instead of backing up and solving them. Systems, unfortunately, will cure nothing. They just add new layers of complexity and potential hazard. Offices that are well managed to begin with usually do very well with systems. Those that aren't, don't. Thus do I often say: *"Whatever you do, don't bring old problems into new systems."*

The first general stage is plain old "housecleaning." Get the office in order. Straighten out management problems. Redesign the drafting space. Update the standard equipment. Get rid of the silly inconveniences that everyone adjusts to in every office. Above all, simplify and clarify the office's graphic standards. When the drawings are cleaned up, move into ink drafting, drawing on polyester, and other elementary advances. Stage 1, "housecleaning," saves offices so much time and money, people feel safer moving on to the more elaborate improvements.

Next comes Stage 2, "reusing simple data." That's something most offices have done to some degree. Reuse, say, through standard details, through appliques or preprinted elements, through use of schedule forms, and so on, is a simple way to introduce and test aspects of more elaborate systems. And, again, it helps finance further developments.

Then comes Stage 3, "new tools and graphic equipment." This involves the use of typing, photodrafting, and plain paper copiers. Again, this is comparatively simple, especially if the previous stages are well handled.

Next is Stage 4: "composite and overlay drafting." These systems will work, and work well, together—*if* the groundwork has been laid.

Finally, we have Stage 5: "Total Systems Drafting." And then you can add the latest that comes down the road without the major transition problems that less prepared offices will face.

It can all come together so smoothly and painlessly that, if you wanted to, you could introduce systems in an office without ever letting people know what you are doing. Just introduce one simple reform at a time. Back up and change direction slightly if you face some strong opposition, and keep moving forward.

How long will it take for the whole process? Plan on a year or so at least. A few firms that have followed the process successfully took 5 or 6 years to make the changeover. They took their time, used the gradualist approach, and now are in great shape. They're the successful innovators and the inspiration for this five-stage approach.

2.2 THE FIVE-STAGE CHECKLIST

One of the first steps in the first stage is administrative planning of the transition into systems. The following is your first tool in administrative review and planning, and a condensed preview of this book:

STAGE 1: HOUSECLEANING

This stage systematizes and simplifies various working drawing procedures. It paves the way for change and helps ensure the success of more sophisticated systems and techniques, which you'll introduce later on. The main steps in Stage 1 are:

____ Initiate an administrative plan, a long-range program for all the appropriate steps outlined in this five-stage checklist. Include a calendar timetable, deadlines, and time and money budgets for planning and research.

____ Start administrative planning checklists of equipment, materials, and techniques to test and/or introduce.

____ Checklist current techniques, materials, and equipment that you'll keep using, items to reconsider, and items to eliminate.

____ Start an administrative journal in which you'll record results of all tests of equipment, materials, and techniques.

____ Begin formal job planning for all new projects. Prepare miniplan working drawing sheets. Design a wall-chart display of miniplans.

____ Plan for reusability of design development drawings during working drawing phase. Ask design and production staff for input on how to improve continuity in the design-to-production process.

____ Start a "quality control" or "quality assurance" theme. Graphics simplification and standardization can be justified on the basis of construction quality and liability protection.

____ Introduce a regular employee review program. Discuss employees and their development in the office at regular intervals,

separately from review of salaries. Introduce this as a *support* program to allow employees to have a basis for measuring their progress.

____ Employee development review requires closer measurement of drawing budgets and schedules. On the binding margin of each working drawing sheet have a budgeted time allowance chart for draftspersons to record dates and time spent on each sheet. Record time spent in a time and cost data bank.

____ Examine and analyze past working drawings. Identify instances of oversizing, over-elaboration, redundancy, error, and irrelevancy. Mark up prints and initiate a reference checklist.

____ Start or refine the office drafting manual. To set new standards of simplification the manual should be short and may begin with the reference checklist just named above.

____ Introduce drafting reforms such as larger-sized lettering standards, larger symbols, more open spacing in patterns and textures, larger arrowheads, thicker lines, etc. All such size increases are necessary to compensate for photoreduction. Photoreduction is part of Systems Drafting. (Oversizing of lettering and symbols is already required in many building code jurisdictions for microfilm storage of drawings.)

____ Gather employee input on suggested improvements. Declare your intent to support employees more in terms of data and facilities, and ask that they cooperate by using simpler graphic standards and drafting efficiencies. Identify staff who are clearly most interested.

____ Introduce simplest door, window, finish, and other appropriate schedules. Find the clearest and simplest schedules appropriate to various building types. Design schedules to fit office typewriter ratchet spacing, so typewriting will be in phase with schedule-form lines.

____ Restudy your job and drawing numbering system. If practical, introduce the "chapter" or "division" numbering system.

____ Review the technical library for completeness, clarity of indexing, and ease of retrieval and filing.

____ If necessary, replan drafting room for better coordination. Provide special space for graphics paste-up and assembly work. (Some reprographic equipment is noisy, and a sound-insulated space may be necessary as part of the graphics work center.)

_____ Begin training staff in new systems with a "soft" approach: Invite repro shop managers to visit and give lunchtime talks on their processes and the problems they have with certain drawings; send staff on lunchtime visits to blueprint shops to get an overview of how they work; introduce staff to appropriate publications, articles, booklets, and workshops on new production systems.

STAGE 2: REUSING SIMPLE DATA

The first stage, housecleaning, will save considerable time and money in itself. It simplifies office procedures and drawing graphics and makes it possible to move effectively into appliques, reference details, typewritten notation, and other slightly more elaborate reforms. The main steps in Stage 2 are:

_____ Identify types of drawing data that appear from job to job: elaborate symbols, schedule forms, standard general notes, legends, titles, details, etc.

_____ Test various applique products for storing reusable units: offset printing appliques, typing appliques, diazo appliques, and office-copier appliques.

_____ Review headliner machines for cost effectiveness. Test other large-title lettering systems.

_____ Test out tapes, pattern films, and various preprinted appliques in design development and working drawings.

_____ Establish a specific graphics work center for storage and manipulation of applique products. Include light table, applique product catalogs, and applique tools. Reserve space for later introduction of diazo printer, typewriter, flatbed printer, office copier, and reference detail files.

_____ If appropriate, switch over to polyester drafting on a target job. Test the most recommended plastic leads and erasers. Test recommended ink-drafting techniques.

_____ Review the construction details you've used on past jobs. Look for types of details that are often repeated, and prepare a list of likely future reference details.

_____ Meet with senior drafting staff, site representatives, and contractors; discuss details and drawing formats in general. Create a quality control system whereby details used on each future job are reviewed for inclusion in the office reference or standard detail files.

_____ Create your detail file. Require all future job details to be done on 8½″ × 11″ format sheets rather than on full-size working drawing sheets. Encourage freehand detailing by senior drafting staff.

_____ Create the position of "production assistant." The production assistant watches over the graphics work center, handles assembly of appliques onto drawing sheets, and manages the standard details file.

_____ Establish graphic standards for reference or standard details for consistency when assembling on working drawing sheets. Consider using working drawing detail books rather than full-size sheets.

_____ Introduce typewriting of simplified working drawing schedules. Introduce typewriting of notes on reference or standard details. This establishes a pattern of typing procedures. Typing should be by the production assistant, although the regular secretary should be gradually trained as backup typist.

_____ Create full reference or standards sheets, if appropriate (such as a "site-work details" sheet or "structural details" sheet), when a large amount of details appears consistently from job to job.

_____ Create a standard fixture heights schedule as a substitute for drawing interior elevations.

_____ Create standard wall construction sections.

STAGE 3: NEW TOOLS AND GRAPHIC EQUIPMENT

Simplification and consistency in drafting standards lead to reuse of symbols, titles, etc., with applique products. Appliques, once mastered, lead to more ambitious reuse of larger items, such as general notes, schedules, and details. That leads in turn to typewritten notation. The equipment introduced during this phase is a natural continuation of the reforms already established.

The main steps in Stage 3 are:

____ Introduce an appropriate typewriter in the graphics work center. Carbon ribbon with "take-off" correcting feature (such as IBM's Correcting Selectric II typewriter) is recommended. Establish typing elements and standards,

____ Test typing methods when doing reference or standard details, and incorporate more extensively on note blocks in selected jobs.

____ Target appropriate job for photodrafting. Use in-house or photoprocessing-shop techniques, depending on extensiveness of project.

____ When using photodrafting, introduce "keynoting"—a typewritten panel of notes referenced by number bubbles on the photodrawings.

____ Review and introduce screened shadow print background sheets for use by consultants on simpler jobs.

____ Shop, test, and introduce a plain paper copier for use with stickybacks, appliques, photodrafting, typewritten note copying, standard details, and composite or "assembly" drafting. Copier should be part of the graphics work center, but can be auxiliary to the front office as well.

STAGE 4: COMPOSITE DRAFTING AND OVERLAY DRAFTING

Standards, module drawing-sheet design, photocopying, typing, etc., all make it easy to shift into simple composite drafting. Overlay drafting can be introduced simultaneously, but it usually pays to focus on learning one technique at a time. The main steps in Stage 4 are:

____ Target specific future jobs and the best personnel for more ambitious composite and overlay projects. Intend to make these projects come out good *despite* the usual start-up problems and the "learning curve." Pick projects most likely to succeed, and work extremely closely with staff.

____ Plan on having key staff who learn methods on first-trial projects become the "teachers" to other staff members when they shift later to other projects.

____ Use photoreduction and enlargement on any project that utilizes many repeat units at varying scales. Have them assembled for paste-up and photocompositing, either with in-house equipment or out-of-house with photoblowback.

____ Introduce drawing-sheet composites as well as plan composites. Convey and review with staff the whole concept of opaque and translucent composite or "assembly" drafting.

____ Acquire a flatbed printer or vacuum frame to facilitate printing of plan and sheet composites.

____ Use the office copier, a camera, or reflex printer to create translucent copies of opaque paste-up units, to be assembled in turn on the flatbed printer.

____ Make checklists and flow charts showing how to create drawings for flatbed printing onto reproducible media: stop points, drawing for consultants, making check and progress prints, etc.

____ Find an experienced repro shop to work with. Treat the repro shop manager as your graphics consultant.

____ Plan your first overlay job with extreme care. Do a miniature trial run through the whole process.

____ Introduce polyester drafting media, leads, and erasers (or, preferably, the ink techniques).

____ If composite systems are mastered, plan on using them to merge with the overlay system. Target the overlay job with top staff, just as was recommended for first major composite project.

____ Introduce the systems to your consultants. Provide checklists and training information for their staff regarding standards, use of overlays, rules for drafting on polyester, proper sizes of lettering, etc.

STAGE 5: SYSTEMS DRAFTING

At this point, everything has been introduced in logical sequence. A gradual approach has softened employee fears. Cost and time controls have convinced principals in the office that the systems are cost-beneficial. The drawings are looking better than ever and are providing bidding, construction, liability, and marketing benefits.

Stage 5 is the final maturity stage. All systems are understood; media, equipment, and techniques have been chosen and refined so they all work with one another. The preceding transitional steps may now be elaborated with the following:

____ If justifiable, purchase your own process camera and film developers. Provide repro services for colleagues to help offset the costs.

____ Incorporate offset printing of small-size working drawings. Install your own printing press if appropriate.

____ Offset-print multicolor drawings. Print on both sides of the working drawing sheets.

____ Consider restructuring office management and breadth of services. The productivity of drafting staff will be much higher than before: fewer numbers will do more work. Some drafting staff will be able to move into work that is at a higher level than was previously open to them. The office will be much better equipped to respond to needs for instant data, feasibility studies, quick changes during projects, construction management, and fast track.

____ Review a changeover to computer-aided drafting systems. Costs will be coming down. Likeliest systems use "menu" system: storage of common drawing components which you can manipulate on a screen, fix, and translate into drawing with a hard-line plotter. Virtually all work done in transition to reprodrafting systems will serve as the preparation necessary for the transition to computer drafting.

SIMPLIFICATIONS AND REFORMS IN WORKING DRAWINGS

3.1 THE GRADUAL APPROACH

A young architect in a rather stick-in-the-mud design office faced a difficult choice several years back. He wanted to move the firm into more advanced procedures but faced a tangle of indifference, skepticism, and outright hostility. No one in staff or management was anxious to get into anything new. Management especially was resistant, reiterating the favorite saying in the office, "We've got enough troubles as it is."

The architect faced a difficult choice: Should he move on to a more progressive firm or adapt to the old one? The old firm had its problems, but it was basically well managed and the young architect was comfortable there.

So the decision was made. The architect decided to stay put and introduce the new systems on his own—gradually, without saying another word about it. He reasoned that if no one knew what he was doing, no one could form any opposition. (That follows the credo I've always recommended: "Beat them *and* join them.")

The architect had to introduce new techniques without calling attention to the process. That meant cautious planning. He'd have to introduce the simplest reforms first and follow a logical, self-validating, sequence of advancement. As one simple new idea worked out, he could move on to the next slightly more complex one.

And that's what he did. His first reforms were simple, mainly the kinds of things most offices know they should do but don't get around to. He established consistent drafting standards and developed some simplified door and finish schedules (this saved many sheets of work on typical jobs). That led the way to establishing a standard detail system, which in turn led to using appliques and typewriting. That evolved into photoreproduction techniques.

Every step of the way, the reforms made work simpler and increased staff and management confidence in new procedures. No one knew, or needed to know, that the isolated "good ideas" that were being introduced were actually integrated steps in a long-term plan.

Ultimately, when the office became a full-blown systems office, it was far more successful with composite and overlay drafting than were most comparable firms. The main reason was— a point I stress again and again when lecturing on the subject—*they didn't bring old problems into new systems.* They didn't use new systems to create redundant, overdrawn, flawed documents. They cleaned up the act first. That made subsequent steps much easier.

Most design offices find themselves in a mixed situation. They've introduced some new systems, somewhat randomly. They're using new systems to do things that shouldn't be done— such as incorporating overly elaborate schedules. Or their drafting standards haven't been reformed, and the lack of standards interferes with successful use of more advanced systems. For example, wide disparities in drawing styles make it awkward to use standard details. Faint-line drafting and "tight" lettering and drafting don't reproduce well, and that blocks effective use of reprographic techniques.

Thus I always recommend that architects and engineers do some backtracking, no matter how advanced they are. They should do some backtracking and clear up any lingering graphics problems. That's the essence of what I call Stage

1, housecleaning. Some firms need a thorough overhaul: management, office plan, business planning—the whole works top to bottom. That varies. But almost universally, design offices need to clean up and simplify basic procedures and basic drafting graphics.

This chapter deals with the graphics, and *some* related aspects of procedure. The chapter to follow will deal mainly with procedure. Don't be fooled by the simplicity of some of the suggestions to follow. They have brought very large, long-term benefits to the offices that have adopted them—all out of proportion to the minor investment of time and effort that is required.

3.2 LINE WORK

Pencil lines on paper are usually classified as "light," "dark," or "medium." People are taught in drafting classes to differentiate elements of drawing by using dark or light lines—for example, dark for outlines, medium for intermediate elements, and light for background elements.

All that is obsolete. You don't deal with dark or light lines in reprographics and Systems Drafting. *You deal with thick lines or thin ones.* All should be equally dense or opaque—preferably extremely opaque—and vary solely by their width.

Why should consistently dense, opaque lines be used? Why should the lines be categorized by width rather than darkness? What difference does it make? The first difference is the guiding one: clarity. Faint, lightweight line work doesn't reproduce clearly. There are other differences, mainly pertaining to the printing and reproduction systems that go with Systems Drafting. For one thing, you'll be working with photoreproductions along the way, with photo washoff and diazo-reproducible drawings on polyester film. The line work on the reproductions will be extremely dense, differentiated only by width, and any changes and additions made on those drawings will have to match the photo line work.

Further, when preparing drawings for photoreproduction, you have to work with the restrictions of the camera. The camera can't photograph very light line work and very dark line work simultaneously. It has to be set for one or the other. If it is set for one or the other, that means something suffers. If it is set in compromise between extremes, you get a weak result. So for reproduction in general, and photoreproduction in particular, you want clean, clear, opaque lines.

If you get into ink drafting later, you won't have problems with varying darknesses—the ink will be consistently opaque. You'll also get around the problem of inconsistent thicknesses or widths of lines—the pen tips give the same consistent gradations in line widths no matter who's doing the drafting.

But before you get into ink, you may need to deal with problems of overly light or translucent pencil-lead lines, and inconsistency. Usually the problem won't be officewide; only a few people will draw with too light or too erratic a touch. If they do, give them a sample of what you want and ask them to practice a bit on their own time to come up to the office standard.

3.3 DRAWING AND LETTERING FOR REPRODUCTION

Here's the rule on lettering in a nutshell: *Keep it large and consistent.* This also happens to be the hardest rule for drafting staff to follow. If a draftsperson is a little shaky, it'll show up much more with large lettering than with small. If a draftsperson is a little unsure of his or her touch, it'll show up all the more with large lettering. In addition, large lettering seems inconvenient sometimes because it may not fit well on crowded drawings. The latter barrier to larger lettering is eliminated through other aspects of Systems Drafting. Crowded drawings become a thing of the past.

Why use large lettering? It is not for size as an end in itself. It is for clarity and for readability. All other things being equal, large lettering is easier to read. That clarifies the documents. In addition, new production systems rely on multiple stages of photoreproduction or diazo reproduction. If lettering isn't large and clear, it won't survive the reproduction stages that it may be subjected to. Especially it won't survive *reduction.* Photoreduction is a very large part of Systems Drafting, and no one should be caught unprepared for it.

Another argument is that the larger graphics make for easier-to-read bidding and job-site prints. On some prints you can't tell the rips, wrinkles, dirt, and scribbles from the drafting.

If clarity and readability aren't convincing reasons for using large lettering, it really doesn't matter. As of this writing, many city building code enforcement agencies require that construction documents be "microfilmable." Eventually, the requirement will be universal.

Building code jurisdictions have storage and retrieval problems. Microfilm isn't well suited for storing large documents with small, detailed drawings on them. Microfilm images—line work, symbols—tend to swell slightly and clog up when enlarged and reprinted. So you have to enlarge and space out drafting elements to allow for this.

It happens that the rules for drawing for microfilm are the same as the rules for drawing for reprographics in general. They are also the same as drawing for half-sized reproductions—an-

LETTERING

For uniformity of Construction Documents it is desirable to have uniform lettering. Since many people contribute to the production of the drawings, lettering is one area where artistic individuality can and should be avoided.

The trend towards machine lettering of drawings may eventually take care of this situation. Still, corrections to these drawings are inevitable and it is usually more practical to free-hand letter them. The ever-increasing practice of issuing reduced drawings makes it imperative that lettering be not only plain and legible, but also larger and wider-spaced.

SAMPLE

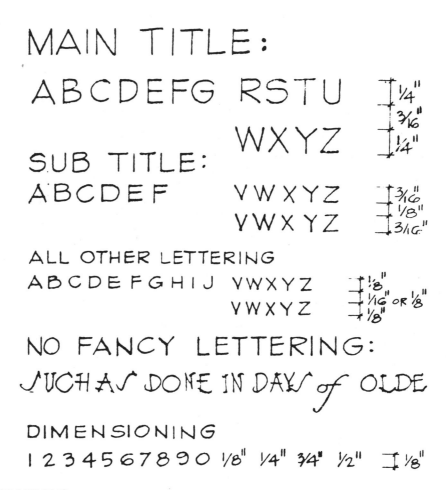

RECOMMENDATIONS

1. All, including Consultants' drawings, to be plain, block vertical capitals.

2. Sizes —
   Main or Major Titles — 1/4'' high
   Minor or Subtitles — 3/16'' high
   All Other Lettering — 1/8'' high

3. Spacing between letters or between lines of lettering shall be adequate to result in clear, legible, ½ size reduced drawings.

4. Fancy lettering is not permitted (see sample).

5. If lettering-aids, such as triangles, are used, care shall be taken that all strokes are of same value and width.

6. Notation to be connected to an item with a simple line ending in a plain, hand-drawn arrow.

7. Avoid **underlining** and exclamation points!

Fig. 3-1. Recommendations for lettering.

(Northern California Chapter of the American Institute of Architects, Task Force on Production Office Procedures.)

Actual Size of Lettering	¾ Size Reduction	⅔ Size Reduction	½ Size Reduction	⅓ Size Reduction	¼ Size Reduction
ABCD abcdef 12345	ABCD abcdef 12345	ABCD abcdef 12345	ABCD abcdef 12345	ABCD abcdef 12345	ABCD abcdef 12345
ABCDEF abcdefgh 1234567	ABCDEF abcdefgh 1234567	ABCDEF abcdefgh 1234567	ABCDEF abcdefgh 1234567	ABCDEF abcdefgh 1234567	ABCDEF abcdefgh 1234567
ABCDEFGHIJK abcdefghijklmno 1234567890°."	ABCDEFGHIJK abcdefghijklmno 1234567890°."	ABCDEFGHIJK abcdefghijklmno 1234567890°."	ABCDEFGHIJK abcdefghijklmno 1234567890°."	ABCDEFGHIJK abcdefghijklmno 1234567890°."	ABCDEFGHIJK abcdefghijklmno 1234567890°."
ABCDEFGHIJKLMNOP 1234567890 °."= % ()	ABCDEFGHIJKLMNOP 1234567890 °."= % ()	ABCDEFGHIJKLMNOP 1234567890 °."= % ()	ABCDEFGHIJKLMNOP 1234567890 °."= % ()	ABCDEFGHIJKLMNOP 1234567890 °."= % ()	ABCDEFGHIJKLMNOP 1234567890 °."= % ()
ABCDEFGHIJKLMNOPQRSTUV 1234567890 ° " = () %	ABCDEFGHIJKLMNOPQRSTUV 1234567890 ° " = () %	ABCDEFGHIJKLMNOPQRSTUV 1234567890 ° " = () %	ABCDEFGHIJKLMNOPQRSTUV 1234567890 ° " = () %	ABCDEFGHIJKLMNOPQRSTUV 1234567890 ° " = () %	ABCDEFGHIJKLMNOPQRSTUV 1234567890 ° " = () %

Fig. 3-2. Lettering reduction guide.

other important part of Systems Drafting. Here are the rules:

1. Use larger lettering—minimum ⅛″-high letters—and ³⁄₃₂″ space between lines of lettering. Letters in major titles should be a minimum of ¼″ high; minor titles, ³⁄₁₆″ high.
2. Space out, stretch out, and enlarge all minor symbols, such as door and window symbols, inch marks, arrowheads, and loops in letters and numbers.
3. Don't let line work touch letters or numerals; don't let fractional numbers touch division lines. Otherwise they'll run together and blob up in the microfilming and blowback process. Similarly, spread out all texture patterns, crosshatching, materials indications, parallel line work, and so on, to about twice normal spacings. Avoid paste-ups or appliques that leave hazy background on diazo prints.
4. Include an arrow or tick line at the midpoint of each drawing border line to aid the microfilm photographer in centering camera focus on the drawing sheets.

3.4 DESIGNING WORKING DRAWING SHEETS

Most design professionals know the importance of planning working drawing sets and planning individual working drawing sheets. But *designing* working drawing sheets is another matter. Every office does it at one time or another, but rarely do they appreciate the great opportunity they have. A *good* working drawing sheet design will expedite the work for everyone: design and drafting staff, reproduction people, and the contractors.

When you start planning for Systems Drafting, a good drawing sheet design is even more important. Here's what working drawing sheet design consists of:

1. Sizing
2. Along with sizing, the creation of a drawing module
3. Tick marks, scales, and other incidental data for the convenience of reprographic staff and others
4. Small recordkeeping forms, borders, cut marks, and title blocks

Start with sizing and a drawing module. Standard engineering drawing sizes are already established. All are multiples of 8½″ × 11″: "A" size is 8½″ × 11″; "B" is 11″ × 17″; "C" is 17″ × 22″; "D" is 22″ × 34″; and "E" is 34″ × 44″. The basic 8½″ × 11″ module is already built-in with those sizes, so the next step is to settle on a division of 8½″ × 11″ as a submodule. The most popular and natural one is 4¼″ × 5½″—a quarter size of the 8½″ × 11″ sheet. The 4½″ × 5½″ is adequate for most single detail drawings and the 4¼″ width is OK for most columns of general notes, indexes, small schedules, etc.

The 8½″ × 11″ sheet module and the submodule are not just a trivial nicety: they're essential to well-organized drawing sheets. They're especially important in Systems Drafting for three reasons:

1. You'll most likely be creating standard details, standard notes, legend, nomenclature, and symbols lists, and you'll want them to fit together and to fit with the overall drawings they go on.

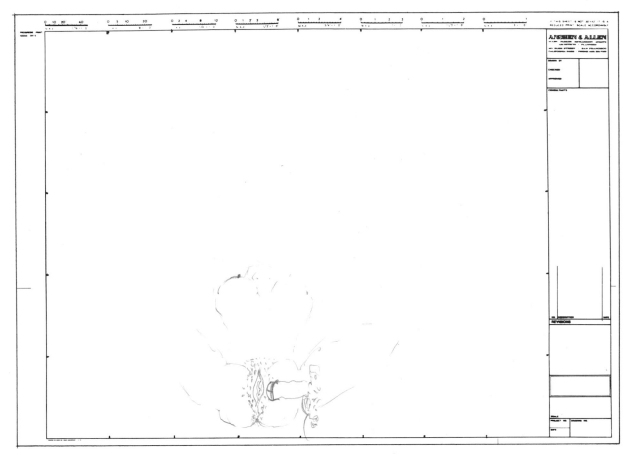

While numerous sheet sizes are now in use by the profession, surveys have indicated that the most commonly used size is 30" x 42".

The reasons are understandable. It is a manageable size, readily available in standard cut tracing and printing sheets, as well as being compatible with the most practical sizes of drafting, reproduction and plan storage equipment.

The recommendation of the 30" x 42" size sheet as a basic standard for the profession is based on the above considerations, as well as the study of layout which divides the drawing body of the sheet into modules that will accommodate details developed on modules of ¼ of an 8½" x 11" sheet.

Letter-sized (8½" x 11") master sheets, containing one or more standard details are easily filed for repetitive use in paste-up and photographic drafting.

While the title block design may be left to the discretion of the individual office, it is recommended that this also be confined to the vertical column of modules

on the right hand of the sheet and that the most pertinent identifying information be positioned so that it is visible when the sheet is folded for mailing or filing.

It is further recommended that all title block lettering be placed parallel to the base of the sheet.

Schematic, presentation or special requirements may dictate that other sizes be used at times. In any event, the selection should be confined to the standard cut sizes now on the market.

RECOMMENDATIONS

1. The overall sheet size is 30" x 42". Both standard cut sheets in tracing paper and diazo paper are available.

2. The sheet is divided into 45, 4-3/8" x 5-5/8" modules.

3. The five vertical modules on the right side are for the title block.

4. Title block should be designed with information in the following areas:

a) Lower corner:
   Job Indentification, Sheet Title, Scale, Sheet Number, Job No., Drawing Date.

b) Upper corner:
   Firm Name and Address, Signature and Initials of project team members, Consultants' Name and Address, Approval agency names.

c) Space between a and b from top to bottom:
   Sheet Notes, Key Plan, Revision identifications.

5. Details may be drawn on one or multiple modules.

6. If standard office details are developed on modules of 4¼" x 5½" (¼ of an 8½" x 11" sheet), they can be assembled to fit any of the modules on the tracing.

7. If drawing is reduced, "Reduced Print" note must be shown.

8. The Graphic Scales indicated on the top margin will help in establishing the actual size of drawing.

Fig. 3-3. Working drawing sheet design recommendations.

(Northern California Chapter of the American Institute of Architects, Task Force on Production Office Procedures.)

2. You'll learn later the extreme value of creating large drawings out of small subdrawings. A partial floor plan may be on an 11″ × 17″ sheet; a few details on a 4¼″-wide vertical strip; some keynotes on a 4¼″-wide strip; a schedule and general notes on partial 8½″ × 11″ sheets. They're all created or derived from different sources. Ultimately they're assembled and made into a single 22″ × 34″ photo or diazo reproducible (a "second original" that is then treated as a single original tracing). If all the pieces are on module, they'll fit easily, and sheet planning, composition, and reprographic reproduction is a relative snap.

3. The reproduction media—diazo sheets, office-copier sheets, photographic products, standard paper for offset printing—all are sized at 8½″ × 11″ or multiples thereof.

The popular architectural drawing sizes, 24″ × 36″ and 30″ × 42″, are "off" size. They're not multiples of 8½″ × 11″. But if they're the sizes you plan to use, you can design border lines to encompass some multiple or division of 8½″ × 11″.

Architectural drawing title blocks are normally top-to-bottom strips on the right-hand side of the drawing. A "half-sheet" module of 4¼″ is OK for a title block for very large sheets, but is excessive for smaller ones. Many vertical title blocks are made at 2⅛″ width—a further subdivision of 8½″.

Many firms include a "general notes" column space adjacent to the left of the top-to-bottom title block. That column can be combined with the 2⅛″ or 4¼″ title block to make a complete module strip.

NOTE: *Drawing design has to allow for likely "half-size" reductions in working drawing prints. If final prints are made half-size, then it pays to hold back typewritten general notes, or strips of keynotes. That is, don't reduce the columns of general notes or keynotes to half size when reducing the rest of the drawing. Instead, have the rest of the drawing photoreduced and have full-sized typed notes stripped in on the final half-size reproduction. That makes for superior readability.*

If you use or will use standard details, you'll design them according to a modular subdivision of 8½″ × 11″—one that will fit either a detail book or your large working drawing sheet sizes.

There's additional data you might want to include. Following are typical items that can be helpful on preprinted drawing sheets:

8½″ × 11″ tick marks around the borders to indicate the large module of the sheet, which aids in composition of graphic units on the drawing. It's also convenient as a guide for folding to 8½″ × 11″ size prints that have to be mailed.

Smaller tick marks at the edges showing the submodule.

Centerline tick marks for short and long dimensions of the sheet. That's an aid for photographers, especially when drawings are microfilmed.

A small printed note at the border stating the actual size of the original drawing. This helps avoid confusion when drawings are reduced and /or blown back at odd sizes.

Scale indication bars.

A date/hours/initials graph on the binder strip to help in recording work time per drawing.

Grids or matrices to aid in controlling drawings and printing in overlay drafting.

_____ Architect's name_____ Address_____ Phone number_____ Registration number or official stamp_____

_____ Project name and address

_____ Owner's name and address

_____ Consultants: Structural_____ HVAC_____ Plumbing_____ Electrical_____ Lighting_____ Soils_____ Civil Engineering_____ Acoustical_____ Auditorium_____ Kitchen and Food Service_____ Landscaping_____ Interiors_____

_____ Consultants' names_____ Addresses_____ Phone numbers_____ Registration numbers or stamps_____

_____ Drawing title and scale

_____ Minioutline key plan of building

_____ Partner in charge_____ Chief or project architect_____ Job or team captain_____

_____ Project manager: Name_____ Address_____ Phone number_____

_____ Designer and draftspersons (a growing preference is to provide full names of participants rather than initials)

_____ Initial or name of drawing checker

_____ Space for revision dates and revision reference symbols

_____ Project number_____ File number_____

_____ Copyright notice or note on rights and restrictions of ownership and use of drawings

_____ Building and planning authority names_____ Addresses_____ Phone numbers_____ Permit numbers_____

_____ Space for approval stamps or initials_____ Dates of approvals_____

_____ Checking dates_____ Job-phase completion dates_____ Client approvals_____

_____ Final release date

_____ Drawing sheet number and total number of drawings

_____ Sheet number coding for drawings of different consultants_____ Coding for separate buildings or portions of project_____

Fig. 3-4. Checklist of title block data.

3.5 WORKING DRAWING NUMBERING SYSTEMS

There is opportunity for improvement in the way working sheets are numbered. Hansen Lind Meyer (HLM) of Iowa City and Jarvis Putty Jarvis (JPJ) of Dallas, leading pioneers in Systems Drafting, have also pioneered in a simplified drawing organizational system.

What's common to the HLM and JPJ systems is that portions of the working drawings are divided into divisions or chapters. The divisions or chapters follow a sequence that matches the sequence of actual construction. General information comes first, then site preparation, then the structural system beginning with the foundations, then exterior walls, roof, and so on, down to the final details of finishing.

Each division or chapter includes *all* work in that section: architectural, structural, electrical, plumbing, heating, ventilating and air conditioning (HVAC), and so on. That's a major deviation from the normal procedure of including each separate discipline's work as one isolated section in the drawing set—the structural section, the electrical drawing group, etc.

The advantages of a division numbering system for a set of construction drawings are as follows:

1. It makes it possible to get most drawing sheet numbers established early in the project even when all drawings aren't identified yet. *Most* of the first drawings to go in a division are known and can be numbered as 2.1, 2.2, 2.3, etc. The less certain drawings, such as special conditions, details, and schedules, go in the latter part of each division or chapter and can be added as necessary without affecting the total sequence of drawing numbers.

2. Since most drawing sheet numbers can be established early in the game, so can many of the detail key numbers. They don't have to wait for a last-minute rush of numbering.

3. As noted earlier, the division numbers are planned to match the sequence of construction on the job. This makes it easier for bidding and construction planning, especially for phased and fast-track construction.

4. Another convenience for contractors is that they don't have to skip back and forth through drawings to pull together all the re-

lated work. Related work, broad scope and narrow scope, is all in one section.

NOTE: *If you establish a standard or reference detail system, consider indexing and numbering the details according to a basic drawing division system such as the one just described. Also, on some medium-sized jobs, consider organizing the specifications in this format rather than in uniform construction index (UCI) format and including them as integral parts of the drawings.*

Both Hansen Lind Meyer and Jarvis Putty Jarvis vary their drawing-section sequence to suit the job. They switch sequence or add or subtract portions as appropriate to the situation.

The basic section formats which are varied to suit need in the HLM and JPJ systems are shown below.

DIVISIONS FORMAT (FROM HANSEN LIND MEYER)

Division 1—General
  Cover sheet
  Symbol sheet
  Equipment schedules
  Project schedule (critical path method [CPM], etc.)
  Key plans
Division 2—Site Development
  Existing site plan
  New site plan
  Mechanical site work
  Electrical site work
Division 3—Structural
  Structural plans
  Structural schedules
  Structural details
Division 4—Building Enclosure
  Exterior wall plans
  Exterior sections and details
  Roof plans and details
  Exterior elevations
Division 5—Building Division
  Interior floor plans
  Interior details relating to walls
  Room finish schedules
  Door schedule
  Hardware schedule

Division 6—Ceilings
  Reflected ceiling plans
  Ceiling details
Division 7—Equipment
  Equipment plans
  Casework
  Millwork
  Miscellaneous equipment
  Interior elevations
  Details
Division 8—Plumbing
  Plumbing plans
  Plumbing details
  Plumbing schedules
Division 9—Piping
  Piping plans
  Piping details
  Piping schedules
Division 10—HVAC
  HVAC plans
  HVAC details
  HVAC schedules
Division 11—Electrical
  Power plans
  Riser diagrams
  Details
  Schedules
Division 12—Communications
  Systems plans
  Riser diagrams
  Details
  Matrices
Division 13—Colors
  Plans
  Schedules
  Details
  Painted graphics
Division 14—Signage
  Plans
  Schedules
  Details
Division 15—Furnishings
  Plans
  Schedules
  Details
Division 16—Landscaping
  Plans
  Schedules
  Details

CHAPTER FORMAT (FROM JARVIS PUTTY JARVIS)

Chapter 1—General Information
  Consultants
  Index
  Legends and project data
  Instructions for use of drawings
  Nomenclature and symbols
Chapter 2—Site Improvements
  Site plans
  Details
  Mechanical-electrical (M-E) site plans
  Landscaping
  Irrigation
Chapter 3—Structural
  Structural plans
  Details
  Schedules
Chapter 4—Envelope
  Floor plans
  Exterior door and frame schedules
  Exterior elevations
  Building sections
  Wall sections
  Roof plan
  Details
  Exterior door and frame details
Chapter 5—Space Dividers
  Plans
  Finish, door, and frame schedules
  Interior elevations
  Details
  Interior door and frame details
Chapter 6—Ceilings
  Reflected plans
  Details
Chapter 7—Fixtures and Fittings
  Plans
  Large-scale plans
  Details
Chapter 8—Heating, Ventilating, Air Conditioning
  Plans
  Equipment room plans
  Schedules
  Details
Chapter 9—Plumbing
  Plans
  Schedules
  Details, riser diagrams

Chapter 10—Electrical
  Lighting plan
  Power plan
  Schedules
  Details, riser diagrams

SUBGROUP NUMBERING SYSTEM (RECOMMENDED BY THE COMMITTEE ON PRODUCTION OFFICE PROCEDURES OF THE NORTHERN CALIFORNIA CHAPTER OF THE AIA)

This system separates consultants' drawings in the traditional way but with differences. It has subgroup numbering within larger groups. For example, "A3" drawings are architectural sections and exterior elevations, and any drawings within that set will be numbered A3.1, A3.2, A3.3, and so on. This allows adding or subtracting drawings without altering the overall numbering system.

Also, there's some consistency in group numbers of consultants' drawings and the architectural drawings. For example, the "A2" drawings are architectural floor plans. The others—S2 (structural), M2 (mechanical), P2 (plumbing), and E2 (electrical)—are all also floor plans.

System Code:—A 2. 1

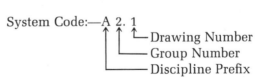

Architectural Drawings
  A0.1,2,3 General (index, symbols, abbreviations, notes, references)
  A1.1,2,3 Demolition, site plan, temporary work
  A2.1,2,3 Plans, room material schedule, door schedule, key drawings
  A3.1,2,3 Sections, exterior elevations
  A4.1,2,3 Detailed floor plans
  A5.1,2,3 Interior elevations
  A6.1,2,3 Reflected ceiling plans
  A7.1,2,3 Vertical circulation, stairs (elevators, escalators)
  A8.1,2,3 Exterior details
  A9.1,2,3 Interior details

Structural Drawings
S0.1,2,3 General notes
S1.1,2,3 Site work
S2.1,2,3 Framing plans
S3.1,2 Elevations
S4.1,2 Schedules
S5.1,2 Concrete
S6.1,2 Masonry
S7.1,2 Structural steel
S8.1,2 Timber
S9.1,2 Special design

Mechanical Drawings
M0.1,2 General notes
M1.1,2 Site and roof plans
M2.1,2 Floor plans
M3.1,2 Riser diagrams
M4.1,2 Piping flow diagram
M5.1,2 Control diagrams
M6.1,2 Details

Plumbing Drawings
P0.1,2 General notes
P1.1,2 Site plan
P2.1,2 Floor plans
P3.1,2 Riser diagram
P4.1,2 Piping flow diagram
P5.1,2 Details

Electrical Drawings
E0.1,2 General notes
E1.1,2 Site plan
E2.1,2 Floor plans, lighting
E3.1,2 Floor plans, power
E4.1,2 Electrical rooms
E5.1,2 Riser diagrams
E6.1,2 Fixture and panel schedules
E7.1,2 Details

BASIC TRADITIONAL NUMBERING SYSTEM

The following basic traditional numbering system is still adequate for small projects.

Architectural Drawings
A1 Index, symbols, abbreviations, location map
A2 Site plan and details
A3 Floor plans
A4 Roof plan
A5 Building sections
A6 Exterior elevations
A7 Exterior details
A8 Window and louver schedule, details
A9 Interior elevations
A10 Ceiling plan and details
A11 Toilet room plans and details
A12 Stairways
A13 Elevators
A14 Partition schedule and details; hollow metal details
A15 Room material schedule; door schedules, details
A16 Casework schedule, details

Structural Drawings
S1 Foundation plan, typical details, and general notes
S2 Floor framing plans
S3 Wall elevation and slab sections
S4 Wall sections and details
S5 Steel stairs, plans and details
S6 Schedules

Mechanical Drawings
M1 Mechanical site plan
M2 Floor plans
M3 Roof air-conditioning and ventilating units
M4 Mechanical equipment room plan and sections
M5 Miscellaneous details
P Plumbing drawings
F Fire protection drawings

Electrical Drawings
E1 Site plan, symbol list and details
E2 Single line diagram, bus riser details
E3 Power plans
E4 Lighting plans
E5 Sections and details
E6 Elevations and details
E7 Communication plan

3.6 SIMPLER SCHEDULE FORMATS

Many schedules in use—door schedules, finish schedules, equipment schedules, and so on—are oversized, overcomplicated, and overly time-consuming to prepare and to use.

The complexity of most schedule forms is ironic since schedules were invented as time-savers in the first place. Schedules exploit the genius of the human species to condense large amounts of data within simple little symbols. The general application of that principle in working drawings is that whenever something is repeated many times over, we stop repeating it and use a simpler symbol instead. Then the symbol refers to a single drawing, note, or schedule that contains the original complex data.

A schedule is overly complicated if *it* has much information repeated within it. For example, suppose a column in a door schedule is titled "height." Looking down the column, you see that every single door has the same height: 6′8″. Sometimes such repetitions are spelled out, sometimes ditto symbols are used. Neither is satisfactory. Spelling out all the repetition conflicts with the purpose of using schedules. Using dittos is better, but it indicates that the overall format needs simplification or the need wouldn't come up. If, for example, all doors in a project are 6′8″ high, it is not necessary to repeat that hundreds of times; it should be stated just once. If almost all doors are 6′8″, but some are other sizes, the general rule can be stated in a clear general note and the exceptions can be noted or keyed separately. That's a great general rule in working drawings, by the way: don't repeat what's most common, just indicate it with a general note and call out the exceptions.

You can't do much better than to follow the simplified schedule recommendations of the Task Force on Production Office Procedures of the Northern California Chapter of the American Institute of Architects.* They might not be *directly* usable; you may have to modify them. Study them; they'll suggest a good general direction to take (see Figs. 3-5 and 3-7).

Some users of the simplified door schedule have run into problems in terms of identifying and keying the door frame connection details. Avoid that problem by varying the NCAIA "door mark" system. Use a number letter number key system, such as $\frac{2A4}{B3A}$. That particular key would provide for six different schedule references. *In most cases only five or even four references would be adequate, for example:* $\frac{2A1}{C2}$. The reference system can take any sequence you like. One would be: Top left number refers to a *drawn* frame size and type schedule. Top middle letter refers to a door type and size schedule. Top right number refers to door facing, type, and fire rating. Bottom left letter refers to hardware set schedule. Bottom right number refers to special conditions such as undercut. *The most important element in this recommendation is: With a drawn doorframe schedule (the one called out by the top left number), you can include detail key bubbles for mounting of frames in various types of wall construction, including sill and floor conditions. Details are keyed on frame schedule, instead of the plans. If the same frame has different mounting construction details in different wall construction, that's easy to handle as a variation—with a different number on the door mark—on the doorframe schedule.*

NOTE: *Doors are frequently far more varied than they need to be on a job. Designers should be asked to shoot for more uniformity in size, frame, finish, and hardware. A large set of doors at one size, for example, rather than a lot of doors in all different sizes, will be less expensive and more convenient all the way around. The fewer the variations, the simpler the door mark and door schedule can be.*

*Recommended Standards on Production Procedure, vol. 1, Committee on Production Office Procedures, NCAIA, 1974.

TYPE 1

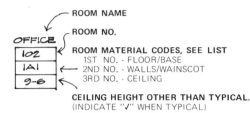

ROOM NAME

ROOM NO.

ROOM MATERIAL CODES, SEE LIST
   1ST NO. - FLOOR/BASE
   2ND NO. - WALLS/WAINSCOT
   3RD NO. - CEILING

CEILING HEIGHT OTHER THAN TYPICAL.
(INDICATE "√" WHEN TYPICAL)

TYPE 2

ROOM MATERIAL SCHEDULE

ROOM NO.	FLOOR/BASE	WALLS/WAINSCOT	CEILING	CEILING HEIGHT*	REMARKS
102	1	A	1	9⁶	
103	1	A	1	√	

*OTHER THAN TYPICAL. TYPICAL IS INDICATED BY "√".

TYPE 1 & 2

ROOM MATERIAL CODE LIST

	FLOOR/BASE		WALLS/WAINSCOT		CEILING
0	SPECIAL, SEE DETAILS	0	SPECIAL, SEE DETAILS	0	SPECIAL, SEE DETAILS
1	RESILIENT/ RESILIENT	A	GYP. BD. & BRICK	1	ACOUSTICAL TILE
2		B		2	
3		C		3	

A schedule usually is a tabulation or list. Making a list of room materials is time consuming and in laying out each room on the floor plan, we are in fact drawing up a list of rooms. Since making another list is repetition, we suggest eliminating the list if possible. For all jobs this is not practical; therefore, we have devised simplified material schedule systems. Both systems do away with a lot of tedious work and·by being compact the schedules can easily be accommodated on the floor plan sheet.

The Task Force recommendation for scheduling of room materials is by code numbers and letters with a legend on the floor plan sheet or once listed with other legends and symbols. These codes are indicated in each room on the floor plans (type 1). If a room plan is so small that the codes will not fit the space, the "box" can be shown outside the room plan. If all the room plans are too small to fit any codes, make a list of rooms and assign the codes to them (type 2).

In all cases this list should be shown on the same sheet on which the rooms are drawn so that one can readily find the required information.

RECOMMENDATIONS

1. Room material schedule indicates basic materials used for room surfaces. Finishes of surfaces such as paint should be covered separately.

2. Room material generally covers from material surface from the room side to the backing material, i.e., ceramic tile on gypsum board or vinyl wall covering on plaster. The construction and fire rating should not be in the Room Material Schedule. It should be covered separately by partition type indications.

3. When more than one material is used for a surface, such as a wall, the extent and type of material should be shown or noted on plans. When a complicated combination of materials are used, assign a special code and refer to details such as interior elevations, ceiling plans.

4. When more than one type of the same material is used, i.e., acoustical tile, rated and non-rated, use a different code for each.

5. It is most desirable to have all schedules standardized in modular master form and set up for typing spacing. Copies of this form can then be filled, typed and reproduced on adhesive backed film that can be applied to tracings.

6. Room material schedule should be placed on the same sheet as the floor plan.

Fig. 3-5. Recommendations for finish schedule simplifications.

(Northern California Chapter of the American Institute of Architects, Task Force on Production Office Procedures.)

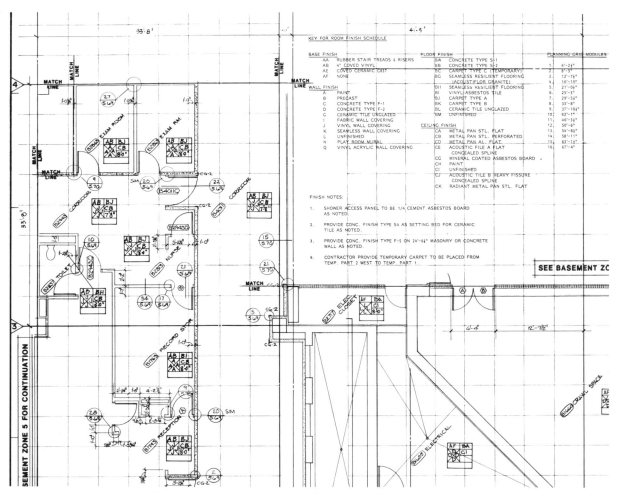

Fig. 3-6. A standard room finish schedule key printed on each floor plan and referenced by symbols and numbers within each room.

(Hansen Lind Meyer.)

Depending on the complexity of the project, a door schedule should be a list of all doors or a list of groups of identical doors. Some projects having typical doors and few variations do not require listing all doors. However, some projects having extensive variations require a listing of all doors. The recommended schedule (type 1) can be used for both types of projects. It is desirable to have the schedule appear on the sheets with floor plans as is the case with the room material schedule.

An alternate schedule (type 2) is a schedule that has an identical master list for every job and covers most door type conditions.

RECOMMENDATIONS

The following should be used in preparing the door schedules for type 1.

1. Items tabulated on the schedule can be added or deleted to fit a firm's requirements. As an example a hardware group column can be added, if desired, which will eliminate paragraph 3 below.

2. Determine the typical items, such as door construction, facing and finish, etc. and verify with schedule notes. The more items that are typical, the simpler the schedule.

3. Schedule 1 does not list hardware. The hardware group is shown in the door symbol on the plans. The hardware groups are covered in the specifications.

DOOR SYMBOL, TYPE 1

DOOR MARK
HARDWARE GROUP

TYPE 1

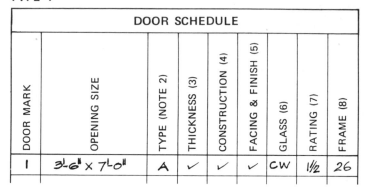

DOOR MARK	OPENING SIZE	TYPE (NOTE 2)	THICKNESS (3)	CONSTRUCTION (4)	FACING & FINISH (5)	GLASS (6)	RATING (7)	FRAME (8)
				DOOR SCHEDULE				
1	3'-6" x 7'-0"	A	✓	✓	✓	CW	1½	26

1. "✓" SHOWN ON SCHEDULE INDICATES TYPICAL
2. DOOR TYPES:

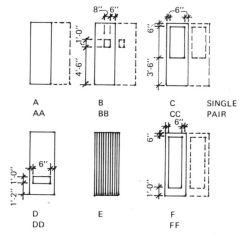

3. ALL DOORS 1¾" THICK UNLESS OTHERWISE NOTED
4. DOOR CONSTRUCTION:
   TYPICAL = SOLID CORE
       HC = HOLLOW CORE
      HM = HOLLOW METAL
       AL = ALUMINUM & GLASS
5. FACING & FINISH:
   TYPICAL = RED BIRCH, TRANSPARENT
       PT = PLASTIC LAMINATE, TEXTURED
      MP = METAL, PAINTED
6. GLASS:
   TYPICAL = CLEAR PLATE
      SG = SHEET GLASS
     CW = CLEAR WIRE
      TP = TEMPERED PLATE
     LG = LEAD GLASS
7. ¾, 1, 1½ ETC. INDICATES HOURS OF FIRE RATING.
8. TYPICAL FRAMES SHOWN "✓". NUMBER INDICATES DETAIL SHOWN ON SHEET_____.

Fig. 3-7. **Recommendations for door schedule simplifications (types 1 and 2).**

(Northern California Chapter of the American Institute of Architects, Task Force on Production Office Procedures.)

RECOMMENDATIONS

The following should be used in preparing the alternate door schedule A for type 2.

1. Verify all typical items in notes.

2. Select door mark and door opening code from schedule. If no door mark fits the requirements of a particular door, use the marks under "other" column and note the requirements under the column "...other than typical" or create a new mark. Add new door types and opening codes as required.

1. PLAN INDICATION

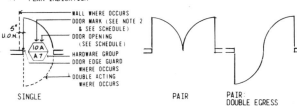

WALL WHERE OCCURS
DOOR MARK (SEE NOTE 2 & SEE SCHEDULE)
DOOR OPENING (SEE SCHEDULE)
HARDWARE GROUP
DOOR EDGE GUARD WHERE OCCURS
DOUBLE ACTING WHERE OCCURS

SINGLE   PAIR   PAIR: DOUBLE EGRESS

2. LOCATE DOOR MARK ON SCHEDULE. READ UP FOR FACING. READ ACROSS FOR TYPE, GLASS, RATING, CONSTRUCT. ETC.

3. DOOR OPENING SCHEDULE

   A   2'-2'' x 7'-0''   E   4'-0'' x 7'-0''
   B   2'-6'' x 7'-0''   F   5'-0'' x 7'-0''
   C   3'-0'' x 7'-0''   G   6'-0'' x 7'-0''
   D   3'-6'' x 7'-0''   H   7'-8'' x 7'-0''

4. ALL DOORS 1-3/4'' THICK. U.O.N.

5. TYPICAL WOOD FACING = RED BIRCH

6. TYPICAL DOOR CONSTRUCTION U.O.N. ON SCHEDULE:

   WOOD = SOLID WOOD CORE. FIRE RESISTIVE CORE FOR FIRE RATED DOOR WITH RATING OVER 20 MINUTES.
   PLASTIC LAMINATE = SOLID WOOD CORE FIRE RESISTIVE CORE WOOD FOR FIRE RATED DOORS WITH RATING OVER 20 MINUTES.
   HOLLOW METAL = STEEL

7. TYPICAL DOOR FINISH U.O.N. ON SCHEDULE:

   WOOD = TRANSPARENT
   PLASTIC LAMINATE = TEXTURED
   HOLLOW METAL = PAINTED
   ALUMINUM = COLOR ANODIZED

8. LEAD LINED WEIGHT AND LEAD GLASS SHALL MATCH ADJACENT PARTITION. U.O.N.

9. ALL DOOR MARKS ON SCHEDULE MAY NOT HAVE BEEN USED

10. DOOR FRAME NOTES

    A   DOOR JAMB DETAILS SHOWN. HEAD DETAILS SIMILAR U.O.N.
    B   CASED OPENING 7'-0'' HIGH U.O.N.   PLAN SYMBOL
    C   LEAD LINED WEIGHT AT DOOR JAMBS SAME AS ADJACENT PARTITION U.O.N.

DOOR MARK SCHEDULE

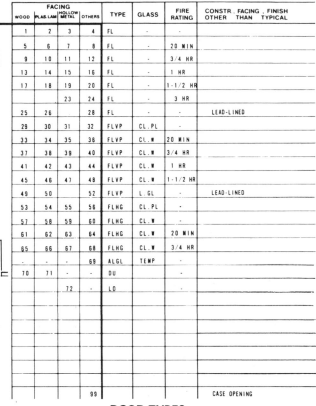

DOOR MARK	FACING				TYPE	GLASS	FIRE RATING	CONSTR. FACING, FINISH OTHER THAN TYPICAL
	WOOD	PLAS. LAM	HOLLOW METAL	OTHERS				
	1	2	3	4	FL	-	-	
	5	6	7	8	FL	-	20 MIN	
	9	10	11	12	FL	-	3/4 HR	
	13	14	15	16	FL	-	1 HR	
	17	18	19	20	FL	-	1-1/2 HR	
			23	24	FL	-	3 HR	
	25	26		28	FL	-	-	LEAD-LINED
	29	30	31	32	FLVP	CL.PL	-	
	33	34	35	36	FLVP	CL.W	20 MIN	
	37	38	39	40	FLVP	CL.W	3/4 HR	
	41	42	43	44	FLVP	CL.W	1 HR	
	45	46	47	48	FLVP	CL.W	1-1/2 HR	
	49	50		52	FLVP	L.GL	-	LEAD-LINED
	53	54	55	56	FLHG	CL.PL	-	
	57	58	59	60	FLHG	CL.W	-	
	61	62	63	64	FLHG	CL.W	20 MIN	
	65	66	67	68	FLHG	CL.W	3/4 HR	
	-	-	-	69	ALGL	TEMP	-	
	70	71	-	-	DU		-	
		72	-		LO		-	
				99				CASE OPENING

DOOR TYPES

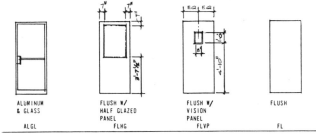

ALUMINUM & GLASS — ALGL
FLUSH W/ HALF GLAZED PANEL — FLHG
FLUSH W/ VISION PANEL — FLVP
FLUSH — FL

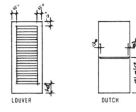

LOUVER — LO
DUTCH — DU

RECOMMENDATIONS

Dimensioning should start with critical dimensions as predicated by design or other requirements.

It should take into consideration the trades using them and the sequencing to their respective work.

It is also necessary to bear in mind that tolerances in actual construction can be as varied as the people involved in the process.

This means that as-built dimensions do not always coincide with design dimensions.

Dimensioning from established grids or structural elements, such as columns and structural walls, assists the trades that, for example, must locate some of their work prior to the placement of floor slabs and of the partition layout that follows.

It can be concluded then, that the practice of closing a string of dimensions running between two reference points, might be useful for office checking, but it can definitely be conducive to conflict when, as in another example, the work of two different trades which must interact at a common point happens to be layed out by each starting from the opposite end of the dimensional string.

1. All numbers 1/8" high.

2. Fractions to have diagonal dividing line between numerator and denominator.

3. Dimensions under 1'-0" shall be noted in inches, i.e., 11", 6", etc. Dimensions 1'-0" and over shall be expressed in feet.

4. Fractions under one (1) inch shall **NOT** be preceeded by a zero.

5. Dimension points to be noted with a short blunt 45° line. Dash to be oriented the same for vertical and horizontal runs of dimensions. Modular dimension points may be designated with an arrow or a dot.

6. Limit fractional dimensions in plans and elevations to 1/8" except for indication of a single material thickness.

7. Dimension all items from an established grid or reference point and do not close the string of dimensions to the next grid or reference point. Dimensioning shall be started with critical dimensions as predicated by design or other requirements. Since there is always the possibility of a variance between the on-job condi-

tions and the design dimensions, all trades on the job should lay out their respective work from the same reference point.

(Check non-dimensioned spaces for adequacy.) If three equal spaces are required in a given 12'-0" space, note it as such rather than noting three 4' dimensions.

8. Dimension; to face of concrete or masonry work; to centerlines of columns or other grid points and to centerlines of partitions. In nonmodular wood construction dimension to critical face of studs. When a clear dimension is required either by code (or other reason), dimension to the finish faces and note as such. Do not use word "clear". Likewise, furred spaces should be dimensioned from face to face or from a structural point to finish face.

9. Dimension as much as possible from structural elements rather than from items that may not yet be installed when the layout takes place, i.e., for plumber or electrician laying out sleeves on the forms for the floor deck.

10. Do not dimension items such as partitions or doors, that are centered or otherwise located on a grid, module, mullion, by schedule or by typical detail condition. The general notes or typical details should cover this fact or any other typical condition of dimension. Dimension unscheduled openings in accordance with paragraph 8 above.

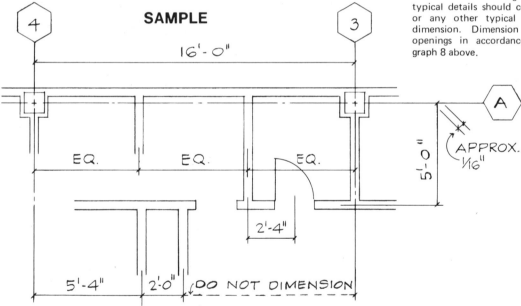

Fig. 3-8. Recommendations for dimensioning.
(Northern California Chapter of the American Institute of Architects, Task Force on Production Office Procedures.)

3.7 OVERDRAWING

Chances are that 10 to 40% of the items in your working drawings are overdone or shouldn't be there in the first place. I've examined hundreds of working drawing sets, and that's the normal percentage range that I've found. The wasted drawing is bad enough. What's worse is that *the extraneous items are a visual noise.* Like static, they detract from the important information.

The following checklist names the most common "noisemakers." There are three main types: redundancies, overelaborations, and irrelevancies. After you read the list, look through your drawings. You'll come up with a pretty clear idea of what percentage of your drawing can be simplified or eliminated. Then set a target, and start an explicit drafting simplification program. Share this checklist with your staff. Photocopy it and spread it around. There will be disagreements over some of our dos and don'ts. That's fine. The arguments help focus attention on the main issue: *graphic clarity and simplicity.* The questions have to be raised again and again: Who are these drawings really for? What is the final purpose of these drawings? The more thinking and talking there is on these questions, the better. The following checklist includes over thirty areas of potential improvement:

NOTATION

____ Notes often describe specific materials, trade names, gauges, and other particulars that should be spelled out *only* in the specifications. Besides being extraneous, such notes often contradict the specs. Generic names and simplest wordings are best. For example, say "flashing" instead of "24 Ga. G.I. flashing" and "built-up roof" instead of "3-ply tar and gravel roofing."

____ General notes are duplicated from job to job and are often hand-copied on many sheets in the same job. There are lots of options here, such as typewriting, adhesive back office-copier appliques, rubber stamps, and custom-printed press-on sheets. If you're using composite drafting with opaque paste-up work sheets, the options are even more varied and are easier to use.

____ A large number of general notes shouldn't be found in working drawings. They should

be in specifications. Ask for advice on this from your specification writer.

____ Reference notes sometimes cite a published trade standard or building regulation and spell out the whole item. In most instances, it's *not* desirable to reproduce the whole item, because there may be an update on it by the time the drawings are out to bid. In most cases, it's only necessary to name the reference source and let the contractor look up the latest data.

____ Space identifications and other titles are repeated from one end of a drawing to another. It's unnecessary to label every office, exam room, or classroom when there are a whole string of such rooms with obvious identical functions.

____ Drawings often include duplications of titles. The title block says "building cross sections," or "exterior elevations," or "site plan." Then the same label appears under the drawings on that sheet. If the sheet title block description is bold and clear, it's not necessary to duplicate it under the specific drawing on the sheet.

DIMENSIONING

____ Feet and inch marks on dimensions don't necessarily improve clarity. Some offices have abolished the feet and inch designations. It has a cleansing effect on the drawings, and dimensions remain perfectly readable. This is obviously a very minor timesaver. You have to institute a cluster of minor items like this to gain any notable overall improvements. (Any such departure requires that you include a preprinted note on each sheet to cite the change from standard practice.)

____ Another minor item worth changing: those dimension-line arrowheads. *Dots or slashes are cleaner and faster.*

____ Dimensions frequently appear where sizes or locations are self-evident or already noted. If a window opening is centered on a room, for example, and its size is established elsewhere, any dimensioning to centerline or sides of rough construction is unnecessary. And such dimensions may be misleading because of discrepancies in actual job-site measurements.

____ Generally a string of the same dimension numbers or the note "equal" is repeated across a whole series of equally spaced mullions, paving dividers, etc. *One overall dimension and a note* like "16 eq. spaces" does it more neatly.

_____ Unrealistically small fractions of an inch are noted in large-scale construction. Sometimes fractions are shown at $\frac{1}{16}$ and even $\frac{1}{32}$ of an inch on rough construction. It's better to avoid fractions altogether; this simplifies both drawing and construction. If possible, go even further, and stick to 4" increments.

_____ Elimination of dimensioning—or at least most dimensioning—has been achieved by offices that use a consistent modular system. A ceiling or floor grid system with number and letter coordinates (such as that used by engineers in designating column locations in bay-frame buildings) can locate and size almost every partition within a plan without numerical dimensioning. Such coordinates, when also applied in elevation, can automatically key the locations of sections and details.

_____ Column or bay lines should be used as reference points for dimensioning of partitions. This cuts the length of dimension chains, helps prevent cumulative error, and reduces revision "fallout" when one portion of the plan is changed during the job.

SYMBOLS

_____ Doors and windows are frequently identified by note or symbol on the exterior elevation drawings. *Door and window reference key symbols should be restricted to plans.* There's no need to duplicate them on other drawings.

_____ Detail and cross-section reference symbols are usually overelaborate and overabundant. They *can* be very simple, yet still clear and graphically acceptable. For example, a cut line with a T cap and a number reference along the T bar makes a good, simple detail reference. If the direction of detail section is important (it usually isn't), then a cut line with a stem pointing one way or the other, plus number reference, does the trick. The simplest number reference is something like 4-3.17, which means detail number 4 on sheet number 3.17.

GRIDS, PATTERNS, AND SYMMETRICAL ELEMENTS

_____ Repetitive fenestration, paneling, paving patterns, floor and ceiling grids, handrails, and so on, *can* be drawn in part, cut with a break line, and completed with a note. They can, but most often they're drawn in their entirety. Some offices have become stringent about this, however, and have managed to get people to change their habits. (Composite drafting eliminates the problem. Repetitive elements are drawn in part, photoduplicated in quantity, and completed as paste-ups.)

_____ Symmetrical details, plans, and portions of plans are also usually drawn in their entirety. But they don't have to be. Just draw one-half of the item, complete with notes and dimensions, then draw the outline of the other half. Add an explanatory note, and it's done.

MATERIALS INDICATIONS, TEXTURES, AND HATCHING

_____ Textures such as plaster dots, masonry lines, wood grain, and even the reflection lines of window glass fill up many drawings. This is an undemanding type of drafting, and it does make the building "look better." But if you want to eliminate overdrawing, then excessive texturing has to go. The best rule is that each element should have just enough notation or graphic indication to show what it is—usually only at corners and boundaries.

_____ Wall construction is usually shown via material indications on floor plans. Although this is usually done by low-cost junior drafting staff, it amounts to a substantial amount of time on larger jobs. Some offices no longer draw in the wall construction or materials hatching. Instead, only the wall outline is shown, and each wall length is identified with a T cut line and reference number. The number refers to the detail drawing of the wall cross section.

_____ An alternative to the above is to include a "wall construction schedule" on each floor plan sheet. This is a small print of the types of wall construction in the building, showing each type with its number code. The schedule is preprinted, of course—not drawn individually on each plan sheet.

_____ There are many new tapes and press-on

sheets available for textures, small patterns, etc. Some will work on tracing paper and diazo printing. Some are best used on composite-drafting work sheets. Check your graphics supply shop.

OVERSIZED DRAWINGS

____ Drafting staff sometimes do half-size or full-size detail drawings. These are essentially shop drawings and shouldn't be part of the architects' documents. *Large drawings, as a rule, take more time to draw* than small ones, and details are frequently oversized. Try doing more ½"- and ¾"-scale details rather than 1", 1½", and 3" ones.

____ Exterior elevation drawings, building cross sections, and interior elevations are usually oversized. These are essentially "empty" drawings and lose nothing by being reduced in size. For small- and moderate-sized buildings ⅛" scale is recommended; 1⁄16" scale is often fine for large, uncomplicated structures.

____ Oversized sheets encourage drafting staff to use large-scale units in order to fill up the empty space. Try keeping sheet sizes down to small and moderate sizes, and avoid the outsizes altogether. Giant-size sheets sometimes seem necessary when planning a job; but they rarely are really necessary, and they're extremely inconvenient for drafting.

____ On larger projects, the utility spaces, toilet rooms, stairs, and so on, are drawn on separate sheets in large scale. Toilet rooms, for example, may be ¼" scale on the "toilet room plans" sheet, and may be shown in essentially the same detail at ⅛" scale on the construction floor plans. *This is a major area of duplication and overdrawing, and it should be examined closely in your office.* There are two ways to approach it: (1) maybe the larger-scale drawings are *not* needed. It may be that all is clearly shown in small scale. This is most often the case. (2) If larger-scale drawings are needed to convey important detail, then the same areas of the building on the smaller-scale plans should be essentially *blank*. A small-scale toilet room, for example, should *not* show floor tile, mirrors, dispensers, toilet stall partitions, etc. (Only basic plumbing fixtures—drains, toilets, urinals, and lavatories—will be shown for the benefit of the plumbing consultant.)

WAYS TO AVOID OVERDRAWING ON VARIOUS WORKING DRAWING SHEETS

TITLE SHEET, INDEX, AND GENERAL INFORMATION

____ The usual data—standard symbols, legend, list of abbreviations—should be right out of the file and assembled virtually as is.

____ Original data, particularly the index, *should be typewritten, never hand-lettered.* Some offices have had basic sheet titles, e.g., "floor plan," "framing plan," "exterior elevations," etc., printed on clear, stickyback polyester labels. These are used to *compose the index of drawings, as appliques on title blocks, and/or as labels for individual drawings.*

____ A vicinity map needn't be drawn if a road map is available to copy onto photocopy-type applique polyester.

SITE PLAN

____ Many of the preceding examples of overdrawing apply to site plans. Textures, entourage, patterns, etc., are all subject to simplification and to applique drafting in ways we've already described. The transparent "clear stamps" at leading drafting supply outlets are especially recommended for trees and foliage.

____ Some offices routinely redraw surveys that are in "engineering scale" and make them "architectural scale." The reasons for doing this are not persuasive. Aim to get a directly usable survey reproducible and add the architectural data directly onto the reproducible.

FLOOR PLANS

The most common points of overdrawing on floor plans have been covered in preceding portions of this chapter.

STAIR PLANS

____ Like toilet rooms and other "core" spaces, stair plans are often repeated in small- and large-scale drawings. The small-scale construction plans that show stairs don't *have* to include treads, handrails, riser notations, etc. All you need is an outline of the stair, an arrow showing direction of slope, and stair identification number. A general note explains that risers, dimensions, etc., are

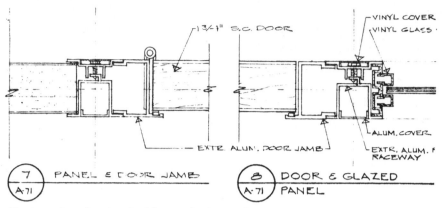

Fig. 3-9. Overdrawing. In this case the internal extrusions of a partition system are drawn as if this were a shop drawing for the manufacturer. Only an outline of a manufactured product and details of its connection to other construction need be shown.

(Guidelines.)

not shown and refers to the larger-scale drawing.

FRAMING PLANS

____ Framing plans for smaller buildings are often drawn complete with every joist and beam. This is a holdover from a common practice on larger buildings. Unless the framing is terribly complex, all you need are framing notes on the regular construction floor plans. Framing notes are double-headed arrows that show direction of the overhead framing, the name of the joist size, type and material, and spacing of the members. The arrow and note are included at every space where framing differs from other spaces.

EXTERIOR ELEVATIONS, CROSS SECTIONS, AND INTERIOR ELEVATIONS

____ These are usually blank-looking drawings, so drafting staff tend to fill them in with excess detail. Try having them done at the smallest possible scale. They'll look less "unfinished" and less tempting to compulsive drawers.

____ Watch for elaborate drawing of doors, fenestration, and louvers. Frames, sills, muntins, and so on, don't have to be drawn. All that's required are single-line openings and header heights.

____ Drawings of lateral and longitudinal cross sections sometimes show background walls with interior views of their fixtures, openings, etc. This background is not relevant to the mainly structural and height data that's to be conveyed by a cross section.

____ Cross sections often include joists, slab or ceiling waffles, and other structural detail. For bidding and construction, generally *all that's needed is a plain outline of floor and roof construction* without any structural detail.

____ Most cross sections in working drawings aren't really necessary. A cross section is justified if it clarifies some situation that's not called out via plan and elevation. If it just shows walls and flat slabs, it adds nothing and should be left out of the set.

____ Interior elevations frequently show no more than floor-to-ceiling heights, baseboards, and occasional fixtures. They serve no construction function in that case and shouldn't be drawn.

____ Sometimes strips of interior elevation are drawn to show heights of fixtures and wall-mounted equipment. It's easier and preferable to show such heights in fixture schedules. That way, each item is drawn only once and not within a backdrop of otherwise useless drawings of walls.

DETAIL DRAWINGS

____ Connectors—screws, bolts, rivets, etc.—are drawn as complete objects with threads and shading. It's hard to convince some people, but all that's required is a dark dash-dot-dash–type of indication and the note that tells the type and size of the connecting hardware.

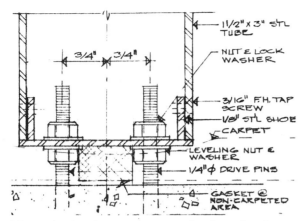

Fig. 3-10. Another common example of overdrawing: detailing of nuts and bolts, including bolt threads. (Guidelines.)

—— Ready-made products that will be installed as is are detailed as if the contractor were to manufacture them. Items most often drawn unnecessarily are: stock windows, skylights, and scuttles; wheel guards, gratings, and manhole covers; fire escapes, ships' ladders, and handrails; linen and garbage chutes; chalk and bulletin boards; commercial movable partitions and integrated ceiling systems; urinal and toilet stall partitions. When details are necessary, it's mainly connections to other construction that should be drawn. *The ready-made or manufactured main item requires only an outline and identifying note or label.*

—— Hidden aspects of construction are excessively detailed. Minor support members and connectors are shown, noted, and dimensioned in detailed drawings of furred walls, closed-in stairways, soffits, dropped ceilings, overhangs, etc. These drawings rarely match actual working conditions, and such construction is usually improvised to match real conditions. *In most cases, such drawings need only show the final result desired and leave the means up to the contractor.*

SCHEDULES

—— Design them small. *It's best to have finish, door, and window schedules on floor plan sheets* instead of combining schedules for all floors on isolated schedule sheets.

—— Design simple schedule formats usable from job to job. Have these preprinted as appliques or strip-ins.

—— Design the schedule forms for typewritten rather than hand-lettered notation. Schedules should be sized to fit the office typewriter, and *the vertical spacing of horizontal lines should match the line-to-line roller spacing of the typewriter.* If the schedule format isn't made compatible with the typewriter, the typist will have to constantly readjust the sheets while typing, and uniformity of appearance will suffer.

3.8 COMMON ERRORS AND OMISSIONS IN WORKING DRAWINGS

In 1973 a British construction research group completed a survey of flaws in working drawings. The group found that certain kinds of problems were extremely common. At *Guidelines* we did a similar study. We looked at drawings from offices of all kinds and sizes, covering every major building type. We confirmed the main conclusions of the British study and came upon a few additional discoveries. Results of both studies are summarized in this chapter.

OMISSIONS

1. Between 25 and 40%* of the details in an average working drawing set are not referenced anywhere in the plans, elevations, sections, or schedules. A slightly smaller percentage of details that *are* referenced in the plans, etc., either cannot be found or are not applicable to the referenced point of construction. As a result, a search for a construction detail in a set of drawings will take anywhere from 30 seconds to 30 minutes. When details are not readily found, contractors usually quit hunting and either call the architect or improvise their own details.

2. Flashing and other waterproofing are excluded in nearly half the relevant drawings. They are most noticeably missing in sections and details of exterior wall openings. It's suggested that technical staff members are not well informed about flashings, moisture barriers, caulking, and sealants. They're not sure of what to draw and tend to assume such items will be covered in the specifications.

3. Over 50% of working drawing sets have insufficient data on fittings. Fittings required in concrete and masonry (such as connections for balustrades, doors, and windows) are not clearly shown and are frequently discovered only after primary construction is completed. Structural drawings, which generally guide primary construction, almost always omit some portion of architectural features which are integral parts of rough construction.

*The percentages cited are rounded off for readers' convenience.

DIMENSIONING

Between 40 and 45% of individual drawings (plans, elevations, sections, and details) have blank spots or errors in dimensioning. The most common oversights are:

1. Locations of existing elements on site plans are in error about 35% of the time. These errors require adjustments during construction in about half the instances. The cause is reliance by drafting staff on locations as shown on surveyors' drawings. The surveyors' "eyeball" approximations are copied, scaled, and dimensioned as is. Any site feature that will affect design and construction should be double-checked for accuracy of size and location.

2. Blank spots often occur in strings of dimensions through interior floor plans. Gaps are most prevalent in complex and/or cluttered plans, or plans subject to many changes during production. A good way to catch these on final-check prints is to overlay sketch tracing paper on the plan and quickly trace the dimension strings. Gaps will show up immediately on the overlay.

3. Drawings may not indicate if dimensions are to finish surfaces, to subsurfaces, or to structure. When intent isn't clear, subcontractors may make conflicting assumptions that will foul up construction coordination. It's recommended that dimensions go to structure, framing, and rough surfaces as much as possible rather than to finish surfaces. State intent in a prominent note, and clearly mark the exceptions.

4. Conflicts arise when a drawing shows a partition centered on a column but dimensions would place the partition off center. When partitions are to align with previously built elements, it's best not to include location dimensions. Such dimensions are either extraneous or contradictory.

5. Location dimensions for drainage lines in slabs are often left out. Drains may then be placed by a contractor with undesired results.

6. Heights of openings, changes in levels, and other features are most often not dimensioned to a consistent reference point. They are frequently calculated on the job, and this is often a source of error.

7. A common lapse, almost universal, is that vertical dimensions of sills and lintels are not provided.

NOTATION

Between 15 and 35% of the notes in the drawings examined were irrelevant or misleading. Two-thirds of the individual drawings contained excessive and redundant notation. Redundancy, in itself, isn't necessarily a problem. It can help assure that the message gets across. Problems arise when drawings and specifications both cover the same ground with different or contradictory wording. Following is a list of the leading trouble spots:

1. Terminology and abbreviations are very often inconsistent within the same set of drawings and specifications. Room names, construction features, and materials are sometimes identified three or four different ways in one set. This is a good reminder that every office should follow a single nomenclature and that every staff member should have a copy of the standard nomenclature.

2. Materials and construction notation is too specific in most drawings. The notes should use generic terms and leave specifics to the specifications (as the word implies). Contradictions are extremely common because of violations of this rule. A note should say "flashing" instead of naming the gauge and the type of metal and "built-up roof" instead of "3-ply tar and gravel roofing." (This rule doesn't apply to drawings for a small building that doesn't require separate specifications.)

3. Reference notes, such as "see structural drawings," "see specifications," "see Dwg. A-77," and "unless shown otherwise elsewhere," are common throughout most drawings and are inadequate as references. They lead to long, fruitless searches by contractors. The only way to make such references useful is to name specific locations and an address that includes location number and sheet or page number.

4. Almost all drawings include lettering that is too small to be readable. The problem is compounded by background, smears, and wrinkled job-site prints.

5. Over 50% of drawings include notation that crosses through dimension lines or parts of construction. This sometimes makes the data unreadable.

6. Many instances of incomplete notation were observed in the drawings surveyed. Sentences are not completed, or words are erased but not replaced. These instances indicate that checkers tend to fail to read notes all the way through. Joke notes and obscenities intended for checkers were also found.

TECHNICAL ERRORS

These are not as common as might be expected. Fewer than 15% of individual drawings had outright technical mistakes in construction, and many of these could be interpreted as overdesign. Mistakes of omission were much more common, as noted previously. The technical errors that recur frequently enough to note here are:

1. Site drainage was ignored in several instances. Ponding could be expected in some cases; flowing ground water would impinge upon the building in others. Parking lot drainage was sometimes very questionable.

2. Roof drainage tended to follow minimal slope requirements for built-up roofing. Severe ponding would be inevitable in a couple of cases if slopes were not increased during construction.

3. Construction joints and expansion and contraction joints were fairly often misplaced, too few in number, and undersized. Some relief and movement joints would clearly fail if built as detailed.

4. Weep holes for masonry walls, for curtain walls, and at flashings tended to be omitted or were too few and undersized.

5. Waterproofing, moisture barriers, and vapor barriers were confused by some drafting technicians and tended to be incorrectly placed.

6. Detailing shown in some furred spaces, under stairs, and in other closed areas would be impossible to execute as shown because of lack of space for workers to enter or maneuver.

7. Some access panels, scuttles, and hatches shown would be unusable because of size and location. Installation and maintenance space was usually bare minimum and sometimes wholly inadequate for mechanical equipment.

8. Gaskets, barriers, or coating to separate dis-similar materials that might interact electro-chemically tended to be omitted or only vaguely drawn and noted.

3.9 "TRADE SECRETS" AND SHORTCUTS IN DRAFTING

There's a lot of time to be saved. People are al-ways finding ways to knock a couple of minutes off some routine task or another. These are small timesavers usually, but they add up. Some of the best timesavers are small ones applied to fre-quently repeated tasks.

Measure the time you spend on repetitive ac-tivities. That will give you the baseline you need for measuring improvements. It will also dram-atize the importance of saving a couple of min-utes here and there. An *easy* goal for any drafts-person is to salvage an hour each day. That'll add up to 250 hours in a 50-week work year. That equals six 40-hour weeks. That's a lot from a little.

Compare your procedures with the ideas in the following checklist. This list, compiled from architects and engineers all over the country, will stimulate many additional ideas. It is a sum-mary of some of the things you will find at the work stations of some of the most productive drafting people in the country.

____ A grid sheet underlay on the drafting board. Those who use grids say they can't under-stand why anyone wouldn't. A grid sheet—which usually includes 1, ½, and ¼″ lines—makes sketching to scale easy. The hori-zontal lines are ready-made lettering guide-lines. The grid aids alignment of various components of the drawing and speeds up dimensioning. (*Caution:* Many grid sheets sold as drafting-board covers are *not* accu-rate. Measure before you buy.)

____ Underlay templates drawn on the drafting-board cover. Some people combine a grid sheet with ink-drawn markings of common measurements. An architect who special-izes in a simple building type laid out the basic vertical dimensions of piers and foot-ings, sills, floor lines, headers, ceiling lines, and roof lines. The guidelines, inked onto the drafting-board cover, eliminate such commonly done dimensioning when draw-ing building cross sections and elevations. Other reference items that have been inked on drafting boards are: registration corner points for quickly aligning tracings before they're taped onto the board; spacing guides for large-scale lettering; and marks to show preferred positions of floor plans, schedules, elevations, general notes, and so on, on drawing sheets.

____ Vertical drafting board and track-type drafter. Some people cannot adjust to these. Those who do adjust seem to improve their drafting pace from 10 to 25% on routine assignments. A vertical or semivertical board is *much* more comfortable to work on than a flat board. But a vertical board won't work if there isn't an adjacent space for flat sketching. The vertical board should also be adjustable for easy change from a vertical to a flat position. The extra sketch space has to be in addition to reference space.

____ Regular drafting machines are a close second in speed to the track-type drafter. Integration is the secret of these devices. They combine scale, triangles, and straightedge in one instrument. The integrated tool definitely aids continuity of work flow in the drafting process. Some users enhance the integration by adding small tensor lamps and tool holders to their drafting machines.

____ Tool holders, erasers, lead holders, templates, and so on, need to be as close at hand as possible. That's one of the first rules of efficient work. Architects and engineers have improvised all manner of tool holders. Some cut holes and slots in blocks of styrofoam to hold their basic drafting supplies. Wood blocks have been similarly drilled and slotted. Some draftspersons tape bent paper clips to their table lamps and hang tools from the clips. There are many options, but some kind of holder is a must, for it is an important timesaver.

____ Strips of runners to keep a parallel rule slightly above the drawing surface are very commonly used. Such strips are usually plastic or cardboard, taped along right- and left-hand sides of the drafting board. The edges of the parallel rule ride atop the strips, which keeps the whole rule slightly above the board. The idea is to reduce friction and dirtying of the drawing and to aid inking: An improvement on the idea is the "hinged" strip. These strips are taped so that they can be lifted upwards to allow the right- and left-hand edge of a drawing to fit beneath the strips. Like a "jig" in a wood working, it speeds placement of the work.

Since the strips lock the drawing down, only one or no pieces of tape is needed to secure the sheet to the board.

____ Heavyweight drafting tape dispensers. These are not often used in drafting rooms, but they are the handiest way to store the tape.

____ "Thin-lead" lead holders. These are fast because they eliminate the lead-sharpening process. Lead sharpening on old rotary sandpaper pointers can eat up 10 to 20 minutes a day. Thin lead takes some adjustment in hand pressure to get the right results. For light layout work 0.5 mm lead is used; 0.9 mm is used for most line work, and 1.2 mm is used for lettering. The leads come in standard gradations of hardness.

____ "Serrated" bar erasers. Erasers lose their grip and may slip and smear on heavily drawn surfaces. The problem is prevented and general erasing is speeded by cutting grooves in the erasing edge with a sharp knife. A series of slots or grooves through the eraser's front edge creates a "tire-tread" surface which will grip the surface being erased.

____ The "bent" metal erasing shield. Erasing shields are notoriously losable, usually under the tracing. When shields are bent into a permanent upward arc, they won't slip under things so readily. After bending, they can still be pressed flat for erasing.

____ Kneaded erasers. Kneaded (not "kneadable") erasers can do most lightweight erasing work quickly. They leave no eraser crumbs, which eliminates the brushing process.

____ Small "nubs" on one surface of plastic tools such as triangles, French curves, and templates. Nubs (or bumps) keep the surface of the tools off the drawing, which keeps both tool and drawing clean. Some triangles are sold with nubs as a help in doing ink drafting. You can make your own by setting small drops of white glue (one near each corner of a triangle, for example) on the tools. Turn the surface with the drops over so they'll dry downwards as nubs. Use erasers or other small items as props during the drying period.

____ Alcohol-moistened towelettes. These are sold in all drugstores and are useful for quick cleaning of tools and hands.

____ A hand-held hair dryer (with the heat button off) is used by some people to blast crumbs and dust off their drawings. It's a very fast and effective cleaner, but not practical where others would be disturbed by the noise. Spray cans of compressed air are sold in some graphic arts supply stores for the same purpose.

_____ A can of nonabrasive cleansing powder is excellent for fast "dry cleaning" of accumulated dirt and graphite off the drafting board. The powder is rubbed across the board surface with a *dry* cloth. This does the cleaning. Afterwards, the residual powder is brushed off, and the final remaining powder is wiped off with a slightly damp cloth or paper towel.

_____ Extra-long drafting scales are much faster for measuring the longer dimensions. A regular scale in 24″ length may cost $40 or $50, so most people opt for the 18″ drafting machine scale, which costs around $10. The extra-long scale also helps prevent creeping plan-dimension errors that occur when you try to make long-string measurements end over end with short scales.

_____ Color coding on the scales. It's easy to misread some figures on scales that combine two measurements on each edge. Such scales become much more readable when the numbers representing the large measurements are rubbed with a soft red pencil. The red color sticks to the numbers and makes it clear which numbers represent what.

_____ A sketch paper roll dispenser and cutter. Unrolling and tearing off portions of "flimsy" or "onionskin" tracing paper is a major drafting room activity. To simplify it, some people have installed holders (such as the 11″ plastic paper-towel dispenser sold in supermarkets) and a steel rule lightly secured to the side of the drafting board. Paper from the roll is fed up to the edge of the board and under the rule. The rule acts as the tearing edge. This way, the rolls of paper are always in place and ready to tear in practically a one-handed operation.

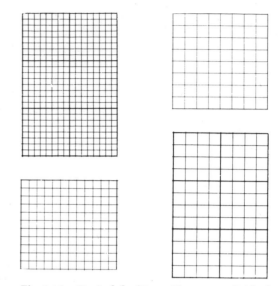

Fig. 3-11. Typical drafting grid patterns. Grids should be used to expedite drafting and especially to guide assembly of appliques and composites. They may be attached as underlayment at the drafting and layout tables or they may be printed in "fade-out" blue on the drafting and carrier sheets themselves.

(Guidelines.)

3.10 EXERCISES

These exercises are among the most important ones listed in this book. I emphatically urge you to do them and follow through on the information you develop from them.

1. After reviewing the sections "Common Errors" and "Overdrawing," obtain some past sets of working drawings. With red pencil, circle all examples of errors, omissions, oversizings, overcomplexities, overdrawing, and overnotation. Watch particularly for items that shouldn't have been drawn at all.

2. In conjunction with the above exercise, give particular attention to schedules in the drawings: door schedules, fenestration schedules, finish schedules, lintel schedules, equipment, etc. An important clue is: Repeated notes or entries in a schedule are a sign that the schedule needs to be simplified, as described in the section, "Simpler Schedule Formats."

3. Examine the dimensioning in the drawings. Is it realistic in terms of job-site conditions, construction sequence, and normal construction tolerances?

4. If practical, carry through some of this examination of prints with another person or a team. Assign a group of employees to study the principles of graphic simplification, and follow through with an examination of office prints.

NOTE: *Examine prints solely for the purpose of improving future practice. Any lapses in the drawings will speak for themselves. Blame or recrimination is unnecessary and will create resistance to the reforms you desire.*

5. As a parallel exercise, examine prints for consistency in lettering sizes, style, nomenclature, and symbols. Look for the most glaring inconsistencies and note them as items for special attention in an office procedures memo or manual.

6. If lettering, patterns, line work, and other elements are drawn too small and close for readable half-size reduction, photocopy some portions. Have prints of half-size reductions printed beside the full-size originals on sheets

to clearly show what's needed in proper graphic sizing and the consequences of not using proper sizing of elements.

4

SIMPLIFYING MANAGEMENT

4.1 EFFECTIVE DRAFTING ROOM SUPERVISION

Many people who are well into new production systems have been extremely successful. Many haven't. All will agree on one central point: *Don't bring old problems into new systems.* That's the idea behind the "housecleaning" concept of Stage 1. That's the idea behind graphic reform. It's dumb to use beautifully conceived systems to produce poorly conceived documents. And that's the idea behind this chapter. Most design firms are not tightly managed. Often enough that doesn't matter when using traditional design and production systems. The whole process is so haphazard and slow that management oversights or misjudgments can be rectified before much damage is done. That changes with the new, faster pace of systems. A problem that remains uncorrected can do more than the usual harm in much less time.

Your office situation will be exaggerated with the introduction of new systems. If your firm has conflicts and political infighting among principals, management, and staff, all that will get worse. If your firm has morale problems, they'll intensify. If your firm tends to teeter from one near-catastrophe to the next near-catastrophe, it'll continue to do so, but at a faster pace. If people don't know how time and money are distributed without systems, they'll know even less with systems. If the office is reactive, just responding to events instead of running according to long-range plans, it'll become more reactive with systems.

On the other hand, if your firm is well managed, chances are its management and planning people have been chafing at the bit running ahead of the traditional end of the business. Many of the best-managed design offices have to diversify to keep management busy, productive, and independent of the snail's pace of the drafting room.

Good management is marked by simplicity, clarity, and logical consistency. Most supervisory management deals with drawing out the most from people and preventing or curing the usual conflicts and people problems. So a large part of this chapter deals with reforms, new procedures, and new techniques that will help employees do their best.

Three major factors mar virtually every work situation:

1. Ambiguity in definition of job roles
2. Vague understanding of what is expected of employees
3. Subjective evaluations of performance

These factors are trouble spots, whether an office is run strictly or loosely, in an authoritarian or democratic fashion, or with or without extensive fringe benefits.

Professor Ralph M. Stogdill of Ohio State University has collected just about all the information there is on the subject of employee management and summarized it in a 425-page volume, *Handbook of Leadership: A Survey of Theory and Research* (New York: The Macmillan Company, Free Press Books, 1974, $19.95). This mass of on-the-job observation and measurement boils down to one central point: The determining factor in successful leadership is clarity in the work situation.

Employees do their best when they know the boundaries of their job roles and know exactly what's expected, what the measurements of performance are, and what rewards can be expected for meeting or surpassing the standards. Employees also need to know that management is personally concerned about helping them do their best work. The concern is best expressed in open, *totally clear*, and rational two-way communication throughout the office hierarchy.

There's nothing speculative or idealistic about this; it's been proven again and again in every kind of work situation with every kind of employee. Where there is *clarity*, the work gets done. Where there isn't, everything just plain goes to pieces.

CLARITY IN JOB ASSIGNMENTS

The owner of one of New York's largest offices was making one of his infrequent tours of the drafting rooms. This is what happened:

He stopped at a young draftsman's board, glared at the few light lines on the tracing, and said, "What are you working on here?"

"I'm not sure," said the draftsman hesitantly.

"You're not sure," said the architect somberly. "Well, what project are you on?"

"They didn't tell me," replied the draftsman.

"I see," said the architect. "Well, how are you coming on it?"

"It's hard to say."

"I see. You don't know what you're working on, or what you're doing, or how you're doing on it. Just what do you know?"

"I don't know," said the draftsman very weakly.

"You don't know. Then how do you expect to accomplish anything today?" said the architect disgustedly. Raising his voice, he added, "I mean, what the hell are you even doing here in my office?"

The draftsman, perceiving the absurdity of the situation that he was in, pulled himself together and voiced his complaint loudly for everyone to hear: "Please, sir! I'm doing the best I can. Please, please, don't hit me!"

Thus did the architect learn that this department of his office had become a textbook example of the worst possible supervision practices.

I had previously interviewed the manager of this department. He repeatedly interrupted the interview with asides to subordinates who came by: "Don't bother me with that. What's the matter with you?" "What are you asking me *that* for? I already told you." "Can't you see I'm tied up? You should be able to figure that out for yourself." These remarks in response to questions were punctuated by head shaking and sighs. "See what I'm up against," he told me. "These guys are helpless. They don't know a damned thing."

The manager's employee relations philosophy included the following key points: "They're supposed to know how to do their job, or they shouldn't be here." "I keep it simple. If they screw up, they're out." "Why should I tell them everything? If they knew everything I know, there's no point in my even being here."

This is an extreme case. The manager had adopted *anticlarification* policies for almost all his dealings with subordinates. But I've seen similar attitudes and heard similar remarks from architects, office managers, and job captains in offices all across the country.

One result of anti- or nonclarification attitudes is that individual job assignments are ambiguous and incomplete. Work systems experts have found that there are about nine key pieces of information anyone needs to do a task properly. Usually only three or four pieces of information are provided. Employees then either have to guess at the rest or keep coming back to ask for the missing data.

The following is a checklist of the nine items that need to be included in any task assignment. Some may be self-evident in particular situations, but it doesn't hurt to be redundant here. What is self-evident to a manager or job captain is often a dark mystery to an employee. Here's the assignment checklist:

____ The name or description of the task.

____ The reason for or purpose of the task (usually self-evident).

____ An estimate of proper duration for completing the task, the *final deadline*, and *deadlines for interim reviews*.

____ The quality of result desired. This is cited by description, an office standard, or existing work samples.

____ The quantity of result desired, the size and scale of drawings, and degree of completeness expected.

____ Where the job fits in, both in time and place; why the task should be done within a certain time; and recommended sequence for doing the parts of the task.

_____ The means of implementation—recommended or required tools, materials, and media—and where these are to be found.

_____ Sources of samples, standards, references, and all further information required to do the task.

_____ Special conditions, abnormalities, departures from standard, and actions *not* to be performed that might normally be part of the task. This requires strong emphasis.

Some engineering firms write out these details on a standard assignment form, with a copy for the person giving the assignment and a copy for the employee. There is a danger of overdoing the paperwork, but some kind of note or memo is very desirable for any assignment that will run beyond a day or more.

Another job-assignment method for working drawings is particularly effective for smaller offices where the boss and/or supervisory personnel are away from the drafting room a great deal of the time. In this method the project architect or job captain draws up a mini-working drawing set, as is usual in most office job planning these days. *After completing the small-scale mock-up of the working drawing set, a more detailed full-scale mock-up is sketched up.*

The *full-scale* mock-up shows almost everything that will be in the final set of drawings. It includes size of components, locations, scales, and special instructions for drafting each component. Technical literature, reference prints from previous jobs, and office standards are clipped to each appropriate mock-up working drawing sheet.

The full-scale mock-up leaves very few questions to be answered. If drafting staff do not have to put something aside pending further clarification, they can move on to another portion of the assignment with a very clear idea of what's to be done.

An office that has used this system for several years says the total time and cost for mock-up drawing and final drafting is *10 to 20%* less than for comparable jobs done in the traditional fashion.

KEEPING TRACK OF ASSIGNMENTS

Assignments, things to do, ideas to try—they all get lost from time to time in the office shuffle. People forget or brush off verbal requests from the boss, other tasks take precedence, or assignments are passed down the line and disappear somewhere. "Oh no, I didn't forget. I asked George to handle it, and he told Helen, and I don't know what happened after that."

One solution to the problem—used by many executives—is the "action list." This is a preprinted notebook page for recording daily assignments. Here's a sample of format and content:

Action List

Date 8/9

Subject	Person Responsible	Action Assigned	Date Due	Date Comp.
Shop. ctr.	H.K.	Impact statement, first draft.	8/12	
	H.H.	Finish CPM, review w/me.	8/14	
	O.M.	Review H.H.'s checkprints, see me.	8/20	
Med. bldg.	O.M.	Interview draftspersons, review applications w/H.H. and me.	9/1	
	Me	Reach B.D. about site trip.	8/10	
Office	Me	Ask D & K about joint venture.	8/9	
	Sec	Pass out vacation schedule.	8/10	

The action list is kept in plain view and checked frequently to confirm compliance with assignments. Completed tasks are crossed off. Past-due assignments are reaffirmed or rescheduled. Items that belong in the appointment book or other records are copied off.

The list notifies everyone that requests and assignments will be remembered and that due dates are part of the assignments. When many discrepancies show up between the "date due" and "date completed" columns, it shows a clear record of problems in time estimation or performance.

DEFINING SUPERVISORY AUTHORITY

Next to the problem of lack of information and direction is the problem of too much from too many supervisors. An old business maxim says that no employee should be responsible to more than one supervisor. The principle apparently isn't well understood by architects. Drafting staff report being caught daily between contradictory instructions from designers, senior drafting staff, job captains, managers, and office partners.

They're told, "Don't listen to that guy, he only *thinks* he's in charge. Now put this nonsense aside and get started on. . . ."

Some offices have put an end to this costly circus by naming a specific division and hierarchy of command for each job in an unequivocal "job control" memo. Once done, such memos have led to the discovery that vaguely defined job authority is one of the least visible but most treacherous barriers to efficient production.

MONITORING AND FEEDBACK IN JOB ASSIGNMENTS

The basic rule for clarification after assigning a task is to ask for a replay from the employee on specifics of the assignment. Sometimes this is done by asking the employee to make up a sequential plan for the task and then going over the plan (which usually takes the form of a short checklist) to make sure the assignment is fully understood.

As a task proceeds, it's necessary to check back to answer questions and to ensure that the instructions *remain* understood. Some employees make decisions that seem sensible to them but that veer 180° from what they're supposed to be doing. So monitoring is essential, and most supervisors know that; but when it is done haphazardly and irregularly, employees run far off the track.

One outstandingly successful monitoring system is the daily after-hours drafting-board survey. The supervisor's workday is scheduled to end an hour or so later than that of the drafting staff. The late hour is used for checking each day's completed work and writing short memos to direct the next day's action.

Employees have worked enthusiastically with this system. They like the consistent clear direction. They like leaving question notes at the end of a day and having answers waiting for them first thing in the morning.

These desk checks have to be done *openly, without recrimination, and strictly in a helpful spirit.* Many offices do such checking without notifying their employees and with the intent of trying to catch people who slough off or make mistakes. Notes left on boards in such offices are typically negative and critical. They create demoralization and resistance rather than cooperation.

THE GROUP CRIT SYSTEM FOR MONITORING WORK

The weekly office crit is the most effective system I've encountered for monitoring long-term job assignments and for reviewing overall employee performance.

Such crits bring all employees in small or medium-sized offices into a single group. The group meets weekly—usually late Friday afternoon. All participants bring *every* sketch and drawing they've worked on during the week. All work is pinned up, and each employee describes assignments and shows results. Then each responds to questioning and comment by other employees. The boss or supervisor asks questions to clarify what's presented, but *withholds any negative comments for later private talks.*

In larger offices, the group crits have to be broken up according to projects or departments. But the same rules and advantages apply. The main advantage is that there's no way major communications problems, work slowdowns, or major errors can slip through this kind of scrutiny. It soon becomes crystal clear what work is getting done and what isn't.

The group crit is multifunctional, serving many important needs in one shot. Besides objectifying task monitoring and employee performance evaluation, it lets everyone know what's happening throughout the office, which is usually a great—and usually frustrated—concern of all better employees. It is also a teaching tool. Employees learn from the techniques and procedures of superior performers.

The crit system won't work if it's used as a put-down session. Some people habitually try to build themselves up by seeking out others' weaknesses. This doesn't help others improve, and it doesn't help the office. The crits have to be positive and should be introduced with this intent explicitly stated.

SUPERVISING THE SUPERVISORS

After close watch on six representative architectural offices, I found a direct correlation between supervision and productivity. At one extreme, an office permits staff to work on large assignments 2 to 3 weeks at a stretch with only cursory checks. This office has the *worst* production record. The office with the best production has supervisory checks at each work station up to *four* or more times daily.

Supervisory checks aren't whip cracking. Effective supervision consists of support services for employees, mainly question answering, elaboration on instructions, suggestions, and general feedback, as needed to keep work flowing.

"I don't have the time," say many job captains and office managers. Various other reasons are offered for avoiding frequent checks on personnel. One problem behind these reasons is: Most supervisory staff aren't really comfortable with the "boss" role. There's an aversion to seeming like snoopers, a fear of being resented by subordinates. These attitudes are strongest where supervisory policy and procedures haven't been clearly delineated by the front office.

Higher-level staff see their supervision time as wasted. Most feel they should be designing, drawing, or consulting with clients—*anything* but acting as a resource for drafting staff. Some job captains say they've tried frequent checking and found things going smoothly enough and that checks were unnecessary distractions. My observations suggest that work smoothed out *because* of frequent checking.

In case you've wondered, work stops when the boss is away. From my observation of twelve offices, team captains tend to participate in work stoppages by disappearing or ignoring office goofing. A watch of periodic, day-long lapses in supervision showed me that many otherwise mature and businesslike staff members are always ready to stop working when the opportunity arises. In most instances, the boss would come out ahead by giving everyone the day off when active supervision can't be provided.

There's a second-level problem of supervising the supervisors. Team captains often paint rosy pictures of job progress to avoid recriminations. Bosses in lower-productivity offices tend to take the assurances at face value until crises force them to check the evidence. The day of reckoning is often avoided by new circumstances. Salvation for managers of trouble-prone jobs comes in the form of last-minute job changes. The turmoil of rushed revisions, overtime work, and added staff is blamed for time and cost overruns that would have been inevitable anyway.

Some designers feel forced to exploit lax supervision. They say 10 to 25% of their work time goes to basic design. The rest of the time goes to refinements. Most refinements are acknowledged to be highly subject to backtracking and change during working drawings or during construction.

A common justification for padding is that work has to be stretched out because of the threat to the designer of being bounced when the job is completed. Designers claim they get by with padding and keep their job security by having (and keeping to themselves) important job data that's hard to pass on to any replacement who might be called in.

There's another motive for designer slowdowns. When doubts arise about new jobs coming in, designers anticipate being transferred to production work. This problem is most acute in offices where high status is reserved for the design staff. Most designers consider working with production staff a comedown. They find all kinds of reasons to do additional design studies and revisions of previously completed assignments.

That's the rundown on some major supervision problems. Now, how can you handle them? One tool found in high-production offices is the "supervision notebook." The book has sections on each employee to record assignments, times, and data referrals. Notations are added several times daily. Similar control records are kept throughout the office hierarchy. Job captains are checked by the manager or principal, not necessarily daily, but several times each week for documented updates of work in progress.

One rule of thumb from high-production offices is: If the manager or job captain can call out the start time, status, and projected finish time of every current, significant job component, he or she is on top of the project. Conversely, questioning of supervisors in low-production offices shows they have only vague impressions regarding the work flow. Highly detailed record keeping is not essential; close, day-to-day observation and support are.

Supervision of designers is tricky but well managed in offices that have frequent in-house crits of work in progress. A large pile of drawings looks impressive on the drafting board, but it is more realistically appraised when the drawings can all be seen simultaneously. When all sketches and studies have to be put on the wall, the designer gains an incentive to solve problems, not to overdraw or overrefine.

A final note on dealing with substandard performance is: Effective supervisors avoid a hands-off attitude that lets workers hang themselves. Problems are raised as soon as they appear. Employees are *asked* how their performance might be improved. They usually know what's needed as well or better than the supervisor. After agreement is reached on the problem to be solved, the situation is closely monitored and guided toward a definite resolution.

4.2 WORKING WITH EMPLOYEES AND NOT AGAINST THEM

THE "CONFLICT" OFFICE

In many offices architectural employees are hampered by extreme stress and confusion. They describe working conditions as a never-ending series of pointless conflicts.

Emotional distractions and excessive waste characterize the "conflict" offices. Employees say they're hamstrung by office secrecy and intrigues, arbitrary shuffling of personnel, and political infighting. The biggest frustration is that there is no way of communicating problems to bosses without fear of reprisals. Communication of problems remains nonverbal, but is expressed by apathy and indifference to the quality of production.

Some offices hum along with a highly cooperative spirit. I've been looking for reasons for the differences and find substantial variation in approaches to management. Some approaches *cause* and some *prevent* major office conflicts.

The greatest difference is found in the quality of information flow. The following paragraphs give a profile of one high-conflict office, with notes on major communication gaps, subsequent problems, and likeliest solutions.

INTRIGUES AND NEGATIVE COMPETITION AMONG ASSOCIATES

Standards for advancement within the office are often vague, undefined, and left to the whim of the principals. Associates feel unsure of personal growth prospects within the firm and see others as competitors for arbitrary favoritism from bosses. Reactions come in the form of empire building, interference in others' responsibilities, and putdowns of others' work to enhance self-reputation.

Negative competition diffuses throughout an office. Designers, job captains, and drafting staff expend competitive energy against each other instead of toward productivity. The problem is most acute where offices lack systematic procedures for employee appraisal, promotion, and delegation of authority.

In low-conflict offices all promotions and bonuses are pegged to specific job achievements. Delegation of authority is established for each project, and a delegation chart is printed and distributed to all job participants.

SECRECY AND WITHHOLDING OF DATA

Principals and higher-echelon staff treat some information as exclusive property, as a privileged part of their positions. There's a feeling that sharing privileged data may diminish status.

Managers and job captains complain of front office secrecy over job prospects, fees, and time and money budgets. A lack of overview diminishes the sense of control over the work and discourages any effort to enforce the work pace or to control quality. Secrecy over salary scales, office income, and prospects for bonuses results in the spread of rumors and misinformation as a result of guesswork.

I haven't found an office with a totally open information policy. But in low-conflict offices a definite effort is made to provide periodic updates on office progress and finance for all staff. Supervisors are encouraged to provide background explanations when directing subordinates.

GENERALIZED QUESTIONS AND EMPTY ANSWERS

Bosses and supervisors ask generalized questions of employees and get empty answers. Offhanded inquiries on job progress and problems get minimal response. The natural reaction of employees is to look good, to give general positive predictions, and to avoid talking about trouble spots.

Productive troubleshooting questioning is nonthreatening and highly detailed. If job progress is at issue, for example, questions should deal with specific deadlines for each component of the work. Questions should be geared to finding all possible points of a bottleneck, and to determining data needs, needs for additional assistance, and conflicts with other staff members, etc.

THREATS AND BLAME

Information flow is blocked by threatening and blaming. Subordinates who feel under attack focus attention away from problems and waste time on defensive excuse making and buck passing.

One management rule consistently applied in smoother running offices is: *Deal with the problem, not the person.* An employee who is not burdened by a guilty or angry response to fault finding is free to take a hard look at the problem at hand and won't resist mutual exploration of options for a solution.

UNRESOLVED GRIEVANCES

Employee grievances are cut off and left unresolved. Any employee complaint is an explicit criticism of management. This usually arouses management defensiveness and a desire to turn the blame back on the employee.

Professional personnel managers and arbitrators increasingly use "active listening" in handling employee grievances. The listener keeps tuned both to the employee's complaints *and* expressed feelings. These are rephrased and fed back to the employee for confirmation or further elaboration.

The listener avoids taking an adversary role and works as an active sounding board. The employee's tendency, once satisfied in expressing complaints, is to drop superficial grievances that build up through emotionalism. The complainant tends to relax and give reasoned reconsideration to the root grievances that remain.

GRIEVANCE AND COMPROMISE

Reports of staff confrontations with management have become more frequent in the past couple of years. Extreme incidents include verbal abuse, shoving matches, and threats.

Some offices vacillate in an off-balance response to unexpected demands. Some adopt a democratic approach to setting policies, take staff votes, then reverse themselves and overrule the voting. One office fired a dissident employee, then went ahead and adopted the dissident's proposals.

Small issues sometimes mushroom. The posting of wages is one example. The scenario goes like this: One or more employees argue to staff that office wages should be publicly posted. The staff is persuaded and asks the boss to comply. The boss refuses. The refusal is taken as proof of boss indifference and exploitation of employees. The wedge is in and may now be driven farther as staff and management polarize themselves into adversary camps.

A minor issue (such as posting of wages) may be blown out of proportion as a result of management rigidity. Bosses argue for privacy on wages. Some refer to the privileged relationship between employer and employee. Some employees agree. Others argue that wages aren't posted because of inequities in money paid for equal work; that subjectivism and favoritism would be exposed; that total wages are too low compared to high office income; that secrecy is used to hold down wage competition and requests for raises. The boss's argument for privacy seems self-serving and carries little weight against those accusations.

The wage-posting controversy has been handled with minimum fuss. Several offices post established wage-scale ranges for various job categories instead of listing individual salaries. Variations within the wage range depend on differences in education, experience, and productivity. Posting of wage scales answers employees' needs without compromising privacy. This example demonstrates an axiom of professional negotiators: Don't get locked into "either/or" positions—there are always other mutually agreeable alternatives.

The question of "dead-end" jobs arises more frequently as unionists point out the lack of upward mobility in most offices. Employee expectations of advancement are soured as they see new personnel brought in to fill higher-level job openings. Dissatisfactions are expressed in demands for job security, pensions, and hefty pay boosts to compensate for limited job-advancement opportunity.

One out, used by several managers, is: If some job categories can't be elevated, *they can be expanded.* Experience suggests many workers remain satisfied if allowed to assume greater responsibility within a static job slot. Added responsibilities justify expanded earnings and satisfy the need for a sense of personal advancement. Some firms set exceptionally high and open-ended wage possibilities in return for equivalent high levels of productivity.

GETTING EMPLOYEE ADVICE

Employees will give a special bonus to the office—if asked. The technique is called the "employee audit." It's born of the fact that employees know more about internal office problems than the boss ever hears about. The trick has been to get the truth out.

Employee audits expose demoralizing personality conflicts; bad job coordination; faulty delegation; day-to-day problems with consultants; impending time and cost overruns; improper use of office facilities; and solutions to problems that may be invisible to the boss.

Employees balk at saying too much directly to the boss. There's a fear of put-downs and reprisals for bringing in advice, criticisms, or bad news. Professional audits of employee problems are available. Outside audit specialists guarantee employee anonymity and find plenty of meaty data. But costs (up to 5 hours of interview time per employee) are prohibitive for most offices.

There is a practical alternative: *Do it yourself and still preserve employee anonymity.* Prepare questionnaires and submit them periodically to staff. Most effective questions are direct: "What's good, what's bad about working here?" "What are the worst bottlenecks you see?" "Do we help or hinder you in your job?" "How?" "Is your salary fair?"

Questionnaires are distributed with a return date set for several days later. Responses are dropped into a "hands-off" box for delivery to an outside typing service that records the data and destroys the originals. This way, employees can say what they mean without fear. Here is a warning from specialists in employee auditing: Some responses will annoy, some will hurt, some will make you want to forget the whole idea. But, objectively evaluated, the "worst" ones can solve problems and prevent unexpected catastrophes.

Here's another way to draw out employee advice: Ask the staff to think about suggestions for improving the office, then circulate a list for employees to fill out a week later. The time lag lets employees take note of problems that might not come to mind on short notice.

The suggestion checklist should include some pump primers such as questions on the adequacy of the lighting or on glare problems; the convenience of work stations; and the possible need for more calculators, more secretarial staff, or faster printing turnaround.

Then conduct a second-phase survey to find the worst of the negatives. Summarize the results of the suggestion checklist and distribute copies so employees can rank possible improvements in the order of importance. The final tally will tell you which negatives to go after first and which can wait.

EVALUATING EMPLOYEE PERFORMANCE

A formal evaluation system reduces errors from snap judgments or prejudices for or against individual employees. It works best when several people (principals, managers, job captains, other trusted employees) participate. Users of systems recommend monthly scorings for new employees and quarterly ones for tenured employees.

Performance scoring helps keep superior employees. An objectified rating procedure permits a faster, surer response to good performance. And when raises must be denied, the chart provides a fair standard for an employee's self-evaluation and points up areas for improvement required for advancement in the office.

Low motivation and low output are not always easily detected. Cover-ups are easy. An employee may be shuffled through a variety of assignments under different supervisors. Ultimately, no one is sure of the employee's actual overall performance.

Losses from problem employees are cut by offices that use a systematic employee performance evaluation system. An evaluation system summarizes observations of employee performance and rapidly locates employees who are mismatched with their jobs.

Evaluation charts ease the discomfort of firing employees. Comparisons of scores and salaries show averages or office norms for workers in various job categories. An employee working somewhat below the norm can compare his or her total score with others. If later evaluation shows no improvement and an employee is to be dismissed, the reasons for firing are a matter of record. Employees working well below the norm who are to be dismissed are shown comparative scores. Many elect to resign under such circumstances rather than be fired.

Here's an outline of the evaluation system used by several well-managed firms:

1. The individual employee's file includes a chart for numerically rating such qualities as speed, reliability, technical knowledge, accuracy of drawing, quality of drawing, initiative, inventiveness, cooperation, leadership potential, plus other factors of concern to the office.

2. Numerical ratings for each factor may be 3 for "excellent," 2 for "superior," 1 for "average," and −1 for "below average."

3. If some factors are considered more important than others, each factor is given a numerical "weight." "Weight"—or importance of a factor being rated—may be 3 for "very important," 2 for "important," or 1 for "desirable." If an office considers drawing accuracy "very important," that factor has a

weight of 3. If the employee is evaluated "superior" in drawing accuracy, he or she gets a rating of 2. The *weight* (3) is multiplied by the *rating* (2) for a final score of 6.

4. An employee's overall performance score is the total of all weight-times-rating scores of various factors shown on the chart. The final total is compared with those of other employees.

UNPRODUCTIVE PERSONNEL

Almost every office has people who act as detours or cul-de-sacs to the work flow. They take work in and they put work out with little noticeable benefit to the office or to the jobs at hand.

A New York architectural firm was jolted when the boss discovered three top-echelon people whose positions added virtually nothing to the work flow. Lower-level employees knew about the problem but didn't feel it was safe to say so. An outside management consultant had to deliver the news.

I've never seen an office with six or more people where the problem didn't exist to a serious degree. Some examples follow:

A senior designer was always first to latch onto new projects. He made numerous flow charts and bubble diagrams, which were turned over to project architects, who then did the preliminaries. The project architects never consulted the charts or diagrams. Each thought that others must use them, but, individually, none found them usable in the process of actual project design.

An office manager was officially responsible for intraoffice coordination and allocation of personnel from project to project. Over a period of time, the office's principals took over these functions. The office manager became an intermediary, carrying messages from principals to employees and, beyond that, performing no actual work. Following Parkinson's law, the manager remained busy long after his job became obsolete and useless to the office.

Job captains have frequently been assigned to run projects only to find an associate or principal repeating most of the same work.

Many times, during cleanup after a large project, architects find drawers stuffed with design studies or detail studies that clearly contributed nothing to the jobs they were charged to. Most architects have also noticed at one time or another that a "key" employee's or associate's prolonged absence from the office had no negative effect whatsoever on overall production.

Finding the cul-de-sacs isn't hard—it just takes a little nosing around. The difficulty lies in acknowledging the problem and doing something about it. It may mean unloading an old friend or a faithful employee with many years' seniority. No one has an easy solution for this one. It's easier to look the other way or invent elaborate projects to justify keeping someone on the payroll.

The problem may be in the job role. A change in role may bring a person back into the mainstream of office productivity. When that isn't possible, most firms opt for generous severance settlements as the most painless way out.

Costs have to be looked at head-on. Most offices are squeezed between rising costs and declining income. It's easy to argue that someone is a "good person" and has done a lot for the firm, but this question remains: Does that justify an expense of $15,000 to $30,000 a year for unnecessary work? My observations indicate the problem is nearly universal and is worth careful scrutiny by any firm.

SMOOTHING THE WAY FOR OFFICE IMPROVEMENTS

During an AIA chapter seminar on office practice, a young architect told me, "I despise your manuals. I work in an office where they take your stuff very seriously. You recommend 5-mm lead holders, for example. They tell us, 'Use 5-mm lead—period!' You can imagine how that goes over." I don't have to imagine it. I've seen numerous examples of heavy-handed implementation of office reform—all totally self-defeating.

The following process is observed repeatedly in numerous offices: The manager bluntly initiates a new efficiency policy and expects automatic compliance. Employees react with varying degrees of indifference or hostility. If there is no follow-through by management, the idea dies out quickly. If there is persistent follow-through, the change may take hold at the cost of considerable disruption and demoralization.

Not all changes will arouse negative employee response. Simpler improvements that require little adjustment are usually readily accepted. The problems arise when more demanding changes appear to add new, unnecessary burdens to the work load without appropriate compensation or consideration. But even minor changes have created extraordinary ill will when presented with an offensive "do it this way, do it now, or get out" attitude.

I've observed a variety of offices establish a pattern of failure in their reform efforts. The pattern includes the following lapses by management and subsequent responses among employees:

1. Little or no explanation of the necessity for the change ("they treat us like children or idiots").
2. Explanations for change that focus solely on office goals or abstract efficiency rather than employee needs for convenient working conditions ("they didn't make their 90% profit this year, so they have to squeeze it out of us").
3. Failure to get employee participation in decisions that bear on their working conditions ("we're just cattle in this place").
4. No evident sympathy or understanding of inconveniences faced by employees who must adjust to new procedures ("I'm not going to put myself out for their stupid experiments").

The problem of motivating employee cooperation in efficiency reforms has been faced squarely by a number of offices in recent years. One architect introduces reforms to single project teams, rather than to the entire office staff. Team members are instructed in the new technique and carefully supervised in its application to their project. Each reform is introduced as a potential source of professional self-improvement, rather than as a moneysaver for the boss. Team members, when assigned to new jobs, are expected to train others in the technique. In this manner, changes become self-promulgating; they work their way throughout the office almost automatically.

Another approach—better suited to smaller offices—centers on a comprehensive, long-term, officewide reform program. A list is prepared of major problems and opportunities, along with selected solutions for meeting them. The list is explained, reviewed, revised, and refined through officewide discussion, before any points are implemented. This sets the stage for cooperative action and eliminates the primary causes of employee resistance or resentment.

USES OF AN OMBUDSMAN

"We always keep the door open; we're always ready to listen to problems." That's the sincere promise of most architects I talk to. But their staffs see it differently—from experience: "You can't talk seriously to my boss . . . he blames you for stirring things up." "He'll sit and read the mail while you're trying to get a point across." "There are some things you learn aren't to be mentioned around here."

The "door is open," but employees don't want to stick their necks out. The result can be expensive, as in these cases:

A job captain delayed checking engineering drawings and failed to transmit architectural revisions to the consultants. His crew of four draftspersons knew about the problem and considered going to the front office. But they feared a backlash and decided to keep their heads down. Extensive revisions required in the final phase of working drawings led to a job cost overrun in excess of $12,000.

A draftsperson warned the designer that program requirements on a new public building were being ignored and would have to be included later at added cost to the office. The designer persuaded a principal to transfer the draftsperson elsewhere because of "negative attitudes." Changes were later required at the office's expense, as the draftsperson predicted.

A project architect ordered his design staff to churn out endless, meaningless design studies on a government agency building to "use up the design budget." This was done without the principals' knowledge. An employee became upset at the apparent fraud and felt compelled to notify the client. Subsequent investigation led to disqualification of the office from future commissions from the agency.

One answer is to institute an "ombudsman" in the office. The ombudsman concept attacks the problem behind upward communication failures. The problem is fear. Employees know that management rewards good news, not bad. Management and bosses have ultimate bread-and-butter power. If a grievance, warning, or suggestion has merit, it makes management or the boss look bad. If a problem is raised but proves invalid, it makes the employee look bad. Either way, the pressure is on to keep silent.

What can the ombudsman do about it? The primary function of the ombudsman is to open up communication from employees to management and, at the same time, block recriminations if management feels insulted or threatened. It removes the fear barrier.

One firm rotates the ombudsman role among three associates. All are required to treat complaints, problems, or suggestions in confidence and to act as agents for the employees when wearing the ombudsman hat. Another office gives the task to a technical staff member who is considered qualified by both management and employees.

The ombudsman assignment requires a few hours a week on top of regular duties in medium- to large-sized offices. The investment may be returned manyfold by catching costly personnel and job problems before they get out of hand. If the ombudsman also activates an effective idea suggestion and implementation system, further time savings accrue from efficiency ideas introduced by employees.

A large number of functions can be assumed by the ombudsman: mediation of disputes and misunderstandings between staff members; watchdogging of overlaps and conflicts in supervision of individual employees; checking of overhiring, misassigning, and underutilizing of personnel; handling an internal audit; drawing out dissatisfaction of employees, especially those who quit or are about to quit the office; spotting racism or sexism and the subtle work sabotage and demoralization that often go with them; general trouble-shooting and stopping of rumors. The ombudsman can also act as a conduit for management proposals for new procedures and policy. Employee feedback will be more candid and detailed than is normally accessible to management.

Some rules for an effective ombudsman system are:

1. The scope and limits of action should be clearly defined in writing. Hiring, firing, and setting salaries, for example, aren't normally considered appropriate ombudsman territory.
2. The ombudsman should be empowered to gather information from staff or management to validate a grievance or problem.
3. The ombudsman's recommendations aren't binding on management, but if more than a fraction of the recommendations are rejected, the system should be reexamined and overhauled.
4. When the ombudsman is asked to investigate or to act upon a problem, the petitioning employee must be given a specific later appointment to review the results.
5. The ombudsman doesn't reject any requests to check out a problem. Even apparently trivial or baseless items are examined, and evidence is gathered for feedback to the petitioner.
6. The ombudsman doesn't handle discipline or rule enforcement.
7. The system is *not* initiated without consultation and input from employees. If an ombudsman system is designed and set up solely by management, it will arouse suspicion and the effort will most likely go to waste.

4.3 NEW CONTENT FOR THE DRAFTING MANUAL

After reviewing dozens of office drafting manuals, I asked drafting staffs what sort of information they needed most often and most urgently when putting out a job. Their needs didn't generally coincide with the usual manual content.

On the other hand, some manuals have met drafting staff's data needs and have been exceptionally well received. The author of one of them explained: "For years I watched our draftsmen go to the plan files whenever they wanted to check on an office standard. All our standards were enforced, and they were in the manual. But it was as if the book didn't exist. Why fight it? It became pretty obvious that they needed to be shown the standards in the context of real working drawings instead of in the artificial format of the manual."

He effectively solved the problem with a minimum of time investment. He assembled partial sheets of old working drawings that contained the most common drawing components and added some notes (including some don'ts) with a felt-tip pen. These were reduced to 8½" × 11" sheets with commercial photoreproduction and added to the "Office Standards" section of the manual.

Another highly valued, timesaving manual compiled from the drafting staff's suggestions has virtually replaced *Time Saver Standards*, *Graphic Standards*, and other technical office literature. Whenever someone is repeatedly looking up the same data, it is copied and bound into the manual. Only a few items need to be specially written or drawn up. Most are already on hand for copying.

This manual is designed for residential and small commercial work, but a list of the data it provides at each person's board should suggest useful ideas for any office. The data include:

Office specifications and working drawing symbols, abbreviations, and nomenclature. (Standardizing of names for types of rooms eliminated a very common source of discrepancy between drawings and specs.)
Favored materials and products, ranging from joist hangers to kitchen equipment to elevators.
(This too eliminated a common source of conflict and indecision.)
Foundation vent sizes and spacing requirements.
Standard girder, floor joist, ceiling joist, rafter, and light wood truss spacing and sizes.
Typical large-opening header spans and sizing.
Water heater requirements according to varying residential occupancies.
Chase sizes for all combinations of plumbing equipment.
Preferred toilet room fixture sizes and spacings.
Roof ventilation requirements; inlet and outlet percentages according to roof type and area.
Roof slopes translated into degree settings for the adjustable triangle.
Local roof and site-work draining requirements.
Masonry block and brick course dimensions.
Standard stair riser and tread chart.
An inch and foot equivalent chart (for example, 6' 7" = 79", and so on), useful in figuring risers between floors.
A decimal equivalent chart.
Explanation and rules of modular drafting.
Some vital building code requirements; building classifications and construction fire ratings; exit requirement formulas; passageway and stair requirements.
Office standard details and specification format.

It was conceded that it took time and money to provide this data for drafting staff, that some data were included that proved useless, and that updating took some extra effort. But it became apparent that duplication of effort by drafting staff seeking the same information had been occurring almost daily in the drafting room. One year of this wasteful effort would cost the office hundreds of times the expense of preparing the manual.

Several offices, in planning or redesigning their manuals, solicited and received some helpful advice from the people for whom the manuals were written. Suggestions included:

1. Call it a handbook instead of a manual. A manual is thought of as an office rule book to be read only once. As such, an office would need only one copy for occasional reference. A handbook denotes a professional tool worthy of constant use and improvement.
2. Don't "update" the handbook with disciplinarian memos. Memos about excessive tar-

diness or abuse of telephone privileges are often misdirected to the entire staff rather than to the specific offenders. Responsible employees have expressed strong resentment of this policy; they point out that it makes no friends for the handbook and its contents.

3. Emphasize design values in the handbook format and in the select office drafting standards. Working drawing standards of keying symbols, schedules, title blocks, and detail sheet format can be simple and readable, but elegant. The use of ugly standards will be strongly resisted by conscientious employees, especially since they must think about the drawings they'll be showing when looking for the next job.

4. Encourage participation in the handbook's growth. Provide some specific, formal system by which employees can present proposals for improving and updating handbook content. Use a three-hole-punch, looseleaf binder for maximum flexibility.

5. Add copies of technical articles and clippings about the work of the office. One office, responding to this staff suggestion, began leaving stacks of helpful technical literature in the coffee area. All copies were snapped up without prompting. As a spinoff, individuals, on their own initiative, began supplying significant articles on materials, spec writing, etc., to fellow employees.

6. Don't contradict the handbook. All changes should be authorized by principal(s) and distributed as formal amendments. When a principal, manager, or job captain makes occasional verbal "exceptions," the contents of the handbook are thrown into doubt and soon will be generally ignored.

7. Don't force the staff to keep reinventing the wheel. When someone has researched some data that might apply to future jobs, put it in the handbook.

4.4 DRAFTING ROOM MANAGEMENT: SELECTED PROBLEMS AND SOLUTIONS

The following pages indicate some of the most common drafting room efficiency problems, along with a variety of tested solutions.

OFFICE PLANNING

Often technical literature is at one end of the office, reference prints are at another, and supplies are in the back room. A staff of eight draftspersons was logging about 4800 feet of travel per day to an isolated reference print table. Relocation of the table to the center of the drafting room cut total daily travel to 800 feet. This not only saved mileage, but stopped the excessive social visits that accompany heavy office traffic.

Most drafting rooms have grown by happenstance, and are rarely planned in the way an architect plans for his clients. Inefficiencies and conflicts become built-in. The simple solution in almost every case is: centralize facilities to minimize average individual travel distances. But don't move people around without first selling them on some advantage. An employee used to a particular, fond niche interprets an unwanted move as an implicit demotion and will take it out on the office in one way or another.

PRODUCTION STANDARDS

Improvement—or lack of it—is impossible to judge accurately without measurements of existing production levels. Faulty guesswork here interferes with job scheduling, budgeting, and setting reasonable salary scales and standards for promotion.

More and more offices are asking draftspersons to record work-time records directly on working drawing tracings. The accumulated job time is added up, then divided by the number of sheets per job, to get job and sheet averages. In addition, time variations common to certain types of drawings are noted.

Objective measurements may reveal gross inaccuracies in previously used rules of thumb. One housing specialist had always allowed for about 1 week per sheet on his working drawings.

Time checking showed real averages running at 2 and 3 work weeks per sheet.

DESIGN CHANGES DURING WORKING DRAWINGS

Draftspersons frequently cite this as their biggest frustration. Employers consider it the biggest threat to job budgets.

The problem generally results from a combination of changes in client needs and desires, and errors or vacillation by the designer. One protection is a "predesigning" system. Predesigning requires designer and client to agree on basic requirements or options of building height, size, configuration, structural and mechanical systems, fenestration, partitions, and materials—before a line is drawn on paper. This approach prevents serious misjudgments by the designer and helps the client settle on major decisions early in the game.

A complementary procedure is to begin each project with a cautious cost check on the client's program. Overoptimistic budget expectations on the part of the client must be hashed out before the architect gets locked into an unrealistic project.

Here is another protection that some offices swear by, once they've learned the habit: use of complete quantity cost surveys during preliminaries, during working drawings, and just before going to bid. This is considered the only insurance available against major construction cost overruns and the inevitable revision (if not abandonment) that follows.

Client-initiated changes are minimized when the design phase is extended sufficiently to do an exceptionally complete and comprehensive set of preliminaries. Once this is accepted by the client as *the* building, with changes billed as fully reimbursable expenses, client-initiated revisions are sharply reduced. It means a shift in traditional proportioning of design and production budgets, but—where practical—the procedure comes highly recommended.

OFFICE "DOWN TIME"

Forced employee idleness between assignments often worsens as work loads increase. Supervision becomes harried and uncoordinated. Draftspersons are told to look busy, and, out of boredom, they interfere with others by drifting and socializing.

One old-time office has a time-tested remedy. An odd-job file is maintained at a central location in the drafting room. Draftspersons who are between assignments can check out an odd job to fill time. These jobs include checking shop drawings, spillover assignments from other current projects, small "accommodation" jobs with long-term deadlines, and office work of filing and office maintenance. One necessary rule is that when a job captain or manager needs the draftsperson back on the main line of work, the draftsperson can't claim that the odd job has precedence. Another rule is: Someone must have responsibility for keeping the file updated and preventing important items from getting lost at the bottom of the pile.

SCHEDULING AND TIME CONTROL

A partner in one of Florida's largest offices complains that: "Job captains often misread the completion level of a job. They try to make the job *look* like it is on schedule to keep us happy, but then the last 5% takes more time to finish than the first 30%."

A schedule control system can solve this problem. Here are the essential steps:

1. Drafting room budget, based on estimated final fee, determines the maximum number of hours available for the job. These hours are distributed among the planned number of sheets (the miniset provides a good basis for estimating allowable drafting time per sheet). One rule-of-thumb budget allows 50% of the gross estimated final fee to cover direct job costs. Of this, 25 to 50% goes to working drawings. These percentages vary depending on office efficiency and job types. Old job records will show average overhead and working drawings costs per job and per sheet.

2. A working drawing sheet–time record can be stamped or preprinted on the inside trim margin of each tracing. Vertical spaces are provided to record date, initials, daily number of hours spent, and total hours to date. Staff members are required to make entries whenever they work on a drawing (including notes of time spent on studies, consultation, etc.). Estimated total allowable hours for the sheet are noted at the top of each record. The form may look like this:

Total hours
scheduled:____

Date	Name and code	Hours	Total hours

The vertical lines can be extended as required during the course of the job. The "code" shown on the form is optional but is recommended as an aid for job control and analysis for future job planning. Coding designates types of items drawn and the types of work done on them. For example, a "D-1" could mean: "details—sketching and research." "P-2" might be: "plan—finish drafting."

There may be resistance to this system by draftspersons who see it as a policing system. Cooperation is improved if it is made clear that the system will benefit everyone by improving office profits and objectifying decisions on future job fees, schedules, and personnel raises and bonuses.

With this system, the status of a drawing is never in question. If the record shows 75% of time allowance used up while only half the drawing is completed, then the bottleneck is clear for all to see. The completion level of a tracing is judged by comparison with the mini-drawing for working drawings described earlier.

A "finish-up" person can provide a cushion for the system. When drawings fall behind schedule, it is recommended that the most experienced senior draftsperson pick these up for completion before deadlines. Some offices meet their deadlines by keeping one staff member solely for this purpose.

4.5 SYNTHESIS

Increasing the clarity of management-staff communication achieves in human terms what Systems Drafting is supposed to achieve in graphic terms. It means simplifying, eliminating clutter and redundancies, and finding ways to recycle and reuse the best of what you already have.

Introducing new techniques of any sort will bring management problems right to the surface. There will be people problems. People on the job are in very vulnerable positions. If they're employees, they're subject to firing at a moment's notice. Management and especially the owners of a firm need to appreciate that employees don't know for sure, from one day to the next, whether they're going to have a job or not. That's an insecure place to be, and that's why employees are afraid of change.

If so much as a new table is moved into an office, rumors that people are going to be transferred or laid off start flying. That's how vulnerable and uninformed people can be.

On the top side of the hierarchy every improvement or suggestion of an improvement is a threat to the bosses. Every improvement has a built-in condemnation. If it's a good idea and answers some long-standing need, it says: "You idiots. Why wasn't this done months (or years) ago?"

No one wants advice on how they can improve themselves unless they're paying a specialist a pile of money for the favor. If the advice comes from a peer or a draftsperson or, God forbid, an office errand person, forget it.

Both employers and employees are threatened by changes, for their own respective reasons. With systems, change—even methodical, logical change as laid out in this book—is going to frighten and worry some people. They'll express those feelings in diverse and obtuse ways that may be very difficult to decipher. The results will be readily understood, however: dissension, confusion, resistance, sabotage, and systems that don't work.

A good time to test for management problems and introduce some management reforms is during the time you're reforming or refining the basics of working drawing graphics and content. That way you'll get double duty from both changes at once and, hopefully, the management changes will save the new systems from an early grave. Study the communications structure of an office. Which way(s) does information flow between people? Is there a strict one-way flow down the hierarchy? Are there "eddies" of information—people who retain information as their property? Do people know what other people are doing? Do they know, in general, what's going on throughout the office?

5

DRAFTING
ON POLYESTER

5.1 THE DREADED PLASTIC

I first used polyester (Mylar) when working on production drawings at a large office in New York City. We were on a large government job, and the government revised its standards almost daily. That meant there was a floor full of drafting staff doing nothing but erasing the previous day's government standards to comply with the next day's government standards. No tracing paper would have survived the abuse, so the production team leaders had wisely chosen polyester drafting media because it was tough enough to survive all the shuffling and revisions and check printing.

The polyester had some interesting characteristics besides its durability. It was horrible to draw on. The sheets were thick and unpleasantly heavy. Graphite smeared terribly. If you overerased, the matte surface came off. It was hard to make a line of decent darkness on it. The abrasive matte surface wore down the leads in no time. It always had an unpleasant static electricity charge that attracted dirt, made sheets stick together, and gave you a shock every time you touched metal. Between the General Service Administration's ephemeral "standards" and drawing on the polyester, it was as if we had been sent to some sort of architects' hell.

That doesn't mean you shouldn't use polyester, though. Quite the contrary. Polyester is mandatory as a drafting medium if you're serious about getting into systems. You just have to use a little finesse to avoid or mitigate its bad qualities. We weren't told about such things in the New York office and so accepted our plight with tortured resignation.

Before explaining how to use polyester most effectively, I need to explain why I don't call it "Mylar" as everyone else does. The reason is that Mylar is a trade name of the DuPont Company. DuPont is responsible for most polyester drafting media, but not all. Therefore, we use the preferred generic word: "polyester." Another trade name for polyester base film is Estar, which is Kodak's product.

There are three main general kinds of polyester:

1. Drafting medium, with a matte surface (lightly textured drawing surface) on one or both sides.
2. Photosensitive polyester. The surface is coated with a light-sensitive emulsion, similar to photographic film. The material is exposed to projected or direct-contact images, developed by a single-solution developer which "washes off" the nonexposed areas. Variations include matte and nonmatte surfaces on one or both sides.
3. Diazo-sensitive polyester. The surface is coated with ammonia-developed coating. The main choices are sepia line or black line. These two come with nonmatte or matte surfaces, one or both sides. The nonmatte films are called "slicks" or "throwaways." The sepia material is most commonly called "sepia Mylar." This is an extraordinarily handy product in reprographics.

Why is polyester mandatory as a drafting medium if you're using new production systems? There are two main reasons: durability and dimensional stability. When you use overlay drafting, for example, two or more layers of drawing *have* to match up in perfect registration, no matter what the temperature or humidity. Tracing paper won't do that for you. When you use composite paste-ups or standard details, there is a lot of physical handling of the medium. Polyester will survive the abuse.

Much of the repro shop's final product *has* to be on polyester, and you have no choice whatever about it. So, for these and related reasons— it's wonderful for ink drafting, for example— polyester has become part of daily drafting room life.

Next I'll cite a few more characteristics of the material that you should know about and then tell how to use the material effectively with a minimum of strain.

5.2 CHARACTERISTICS AND SOURCES OF POLYESTER

Besides the choices of light-sensitive emulsion, or no emulsion, and draftable matte surface or nonmatte surface, there is a choice in thicknesses. The thinnest practical polyester is 1.5 mil (0.0015"); the thickest practical polyester is about 7 mil (0.007").

Thin polyester tends to curl and bubble up from the drafting board. For most drafting purposes, use 2, 3, or 4 mil. Use 1.5 mil for the smallest sheets, 2 mil for sheet sizes such as 11" × 14" or 18" × 24", and 4 or 5 mil for large sheets such as 30" × 42". Generally speaking, use 3 mil for the popular medium-range sheet size of 24" × 36".

An architect told me that he bought his polyester from a local blueprint shop and they refused to sell him anything less than 7-mil polyester. You never have to be stuck with that kind of dealer, or the kind of prices you may have to pay in smaller communities. There are always reliable mail-order sources. (Remember, *Guidelines* will send you an update of reprographic materials sources. See Resources at the end of the book for address and ordering information.)

People who have had years of experience with polyester drafting say it's definitely best to stay with products from major manufacturers. There's always such a thing as the "bad batch," and the bigger companies are better about throwing theirs away.

It's also recommended that you use the same brand drafting polyester as photosensitive or diazo-sensitive polyester. There's a compatibility factor. Each brand has its own "feel," and it's easier for staff if they can adjust to just one product.

5.3 COMPATIBLE DRAFTING MATERIALS

Standard drafting leads and standard drafting erasers don't work well on polyester. That's mainly why people become so frustrated when working with the material. True, the standard graphite lead grabs better and has a better drafting feel on the plastic film, but it doesn't lay down a good dark line, it smears easily, and it murks up the whole sheet after a while.

The standard drafting erasers are designed to scrub and grind out graphite particles that are ground into paper fibers. Line work on polyester is strictly on the surface and requires only surface erasure. The abrasive erasers are very harsh on the polyester matte coating and will wear it away quickly. *That is especially true with abrasive electric erasers. They'll burn away the matte in no time.*

There are leads and erasers that are chemically designed to work best on polyester. They do work the best, and they're the ones to use. Since there's often resistance to the most minor change in personal drafting habits, you'll find draftspeople refusing to use the proper leads and erasers. In such a case your office may use this approach: Send a cart from work station to work station. Have each draftsperson empty drawers and shelves of all graphite leads and all standard erasers. Then distribute the appropriate polyester-compatible products.

I don't mean to imply that drafting staff are necessarily willful in their resistance to polyester-compatible products. The compatible "plastic" leads have a greasy feel to them when you draw with them. They tend to be brittle and require constant sharpening. And the sharpening may break the leads as much as sharpen them. It takes some adjusting.

One popular adjustment is the mixed lead—part graphite, part plastic. Many offices have settled on this as the happy medium (or unhappy compromise, depending on viewpoint).

There is an even more popular adjustment: a switch to ink drafting. People who get the hang of it do ink work as fast or faster than lead drafting, save on materials, and draw work that's properly dense for reprographics. There is more on that in the next chapter.

DuPont has some good, realistic advice on drawing with pencils or leads on polyester.

1. Rotate pencil while drawing lines. This helps maintain line width.
2. Hold pencil at slight angle to the direction of the line. There is more chance for matte damage if the pencil is held near the perpendicular. Keep the angle constant while drawing the whole line.
3. Do not retrace lines. This may lead to smearing. (Select the pencil hardness to produce the right line density.)
4. Use a slightly blunted point. This reduces the possibility of gouging the surface. Drawing a few lines on paper will suffice for smoothing the point and eliminating any burrs.
5. Do not press too firmly, as this may emboss the film. Actually, relatively little pressure is needed to produce a good line. A firm rather than pliable backing sheet is best.

Here are some of the plastic leads and plastic/graphite combinations that have proven acceptable on polyester drafting film:

Ruwe #205
A. W. Faber-Castell Dri Line #1915
Eberhard Faber Microlar
Dixon-Crucible FTR; FTR matte
Eagle Turquoise Filmograph
Staedtler Mars Lumograph Duralar
Hardmuth Koh-I-Lar 1500M
Dur-O-Lite Film King

And acceptable erasers for drafting and photo or diazo matte drafting films are:

Plastic
 NIJI #101, 300
 Pelikan Plasto/10

Vinyl
 A. W. Faber-Castell Magic-Rub
 A. W. Faber-Castell #1960
 Best TAD
 Dur-O-Lite Film King
 A. W. Faber-Castell Filmar #1956
 Eberhard Faber Race Kleen #521
 Koh-I-Lar #286
 Eagle Turquoise

Rubber
 Eberhard Faber Pink Pearl #101
 A. W. Faber-Castell Parapink #7021

5.4 EXERCISE

Do a literal materials comparison. Draw, or have drawn, one polyester sheet with graphite lead and use standard eraser. Draw another with plastic lead and use vinyl eraser. Draw a third with mixed plastic/graphite lead and use vinyl eraser. Draw a fourth with graphite lead and use regular eraser on 1000H tracing paper. Judge the results: Which drawings reproduce best? Which are cleanest? How long does it take to adjust to a new drafting medium?

6

INK DRAFTING

6.1 FASTER DRAFTING WITH INK

Most architects and engineers aren't sure that I'm serious when I recommend ink drafting. When someone says "ink" to people of one generation, it means ruling pens. Ruling pens were sort of a glorified tweezer with a screw device that opened or closed the pincers. It held ink through a combination of fluid surface tension and luck. And usually luck would run out quickly. If you ran the pen across a piece of eraser crumb or dust, or if you twitched, all the ink would pour out onto the drawing.

To another generation, "ink" means the old technical pens—a great improvement over the ruling pens. But the pens dried up or clogged up constantly. Users had to spend half their time at the wash basin washing and unclogging their pens. Drafting was no breeze, either. It took great care not to smudge a wet ink line. And repairing errors in ink on tracing paper takes much of the fun out of life.

To the current generation, "ink" means faster-drying ink, much more reliable pens, and much easier cleaning. But it's still not perceived as a drafting method that can compare with drafting lead for speed and versatility.

Many architects and engineers now say that the latter is a false perception. They say that in reality ink drafting, with the latest tools and materials, is fully competitive—even better—than drafting with leads. Part of the reason is that it is better—faster and cleaner as a drafting method—if you use ink on polyester.

In fact, the new technical pens and polyester solve each other's problems. Polyester is difficult to draw on even with the best choices of lead and erasers. But it's exceptionally easy to draw on with ink. Conversely, one of the remaining drawbacks of ink drafting is time lost in making corrections or revisions on paper. Corrections and/or revisions of ink on polyester are easy. Add the auxiliary advantage that ink drafting gives the best line work for sharp photoreproduction. Also, when adding drafting to a photoreproduction, only ink will match the density of the photoemulsion line work.

It's a complete set. Ink solves the problem of drawing on polyester. Polyester helps solve the problems of drawing with ink. And both of them solve some of the limitations of drafting for photoreproduction.

It will take staff some time to adjust—mainly because of fear of the permanence of ink. Most people start off unsure and shaky. The technical pen manufacturers say it takes draftspeople a day to adjust and a week to gain normal drawing speed again. Henry D. Norris, a Georgia architect who has all his working drawings done in ink, says 10 days is more like it. But after that learning period, it's all gravy.

Staff have to adjust to the ink drying time. There are new inks that dry fast, almost immediately. But draftspeople usually start out using pieces of tape to lift their straightedges above the drawing surface and keep tools away from "wet" ink. Before long they find that, with nominal care, the wet-ink protection isn't necessary.

When you introduce ink drafting in an office, you'll run into people who will not use the right equipment or materials or will not use them according to directions. When the ink drafting

63

doesn't work for them, they'll blame everything but their own indifference to correct procedures. It's imperative that the rules of good use of technical pens be clearly and expressly emphasized. A draftsperson may have been drafting for 20 years, as some of them like to remind people, but that doesn't mean they know how to do everything correctly. *The rules are provided by the manufacturers. Don't overlook them.*

The leading brands and manufacturers of technical drafting pens are Rapidograph by Koh-I-Noor, Leroy Technical Pen System by Keuffel & Esser, and the TG Technical Pen by Faber-Castell Corp. You can get the latest list of manufacturers and products from Resources, the *Guidelines* resources update cited at the end of this book.

6.2 THE RULES

Ink drafting is most efficient when done on polyester. That will require that you use jewel-tip pens. Regular tips wear out in no time on the matte surface of polyester drafting film. Jewel tips require some care; they'll break easily if dropped on the floor. But that's no reason not to use them. They'll more than pay for themselves because of their extraordinary longevity. Steel-tip pens are for drawing on tracing paper, and tungsten carbide tips are for computer-driven plotters. (Tungsten carbides are hard enough for polyester work but feel a little "scratchy" in use. Jewels feel smooth.)

Buy pens with the newest anticlog tip protectors. These virtually assure instant start-up regardless of long periods of disuse of the pens. If you do much ink drafting, invest in a small technical pen ultrasonic cleaner. That will give you quick, effective cleaning if and when the pens do clog up. If many staff people are using pens, the ultrasonic cleaner will pay for itself in no time.

Technical pens are basically fountain pens. They have a reservoir that holds the ink supply and a small tube that transports the ink to the drafting medium. You can get hours of uninterrupted drafting from one reservoir full of ink—or 1200 linear feet of line according to one manufacturer—if you'd like to draw a 1200-foot line. Here are some rules for using the pens properly.

Fig. 6-1. Ink drafting with a technical pen on polyester. (Du Pont Photo Systems.)

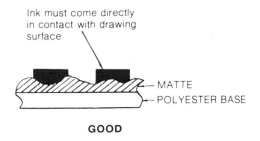

Ink must come directly in contact with drawing surface

MATTE
POLYESTER BASE

GOOD

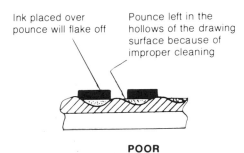

Ink placed over pounce will flake off

Pounce left in the hollows of the drawing surface because of improper cleaning

POOR

Fig. 6-2. Ink adhesion.
(Koh-I-Noor Rapidograph, Inc.)

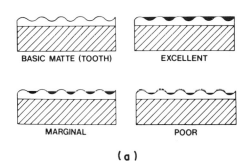

BASIC MATTE (TOOTH)   EXCELLENT

MARGINAL   POOR

(a)

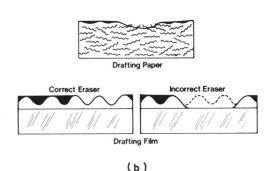

Drafting Paper

Correct Eraser   Incorrect Eraser

Drafting Film

(b)

Fig. 6-3. Draftable surfaces. (*a*) Line creation. (*b*) Effects of erasure.
(Eastman Kodak Co.)

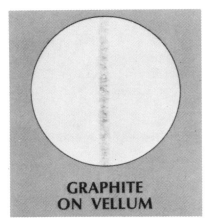

GRAPHITE ON VELLUM

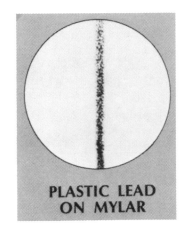

PLASTIC LEAD ON MYLAR

DIRECT INK DRAFTING ON MYLAR

Fig. 6.4. Line quality comparisons.
(Koh-I-Noor Rapidograph, Inc.)

1. When you start, shake the pen slightly. That jiggles a little wire that helps keep the ink supply tube clear. If you don't hear a little "click-click" when shaking the pen, it means it may be jammed up and may require a little more shaking or a run in the ultrasonic cleaner. *Never strike or tap the tip against a surface.*

2. Test a couple of short lines on a scrap of paper or card to check the ink flow. If all's well, you're ready to draw.

3. You'll most likely be using some guidelines or construction lines to guide the inking. For such line work, use 7H or 8H leads, very lightly. You can ink right over those. After a little practice, draftspeople rely less and less on construction lines to guide their inking.

4. When drawing, you may want to keep the pen moving slightly as you touch down on the drafting surface, and continue the movement as you raise the pen. This is suggested

as a way of avoiding slight enlargements of line at the beginnings and ends of lines. On the other hand, some people like that "bulbing" effect.

5. Use a light touch, a feather touch. Don't press the pen down; don't indent the paper or polyester; and don't grasp the pen in a hard grip. One of the great advantages of inking is that it's smooth and easy—less strained and fatiguing than lead drafting. But some people apply pressure out of habit and maintain the strain and fatigue regardless.

6. If you're just starting out in pen use, get a basic set of the most often used tip sizes: 00, 0, and 1. Get the proper erasers and film cleaners, as I'll describe in a moment. Mainly, avoid expediencies. Get a complete, if modest, setup before you get into it. There are other instructions that come with the pens: the proper way to fill the pens, care and maintenance, etc. These instructions are usually ignored in direct proportion to their importance.

7. The drafting medium also requires some care and preparation. Spots of dirt, oil, or perspiration are barriers to ink. Cleaning polyester film is easy. Just wipe clean with a dry industrial paper wipe. Clean small areas with kneaded rubber or vinyl erasers. You can use a nonresidue solvent such as rubbing alcohol. Make sure dirt or oil on the surface is cleaned off, not just dispersed.

8. Pounces and powders are used to prepare surfaces for inking. The technical pen companies and the polyester companies either recommend against it outright or express skepticism as to its value. Main anticipated problems are: The powder will clog up pens, and inked powder surface may eventually flake off the drafting surface.

9. The best rule for novices is: Just start drawing. Make some mistakes so you can see how easy they are to correct.

6.3 INK, INK ERASING, AND PHOTO IMAGE ERASING

Don't be haphazard about your choice of ink. There are many varieties, all with unique characteristics of drying time, opacity, suitable drafting medium, and erasure methods. Pen manufacturers and dealers will tell you best choices. The fastest drying ink at this time is Rapid-O-Ink, for use just on drafting polyester. Especially don't use plain India ink on polyester—it will chip off.

For effective erasing, rely on what the manufacturers say. Even then, don't jump to conclusions. Some people, for example, mistakenly use super-strength liquid erasers on new work. The liquid is designed for very stubborn old ink lines and can affect the drafting surface.

In general, you don't need much to erase ink from polyester film. Generally, moist cotton swabs will do it. DuPont says you can add a small amount of household ammonia to help in ink release. If you use moist erasing, allow drying time before redrafting.

If you erase dry, use a plastic nonabrasive eraser. Vinyl erasers may leave a transparentizing shine from material in the eraser. This is sometimes mistaken as damage to the matte of the polyester.

The pen and ink manufacturers have special formulations—eraser and liquid combinations. They even have one eraser, Pelikan PT 20, that has erasing fluid in its pores. That one works for ink on drafting film and emulsion-surface films such as photoreproducibles or diazo reproducibles.

People generally use electric erasers on polyester, especially when ink drafting. Unless the eraser is extremely soft and the touch exceptionally light, this will eventually damage the drafting matte surface (as will, of course, any hard or prolonged erasing). When that happens, you can roughen up the hard nonmatte area that's been damaged by rubbing it with a typewriter eraser, or by spraying some fixative matte surface on the spot. That should give enough tooth to hold some line-work repair.

Erasing emulsion material—photo washoff, silver line, and diazo reproducibles—is similar to but different from erasing ink lines. The two often go together, since ink is visually compatible with the dense line work of emulsion films and pencil lead isn't.

The best advice is: Get instructions from the manufacturer of the emulsion film you're using. Anything else is risky.

6.4 EXERCISE

Buy or borrow a basic technical pen set. Be sure pens are filled with fast-drying ink. Tape a small drawing on the drafting board, lay tracing paper over it, and trace it with regular drafting lead. Then lay a small sheet of polyester over the same original drawing and trace it again, this time with the technical pen. Hold the pen lightly (follow instructions laid out in this chapter). Notice the light feel. Draw somewhat faster than you think is safe, and see what happens. Test the erasing. Evaluate whether ink might be competitive with drafting lead in terms of drafting time, erasing time, and cleanliness of the final result.

FREEHAND DRAFTING

7.1 INTRODUCTION

I don't like to draw freehand myself. I don't feel competent at it. If I were a draftsperson and were told to draw some details freehand, I'd be very tempted to do what many persecuted draftspeople have done in similar circumstances. I'd want to draw the details with drafting tools first and then trace them freehand. That way I'd feel confident about getting a good-looking result.

If someone as proefficiency as I am would be tempted to waste time doubledrawing to get a fake freehand drawing, you can imagine how tempting it is to others.

Freehanding *is* a major timesaver (when people don't sabotage it), so much so that many offices count on it as a last-minute hedge when under severe time pressures on a job. One architect told me he had to do a large set of residential working drawings single-handed in one weekend. He did the whole set freehand—plans, elevations, everything (of course, he had preliminaries and design development drawings to trace). He said the drawings came out just fine and he made his deadline. But, same old story, he hadn't thought about doing such drawings that way again except when faced with another time crunch.

Another firm discovered freehand strictly by accident. A project architect begged the office manager for three or four draftspeople. It was an emergency. He needed a team for a couple of weeks to draw up a large interior remodeling job that had fallen behind schedule. The office manager didn't have three or four spare draftspeople laying around, so he asked to look at the project. What he saw were many sheets of originals drafted by the designer and project architect on flimsy, yellow tracing paper. Many were oversized freehand studies. "Just use these," said the office manager.

The office manager showed the project architect how to beef up some of the overly light-lined tracings; how to sort some out for photoreduction; how to paste up others on poster board for direct photography. Ultimately, all yellow-paper drawings that were to be redrawn by "three or four" draftspeople for a couple of weeks were transformed by paste-up and photography into working drawings by two people within 4 days.

Speed isn't the only benefit of freehanding, nor is it the major one. The main value of freehanding is that it enhances control and integration of design and production processes. The drawings of the designers, architects, and senior draftspeople are used directly instead of going through a redrawing phase. That's a step saved (sometimes two steps), and it bypasses distortions and compromises of the designers' or senior detailers' intent. It's all much more direct and to the point than the traditional system. Following is a description of how it works:

You've laid out freehand sketches at various times—studies of details, plans, sections, etc. You've most likely drawn them on buff or white "onionskin" tracing paper—"throwaway" paper. You've generally drawn them fast and loose because you sketch to *develop* ideas rather than present them. A final sketch provides a pattern, something for someone else to copy and make into a finished piece of drafting.

Freehand drafting is like freehand sketching—with two main differences: (1) The sketch is not so sketchy. You draw it with somewhat more care than you would normally. (2) You draw it twice as large as it will appear on the final construction-drawing print. Drawing twice as large is a trick for dealing with the appearance problem. The photoreduction irons out the irregularities. A reasonably "straight" freehand drawing will appear to be completely straight when photoreduced to half size.

The oversized sketch details are usually done on the customary flimsy tracing paper. They're assembled with transparent mending tape onto a vellum, linen, or polyester carrying sheet. The carrying sheet is photoreduced as a whole down to regular construction drawing sheet size. The reduced-size photoreduction is on erasable or washoff drafting media. It becomes the new reproducible "second original" to use as you would any other tracing during the checking and finish-up phases of the job.

There are some obvious complexities and disadvantages: sketching with more care, sketching large, using photoreproduction. What are the benefits? The immediate benefit is that the sketch is not redrawn. You don't have to give it to someone to "draft it up." You don't have to redraw it yourself with tools. (In some old-time offices, details are done in three phases by three levels of personnel. The chief honcho does an "idea sketch," a senior draftsperson translates that into a sketch "to scale," and a junior or intermediate-level draftsperson traces or redraws it on the working drawing sheet.)

You'll see an acceleration in work flow when you eliminate the secondary redrawing process. Despite having to slow down a bit when doing the original sketch, the slowdown is minor compared with the overall gain. Many senior draftspeople and project architects already make their final sketches quite accurately. They don't need to change their technique a bit. The only change is that no one has to *redraw* their work.

One of the pioneers of freehand detailing "conservatively" estimates general cost savings at 20%. Robert Stauder of Hellmuth, Obata & Kassabaum (HOK) says typical savings are *at least* 20%; time savings on one university building were about 35%. Once a firm achieves that kind of production savings, there's no way they're going to revert to old ways. HOK and other offices that use freehand drafting note other gains:

1. Construction details are more accurate. Freehand detailing generally necessitates origination by more mature and experienced staff. The extra experience and care they give to

the work is reflected in fewer errors, faster checking, and easier construction.

2. Drawings are cleaner and more accurate. Some project architects say this is because intermediate personnel don't have the opportunity to add extraneous elements and flourishes.

3. There are fewer details and less drawing. When less experienced personnel are allowed to originate or embellish details, they tend to draw items that are irrelevant for construction. And they draw items that are easiest—mainly copies of manufacturers' or trade associations' product standards that are of no use in bidding or construction.

4. The faster job pace of freehand work reduces boredom. The drafting room is livelier, less subject to dog-day slumps. The higher speed meshes with the demands of fast-track construction. Some offices have had to switch to freehand detailing on fast-track jobs, but have done so reluctantly as a desperate means of keeping up. Some still haven't realized that it's a *good* way to draw and *not* just an unfortunate expedient.

5. The system fits right in with "half-size" bidding and construction drawings. If final prints will be reduced anyway, there's even less reason to draw details with tool-drafted precision.

6. Freehand drafting expedites the creation of standard or reference detail files.

7. There's less time and cost loss and less damage to staff morale, such as happens when job changes force abandonment or wholesale revisions of detail drawings.

There are other advantages that will come up later in this chapter, but those are the basic ones to look for and shoot for when introducing a freehand system.

7.2 FREEHAND DETAILS

Freehand detailing is the most popular application of freehand drafting. Most architects sketch out their details while designing them, so this is just a refinement of a familiar procedure.

The first refinement is to draw a little more accurately than you might customarily do. You'll have to establish some reasonable standard of accuracy, a specific tolerance. Drawings can't be *too* shaky, despite photoreduction. And if they're overly precise, you lose the advantage of going freehand.

If a straight line wiggles much beyond its own thickness, it'll be noticeable in the photoreduction. A good standard of accuracy, then, is to keep lines pretty much true within 1/32″. That will photoreduce to an accuracy tolerance of 1/64″, which is adequately straight. You'll use softer drafting implements—felt-tip pens or extra-soft lead—so your original lines will be twice as thick as they would be in ordinary, regular-size drafting. That thickness allows greater deviations from plumb than would be possible with a very fine, thin line.

You can be more liberal in size tolerances. An element that's drawn 1/8″ oversized will come out 1/16″ over in the reduction—no big problem in most cases. A tighter standard would allow 1/16″ deviations in size. That's no great strain, and it translates to 1/32″ deviations in the reduced-size final print, which will be perfectly acceptable.

Very few people can draw reasonably straight lines without using some kind of guide. The guide for freehand drafting is the grid sheet. Some people use a grid drafting-board cover. Some lay grid sheet tracing paper under their sketch drawings. Some sketch directly on pads of no-print, blue-line grid paper. The most useful grid pattern is eight squares to the inch, with varied line intensities to indicate quarter-inch and inch divisions.

A grid is a great drafting instrument. It provides scale measurements, acts as a visual straightedge, and provides guidelines for lettering and numbers. However, here is a warning: Not all grids are accurate. Some grid drafting-board cover sheet material is very much off-scale. Lined, heavy paper stock (sold in many art stores) is also inaccurate. Drawing pads made for architects and engineers—no-print, blue-line grid sheet pads—are usually exact.

Drafting supply houses sell very accurate grids on polyester (Mylar) sheets. The polyester is stable and long-lasting and makes a good freehand drafting guide when used as an underlay sheet.

You can make or buy small auxiliary drafting boards just for sketching. You can set a small board atop the regular drafting board when doing small sheets of sketch details. For greater comfort, some people use a rotary board like the ones film animators use (they revolve in a circle for great ease of drawing).

Small light tables are helpful in sketch drawing. Sketch drafting often entails some degree of tracing from existing materials, and the light table greatly expedites tracing jobs. The back light of a light table also makes grid underlayment easier to follow and speeds up the drawing process.

Most people do their freehand detailing on onionskin sketch paper, because that's the medium they're already used to. It isn't necessarily the best way to do it, but it's the most popular. We'll tell about other options later, but first, here's a step-by-step description of the most common technique using onionskin:

1. Block out the detail lightly and roughly. This is the development stage, where you do some testing and comparison in sketch form before deciding on the final drawing. It's a process most people already know. It differs from the normal process of sizing the drawing, since you'll probably do the original at twice its final size. A common final detail size is 1½″ to the foot, so the originals are done at 3″ to the foot.

2. After you've designed the detail, it will usually undergo some changes and refinements. You may add elements or subtract or revise them through a series of overlay tracing sketches. If changes are few, you might erase and redraw right on the original rough.

3. When the detail is OK in its light, rough form, it's finalized in dark line. Drawing methods are optional. You can use soft pencil—HB or softer leads—or felt-tip pens.

4. Once drawn, you assemble details on a large linen or polyester carrying sheet. This sheet is a double-size, paste-up version of the final total drawing. You'll photoreduce the large paste-up to regular size on translucent drafting media.

5. Check prints can be a problem. If you have access to a large-format copier (such as Xerox

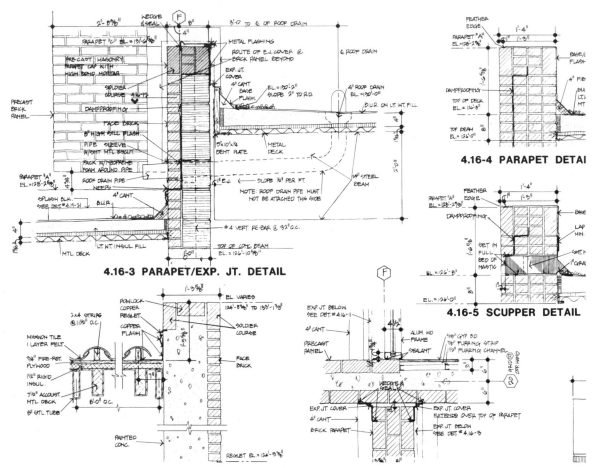

Fig. 7-1. Freehand details.
(Jarvis Putty Jarvis.)

840 or 1860) or AB Dick Design Master, you can make reduced-sized check prints without too much fuss. You'll have to take special precautions if you have to run your carrying sheet through a diazo printer. The main danger is that the flimsy tracing paper will catch and tear or wrinkle while going through the print-machine rollers. One precaution: Tape only the top edges of the thin tracing paper sheets (or side edges, depending on which way you'll send the large carrying sheet through the print machine). Taping just the leading edge allows the tracing paper to smooth out as it's pressed through the rollers. Another precaution: Run a clear 2- or 3-mil polyester cover sheet on top of the carrying sheet. That protects the taped-on tracing paper sheets from snagging and getting torn up in the diazo print machine.

Those are the main steps leading up to the photoreduction process. Questions natually arise: What do you do about the mottled or patchwork mosaic effect resulting from a number of tracings taped on a carrying sheet? How do you deal with the shadowing on the final print? The thin tracing paper you've taped to the carrying sheet will *not* show up in the photograph that's made. The photo will be of high contrast—black or white—and won't reproduce light variations of shading. The patchy effect *will* appear in diazo check prints, but that's no problem unless the checker is unduly sensitive about appearance.

You can avoid large-sheet photoreduction by reducing the large-scale sketches individually before mounting them on a carrying sheet. Use a reducing copier to copy them onto plain acetate or onto clear stickyback appliques. Then assemble the reduced copies onto a work sheet and diazo-print the work sheet on erasable sepia transparency paper or polyester.

Maybe you (or others in your office) draw so well, you won't need to have drawings reduced in size to fudge out the rough spots. If so, that's great. Don't draw at double scale and go through the photoreduction process if you don't need to.

Photocopying and photoreduction provide a special opportunity for time saving in drawing up details. If you draw on small sheets that are transferred to drafting media via photoreproduction or plain paper-copier appliques, *the originals don't have to be completely translucent.* They don't have to be translucent because the next phase reproduction system isn't diazo. Diazo, the most common working drawing reproduction method, requires translucent media. As you probably know, ultraviolet light passes through the original drawing to expose the light-sensitive diazo-print paper. Where there's a line on the original, there'll be a shadow on the sensitized print as the surrounding diazo emulsion is burned away. Then the whole thing is developed with ammonia. It's obvious why the original medium has to be translucent for diazo printing.

If your original drawings don't have to be translucent, you can use more varied timesaving drafting techniques. You can paste elements over existing elements, cover up an area with white paper, use white ink or paint to make fast corrections, or use various opaque press-on appliques. You don't have to worry about erasability or damage to the drawing. Overall, you just don't have to be as fussy as usual and can speed up your sketching.

IMPORTANT NOTE: *Plan the stages of a freehand job, with sketches, before implementing it. If, for example, you will end up printing "half-size" working drawings, your originals might be reduced twice, instead of once, and become unreadable. This often happens, and even if the drawings are large enough initially to stand two stages of reduction, the lettering and dimensions rarely are.* **Allow for whatever reduction steps you'll be taking for the job.**

If original freehand drawings, such as details, are to be photographically reproduced, be careful with your line work. Gray lines, faint lines, and very thin lines are trouble for the photographer. Think in terms of thick or thin lines—*all* lines must be dense and dark. Also keep in mind that small lettering, numbers, textures, and close line work will "clog up" when photoreduced. So when drawing for "half-size" reductions, make everything twice as large as you normally would. If you want 1/16"-high lettering on the final print, for example, make the originals 1/8" high.

7.3 THREE-DIMENSIONAL (3-D) ISOMETRIC AND PERSPECTIVE SKETCHING

3-D isometric or perspective sketches are rarely seen in working drawings, but they definitely have a place. You can appreciate that when you're on the job site and have to draw thumbnail sketches to clarify the formal orthographic drawings.

3-D sketches are useful elaborations on broad-scope section drawings. A British office does all wall construction detail sections as sketch isometrics. They're enclosed in "bubbles" and tied by line to the relevant points on the smaller-scale, formal wall-section drawing.

Tricky connections—flashings, parapets, roof intersections, beam and joist hangers, soffits, spandrels, etc.—are prime candidates for clarification sketches. One office has outline isometrics of 30 or so common wall, roof, spandrel, head, jamb, sill, floor, and foundation conditions. Draftspeople slip the isometric outline drawings under a working drawing tracing. They freehand trace the isometric outline drawings and modify them as required to match conditions of the job at hand.

Use isometric grid paper underlay sheets when doing freehand isometrics. These give line and dimensioning guidance, such as you get from regular rectangular grids. If you're doing a series of perspective sketches, use some small perspective charts. Most drafting and/or graphic arts supply stores have a variety of isometric and perspective grid charts.

You avoid problems when you sketch in sequence from the general to the particular. Start with the axis and a very lightly boxed-in outline of the overall object. Show size and proper proportion of major parts in the light outline. When the general configuration is right, the hard-line work and detail will fall into place.

You have several choices of 3-D types. Freehand perspectives are pretty much standard, although you might have an "exploded view." That's the type you see in industrial manuals that show all the parts disconnected but lined up with their final assembly.

Isometrics are 30° on both sides of a vertical axis. Some people make drawings like this at 45°;

some make them 30° on one side of the axis and 60° on the other. The principle remains the same: the extended sides are not foreshortened as they would be in perspective; they remain at actual scale size.

"Assembly sketches" or installation sketches specifically show the relationships of parts to parts and the relationships of parts to the whole. They're designed to show someone how to put things together, rather than just how the thing will work when it's finished.

"Section" and "partial section" is another variation of isometric or perspective sketch. This is most common in drawing construction details. You draw the component in cross section and extend its elements to include a view of one or more sides of its construction.

In the "oblique drawing," the item is shown head on, the elevation view is parallel to the viewer, and one side and top are shown at a 30° angle. Oblique views are customary in cabinet-making drawings.

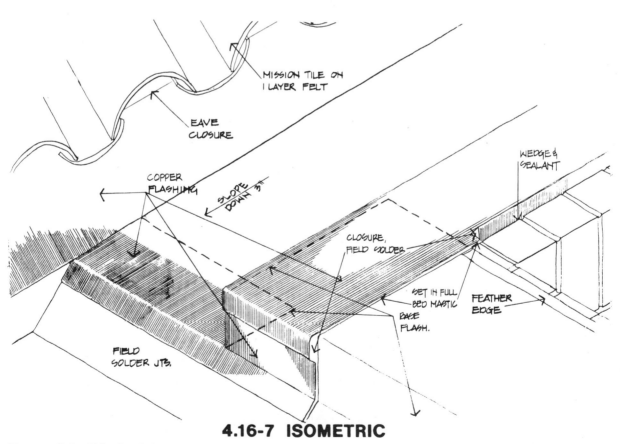

4.16-7 ISOMETRIC

Fig. 7-2.   A "3-D" freehand sketch of a construction detail.

74   (Jarvis Putty Jarvis.)

7.4 FREEHAND PLANS, ELEVATIONS, AND SECTIONS

Freehand can be a great timesaver on broad-scope construction drawings, as well as on the larger-scale details. There are obvious limits; it wouldn't pay to freehand a large reflected ceiling plan, for example. But you can do some kinds of plans, elevations, and sections successfully in freehand.

You can start the process with design development drawings. Most architects usually sketch schematics freehand at small scale to begin with. They're traditionally redrawn accurately to scale with drafting tools, to become preliminary design and/or presentation drawings.

Instead of copying by hand, you can use photographic or photocopying techniques to translate the schematic into a more finished drawing. Here's how: First complete the design study as you usually would, perhaps with somewhat greater care. Photoenlarge the study to twice the size. If you sketch at $1/8''$ scale, for example, blow it up to $1/4''$ scale. An enlarging photocopier or platemaker will do the job. If you don't have one in the office, you can probably find one at an "instant print" shop or your reprographics shop. The blowup will be rather ragged. You refine the enlargement and sharpen the image by adding tape, ink, and correcting fluid, as necessary. Then, when it's photoreduced again, it'll have a tool-drawn look. This small sketch, blowup, refinement, and blowdown process will often be considerably faster than redrafting the original small sketch.

You'll gain a major savings if the building consists of many repeat units. In one case, an architect sketched a typical suite at $1/8''$ scale, then enlarged it four times, to $1/2''$ scale. He cleaned up, retouched, and blew back down to $1/4''$ scale for the detailed room plan sheet. He then made multiple photocopies of the $1/4''$ scale plan and cut out and taped them together as a string of suites. (Repeats of this suite comprised the bulk of the building floor plans for most stories.) The taped-together layout was touched up and photoreduced again to $1/8''$ scale. The $1/8''$-scale prints formed the basis for overall building floor plans. Then the $1/8''$-scale overall plan was reproduced and photoreduced down to $1/16''$ scale, to be used for the site plan. Screened reproducible prints were made from these for the consultants' drawings. The net result is: *Most of the floor plans on about 40 sheets of drawings were created from one freehand sketch that originally took up less than one-fourth of an $8\frac{1}{2}'' \times 11''$ sheet.*

You can apply a similar blowup and blowdown method for any major repeat element. If the exterior elevation and/or through-building cross sections are made up of repetitive bays, for example, you can make a whole assembly of photocopy cutouts of a drawing of a single bay. (Other aspects of this procedure are described in Chapter 12, "Composite Drafting.")

Small-building plans, elevations, and sections are especially open to freehand treatment. They can be treated much like detail drawings—they're just somewhat larger to begin with. Some have been successfully drawn directly at their final scale. Of course, you'll get better accuracy and sharpness by drawing large and reducing the original, as we described in the section on freehand details.

Most of the foregoing depends on reprographic or photocopying facilities. But it's still practical to do the more complex, smaller-scale drawings freehand without such facilities. The trick to that is to augment the freehand system by using *some* tools. We'll tell how in the next section.

7.5 HYBRID FREEHAND DRAFTING

Hybrid drafting is extremely simple. It's so simple, some people have trouble understanding it. Some call it "cheating," as if you're breaking a moral code when you use a tool a different way than you were taught in school.

The main tool is a long architectural or engineering scale. You lay it down, aligning it with guidance grid lines, and draw directly against the scale's edge. One unattached scale, then, serves the functions of parallel bar, triangles, and/or drafting machine.

Test it yourself. Take a small sheet of gridded tracing paper, conceptualize something to draw, and draft using only lead holder and scale. Most likely you'll find it faster and easier than using the usual bunch of traditional drafting tools.

Use a standard-size scale for small drawings, such as details. Some freehand drafting staff members at Hellmuth, Obata & Kassabaum, for example, use small scales as straightedges to aid their freehand detail drafting.

The practical maximum length for long scales is about 24″. Scales made for drafting machines are least expensive and are limited to 18″, which is adequate for most drafting. (The extra-long standard wood-base scales are very expensive and generally no more useful than the lower-cost drafting machine scales.)

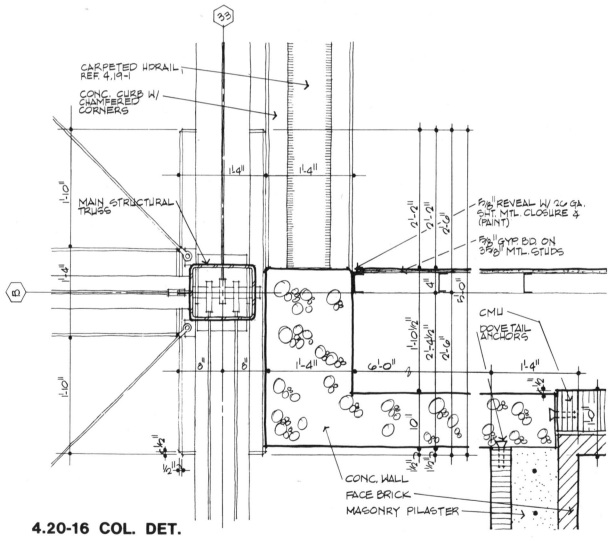

4.20-16 COL. DET.

Fig. 7-3.   A sample of freehand drafting combined with tool drafting for the dimension lines.

(Jarvis Putty Jarvis.)

A common point of resistance to using a scale as a drafting straightedge is that you're "not supposed to." At least that's what every good drafting instructor has told generations of students. If you learned that rule years ago and have obeyed it ever since, you'll probably feel uneasy about changing the habit. A little practice will take care of the habit problem; practice should improve speed enough that the advantages of drawing this way will become unmistakably apparent. (The likely reason for the old rule is that the constant friction of hard lead against the edge of a scale would eventually damage the scale. Damage isn't likely with semifreehand drafting because you're using the "soft" drawing implements. And even if it did eventually wear or nick the scale, you just buy another one.)

7.6 QUICK EXERCISES FOR FREEHAND SKILL

Anyone weak in freehand skills will improve markedly by practicing for a few hours the exercises described here. The main problems people have are shakiness, stiffness, and difficulty in proportioning. The first two result from a combination of muscular habits and self-consciousness. The third can be solved by learning a couple of simple rules about "eyeballing" and sizing the parts of objects.

We have two kinds of exercises that art schools have used for many years. One kind is used to sharpen plain, two-dimensional (2-D) freehand drafting skills. The other deals with sketching 3-D views of real or imagined objects. You can augment these greatly by sketching things during odd moments. Carry a small sketch pad and draw what you see when you're commuting, waiting in lines, during coffee breaks, etc. Date all sketches and exercises so you can measure your progress. Practice with a soft pencil. Don't bother erasing where you botch up on simple exercises. But it's okay to erase on 3-D sketches. The eraser is as much a drawing implement as a pencil or pen and should be used as a tool of drawing rather than a device for removing errors.

EXERCISE 1: STRAIGHT LINES

This and other exercises in this section deal with tenseness that leads to shakiness and sometimes exaggerated errors. Secure a fairly large sheet of scratch paper—say 18″ × 24″—and make a series of large, equally spaced dots down the left-hand and right-hand sides of the sheet. You'll draw horizontal lines, starting at the left-hand dots and connecting with the right-hand dots.

Look at the destination point when you draw your freehand line. You don't need to look at where the line has been or where it is. Draw fairly fast; get some continuity of shoulder and arm action. Use your shoulder as the pivot for your arm. Draw in a continuous sweep and not in a series of short spurts. Don't go over the lines twice.

Do the same exercise on smaller paper—for example, legal size—and concentrate on continuous arm motion. With shorter lines, use your elbow as the pivot for your forearm. Fill up the sheets.

Do the same connect-the-dot exercises with vertical lines, and then with 30°, 45°, and 60° diagonal lines in both directions. These are satisfying exercises, because you're likely to see distinct improvement after only a couple of sessions.

EXERCISE 2: LINE DIVISION

Now you can begin to deal with proportioning problems while still working on line control. Sketch some freehand lines. Then eyeball measure, and mark off their midpoints. Mark off quarter points and eighth points. Make other lines and mark off thirds and sixths. Check your estimates with a scale, and discontinue the exercise when you rate your accuracy as "good."

EXERCISE 3: FREEHAND TRACING

For some people this is the most valuable exercise of all. Use a grid paper underlay, and sketch on flimsy tracing paper. Trace outlines of squares, rectangles, diagonals, etc., right off the grid. Lay down some previously drawn detail drawings, and freehand trace them. Don't labor over them. Sketch with fluid and fairly rapid line strokes.

EXERCISE 4: THE "GESTURE" EXERCISE

Art teachers use this as a loosening-up exercise. Its value to freehand drafting is indirect, but it's very useful if you're a little tense when you draw.

Check your grip on the pencil. Is it tight? Are the muscles under your forearm tensed? Do you feel shoulder tension or stiffness? Think about each muscular area; close your eyes, and direct your awareness into the fingers, forearm, upper arm, and shoulder. Tell each area to relax. That'll usually do the trick.

Then draw some objects just as fast as you can, without letting your pencil leave the paper. This is "gesture" or "scribble" drawing. You'll see the object and then translate the *essence* of its form in a series of scribbly lines. Watch out for tensing in your arm. If you can do a few "scribbles" and still retain a relaxed drawing posture, you're in pretty good shape. You can draw the objects large or small, simple or complex, angular or curvy. Some of them may come out so well, they'll surprise you.

Aim to get the feel or substance of the object you're sketching (rather than the outline). Get its action. Identify yourself with it. Don't think about the look of it. And remember to keep the pencil on the paper throughout the sketch process.

EXERCISE 5: LINE WEIGHTS

Check yourself to see whether you can draw three or four distinct line weights. If you have some trouble keeping weights clearly distinguishable, do a few practice sheets. Your main weights, or thicknesses, are as follows: *Bold and heavy* lines are used for the outlines or profile lines of objects. *Medium-weight* lines are used for basic detail and contour lines of objects within their outline. *Lightweight* lines are thin but distinct; they are mainly for dimension lines and materials indications. *Construction lines* are the lightest weight of all; they're just sketching outlines for approximating final shapes and proportions before drawing in dark hard line.

Do freehand practice sheets similar to Exercise 1, but alternate the heavy, medium, and light line weights.

EXERCISE 6: SQUARES AND RECTANGLES

This exercise is for developing accurate sizing and proportioning skills—usually the weakest area with people who aren't practiced at freehand drawing. People who are trying to draw an identifiable plan, elevation, or construction component often apologize and say their "scale" is a little off. What they mean is that they missed on some relationship of size. Either the length-to-width relationship is off, or some total item is incorrectly sized in relationship to another.

First draw some squares and rectangles at various sizes and various relationships to one another. Then redraw them carefully, using the first sketch as a "model."

Think of all rectangles as representing some specific ratio as 2 to 1, 3 to 1, 4 to 3, and so on, and draw them as discernible ratiomatic proportions. Use construction lines, diagonal construction lines, whatever you need to sketch the proportions fairly accurately.

EXERCISE 7: THE "CONTOUR" EXERCISE

This exercise helps in learning to put ideas on paper as 3-D images. Use 8½″ × 11″ sketch paper. Pick out some existing object to draw. Lean over your drawing surface with your pencil close to the paper. Focus on the object you're going to draw. Focus on the outline of the object, and find some starting point on the outline. Focus hard and get the sensation that your pencil is on the outline of the object and that you're about to literally run the point of the pencil around that outline. You'll be mentally *tracing* the object without looking at the drawing.

Start tracing the object slowly. Don't rush ahead of yourself. Move your eyes slowly around the contour and guide your pencil accordingly. Don't glance at the drawing unless your line goes off the edge or gets "lost" from what you're looking at. If there are inside contours or features, draw them the same way, by mentally tracing them and without watching the drawing.

This exercise lends a special "feel" for sketching. If you do it a dozen times, you will notice a distinct difference in the way you do your informal sketches. You will feel more involved with the subject being drawn, and it will appear more readily on paper the way you want it.

EXERCISE 8: BLOCKING OUT SOLID OBJECTS

Choose some simple construction features to sketch in freehand isometric or perspective. Draw from real things, pictures, or your imagination. Practice roughing or blocking out overall proportions and sizes before you do hard-line sketches. A block outline can be extremely faint and made up of only the merest suggestion of lines or dots. Most people have trouble with 3-D sketches for want of any rough outlining. Once there's an overall sizing and proportion noted on the sheet, the rest comes relatively easily and accurately.

7.7 INTRODUCING FREEHAND DRAFTING TO THE STAFF

You may be surprised at the extreme resistance some draftspeople have to using freehand techniques. There are ways to make it easy for people to switch over to freehand. But some won't draw freehand under any circumstances—not ever.

You're making an extraordinary demand when you ask people to change to freehand. You're creating a potentially embarrassing situation for them. Most draftspeople aren't good at freehand to begin with, and their first efforts may come slowly and look lousy. An older draftsperson particularly isn't going to appreciate the opportunity to look bad.

People need to do good-looking work—self-esteem and job security are at stake. That's why some will surreptitiously trace and retrace a freehand drawing until it comes out looking right. If you can understand and accept the resistance, that will go a long way toward dissolving it. If you take a hard-nosed approach, that will add energy to the resistance. Like the old-time movie space monsters, the resistance will get bigger and tougher the more you fight it.

Hellmuth, Obata & Kassabaum have developed a good compromise. A large amount of drafting is nonfreehand anyway, so that work goes to the staff members who won't adjust to freehand work. Those who *are* willing and able to draw freehand get the freehand assignments. Since detailing is all freehand and that's the senior-level work, there's incentive for staff to develop freehand skills.

Some offices, such as HOK, have made freehand ability an important consideration in evaluating job applicants. That helps assure a pool of freehand talent. New employees who aren't proficient at freehand are usually willing to learn when it's built in from the outset, as a natural part of the job.

You can introduce freehand painlessly if your office has after-hours, "professional advancement" seminars or lectures for employees. Most people will pick up freehand skills with a little practice in your seminars. Some employees need a little nudging but respond well when they're given practice assignments like the ones described in Section 7.6.

You can deal with employee resistance more effectively when you perceive the main "reasons behind the reasons" of their resistance. One subtle reason is the way the schools teach drawing—if and when they teach it at all. Most schools reinforce the "either you got it or you don't" attitude about drawing skill. Every class has a couple of students who, because of aptitudes and/or previous experience, can draw like Michelangelo. Everyone else's work seems amateurish by comparison. Drawing in such competition is an annoying chore if not a distinct pain that pretty much discourages intensive effort to raise one's drawing skills.

A related problem pertains to people's egos and self-images. People in the design professions often have a high opinion of themselves or their capacities. When they confront an area where their talent doesn't meet self-expectations, they tend to steer clear of it. People with exaggerated standards of quality usually would rather not do something at all than be second rate at it. If they can't be *great* at drawing freehand, they don't want to draw at all.

Finally, resistance to freehand drafting may reflect a general employee conflict. Employees always resent putting out extra effort for management without receiving extra compensation in return. It definitely takes extra effort to switch to freehand when you're not used to it. The office may benefit while the employee thinks: "What am I getting out of this? Just more exploitation."

The best way to handle concerns and reservations is to say them out loud. Most employees aren't willing to say to a boss: "I'm afraid I'll feel inferior if I try to do freehand." They won't say it even if the realization is crystal clear. Instead, they say: "What's the point? That's not going to do any good. It's just more trouble than it's worth. Blank and Blank tried that last year and it didn't work. . . ." If you can say what might cause resistance, it takes some pressure off the employees. They don't have to worry about saying or not saying what they feel when you say it for them.

After saying what the concerns and problems might be, ask for further feedback. Tell the facts (as enumerated in this chapter) about how freehand is done and its potential savings to the office. Point out that it *is* a valuable skill that will eventually enhance one's career. Then ask: "Now what do you suggest as the best ways to implement it in this office?" Chances are they'll be able to solve the problem for you.

7.8 SYNTHESIS

Freehand drafting is an optional phase of transition to new working drawing systems. It fits right in at some offices, and it never will in others.

A few firms start with freehand drafting before using other systems and discover it's a convenient, low-risk way to get used to graphic reforms and the processes of photoreproduction and photoreduction.

It also fits right in with the creation of a standard reference detail bank. Some firms have expedited their detailing by making freehanding an integral part of the system.

Freehanding fits in with applique drafting systems, with ink drafting, with composite systems, and even with overlay drafting. It can fit in with all those, or it can be left out entirely.

There are usually pretty clear clues as to whether you should pursue freehand drafting in your office. The main positive clue is whether there are people who like freehand and are enthusiastic about it. If staff resistance is high, on the other hand, it's probably just as well not to pursue the matter.

If you or others in the office have used freehand successfully in normal practice or in "emergencies," you have something good to go on. If it's been tried without success, then go easy.

If you have reason for caution, put freehand drafting aside for the time being. After you read further chapters in this book on appliques, using photocopiers, standard or reference details, composite drafting, etc., you may have a different perspective. What may not be practical right now may become very practical and beneficial at a later stage in your production development.

7.9 EXERCISES

1. Make a sketch flow diagram or storyboard to plan making a detail sheet from double-size freehand detail sketches. Assume the final prints will be half-size. Then what scale do you want for the final prints? What size or scale should the original sketches be?

2. Plan a freehand detail sheet and make the following decision: Should the original over-sized sketch details be photoreduced individually and then assembled on a final-size carrying sheet? Or should they all be assembled on a double-size carrying sheet and photoreduced as a single composite? Consider the advantages and disadvantages of either option.

3. How could you make a diazo-reproducible transparency print of assembled, reduced-size freehand details without using photography?

4. Draw or obtain some original design or detail development sketches. Have them reduced by the least expensive means to half-size (photostat, reduction office copier, and so on—whatever is available to you). Study the reduced-size sketches and analyze what the originals should have been like to achieve a fully satisfactory reduction.

8

DRAFTING WITH APPLIQUES

8.1 USES OF APPLIQUES

I have a pile of applique products on my desk: tapes, a tape applicator, "instant letters," sticky-back sheets, press-on strips, and various tools. It looks like a closeout sale at a graphic arts store.

How many of these items include printed instructions on how to use them properly? One does—only one out of dozens. If you ask a sales representative about instructions, he or she will say: "The directions are in the catalog." And where's the catalog? It is at the store, most likely, or maybe on a shelf in the drafting room. That doesn't help drafting staff members who are supposed to make the products work. Members won't look for a catalog's instructions if no one has told them there *are* instructions. Besides, these are simple things. People can figure them out for themselves. Now, let's see what often happens:

We'll apply these dry-transfer letters on this title sheet. We'll rub the carrier sheet with a pencil, and the letters will stick to the tracing that's underneath. Oops, the letter broke apart; try that again. . . . Spacing's getting a little off. . . . Better scratch that last letter off with a razor blade. Oops, a little too hard. . . . Too bad no one told us about burnishing the letters through the backing sheet and not through the carrier sheet. Since we didn't burnish properly, the letters are going to come off in the diazo printing machine.

These stickyback sheets look handy. We'll just copy a detail on the diazo machine or office copier, peel off the backing, and stick it on the tracing. That will be a lot faster than having someone trace the drawing. . . . Unfortunately, we hadn't

heard about how to minimize background haze, or how to make revisions on such material without resorting to major surgery.

These tapes might be better than hand-drawn walls. We'll pull this out here and stick it on the sheet. . . . Hmm, doesn't go on straight. . . . There, now it's on, but that was slower than drawing. . . . Now why did it pop off the tracing like that?

So it goes. The foregoing includes a *few* of the reasons appliques are often tried and, nearly as often, abandoned. It's not that they don't work. It's that most drafting people don't know how to make them work.

8.2 DRY TRANSFER

Dry transfer is the best known kind of "appli-que": the letters, symbols, lines, and so on, that you transfer just by pressing down and rubbing.

Dry-transfer products come in great variety from many manufacturers. And you can have your own made up. You submit camera-ready art work at full size or double size, and the manufacturers do the rest. The cost isn't high, but you have to buy fairly large quantities (usually 50 sheets at a couple of dollars per sheet). See manufacturers' catalogs for details and prices. Prices vary considerably. Be sure to find a brand of ready-made sheets that works well for you before designing and ordering custom sheets.

Even when you find a good product, it may be used inefficiently and incorrectly. All the points listed in this section are important for making these products work properly.

Dry-transfer letters, symbols, etc., come on translucent plastic or paper carrying sheets. Each has a pink, blue, or white paper "backing sheet." The backing sheet protects the printed side of the carrier and is used as a burnishing sheet when you're transferring an element to the drawing surface.

The basic dry-transfer directions are:

1. Position the letter or symbol, and hold it *very* steady.
2. Rub the carrier in circular strokes, using medium-hard pressure, with a burnisher until the element "grays." The graying shows that it's loosened from the carrier sheet and is sticking to the new surface. (Some products pop right off with no more than thumbnail pressure.)
3. Carefully lift off the carrier sheet. When you want to finalize the letter, lay the *backing sheet* (*not* the carrying sheet) over it and give it a good, hard burnishing.

Those are the *basic* instructions. Make note of all the following points:

1. When transferring a letter, start at the top edge and move downward with the circular strokes of the burnisher. A broad rubbing motion loosens the element in one piece and transfers it in one piece.
2. Don't use a hard, back-and-forth burnishing motion. This tends to transfer part of the element to the sheet below while the other part is still attached to the carrier. The slightest twitch during the process will rip the element being transferred.
3. Very small elements can be burnished with a ball point pen. Larger elements require a larger burnisher to avoid uneven pressure that can tear the element during transfer. Use broad spatula burnishers for large elements; medium-sized, rounded burnishers are best for medium-sized elements. Keep the pressure medium the first time through—just enough to transfer the element. *Final adhesion comes with the second-phase burnishing.*
4. Take special care with the edges when transferring large elements. They're particularly likely to stick to the carrier and rip when you lift the carrier sheet.
5. Another tip on large elements is: Finger-press them down before doing the first transfer burnishing. That will give them a bit of grab and help prevent cracking.
6. An alternate transfer method suggested by the Letraset Company is called the "prerelease" or "stretch technique." It's possible to release elements by distorting the carrier and popping the element off. It's faster than the usual first-phase burnishing, but it takes practice.
7. Some carrier-sheet materials become permanently grooved when heavily burnished. The grooved indentations tend to loosen adjacent elements on the carrier sheet. The problem is compounded when the drafting staff mistakenly use the carrier as the second-phase burnisher sheet. Laminated paper carrier sheets won't groove.
8. Sometimes the pressure of your hand resting on the carrier sheet will loosen and transfer unwanted elements. Whenever elements seem very lightly stuck to their carrier, use the backing sheet as protective underlayment between the carrier and the drawing.
9. In rare instances, a backing sheet may become stuck to the carrier sheet. If this happens, gently roll the sheets up together. That will separate them without ruining any elements.
10. Storage in a hot, cold, or damp place can alter dry-transfer elements quite a bit and make them crack and break easily.

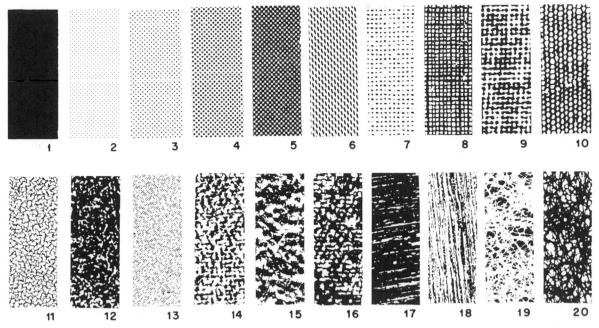

8-1. Dry-transfer textures.
(Geographics.)

11. Don't rush to blame yourself if you experience a lot of cracking, breaking elements. Try another sheet—or another brand. You'll often see instant improvement.

It isn't easy to space and compose letters, especially large titles, without experience. The best help in composing and spacing letters comes from the Letraset Company. Letraset sheets come with "spacematic" bars printed as part of the transfer letters. The bars show both bottom-line alignment and approximate best spacing between letters. Some dry-transfer lettering sheets provide bottom alignment guidelines, *but they're not always straight.*

The most common method of aligning and spacing large letters is to draw guidelines on the original work, and trace-sketch the letters in their exact desired positions. Use a "nonphoto" blue pencil for layout drawing. The lines won't print, and you're spared the problem of erasing guidelines adjacent to the transferred letters.

NOTE: *There's a special method of aligning and laying out letters which isn't mentioned in dry-transfer catalogs. This consists of cutting out the letters, positioning them, and lightly tapping them in place before doing the first burnishing. The cutouts are simple—just rough rectangular shapes around the letters. Some old hands swear this is the fastest and best way of working*

*with large letters. (It's similar to the **Formatt** system, which makes use of a cutout, stickyback material that's sometimes confused with dry transfer.)*

There are three remaining problems: (1) creep and blistering from the heat of diazo printing; (2) erasing or removing dry-transfer elements after they're transferred; and (3) dirt and abrasion. Each of these problems has caused offices to stop using what could be a valuable product.

There are two main reasons why dry-transfer elements fail during diazo printing: (1) Users purchase a product that isn't intended for diazo. (2) Users don't know the elements are supposed to be finish-burnished to complete the adhesion process.

Most manufacturers say their products can take the heat of diazo printing—and they usually can. If in doubt, pretest some elements. Rub them on, finish-burnish them, and run them through a warm machine a few times.

NOTE: *If such products have been applied and they act up in the print machine, **overlay clear polyester film on the top sheet when running diazo prints.** That will protect the applique.*

Sometimes dry transfer that adheres without any problem when printed on the office diazo machine comes right off in the blueprint shop's diazo machine. The likely reason is that commercial diazo machines run at much higher temperatures than office machines. The high temperature tends to raise rosins in the tracing paper to the surface, and they "float" the appliques away. One way of preventing this possibility is to very lightly prespray, or "dust spray," tracing paper with clear unscented hair spray. The plastic dusting on the paper blocks the rosin from undercutting the dry-transfer appliques.

If your drawing has a large amount of dry-transfer material, it will pay to make an erasable, reproducible, transparent print. Let that print be the "original." Then you won't have to worry about heat, dirt, or abrasion problems.

Erasing dry-transfer images is easy. Elements will generally come off if you press tape atop them and lift the tape. Crepe or rubber cement pick-up bars will roll most dry-transfer material off the sheet. If dry-transfer material is particularly ground in and resistant to erasing, coat the element lightly with a very small amount of lighter fluid. Let it sit for a moment, and then apply tape.

Sometimes you'll have to remove a small element that's crowded in by others. Then you risk picking up the adjacent elements. You can handle this by laying the backing sheet over the element and trace-cutting a small hole around it. Apply tape or pick-up bar over the hole to remove the element.

Dirt accumulates around dry-transfer elements, and they're subject to damage by drafting equipment. The best rule is to hold back applying these materials until the regular drafting work is nearly completed. As with any applique, *keep all portions that aren't being worked on at any given moment thoroughly covered with protective paper.* All graphic arts supply stores carry protective sprays that will further help prevent dirt buildup and surface deterioration.

8.3 TOTAL TRANSFER AND CUTOUT FILMS

"Total-transfer" material has a thin, clear, lacquer "carrier" that holds the printed image that's to be transferred. A decal, like a parking sticker you put on your windshield, is an example of total transfer.

Use total-transfer material for preprinting somewhat elaborate elements. Elements such as small blocks of standard notation, room names, drawing titles, building equipment, furniture, key plans, trees, and cars have been done successfully this way. The elements are transferred in one piece via the lacquer. They won't crack or break apart, as sometimes happens with dry-transfer material. Also, you don't have to burnish off each little element.

Total-transfer films are mainly custom-made. C-thru Better Letter Company calls theirs "complete unit transfer sheets." The Letraset Company offers them as "clear carrier film." Chartpak calls them "custom templates," and Mecanorma's name for the product is "transfer strip." Please note that unlike the matte finish cutout films, these are glossy and *you can't draw on them.* And some don't print well with diazo.

Preprinted cutout films are similar to the total transfer films. The main differences are that the carrier film is thicker and you have to cut each applique element off for yourself.

Letters of all sizes, similar to the choices in dry transfer, are available on cutout film. Graphic Products Corp. (Formatt) has cutout letters. Cello-Tak includes cutout letters in its catalog. The material is best for large elements, such as schedules, blocks of notation, your own texture and pattern designs, expansive titles, key plans, title blocks, etc.

You'll find cutout film useful mainly for sheets printed according to your designs. You can send orders for such work to applique manufacturers, blueprint shops, and some graphic supply distributors. Stanpat Products Inc. has specialized in this for years, for example.

Another option is to buy blank stickyback sheets and have them printed at a local print shop or on an office offset printing press. There's considerable potential savings in taking this route. You can turn out hundreds of copies at very little per sheet over the price of the material. Most manufacturers offer the blank films.

RESTROOM	**OPERATORY**
HYGIENE	**OPERATORY**
UTILITY ROOM	**OPERATORY**
DARKROOM	**OPERATORY**
LABORATORY	**OPERATORY**
PRIVATE OFFICE	**RESTROOM**
CENTRAL SUPPLY	**RECEPTIONIST**
STERILIZING	**ADMIN. OFFICE**
CONTROL ROOM	**ACCOUNTING AREA**
RECEPTION ROOM	**X-RAY ROOM**

Fig. 8-2.   A sample of "total-transfer" titles.
(Letraset USA, Inc.)

Special ink has to be used when offset-printing onto acetate or polyester films. Even then, great care has to be taken to avoid smearing the sheets during the drying period. Before ordering or printing your own custom-made sheets, get hold of some samples of the material and test them.

Most cutout material will work on tracing paper or polyester and will print OK by diazo. To avoid printing problems, use a clear polyester cover sheet over the original when running it through the print machine. Have a good reproducible print made before running any large number of diazo prints, and use the reproducible rather than the original for printing.

Make note of the following points:

1. Cutout films are usually made out of thin stickyback acetate. *Acetate is vulnerable to tearing and ripping.*

2. Use only the sharpest of blades. Anything less will affect the control of your cut, leave ragged edges, and, at times, cause snagging and tearing of the film.

3. A "conde" cutter is recommended. This is a knife with an adjustable blade that will cut through only one layer of film or paper. Most art or drafting supply stores have them or can order some for you.

4. When cutting film with a blade, keep the blade angle low relative to the work. If you hold a blade at a high angle, little wobbly movements creep in that affect the accuracy of cut. This is especially important when cutting along a straight edge.

5. Don't use your fingers to pick up a piece of thin film after you cut it out on the backing sheet. Instead, after cutting with a sharp blade, lift a corner with the blade, press the film lightly onto the metal, and use the blade to lift and transport the piece of film to the drawing.

6. Films are most likely to catch and be pulled away from the drawing at their sharp corners. You can reduce the danger by trimming right-angle corners off at 45°.

7. Small concentrated spots of rosin or oils in drafting vellum will prevent proper adhesion of dry-transfer or stickyback films. Don't apply appliques on affected areas of drafting media.

8. The precautions cited in the last section about protecting the work from dirt and abrasion apply equally here.

☆ available in 15" x 20" sheets.

Fig. 8-3. A sample of the variety of textures and patterns available as stickyback films.

(Letraset USA, Inc.)

88

8.4 TEXTURING, PATTERNING, AND SHADING FILMS

Most of these products are on stickyback film. That is, the texture, pattern, or shade is printed on a thin, transparent polyester or acetate sheet, with an adhesive on one side. The adhesive on these films is lighter than "pressure-sensitive" products. It won't stick firmly until burnished.

To apply a film, lay it down with its backing sheet on the area of drawing to be filled in. Cut roughly around the area. Slip the cutter blade under the film, lift it off, and set it gently on the area of drawing. Lightly burnish the film into place. Cut exactly around the border of the area, and do a final burnishing.

That's the basic instruction; it applies to most products. A variation is to lay the film, without the backing sheet, onto the area to be filled in and let it stick lightly. Cut around that area, press it down a little harder, and remove the excess film. Then cut exactly around the edge of the area, and do the final burnishing.

Some products have wax adhesive and aren't suited to diazo copying. Be sure not to buy wax-adhesive material unless your work is to be photoreproduced.

Zipatone Inc. has a fairly good selection of patterns and textures, and their adhesive is encapsulated. It has no tack prior to burnishing and is convenient for application on large areas of drawing.

Air bubbles are a distinct problem with some films. If you're working with small areas and have a broad burnisher, it's nothing much to contend with. If you run into a problem sheet, use a pin to let the air out of the bubbles as you burnish them.

Remember that these are thin acetate films that can rip and tear easily. The final notes on cutting that conclude the last section apply equally here.

An exception to the typical adhesive texture product is textures that are dry-transfer rather than printed on a film carrier. These should be protected with a thin, clear polyester film when run through a diazo machine.

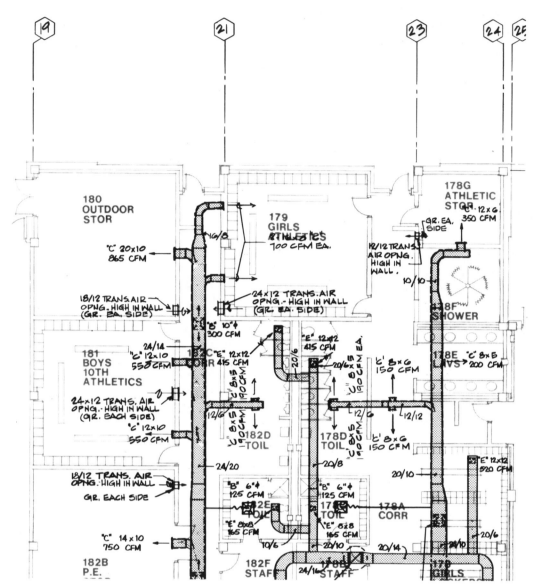

Fig. 8-4.   Dot-textured shading film applique to differentiate ductwork on a mechanical drawing. Building construction is shown as screened shadow print.

—Jarvis Putty Jarvis.)

90

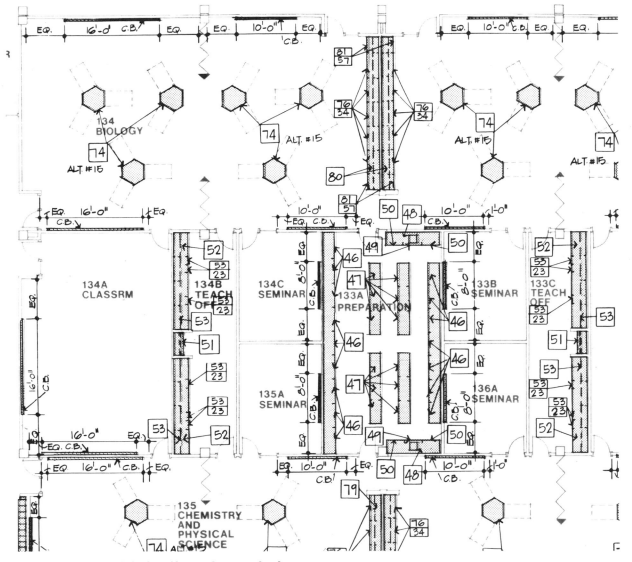

Fig. 8-5. Dot-textured shading film applique to clearly show fixtures and furnishings.

(Jarvis Putty Jarvis.)

8.5 TAPES

Tapes are easiest to use with opaque work sheets, as in the composite drafting system. But some offices have successfully integrated tapes with standard drafting and diazo printing processes.

Tapes are most often used for elaborate line work such as special indications for fencing, boundaries, setback lines, utility lines, match lines, and cut lines. Tapes provide good solid line work for sheet borders and borders around portions of drawings, such as on detail sheets.

Some offices use tapes to "draw" walls and partitions. They've been used on both preliminary design drawings and working drawings.

Tape drafting, whether for diazo reproduction or photoreproduction, gives inklike precision in the final print quality. And, *you can draw remarkably fast with tape.* A finish floor plan "traced" with tape over a rough sketch will firm up very quickly. Here's how to make it work:

1. For fast and accurate straight-line application, *don't* hold the tape roll in one hand and pull out the tape with the other. Almost everyone does this and it slows them down. The best method is to press down the edge of the tape at the starting point of the line (with some overlap) and then *press the tape* in place as you pull the roll away from the starting point.

2. Don't stretch the tape as you lay it out. The tape has a "memory" and tries to pull back to its original length. This can wrinkle a tracing or sometimes result in the tape popping off the sheet.

3. Burnish the tape to finalize the adhesion process.

4. The applicator supplied by the Chartpak Company is useful for fast, straight line work. *Apply it against a straightedge.*

5. When cutting tape, protect the tracing or work sheet by using a plastic cutter or a conde cutter that gives controlled depth of cut.

6. You'll need guidelines for drawing with tape, either an underlay drawing to be traced or a guide drawn in nonphoto blue pencil line. *Use a light box or tracing table.*

7. If you're drawing an item that will be photoreduced, don't assume that wiggles in tape lines won't show up. They will. They'll be smaller, but they'll still be visible.

8. Use flat matte-finish tape rather than glossy tape for photoreproduction. Shiny surfaces create "hot spots" in photorepro. Use crepe tape for curved lines such as contours on a site map.

9. Transparent tapes have two layers laminated together. *You might accidentally unroll only the top layer.* This will show up as a distortion of the printing on the tape. If it happens, *cut through and unwind the tape by one revolution* until the laminates are in their proper place with the protective layer on top.

10. All the rules about cleanliness, protective covers, use of a protective clear film when printing diazo, etc., apply especially to tape applique.

11. Don't use tiny tape pieces for small nubs of walls on plans, such as at door jambs. They come off very easily and are time-consuming to apply. Do small touch-ups such as jambs with ink rather than tape.

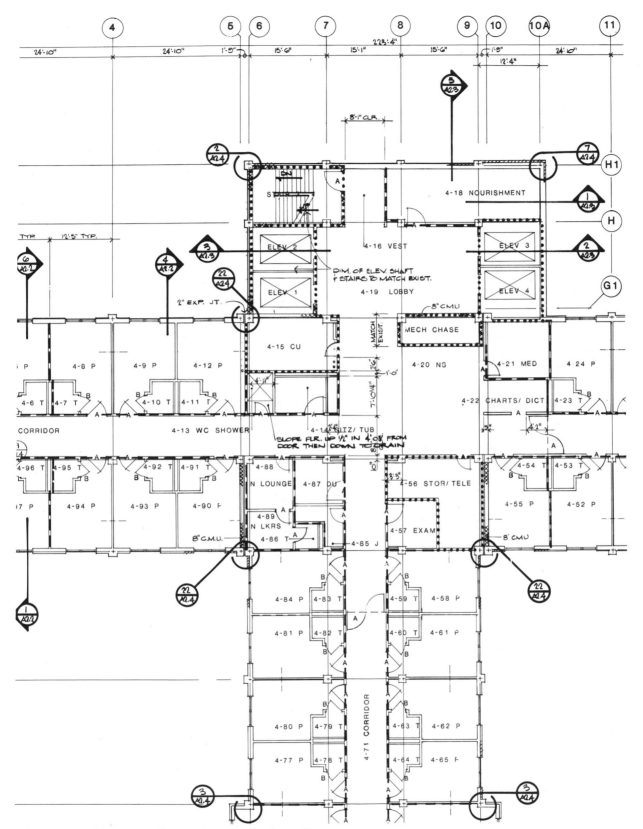

Fig. 8-6. Graphic tape applique to show varying fire-wall construction.

(Gresham and Smith, Architects.)

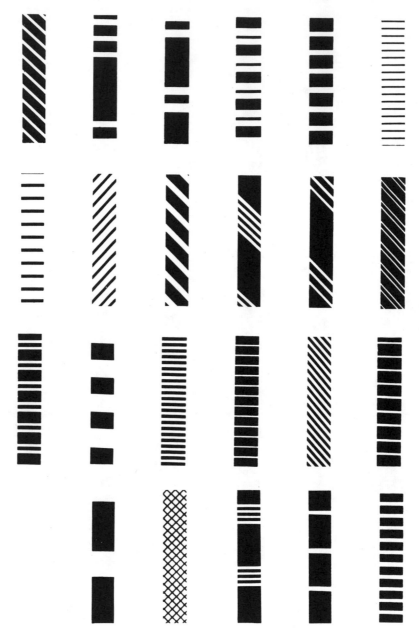

Fig. 8-7. Samples of graphic pattern tapes that can be used in architectural and engineering drawing. Each pattern is available in different widths ($\frac{1}{32}''$, $\frac{1}{16}''$, $\frac{1}{8}''$, $\frac{1}{4}''$ and $\frac{1}{2}''$).

(Guidelines.)

8.6 VARIETIES OF DO-IT-YOURSELF STICKYBACKS

Items from previous work are often copied for use on new drawings. Most times, the copying is done by redrawing or tracing. The items are usually of a type, such as special schedule forms, construction details, sections from preliminary drawings changed into working drawings, blocks of notation, etc. They're mainly the kinds of things that may be reused occasionally but not often.

Since the redrawn items aren't reusable time after time, it doesn't pay to have a batch of custom appliques printed up. Here's where the do-it-yourself appliques come in. One kind of do-it-yourself applique is a stickyback film that can be printed by the use of diazo, the office copier, or the offset printing press. That's not to say that the same film can be printed by all three processes. Some films are diazo-sensitive, some are designed for the office copier, and some are for offset.

You can see the handiness of the do-it-yourself option. Here's a good, usable, large detail on one sheet, and you'd like to transfer it to another without photography or redrawing. Just slip the special applique into your office plain-paper copier, expose the original, and there's the image on thin, clear, stickyback film.

Background haze or "ghosting" depends upon the transparency of the film and adhesive. An adhesive may look clear but be resistant to the ultraviolet light of the diazo machine. The better-known products have transparent adhesives, and virtually all are nonyellowing over time.

Films are either acetate or polyester. Polyester with a matte surface will be somewhat less translucent than the acetate. The thicker the film, the more resistance it will have to light. Keuffel & Esser's Herculene is fairly thick polyester and tends to leave a shadow, for example.

If you run into a background haze problem when running prints, reduce the printing speed by a couple of feet per minute. By reducing the printing speed, you're increasing the "burn" of the print process. This can mean a loss of very light or thin line work that's drawn on the original. *Avoid light line work under any circumstance.*

Fairly dark background haze is unavoidable in some instances. When it is unavoidable, you can incorporate the shadow haze portion in the working drawing sheet by means of a border line around the applique. For example, you might have a sheet of details with the details separated by borders anyway. Hazed prints of applique details that fit within their borders won't be a serious visual problem. Haze ghosting is mainly a problem when the applique shadow is misshapen or so misaligned as to be glaringly out of whack with the rest of the drawing.

Border lines around applique elements can serve another purpose. They'll hide dirt and fuzz that tend to accumulate along the edges of stickyback films.

When revisions are anticipated, the transfer films should be erasable and repositionable. Most of the plain paper copier films are erasable to one degree or another. K & E's Herculene, Chartpak's applique film, and Saga-photocopied images can be erased. An electric eraser is a help in some cases.

The adhesives in most products allow repositioning, but most adhesives get stronger after repeated runs through a diazo machine. The best general solution for dirt and erasing and repositioning problems is to make an erasable reproducible of the original sheet as soon as practicable.

Is it better to adhere transfer films to the top side or the back side of a tracing? The argument for having the image reverse-printed and applied on the back is that it cuts down the dirt and abrasion problem. The argument for putting films on the front or top side is that changes are easier to make and the image will be photographable for making a photoreproducible and for microfilming. *Generally, top-side application is the most practical and convenient.*

One of the frustrations of working with transfer films is separating a film from its backing sheet. When a film doesn't separate readily, slip a very sharp blade or needle along the edge to create a separation. Sheets of transfer film usually come with one edge strip without adhesive, or the backing film is split in such a way as to make separation easy. When one edge strip is without adhesive, be sure to trim that edge off *before* applying the film to a drawing. It's much harder to trim after the film is on the drawing.

Most copiers distort the size of copy image to some degree. This doesn't present a problem for most types of transfer items unless the distortion

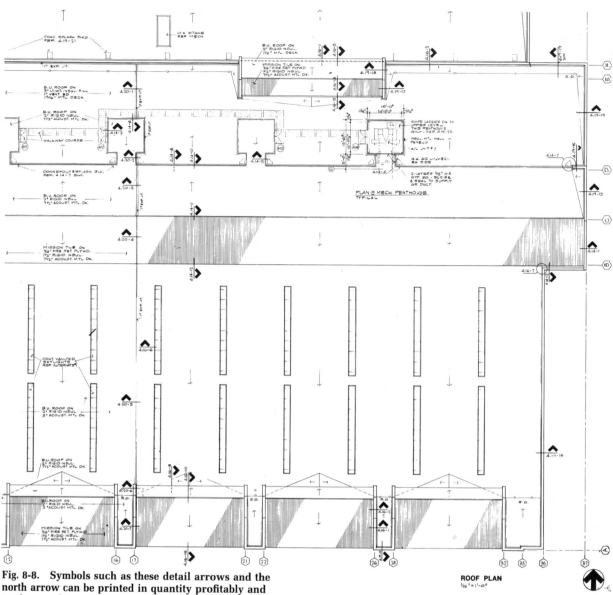

Fig. 8-8. Symbols such as these detail arrows and the north arrow can be printed in quantity profitably and used as appliques instead of being hand-drawn throughout a job.

(Jarvis Putty Jarvis.)

ROOF PLAN

is gross. The precise size of notes, details, etc., isn't critically important.

As mentioned in Section 8.3, "Total Transfer and Cutout Films," many films are usable "plain" for typing, drawing, or offset-printing your own applique designs.

The most convenient and least expensive applique system is old-time "scissors" or paste-up drafting. That's a large part of composite drafting, covered in Chapter 12. The convenience and economy come from the flexibility; you're not dependent on films, dry transfer, and so on, that have to be used with care for diazo-print processing.

Your work sheet doesn't have to be translucent; it can even be pasteboard. The work sheet will be photoreproduced as a washoff intermediate which can be revised and drawn upon, just as any tracing can be.

The opaque paste-up work sheet is a great liberator:

You don't have to worry about the heat of diazo reproduction.
The relative transparency and adhesive qualities of various applique products aren't a concern.
Revisions are easy. You can lay a new print or drawing anywhere over the old. You can "erase" with white paint or paper.
You can use any kind and combination of applique you want: films, tapes, dry transfer, cutouts from diazo prints or from catalogs, typing paper, office-copier prints, photostats.

When you use opaque paste-up work sheets, you gain a special savings in the cost of applique materials. Instead of having custom dry-transfer sheets or films made for a couple of dollars per sheet by a manufacturer, *you can have them printed on paper for a few cents a sheet.*

If there's a quick-print offset shop near your office, *you can have hundreds of custom-design opaque applique sheets run off for you in an hour.*

The offset-printed paper appliques are mainly practical for larger repeat elements: schedules, key plans, standard details, blocks of notation, patterns, grids and textures, etc. Smaller elements are best as ready-made cutouts such as on custom "roll-on" tapes, total transfer, or precut transfer films by Stanpat. That's to avoid having to scissor tiny elements.

Stickyback label paper can be printed on by offset or by office plain-paper copiers. The smaller

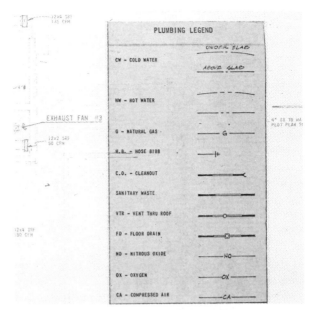

Fig. 8-9.   An example of the shadow left on a diazo print by old-style stickyback appliques. New techniques and materials eliminate this telltale "ghosting."
(Guidelines.)

pressure-sensitive labels have been used by some offices to print detail section symbols, north arrows, and other small, often repeated symbols and notes.

Some offices use their own diazo machines to make low-cost custom appliques. They print on plain diazo paper—crisply and as ghost-free as possible—and use the prints for applique cutouts. Repositionable spray adhesive is used as applicator.

8.7 SETTING UP THE OFFICE GRAPHICS CENTER

There are problems in setting up an applique system and getting it well stocked with supplies. One problem is that most art or drafting supply stores handle only a couple of manufacturers' products. Even a store that's well stocked with the goods of one applique manufacturer still won't have the whole line.

Try to settle on just one or two basic letter styles. Find the few tapes that are going to be useful. Test and decide on one kind of make-your-own applique product. Some offices have destroyed their chances of utilizing appliques by stocking up with too many products from too many sources. Then they lose control of quality, they are unable to keep up on the inventory, and the whole thing falls apart.

I suggest these steps to smooth the way for yourself:

1. Order catalogs or brochures from everyone you can find in the applique business. Your local art and/or drafting supply dealers will supply you with some. (Some catalogs have prices on them to discourage idle browsers, but they're free to potential buyers in almost all cases. For an update of applique sources, order the supplement *Reprographic Resources Guide* cited at the end of this book.)

2. Get samples to test. Dealers usually have small sample sheets or partially used dry-transfer and cutout materials to give away.

3. Test options. Compare cutouts with dry transfer. Try some items, such as tapes, on your next preliminary drawings. See if the product can be continued through the design process into working drawings. Try some custom applique products. Ask the advice of your blueprinter. Write down results of tests for those who will follow you.

NOTE: *Don't use any appliques without the proper backup materials and tools. You'll lose the timesaving value of these products if you don't have the right tools and clean, well-stocked work stations.*

Here's a shopping list of the main items you should have on hand:

____ Light tables, also called tracing tables. A 36″ × 40″ table will cost between $500 and $600. Fancy ones cost $1000. This is an *essential* piece of equipment. Some offices build their own. Good, homemade tracing tables shouldn't cost more than $200 for a 36″ × 40″ surface. Remember: These units are a *must* for doing proper applique work.

____ Anti-static spray such as Static Guard, available at most supermarkets in the laundry supply department.

____ Pressurized can of air to blow dust and crumbs away. (Some graphic artists use a hair blower to clean off work boards.)

____ Fixative sprays. See catalogs for types and uses.

____ Repositionable spray adhesive.

____ Mending tape (such as Scotch Magic Mending Tape).

____ Double-sided adhesive tape.

____ Weighted tape dispensers.

____ Steel T square, triangle, and ruler (24″).

____ Large and small shears, extra sharp, best quality.

____ Small paper cutter, extra sharp, best quality.

____ Mat knife, extra sharp blades.

____ Single-edge razor blades and "piggy-bank" can for used razor-blade disposal.

____ X-acto and blades. The pointed blade #11 is recommended for cutout film materials. Blade #16 is designed to ride along a straight edge.

____ Frisket needle knives (round wood or plastic handle with needlelike blade).

____ Conde cutter and blades (an adjustable blade; it will cut only the thickness of one layer of paper or film).

____ Whetstone. (Just takes a quick swirl and a couple of wipes to sharpen and hone a dull edge. It will save many, many blades.)

____ Nonphoto blue pencils. You can write notes with these, and they won't print on diazo or photoreproductions.

____ Soft erasers. Pink pearl and kneaded (not "kneadable") erasers are good for any erasing required near dry-transfer images that have been transferred.

____ Rubber cement, rubber cement thinner, and small, "oil-can"–type thinner dispenser.

____ "Crepe" or rubber cement "pick-up" bar.

____ Long, flat, thin-blade tweezers.

____ Opaquing fluid for photocopies.

____ Correcting label paper.

____ Long-pointed #3 sable brush for white paint on detailed opaque corrections.

____ White paint or ink.

____ Large rolls of flimsy, onionskin tracing paper as flap or cover paper to protect work sheets from dust and abrasion.

____ Burnishers: "thimble"-type that fits over forefinger; dry-transfer burnisher; dry-transfer final bond burnisher; broad plastic burnisher; roller burnisher; rolling ball, adjustable, pressure-type burnisher. (You won't need all of these in the long run, but it will pay to test them all on different products and settle on those you like best.)

____ Dustproof cabinets or drawers for tapes, films, dry-transfer sheets. (Most manufacturers offer units to fit their products.)

8.8 SYNTHESIS

You've almost certainly used appliques of one sort or another. The only difference, as you pursue this stage of systematization, is that applique use becomes formalized.

The normal practice in buying and using appliques is that someone picks up whatever product is available and uses it in whatever way he or she thinks will work. If several different design and production personnel in a firm use appliques, chances are they're using divergent types, brands, tools, and techniques.

Use of appliques is usually haphazard; storage is even more so. That's one of the main reasons that attempts to encourage office-wide use of appliques fall apart: there's no storage system, no inventory control, no filing and retrieval system. The materials are either around or they're not—usually not. Then, when someone needs some letters or tape, it's a question of whether it's worth running down to the graphic arts supply store to pick some up. Usually it isn't worth it, and it's back to graphite on paper.

You start to formalize the use of appliques by establishing the "graphics center." This little workspace is designed to grow, but it can start modestly enough, mainly as a "paste-up" work counter, with light table and storage units for various applique products. Later, it may include diazo equipment, flatbed printer, drafting typewriter, lettering machine, standard or reference detail files, etc.

Now, with a graphics center underway, along comes the need for someone to be in charge of it. This is a special category of assistant: not a draftsperson, not a graphic artist, not a secretary or file clerk, but someone with some degree of knowledge and skill in all these areas.

Why have a production assistant? Mainly because the graphic assembly processes are so simple. Drafting staff who earn $7 to $12 and more per hour shouldn't do work that can be done as fast or faster by a $4- to $5-an-hour person. Of course, there are times when the design or production people should or have to do their own applique work, typing, and so on. But a sharp production manager will get those times to an absolute minimum to keep work flowing and to keep personnel working at their optimal levels.

Offices also often need to create the job role of manager or *coordinator* of production systems. He or she plans, administers, and monitors the evolution of the office through and beyond its five stages of development, as outlined in Chapter 2. The first big step was the graphic reforms and strategic planning described in that chapter. The next major step was the entry into *systematic* reuse of simple data and systematic use of appliques—simple ones at first, then increasingly more complex ones.

Subsequently or concurrently with the development of the office's applique-drafting system comes the creation, revision, or refinement of the office's standard and/or reference detail system. Standard details may themselves be appliques, or appliques may be used in their creation. They'll most likely include typewritten notation—another subsequent step described in Chapter 10—and maybe photodrafting as described in Chapter 11.

In the next chapter, I recommend setting up a very specific system for creating, filing, using, and reviewing standard or reference details. Similarly, when working with appliques, think in terms of establishing the best possible consistent *system* for appliques: a system for testing products, a system for inventorying them, a system for filing and retrieval, a system for applying those that you've learned are most reliable, and a system for creating and testing custom appliques. And, as at any step or stage in creating a production system, keep a simple, concise journal of what decisions have been made and why. That will save people who come after you an enormous amount of time and wasted effort.

8.9 EXERCISES

1. Obtain catalogs of leading manufacturers of applique products. Use the office copier to copy pages that show the types and patterns of applique products you're most likely to use. Post the copied pages from various catalogs side by side, and compare their stated qualities. Do some manufactured products look best-suited for architectural applications? Do others look best for engineering? Which manufacturer or supplier looks like the best all-around source?

2. Request samples of competitive applique products: letters, tapes, films, etc. Have a comparative use test. Which products adhere most easily? Which adhere too well? Do you run into some unexpected problems in using them?

3. If there are sales representatives for major applique products in your vicinity, call them. Ask why they think their brands are superior. Ask why they think their competitors' brands are inferior.

4. What words, titles, fixtures, furnishings, symbols, etc., do you anticipate using that might be appropriate to have custom-printed as appliques for you? What custom elements work best for you as dry transfer? Which might be better as total transfer? Which as offset-printed stickyback cutouts?

STANDARD AND REFERENCE DETAILS

9.1 WHY STANDARDS?

There are two main arguments for using standard or reference details:

1. Construction details make up 50% or more of the drawings in many sets of construction documents.
2. A large percentage of construction details—sometimes half or more—are repeated in various projects.

Add up those two arguments and it seems a design firm might cut out 25% of its drafting by systematically reusing repeat details instead of redrawing them each time. It's true—potentially. But usually it doesn't work out. Here's why:

Standard details are often started without a complete long-range plan as to what should be standardized and why. One result is a file full of details of stock items traced from manufacturers' catalogs and other items that don't need to be detailed and will just clutter up the documents.

Standard details are often initiated with impractical or expensive ways of transferring the details to new sets of drawings. Some offices have started detail books only to find that their local building code agency (unjustifiably) won't accept them. Some firms do paste-up sheets that are photoreproduced with full-size negatives. That's a costly process that greatly offsets the original time and cost savings.

Even if a system gets off the ground, someone has to watch over it, *manage* it. Most systems fall

into obsolescence and disarray within their first year. Filing, storage, and retrieval systems disintegrate from misuse and neglect.

Then there is the problem of staff and/or management resistance: "This isn't supposed to be a factory," or "We do creative design—no chance for standardization in our work." If that resistance comes from a high position in the office or otherwise has power behind it, it will be virtually impossible to create and maintain a successful system.

So, there is all that potential and there are all those barriers. How can you break through it all with a successful, long-lived system? I will list the main steps—an outline of how some people are doing it. The remainder of the chapter will elaborate upon these steps.*

1. Do the exercises listed at the end of this chapter. Review old working drawings and identify repetitive details. Work out some numbers as to what the actual savings will be for your firm if you establish a bank of reusable details. This step is essential for further planning and budgeting, and it's an important tool for dealing with skepticism or resistance. (Creative people sometimes misunderstand how much design work is really original. Most construction of any kind is highly standardized. No office invents a whole new structural system, flashing system, and roofing system, or unique wall construction, partitions, floors, fixture mountings, stairs, hatchways, and so on, for each new project. But it's often unclear as to how extensive the

*If you already have a working system, consider some of the following points as possible refinements or a profitable restructuring of what you already have.

repetition really is. There's no substitute for counting details to find out.)

2. When reviewing repetitions of details from project to project, look too for *partial* repetitions. For example, many wall sections are alike in most ways and different in others. Curbs, flashing, slabs, etc., may have 90% similarity from job to job without being literal repeats. Plan on reusing the *common portions or backgrounds* of such details that will likely repeat from project to project.

3. Prepare a list of all detail types that you would consider storing in your detail bank. You'll use the list to plan and schedule the creation of your master detail file. When the list exists, you have a basis for gathering reference materials and sample details. You can keep the compiled materials in an "in-process" file, ready for people to work on whenever they're between assignments or otherwise on down time.

4. Plan to create all future details for each new job as if they were for the detail bank *first*. This is an ingenious way of maintaining the integrity of the detail bank system and ensuring that it doesn't get bypassed and ultimately abandoned. You'll prepare *all* job details as if they were standards. Some will be unique and unusable on future work. They'll go in a special "reference section." Some will be of a type that might be reused but only in part. Those will be completed up to the point where they might have further use. They're frozen at that point as "masters." The masters are photo- or diazo-copied to be finished as needed to meet the needs of the special project at hand.

5. When preparing to create all future details as masters for the detail bank, keep the variables as nonspecific as possible. For example, if creating a wall fixture attachment that would use the same screws, bolts, and so forth, regardless of whether the wall were masonry or concrete, then don't show the wall construction or note it on the master. If an opening or material might vary in size in different projects, leave it undimensioned. The opening or material can be dimensioned as needed to fit specific jobs and noted "N.T.S." (not to scale).

6. Classify and label some details as "in process," some as "reference," and some as "standard." That will help keep the files properly segregated. If there's considerable resistance and resentment toward standards, then call them all "reference details" and call the detail bank a "reference detail library." No one seriously objects to using detail references. It's done—it has to be done—all the time anyway.

7. Create a drafting guide of graphic standards for detail drawing. List standards that are necessary for all reprographics:
   a. Minimum lettering height: $\frac{1}{8}$" high with $\frac{3}{32}$ to $\frac{1}{8}$" space between lines of lettering. Minimum minor title letters: $\frac{3}{16}$" high.
   b. Space out and enlarge all minor symbols such as inch marks, arrowheads, and loops in lettering.
   c. Space out all patterns, textures, and cross hatching.
   d. Use very solid line work: thick, medium, and thin. No "faint" or "light" lines permitted.
   e. No back-of-the-sheet pocheing or shading. If any "halftone" or other shadings are used, they have to be large enough in pattern spacing to survive clearly if they are later photoreduced to half size.
   f. Don't allow line work to touch letters or numerals, or fractional numbers to touch division lines.
   g. Establish consistent notation standards— nomenclature and standard abbreviations.
   h. Establish a consistent left or right point of view for construction details. I recommend that the "interior face" of a detail section be to the right with a straight strip of notes down the right-hand side of the detail. Vertical dimensions are on the left or "exterior face" of the construction section being shown.
   i. Establish a consistent spacing between the right-side surface of construction details and the strip of notation.
   j. Establish a consistent spacing for dimension lines along the left face of a construction section.

NOTE: *Keep in mind that details, while prepared at different times on different sheets and put in different parts of the file, will ultimately be assembled together on the same large working drawing sheets. Consistency in composition, lettering, and so on, will pay off in coherence and readability of assembled detail sheets.*

8. While doing preliminary planning and preparation for a detail bank, consider the following possibilities (but don't make immediate decisions on them):

   a. You may decide to have all notation for details typewritten. This solves the problem of consistency in detail lettering. And it's an excellent way to introduce typed working drawings in general because the same basic procedures will be required for typing standards as for any other part of the drawing. Refer to Chapter 10, "Typewritten Notation."

   b. You may choose to draw standard and reference details freehand. This can be very economical and speedy. If final details or drawings sheets are photoreduced, freehand work is "straightened out" in the process. Review Chapter 7, "Freehand Drafting."

   c. You may want to do your original standards in ink. Ink on polyester can be faster than using drafting leads. If you're not familiar with current ink-drafting technology, see Chapter 6, "Ink Drafting," for an explanation of its efficiency. Ink is much better suited for reprographic systems than lead drafting, and it's completely adaptable—and even faster in use—when combined as felt tip pens and freehand drafting.

   d. You may wish to separate detail drawing from notation and dimensions by means of transparent overlays. Some offices do this to gain more flexibility in allowing variations in details that occur from job to job.

   e. You might establish a composite-drafting system in preparing detail drawings. That is, if there are portions of construction that reappear as "background" in varying details, you would use photocopies or diazo copies and paste-ups instead of redrawing them on each original detail drawing. Chapter 12, "Composite Drafting," will stimulate some ideas in this direction.

   f. You can use photographs of actual construction in standard and reference detail drawing. This is another easy, small-scale way to become accustomed to an important technique. See the photodrafting chapter.

   g. You can also make extensive use of appliques: tapes, films, ready-made symbols. Applique drafting can be done by lesser-rank graphic personnel—often faster than drafting by trained draftspeople.

   h. Give extended consideration to the final format, the materials, and the assembly and reproduction method you'll be using. You'll be stuck with the choices for years to come, and they will have to be compatible with the larger overall drawing production system you decide to use most. The choices will be laid out further on in this chapter.

9. Coordinate your standards format with a modular, overall drawing sheet design. Both the popular size sheets—24″ × 36″ and 30″ × 42″—can be designed as composites of 8½″ × 11″ units. Although standard details are prepared and stored on 8½″ × 11″ sheets, that doesn't mean each detail will take up that much space in the final drawings. Your actual "detail module" will be some subunit of the 8½″ × 11″ detail master sheets. Some firms use 4¼″ × 5½″ as their basic detail module size. Then all details drawn henceforth fit either within that 4¼″ × 5½″ unit or in multiples of it.

10. Plan on making each detail complete in itself, without cut lines. Avoid having parts of a detail on different 8½″ × 11″ masters unless they can be used as single details in themselves.

11. Select a filing indexing system. This deserves some careful thought—it's another one of those decisions that you'll be living with for a long time to come. Some firms use an adaptation of the CSI division system so the detail bank complements the organization of specifications files. Some firms, including quite large ones, use a very simple alphabetical system: doors are under "D," roofing under "R," for example. Still another option is to use the drawing division method I recommended in Chapter 3, "Simplifications and Reforms in Working Drawings." If your sets of drawings will be organized according to divisions that match the construction sequence, then that might be a logical way to subdivide your standard detail file.

12. Be sure that someone will be permanent overseer of the detail system. New details have to be processed, approved, and filed. Old details will have to be backchecked when there are complaints or suggestions from the

construction sites. Files will have to be sorted and updated periodically as items get misfiled or lost. New staff will have to be shown how to use the detail bank and how to prepare original details for it. Old staff will have to be reminded of all that occasionally. It's an ongoing process, and, except in some small offices, it won't take care of itself. A production assistant or production coordinator, or both, may be in charge. Or, if a traditional structure is maintained in the firm, maybe it should be watched over by the chief draftsperson, office manager, or specifications writer. Ideally, the person who conceives and implements the file should have ultimate responsibility for its upkeep.

13. Acquire basic storage equipment: a couple of file drawers, a set of hanging file folders, file-out cards to indicate materials that have been removed, and a three-ring "reference binder" that will contain the index and photocopies of all details in the detail bank. (Some firms provide a complete master index three-ring binder to all drafting staff.)

14. Design the detail master sheet format to include the following reference information:
   a. File or index number at upper right-hand corner for easy identification in file folders.
   b. Detail name, also at upper right for easy visibility.
   c. Detail scale, person it was drawn by, original drawing date, and revision dates.
   d. A column to record where and when detail has been used and when last updated according to use. (If ever a detail presents a job-site problem, it can be backchecked through other jobs under construction or nearing construction.)

15. Design a preparation, filing, and retrieval system that will keep the file organized and under control. A recommended system is described in the next section of this chapter.

16. Design a system for assembling details for check printing. Coordinate that system with your method for the assembling and final printing of details on working drawing sheets.

17. You may opt for assembling details in detail books rather than on full-size working drawing sheets. See Section 9.6, "Standard Detail Books."

9.2 STORING AND USING THE DETAILS

There are three main variations of detail storage and assembly systems:

1. Details are filed as opaque or translucent originals which are photocopied with a high-quality office plain paper copier onto sticky-back applique sheets. The appliques are assembled onto the working drawing tracings. Usually changes and additions are made to the details before they're photocopied. It's difficult to make changes later with the stickybacks unless the applique sheet is recopied as an erasable diazo reproducible with draftable matte surface.

2. Details are filed as opaque or translucent originals as above. Copies are made as needed, either with the office copier or diazo printer, and the copies are pasted up on a blank carrier sheet. The carrier sheet is photographed at the repro shop, and the image is recreated on moist-erasable drafting media.

3. Details are filed as above. Reproducibles are made on clear nonstickyback polyester film (nonmatte surface). Reproducibles are made either as diazo polyester prints, plain paper copier prints, or photographic reproductions on washoff polyester. The clear polyester reproducibles are lightly adhered with transparent tape onto a polyester carrying sheet. The taped "paste-up" is run through the diazo machine to make a blue-line check print. Revisions are made on the reproducibles, and the final composite is reprinted as a full-size reproducible on erasable or moist-erasable, matte-surface polyester.

This last variation seems to provide the greatest flexibility. It's flexible enough to adapt to different job or procedural situations with least fuss and expense.

9.3 PREPARING AND FILING DETAIL MASTERS

Following is the procedure for making original detail masters for the standards file:

1. Prepare the original drawing on 8½″ × 11″ sheets according to whatever techniques you've decided on: freehand, ink, typewriting, applique drafting, etc. For the most flexibility, use blue-line grid tracing paper, or a grid underlay beneath polyester drafting media.

2. If you're reusing details already drawn for other jobs, have them photoreproduced or diazo-reproduced on your 8½″ × 11″ master sheets.

3. After checking, approval, index numbering, etc., make two clear polyester copies and a diazo (or office-copier) copy on paper.

4. File the diazo or office-copier paper copy in the three-ring reference binder. The reference binder retains prints of all details on file. When people want to review standard and reference handrail details later, for example, they'll go to the appropriate section in the reference binder and *not* directly to the detail storage masters file. In fact, direct staff access to the masters file may not be permitted. Staff may make office-copier prints of detail sheets directly from the binder if they want to paste up a mock-up or check print, but they're not to remove any of the pages from the binder. The binder also includes a masters index—a list of all details and their index numbers.

5. File a clear polyester film copy of the detail in the masters file. This is the actual "detail bank" or "standards and reference file"— whatever you want to call it. Generally, there is a hanging folder for subdivisions of the file, and reproducible copies of details on polyester are filed in numerical sequence within each folder.

6. The masters file also contains a masters file index. Whenever a new detail is entered or an old one eliminated or renamed or renumbered, it's recorded in the masters index. At the same time, record additions or changes in the masters file index in the front of the reference binder. Ongoing changes can be noted in pencil in the masters index. Type

up a new copy of the index whenever it gets crowded with revision notation.

7. File the original detail, along with a reproducible film copy of it, in a separate "original masters" file drawer. Keep this drawer locked to all but the production assistant and production coordinator (or whoever has equivalent responsibilities).

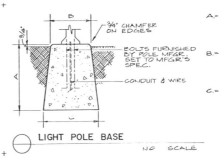

Fig. 9-1. In this standard detail the dimensions that may vary from job to job are not shown but can be keyed in as *A*, *B*, and *C*.

(Hansen Lind Meyer.)

9.4 DETAIL-FILING INDEXES

Offices that use a division system for numbering their working drawings usually file their standard details according to the same division categories. Here's an example of an index list that follows division headings. The division sequence matches the normal sequence of construction.

1	General Information	(Standard schedules, symbols, legends, etc.)
2	Site Development	(Standard planters, drains, paving, etc.)
3	Structural	(Details, schedule forms)
4	Building Enclosure	(Exterior wall sections, fenestration, storefront details, roof details)
5	Partitions	(Interior wall details, door schedule forms, door frames and details, finish schedule forms)
6	Ceilings	(Ceiling details, soffits)
7	Fixtures and Equipment	(Casework and millwork, fixture connections, schedule forms)
8	Plumbing	(Details, schedule forms, fixture photos)
9	Heating/Vac	(Details, schedule forms, equipment photos)
10	Electrical	(Details, schedule forms, equipment photos)
11	Communications	(Details, schedule forms, equipment photos)
12	Conveying Systems	(Details, schedule forms, equipment photos)
13	Color	(Details, schedule forms, equipment photos)
14	Signage	(Details, schedule forms, equipment photos)
15	Furnishings	(Details, schedule forms, equipment photos)
16	Landscaping	(Details, schedule forms, equipment photos)

Often a simple alphabetical system is perfectly adequate for the filing and retrieval of standard details.

A   Master Manual
B   Building code and zoning data blanks, drawing numbers
C   Curtainwall, windows, entrances, store front
D   Door and frame details and elevations
E   Exterior details
F   Finish schedule, door schedule
G   Graphic symbols, abbreviation
H   Handrails, stairs, ramps
I   Interior details
M   Millwork
P   Partition-type sections
S   Site-work details
T   Toilet details and mounting heights

"A" & "B" are reference sections. Following is a list of one office's details filed under the alphabetical section titles from "C" on:

C   Curtainwall, Windows, Entrances, Storefront Details
   1. Typical aluminum entry doors
   2. Sliding glass doors
   3. Typical aluminum window sections
   4. Brick sill sections
   5. Sloping "greenhouse"-type skylight
   6. Concealed overhead closer mullion
   7. Drive-up bank-teller window
   8. Wood guard railing on entry doors and sidelights
D   Door and Frame Details, and Elevations
   1. Typical hollow metal frame sections
   2. Typical hollow metal and wood view panel
   3. Door louver detail
   4. Door and frame elevation sheets
   5. Hollow metal borrowlight frame
   6. Wood doorframe and sidelight frame
   7. Overhead door and track
   8. Roll-up grille and door
   9. Pocket door detail

10. Door thresholds
11. Penthouse door sills
12. Elevator doors
13. Masonry block door lintel types

E Exterior Details
1. Typical roof parapets
2. Typical gravel stops
3. Typical window head flashing
4. Typical masonry wall flashing blowup
5. Roof expansion joint curbs
6. Brick control joint detail
7. Bank or book depository
8. Roof scuttle
9. Prefab metal canopy
10. Wall louver details
11. Roof dome skylights
12. Loading dock details
13. Metal fence and gate
14. Roof drain and sleeve
15. Roof flashing
16. Roof equipment screen
17. Service yard screen
18. Foundation
19. Wall-mounted roof ladder

H Handrails, Stairs, Ramp Details
1. Wall-mounted brackets
2. Various typical railings
3. Tread-riser detail
4. Ships' ladders
5. Typical stair stringers
6. Areaway railing
7. Balcony railings
8. Ramp railings and slopes
9. Metal spiral stairs

I Interior Details
1. Base types
2. Divider strips and saddles
3. Folding partition details
4. Ceiling expansion joint detail
5. Brick column plan section
6. Fire extinguisher mounting height elevation, lettering, and section
7. Drapery track alcove
8. Strip electric heater mounting
9. Partition expansion joint
10. Floor expansion joint
11. Light cove detail
12. Wall-mounted light strip
13. Movable panel partition track and jambs
14. Toilet room soffit light
15. Door mat recess and frame
16. Typical lay-in ceiling details
17. Chalkboard and tackboard

18. Directory-mounting detail
19. Hospital corridor rail
20. Drinking fountain heights
21. Drywall column furring plan
22. Acoustic ceiling coffer
23. Kitchen equipment base

M Millwork Details
1. Cabinets and counters
2. Open shelving and adjustable standards
3. Coat rod and hat shelf section
4. Projector window and shutter
5. Interior borrowlight details (wood)
6. Coat hook strip mounting
7. Wood grille ceiling or soffit
8. Projector screen cabinet
9. Reception counter

S Site-Work Details
1. Walk expansion and control joint
2. Railroad tie retaining wall
3. Bollard details
4. Trench drain detail
5. Bike rack detail
6. Concrete curb detail
7. Concrete drive section
8. Concrete walk section
9. Brick paving
10. Asphalt curb detail
11. Asphalt paving section
12. Parking light standard base
13. Flagpole base
14. Bank drive-up island and culvert
15. Pipe guard for driving
16. Landscape planters
17. Traffic island
18. Concrete tire stop
19. Concrete or stone bench
20. Paving pattern plan

T Toilet Room Details and Heights
1. Toilet room accessory heights
2. Handicap rail and fixture dimensions
3. Toilet partition bracing above ceiling
4. Lavatory counter section
5. Mirror mounting trim
6. Shower receptor detail
7. Recessed towel and wastepaper wall section

Offices often file standard and reference details according to Construction Specification Institute Uniform Systems Divisions. The major headings are:

1. General requirements
2. Site work

3. Concrete
4. Masonry
5. Metals
6. Carpentry
7. Weather protection
8. Doors and windows
9. Finishes
10. Specialties
11. Equipment
12. Furnishings
13. Special construction
14. Conveying systems
15. Mechanical
16. Electrical

Subdivisions are given appropriate number classifications that continue the CSI sequence, and individual details within each subdivision are numbered consecutively as they're introduced into the system. Here's an example from "Division 2, Site work":

02500	A-1	Headwall
	A-2	Footing and subsurface tile
	A-3	Yard cleancut for footing drain
	B-1	Area drain
	C-1	Planter drain
02550	A-1	Light pole base
02600	A-1	Asphalt paving
	A-2	Service drive paving
02620	A-1	Type A curb
	A-2	Expansion joint in curb
	A-3	Concrete entrance apron
	A-4	Combination curb and gutter
	A-5	Combination curb and gutter
	A-6	Combination curb and gutter
	A-7	Concrete curb
	A-8	Integral concrete curb
	A-9	Integral concrete curb
	A-10	Integral curb and sidewalk
	A-11	Type M6-12 curb
	A-12	Expansion joint at curb
02630	A-1	Walk paving
	A-2	Concrete walk section
	A-3	Expansion joint at walk
02700	A-1	Flagpole base
02760	A-1	Site furnishings

Here's another example of a filing indexing system based on the CSI division format:

01-000 General Conditions
02-000 Site Work

02-001	Miscellaneous details
02-100	Paving and walk details
02-200	Planting details
02-300	
02-400	
02-500	
02-600	
02-700	
02-800	Track details
02-900	

03-000 Concrete

03-001	Miscellaneous details
03-100	
03-200	
03-300	
03-400	
03-500	
03-600	
03-700	
03-800	
03-900	

04-000 Masonry

04-001	Miscellaneous details
04-100	Cavity wall details
04-200	Solid masonry details
04-300	
04-400	
04-500	
04-600	
04-700	
04-800	
04-900	

05-000 Metal

05-001	Miscellaneous details
05-100	Railings
05-200	Special stairs
05-300	Metal pan stairs
05-400	Concrete stairs
05-500	Utility stairs and ladders
05-600	
05-700	
05-800	Expansion and seismic joints
05-900	

06-000 Wood and Plastic

06-001	Miscellaneous details
06-100	
06-200	
06-300	
06-400	
06-500	
06-600	
06-700	
06-800	
06-900	

07-000 Thermal and Moisture Protection
    07-001 Miscellaneous details
    07-100 Roof accessories
    07-200 Roofing details
    07-300 Waterproof membrane details
    07-400
    07-500
    07-600
    07-700
    07-800
    07-900

08-000 Doors and Windows
    08-001 Miscellaneous details
    08-100 Door types
    08-200 Frame types
    08-300 Door details
    08-400
    08-500
    08-600
    08-700
    08-800
    08-900

09-000 Finishes
    09-001 Miscellaneous details
    09-100 Base types
    09-200 Wall types and details
    09-300 Ceiling types and details
    09-400
    09-500
    09-600
    09-700
    09-800
    09-900 Column enclosures

10-000 Specialties
    10-001 Miscellaneous details
    10-100 Toilet partition and accessories
    10-200 Wardrobe and locker details
    10-300 Louvers, vents, covers
    10-400 Wall and louver guards
    10-500
    10-600
    10-700
    10-800
    10-900

11-000 Equipment
    11-001 Miscellaneous details
    11-100 Educational
    11-200 Laboratory
    11-300 Medical
    11-400 Food service
    11-500
    11-600
    11-700
    11-800
    11-900

12-000 Furnishings

13-000 Special Construction
    13-001 Miscellaneous details
    13-100 Radiation protection details
    13-200 Sound and vibration control details
    13-300
    13-400
    13-500
    13-600
    13-700
    13-800
    13-900

14-000 Conveying Systems
    14-001 Miscellaneous details
    14-100 Elevators
    14-200 Moving stairs and walks
    14-300 Dumbwaiters
    14-400 Conveyors
    14-500 Pneumatic tube
    14-600
    14-700
    14-800
    14-900

15-000 Mechanical

16-000 Electrical

9.5 RETRIEVING MASTER DETAILS

Here are basic steps (and some variations) for finding and pulling standard details to use on a project:

1. Details that will probably be used on a job are noted in the project miniplan. As the project develops, specific detail titles and reference numbers are noted on the miniplan or working drawing mock-up.
2. To find and select a detail, first look in the appropriate sections of the three-ring-binder masters file index. Make copies of desired details on the office copier. (The masters file should be located near the graphic work center and there should be a good plain paper copier in or immediately adjacent to the work center.) Use the copies as check prints and, later, as a means of ordering reproducible standard details to assemble and mount on the final detail work sheet or carrier sheet.
3. If there are changes or additions to be made on a standard detail on file, order an erasable reproducible copy. If the changes are such that they might be useful in future jobs, give the revision a new index number, have a final clear reproducible made for the job, and file the revised version in the masters file and the originals file. If revisions or additions aren't going to amount to much, just assemble and mount details on a clear carrier sheet. Make an erasable polyester reproducible of the carrier sheet that has a matte drawing surface, and make the final changes or additions there.

NOTE: *It takes experience and trained judgment to make correct decisions as to when to make reproducibles and what methods and materials to use. It's important to avoid running the original reproducibles through too many generations of copy and recopy. Even very sharp work can begin to lose definition after a couple of copying cycles. Some firms use detail originals as masters instead of a first-generation reproducible. That helps keep the quality of the final prints high, but requires care so as to avoid damaging or losing the originals.*

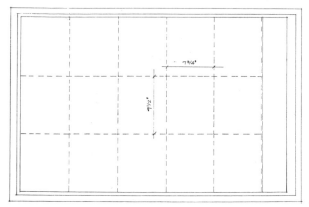

Fig. 9-2. A working drawing sheet module designed for assembly of standard details.
(Guidelines.)

4. Cut out the details to final size from their 8½" × 11" sheets. Mount final detail reproducibles on a nonmatte-surface working drawing carrying sheet with clear tape. The carrying sheet will usually have title block and border preprinted on it. Run the taped paste-up through a diazo machine to make either blueline paper diazo check prints or to make a final working drawing reproducible. Or, the original taped paste-up can be the final transparency for volume printing later. It all depends on how much wear and tear it might be subjected to. If it's subject to damage, make a reproducible. If not, use it as is. When running a taped paste-up through a diazo machine, cover it with a thin, 1.5- to 2-mil clear polyester sheet to protect the taped-on detail sheets.

NOTE: *Item 4 describes one of the three basic popular methods for creating the final prints from assembled standard details. Other methods are described elsewhere in the chapter.*

When dealing with assembled transparencies on a transparent carrying sheet, you're likely to run into the "ghosting" or "shadowing" problem. That is, a darker tone may appear on final prints where the original transparency materials are mounted—including tape marks. This is not a problem if the whole sheet is photographically reproduced—because any paste-up lines are opaqued out on the negative. And it's not a problem if the original masters are created with extremely dense lines because they can be exposed for an extra long time in diazo printing of a diazo

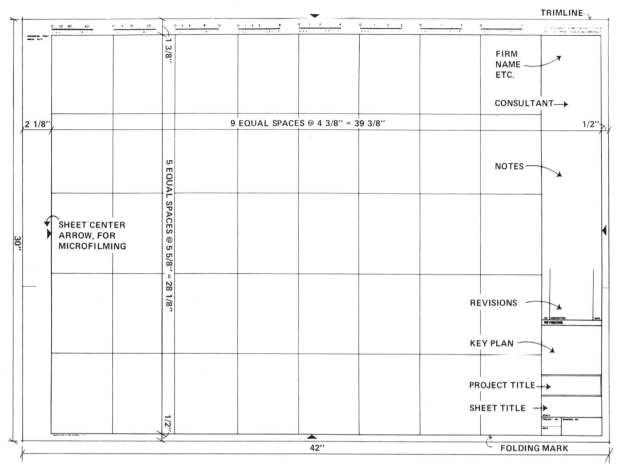

Fig. 9-3. A working drawing sheet module and design.
(Northern California Chapter of the American Institute of Architects, Committee on Production Office Procedures.)

reproducible. The extra "burn" wipes out the shadowing or ghosting. Also, if some shadowing or ghosting appears on a sepia Mylar or other type of transparency, it will most likely not show up on diazo reprintings.

There's another way of handling ghosting or shadow lines of translucent paste-up details. That is to design the sheets as a grid, in specific subdivisions of 8½" × 11", and provide a wide tape border to delineate the grid. The tape border covers up the match (or mismatch) points of the cutout and taped-on details.

Two final options for doing check prints are illustrated in the following:

A firm in Phoenix keeps a number of polyester cutouts of each standard detail in the file. When someone wants to mock up a detail sheet, they take the desired polyester cutouts and slip them into pockets of a transparent vinyl carrying sheet. The pockets are the size of the detail module

units. These are similar to the vinyl-pocket photocarriers in photographic or photoslide albums. The check prints are a little hard to read, but they're very fast to assemble. (This office had the vinyl-pocketed carrying sheet assembled by a local plastics shop.)

A small design office in Atlanta created a similar idea. They keep a polyester carrying sheet that has diagonal slots in it. They slip their master cutouts into the slots for a quick diazo check print. Again, prints aren't of final document quality, but they're very easy to put together as a mock-up for designing the final sheet.

9.6 STANDARD DETAIL BOOKS

Standard detail systems are most often described in terms of assembling details on large working drawing sheets. The following question inevitably arises: If you're keeping your standard masters on 8½″ × 11″ format sheets, why not just use them at that size directly in detail books?

That's definitely more convenient, and many offices do their details in book form. Sometimes they're incorporated with the bound specifications; sometimes complete working drawings, details, and specs are all bound together as one book-sized unit.

There is controversy about standards books. Many contractors say they're inconvenient to use and easy to lose (or ignore) on the job. They also complain that they don't know if details included in such books are real and actually apply to the job as shown. They've seen book details that were just randomly applied boilerplate with only the vaguest application to the job at hand.

On the other hand, some contractors and subcontractors say they're extremely handy. One fabricator told us: "It saves me and my men a lot of time to be able to pull a page and carry it right up the ladder instead of wandering back and forth to the print table."

In general, if the drawings are applicable to the job, and if the addressing and referencing system is very simple and clear, there needn't be much objection to using detail books.

Detail books can be improved by including reduced-size prints of key plans, elevations, and sections. That helps people to see the isolated details in context.

Some building code jurisdictions reportedly will not accept detail books. This is wholly unacceptable behavior by such agencies. Local professional societies should oppose such incursions until the agencies come to grips with their actual limited functions.

9.7 STANDARD DETAIL SHEETS

Certain kinds of details may be treated as standard sets or clusters rather than individual unrelated drawings. Site-work details, for example, often repeat themselves as a group from project to project.

Another, most obvious example is the "nomenclature and symbols" sheet that shows the abbreviations, standard notes, symbols, etc., that are office standards for all projects. Such sheets can be prepared just as standard details would be except they're filed as full-size drawings rather than units of 8½″ × 11″.

Other drawing types that may be prepared as full-size sheet standards include: cabinet work, wall construction, doorframe schedules and details, and integrated partition and ceiling systems.

Every discipline has its group of consistently reusable elements. Many structural engineers, for example, prepare an "S-1" drawing which contains all the most commonly repeated structural details.

A very important type of "standard" sheet is the "interior elevation fixture standards." If your firm does any particular building type repeatedly, there'll be a set of fixtures that commonly recur, such as hospital fixtures, housing cabinetry, plumbing fixtures, library fixtures, penal institution fixtures, etc.

Often drawn are interior elevations that really only have the function of showing the heights and, perhaps, appearance of wall-mounted fixtures. Since the horizontal location of fixtures such as drinking fountains, phone booths, fire hose cabinets, and so on, is shown on plan, all that's needed is the height indication and possibly some detail key reference. That can be provided in a standard elevation drawing that shows the fixtures, their heights, sizes, appearance, and any necessary fixture mounting detail keys.

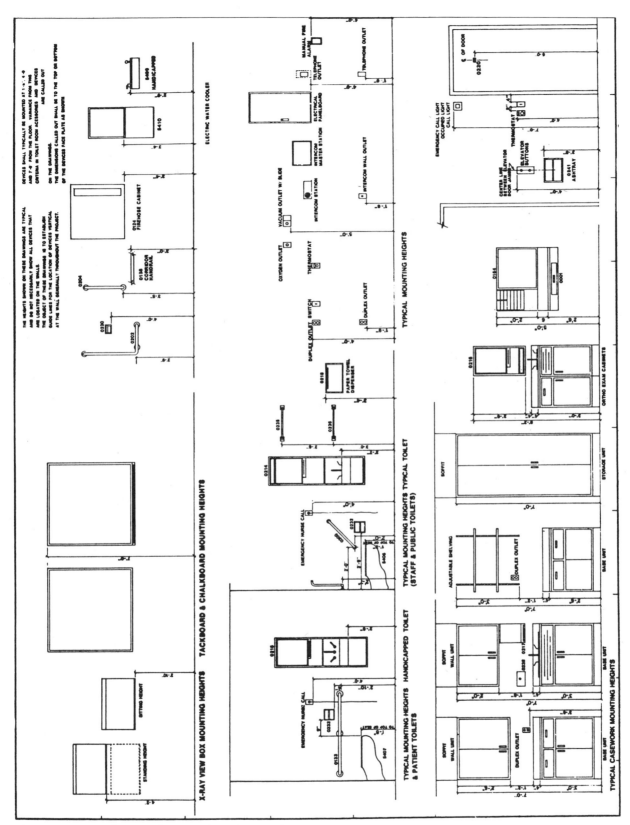

Fig. 9-4. Interior elevation drawings show fixtures and fixture heights but are often unnecessary. They can be covered with a standard fixture mounting height drawing such as this one (fixture locations are shown on the plan).

(Hansen Lind Meyer.)

113

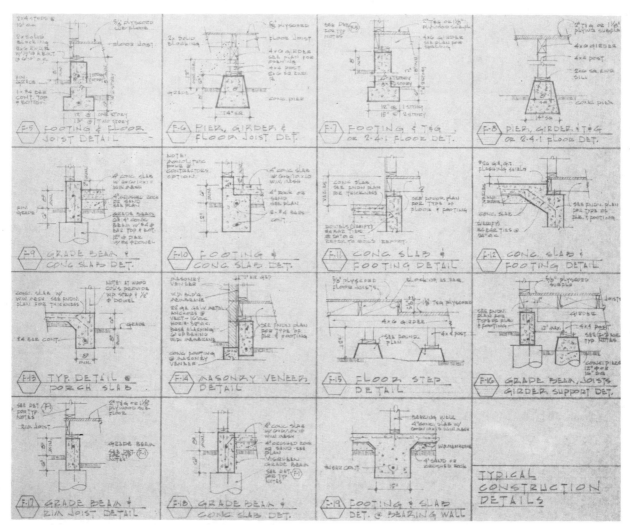

Fig. 9-5.   A portion of a standard detail sheet used by a
housing designer. Virtually all the construction details
of light-frame construction will repeat from one project to
another. Notation and dimensions are lettered in normal
size on the original—note how they clog up on this
reduced copy.

(Guidelines.)

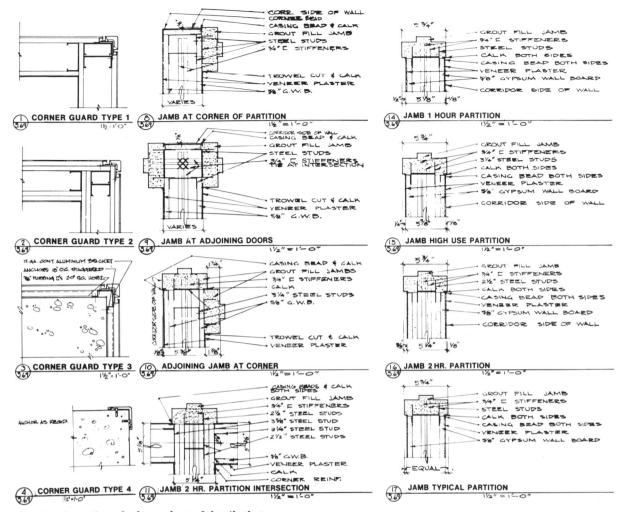

Fig. 9-6. A portion of a large sheet of details that occur from job to job.

(Hansen Lind Meyer.)

9.8 SYNTHESIS

This chapter's subject—standard and reference details—comes early in the five stages of transition. It's one of the first systems because it's comparatively easy to implement. It *is* a simple form of reuse of existing data, it is familiar, and it is easy to adjust to. Many or most offices have used, or are using, a standard detail system of some sort.

If you get sophisticated in making and using standards, it will lead you into every major system described in this book. Standard detail drawings are like any other drawings except for size. Since they're small, they're a convenient learning vehicle for any advanced production method. You can test everything: graphic reforms, appliques, typing, photodrawing, freehand and ink drawing, composite drafting, and overlay drafting. All have their applications in making standard detail drawings. You can also test any and all the reproduction systems, reproduction media, and drafting media.

I make the point repeatedly that each component of Systems Drafting will augment and simplify the other components. This is most obvious, and most rewarding in terms of quick and tangible time and cost savings, in the case of standard details.

9.9 EXERCISES

1. Do a follow-through on the working drawing examinations and red marking I've cited in Chapter 3. Review old working drawing prints, upwards of half a dozen typical sets of drawings. Estimate the percentage of drawing that goes to construction detailing. Count the number and kinds of construction details that are repeated in two or more jobs.

2. How would you answer the argument that all details done by a design-conscious office should be completely original because every project is unique?

3. Can you list three main potential problems that might arise once staff start using and relying on standard details?

4. Invite a contractor to go over several sets of construction drawings, and then present to an office or school group his or her most candid possible critique of the value of those details for bidding and construction.

5. Invite specification writers and/or site representatives to review office details, and give a critique as in Exercise 4.

6. Review Section 3.7, "Overdrawing," and Section 3.8, "Common Errors and Omissions in Working Drawings," as a guide toward creating cleaner, more accurate, easier to find, and more usable construction details.

7. Do a brainstorm exercise. Conceive of three or four ways to convey the kind of information that construction details convey without using drawings of construction details.

8. If you already use a standard or reference detail system, compare it with the important points described in this chapter. Could your system be simplified or made easier to use? Could it use some elaboration? In what one or two principal ways could your system be improved?

10

TYPEWRITTEN NOTATION

10.1 INTRODUCTION

Typing has three great advantages over hand lettering: legibility, consistency of appearance, and *speed*. How much faster is it? That mainly depends on what's typed, how it's done, and who does it. Most people can type a sheet full of notes (such as a large equipment or finish schedule) about four to six times faster than they could letter it by hand.

Speed diminishes as the notes get shorter and more scattered. Medium-size blocks of notes can be done two to five times faster than hand lettering. Short one- or two-line notes may be as slow as hand lettering—or faster, depending on the typing system.

There's no question about the time savings possible with typing. So why don't more offices use it? It's mainly a matter of knowing how. There are tricks to typing working drawings. When there are tricks involved, it means special procedures to learn, a start-up time investment, and some initial inconvenience. There's none of that fuss with hand lettering. There is no special investment, no new techniques. People just do it, and that's that.

When you switch to typing, you don't just bring in a typewriter and start typing on the working drawings. You have to introduce a typing *system*. You need the system to avoid problems. There are going to be problems in getting sharp reproducibility, in making revisions and corrections, and in coordinating between drafting and typing processes. You choose a system to solve these problems.

Setting up the typing system may mean a change in other production procedures. You might change working drawing sheet sizes, formats, drafting media, etc. All the changes, the choices, and the components of a system best suited to your work are laid out in this chapter. You'll be able to choose the typewriter, the typing medium, and the typing procedure that's probably best for you from the many options available. You'll have to test things for yourself, of course, but all will go much smoother with this information than it would without it.

I have some special recommendations regarding the simplest and least expensive typing systems. These will be clearly identified. I have one very definite general recommendation: *For greatest overall simplicity, convenience, and flexibility, combine typewritten notation with composite drafting and photoreproduction.* That will give you maximum latitude in typing media, in ease of making corrections and revisions, in control of graphics, and in sharpness and clarity of the final reproductions. There's more on that in Section 10.9, "Typing for Composite and Overlay Drafting."

For those of you who prefer to type your own notes, make note of the following point: *It isn't necessary to know how to touch type.* After a little hunt-and-peck practice, any draftsperson will be able to punch out the letters many times faster than he or she could letter them. And that will be *net* improvement, after allowing for special procedures, fooling with the machine, and making corrections.

Finally, don't worry about abandoning the tradition of hand lettering that stretches back hundreds, even thousands, of years. It isn't much as traditions go, and it won't be missed.

10.2 THE OPEN-CARRIAGE TYPEWRITERS

"Open-carriage" typewriters are specifically designed to hold large drawings, charts, tables, and so on, of virtually unlimited width. The Varityper Engineering Lettering Machine was the only such machine of its kind for many years. Then IBM made one for a while but bowed out. As of this writing, the Music Print Company in Boulder, Colorado, will modify your IBM Correcting Selectric II typewriter to be an open-carriage machine. It is costly, but for many offices such machines have paid for themselves in less than a year.

It is possible to track down an old IBM open-carriage or Varityper engineering typewriter at a reasonable price and, after some experimentation, put it to good use. Also watch for new products. By the time you read this text, the market may have encouraged many variations of mechanical or electronic open-carriage or "on the board" lettering machines.

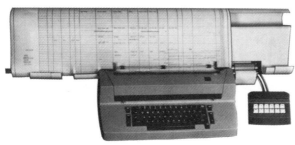

Fig. 10-1. An open-ended carriage modified IBM Selectric typewriter that can hold original drawings of virtually any width.

(Music Print Company.)

10.3 LETTERING MACHINES

Typewriters are clearly limited in lettering size. For sheet titles, spatial identification, drawing titles, and so on, most offices draw their letters or use applique letters or "Leroy"-type title lettering. Stencils are a help for large titles, but still comparatively slow.

The fastest large-lettering system is the lettering machine. Lettering machines take about one-

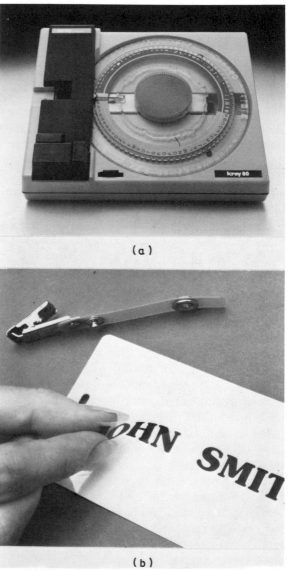

(a)

(b)

Fig. 10-2. (a) A "lettering machine" that prints titles onto clear tape. (b) The tape is a stickyback applique that can be adhered to drawings.

(Kroy Industries, Inc.)

third as much time to use as the "Leroy" system, for example, and about one-fourth the time required for dry-transfer "instant-letter" appliques.

Lettering machines have the appearance of a typewriter-sized "Dymo" label maker. There are a large circular letter dial, a tape output, and some buttons. Lettering machines are very simple to operate, and it is easy to change letter sizes and spacings.

The machines print letters on a clear adhesive film strip. Letters are dark and crisp in outline. The carrier film is clear enough not to leave a ghost shadow on diazo prints *if* your other drafting procedures are geared to a slower, "burn-out" diazo printing. You can also print on opaque tape, which might be appropriate if you're doing composite drafting on opaque paste-up sheets that will be photographed rather than diazo-printed.

There's a limit on letter sizes—about ⅜″ high. Larger types will most likely be available by the time this text is published.

NOTE: *After you review Chapter 8, "Drafting with Appliques," you may see other ways of handling large titles more efficiently and economically.*

Considering the "reusability" principle, you might note that most larger titles used in construction documents are repeated from job to job. Obvious examples are titles such as: "floor plan" (with scale), "cross sections," "wall sections," "exterior elevations," "interior elevations," "site plan," "roof plan," "vicinity map," "cabinet work," and so on.

The fact that they are reused from project to project suggests that they should just be preprinted in full in one form or another and reused over and over again. They can be preprinted as a cutout or total-transfer, custom-made applique by the applique companies, which can be rather expensive. Or you can make up some master sheets and have them offset-printed or plain paper copier-printed onto thin, stickyback matte acetate, which is much less expensive.

Similarly, if you specialize in certain building types, the room names and other special titles within drawings will be repeated job after job. There are ways of reproducing those titles cheaply, storing them, and applying them whole as needed without resorting to lettering machines or to letter-by-letter stencil or applique methods.

Fig. 10-3. A sampling of the range of type sizes and styles that can be made with a lettering machine. (Kroy Industries, Inc.)

ABCDEFGHIJKLMNOPQRS TUVWXYZ &?!)(:',.-/#%$ 0123456789

ABCDEFGHIJKLMNOPQRSTUV WXYZ &?!)(:',.-/#%$ 0123456789

ABCDEFGHIJKLMNOPQRSTUVWXYZ abcdefghijklmnopqrstuvwxyz .,?!:'-&

10.4 USING STANDARD AND NONSTANDARD OFFICE TYPEWRITERS

The question arises: How do you get a 42″-wide drawing into a 13″-wide typewriter? The various ways of transferring type from standard-size typewriters onto larger drawings are dealt with in later sections, particularly Section 10.8.

Some drawings are done small enough to fit directly into standard typewriters. One architect always does small-size working drawings—13″-wide sheets—and fits them into his office typewriter. This doesn't seem so strange when you consider that many sets of drawings are photoreduced by half anyway for bidding and/or construction. Now some offices just draw them small in the first place.

There are wide-carriage typewriters that can take medium-size drawings. Olympia and Remington manual models can be ordered with 36″-wide carriages. IBM, unfortunately, has a 13″ maximum on its standard wide-carriage Selectric.

There are also extra-large typefaces available. The Bulletin, for example, comes in sizes larger than the IBM Orator and is available from Remington and Olympia.

Special-order, wide-carriage, large-type machines might be useful in certain cases. Their prices are comparable to the IBM Selectric II, but there's a several-month waiting period in most cases, the type is limited to the style ordered (no interchangeability), the widest-carriage machines are nonelectric, and the quality of inking and type image is poor to medium. We can't make any recommendations, but you might check out some of these for yourself. Sometimes there are bargains available in used special-purpose equipment, such as wide-carriage and/or large-type machines.

Regardless of make and model, chances are your regular office typewriter is usable for working drawing notation. It's just a matter of using the right combination of materials and procedures.

As of this writing, many or most design offices are equipped with at least one IBM Correcting Selectric II. This popular machine has some exceptional features that are very helpful in the drafting room.

First, for those who don't know the machine, we need to deal with a common misconception. The IBM correcting typewriter is not a "cover-up," chalk-ribbon machine. Most people assume that's what "correctable ribbon" means. The confusion is compounded by the fact that you can *also* use such a ribbon (Tech III ribbon and Tech III cover-up tape) with the machine.

The IBM correctable ribbon has a special-formula ink. After typing, any of the letters can be pulled off the paper by restriking with a special key that activates a "lift-off tape." This nonerasing correcting system makes life easy, especially for nontypist drafting personnel.

The correctable ribbon types well on drafting media: tracing paper, matte acetate, and polyester films. (IBM representatives aren't usually aware of this capacity.) The ink is smear-resistant, and letters reproduce well. If a sheet needs to be erased when it's out of the typewriter, the ink erases relatively ghost-free with a vinyl eraser.

There is the added convenience of varied type styles. The IBM Selectric is what they call a "single-element" typewriter. It uses "golf balls" instead of a set of typebars. The elements are, of course, interchangeable.

IBM has an extraordinarily handy type element, the Orator. Orator has oversized uppercase letters—over ⅛″ high. The Orator's "lowercase" letters are still capitals. The upper-case letters look good for medium-sized titles, especially when spread out by double spacing between letters. Also good: the Presentor.

IBM has other elements acceptable for architectural or engineering lettering. The combination of Orator in upper and lower cases, along with a Manifold or Letter Gothic element, covers three general-purpose letter sizes. The Orator is especially useful, incidentally, for microfilming or other photoreproduction requirements.

The Orator element, which can be extremely useful, has some problems. If the typewriter is slightly out of adjustment, the large upper-case Orator letters won't type clearly. IBM doesn't recommend the Orator for diazo reproduction. As far as I can tell, the reason is that the upper-case letters don't always print with 100% density. This problem can be handled by setting the machine for extra-heavy typing pressure; using the Tech III ribbon when you're not typing on translucent media for diazo copying; or on occasion, just double striking faulty letters.

I must emphasize that the oversized letters of

the Orator are used on a *standard* Selectric typing element. People often assume a special typewriter is needed to make such large letters. The element will work on any Selectric model, but, of course, I'm advocating use of the IBM Correcting Selectric II in particular.

10.5 TYPING AND TYPEWRITERS IN GENERAL

There are a few technical details you should know about when shopping for and otherwise dealing with typewriters. For instance:

1. The "single-element" typewriters are those that use a ball or cylinder that contains the typing "keys." The IBM Selectric is the best known, with its "golf-ball" element. Royal has one for its better electric typewriter, and Varityper Company has used interchangeable elements for many years. Interchangeable elements are also often called "fonts." Single-element machines are simpler, lighter, comparatively less expensive. and, of course, more versatile than typebar machines.

2. The "typebar" is the traditional typewriter system—the familiar metal arms that hold the type. Typebars are still used in the less expensive electric typewriters, in manual typewriters, and in the "proportional-spacing" machines. We'll discuss proportional spacing later in this section.

3. The basic choices in ribbon are simple: "fabric" or "carbon." Virtually all professional work is done with the carbon ribbon, which is actually a plastic film. When struck with a typebar or element, the ink letter literally comes off the ribbon and adheres to the paper. This makes a precise, dense image that is not possible with fabric ribbon. Many brands of typewriters now offer easy-in, and easy-out ribbon cartridges that include choice of fabric or carbon. There are special ribbons for typing on tracing paper or polyester.

4. IBM introduced a new error-correction technology with its IBM Correcting Selectric II. The carbon ribbon has a special-formula ink, and the ribbon mechanism includes a spool of "lift-off" tape. When you strike over a typed letter with the lift-off tape, the ink sticks to the tape and leaves the paper. This is quite different from covering over the retype with chalky paint, tape, or ribbon.

If you're a nontypist, you should learn the various impression and spacing controls. Your best reference will be the manufacturer's operating manual. The main controls that affect the quality of typing are:

1. The impression control, just as it sounds, increases or decreases the intensity of force with which the type hits the paper. Although you want a dark image for good reproducibility, you may not want maximum impression on the paper. Too deep a type impression on the sheet may show up in reproduction, even after complete erasure. Test the different impressions on the materials you will be typing on. Include corrections, and test different degrees of impression with corrections, to see how they show up after reproduction.

2. The line-space lever controls the number of lines the paper will move up when you hit the carriage return key. Usual choices are one, two, and three line spaces. For more flexibility, you can order a "66" ratchet from IBM, for example, that lets you move the roller (also called the "platen") up or down half a line.

3. The paper-release lever lets you release the grip on the paper, so you can shift it up, down, or sideways on the roller. When the paper is positioned where you want it, you flip the release back to grip the paper in its new position.

4. The multiple-copy control lever adjusts the closeness of the roller to the element or typebars. It's normally used to adjust for extra-thick copy in the machine. It's often accidentally flipped back, which can cause a sheet to lay loosely against the roller. When the sheet isn't firmly against the roller, air bubbles appear, and the typing may appear fuzzy, uneven, and otherwise marred. (If the sheet doesn't lay flat even with a correct multiple-copy lever setting, give it a slight tug upward while still holding it firmly to the roller with the other hand. That will push air bubbles out and get the sheet pressed down properly.)

5. There's usually a roller-release button on the end of the roller. When you press this, you can move the roller, and sheet, up or down independent of ratchet spacing.

6. The carriage length of your typewriter limits the width of copy you may fit into the machine. An 11" carriage restricts you to 11"-wide copy. The IBM Selectric II has a 13"-wide carriage option. The Olympia Model 50

has interchangeable carriages, with a 24" maximum. Some machines, such as manual Olympia and Remington machines, can be ordered with 36"-wide carriages.

Some architects and engineers like the option of "proportional spacing." Most typewritten letters are the same width, but on a proportional-spacing machine, letter widths vary. The appearance is more like regular typeset printing. The IBM Executive is the best known proportional-spacing typewriter. A competitor is Olivetti's Editor 5. Both are typebar rather than single-element typewriters.

There are also different typestyles and type sizes. The two basic typewriter typestyles are "elite" and "pica." Elite is the small one (think of petite) and isn't likely to be used in working drawings. Pica is larger. Capitals are called "upper case," and small letters "lower case."

Pica capital letters are about $\frac{1}{10}''$ high. That may be a little short if you need letters $\frac{1}{8}''$ high. IBM's Orator capital letters are slightly larger than $\frac{1}{8}''$ high. Presentor capitals are $\frac{1}{8}''$ high.

Your standard typewriter will be either "10 pitch" or "12 pitch." That means the horizontal spacing of letters is either 10 to an inch or 12 to an inch. The pica-size letter goes with a 10-pitch spacing, the small elite with the 12 pitch. For working drawings, the larger 10 pitch will be preferred.

10.6 TELLING THE TYPIST WHAT TO TYPE

You can type directly on working drawing tracings with the special machines described in Section 10.3, "Lettering Machines" and, as you've seen, with regular office typewriters, too.

The main question, no matter what system you use, is: How do you tell the typist what to type? One way, a good one, is to write rough notes on the tracing with a nonphoto blue pencil. The blue doesn't show in later reproduction. It's a direct approach that lets the draftsperson jot down what's to be typed right on the spot. A problem is that many drafting staff can't stand the idea of scribbling on their original tracings. Appearance of the original sheet is important to them, even if the blue pencil items are invisible to the print machine or camera.

The check-print method is most popular. A sheet is more or less completed in terms of drawing, a diazo print is made, and the rough notes are written on the print.

Some people rebel at rough-writing any notation. "Why," they ask, "should we write the words when it wouldn't take much more time just to letter them in the first place?"

The question includes a misleading premise: ". . . it wouldn't take much more time. . . ." Finish hand lettering is many times slower than the combination of quick rough notation and typing. This is another equally important consideration: *Most drafting staff don't originate their notes in the first place.* They're shown what notes to letter by reference prints and check prints.

Reference prints are a great timesaver. If any previous job has drawing and notation similar to the job at hand, then it may not be necessary to do a check print. Instead, a print of the old job is made and items to be typed on the new job are marked in colored pencil. This, of course, is how notation instructions are often given to drafting staff.

In general, if you're preparing work for someone else to type, the most convenient system is a combination: no-print notes on tracings, check prints, and reference prints.

Always date each check print, each reference print, and each typing episode. When there are more than one set of marked-up prints, it won't be clear which prints are current and which are completed if the work isn't stamped with the date.

As further protection against confusion, be sure corrections are marked in red on the prints, additions marked in green, and red and green notes crossed out in yellow as they're completed. This keeps clear which work is done and which isn't. Similarly, whenever a nonphoto blue pencil note is transferred by typing to the tracing, check or cross off the original blue pencil note.

Results are often excellent when the draftsperson is also the typist. The principals at some small-office firms have taken on this role and are very productive at it. The main advantage, of course, is that the draftsperson can alternate between drawing and typing, without taking time to write the rough notes. That saves a step and augments the time savings.

Timesavers sometimes lead to time wasting because they make tasks so much easier that it's tempting to elaborate on them. In typing notes, for example, the typing is so fast that it no longer seems necessary to use abbreviations and contracted words. Thus, "N.I.C." is spelled out as "not in contract." Such elaboration doesn't really clarify the drawings; it clutters drawings and subtracts from the hard-won time savings.

NOTE: *Some offices manage to do typing much slower than hand lettering. First the rough notes are done lightly but meticulously—just a shade removed from finish lettering. Then, instead of being transcribed by a capable production typist, the notes are typed painstakingly, letter by letter, by a nervous junior draftsperson.*

10.7 BLOCK NOTATION: GENERAL NOTES, INDEX SHEETS, SCHEDULES, AND DETAIL DRAWINGS

These are the easiest kinds of notes to type. You don't have to worry about using a special typewriter. Even if you're typing on working drawing tracing paper, you don't have to type on full-size sheets. You type on strips.

Thick boundary lines are used to mask splice lines of cut strips of working drawing. This is self-evident on "all-notation" sheets such as a drawing index. Drawings are listed column by column across the sheet. The columns are separated by boundary lines. It's a natural setup for cutting the sheet into vertical strips, typing each column of index, reassembling with mending tape, and covering up the splice lines with wide, black-tape border lines.

Columns of general notes and schedules are handled the same way. They're designed in modules: 4¼" and 8½" widths are common modules for strips of schedules and/or notes. If there's to be a strip of notation at the right-hand side of floor plans, for example, that strip is cut out, typed on a regular typewriter, and spliced back onto the tracing. A border line is used to mask the splice line as described above.

Splicing is one technique; typing appliques provides another way to gain the same end result. Appliques come in two materials: acetate and polyester, with a matte surface on one or both sides. Acetate films are usually thinner and more transparent than polyester films. This means they're less likely to leave a shadow or "ghost" on a diazo print. Thin acetate is fragile, however, and easily torn.

Polyester films are very strong, but some products are thick and may leave a shadow when diazo-printed. You can usually get rid of shadow by slowing down the speed of the print machine to get a longer exposure. In that case, other drawing on the sheet has to be dense enough not to fade out.

There are special typewriter ribbons for typing directly on plastic films. They're sold by major drafting supply outlets.

NOTE: *I have found that the best ribbon is the standard correctable ribbon used on the IBM*

Correcting Selectric II. Although it wasn't intended for this use, it adheres well to most films.

When typing on films, use a thick backing paper for a cushion, and use the maximum typing impression setting.

Another option is: Instead of typing directly on the films, you can type on regular bond paper and transfer the image to film with an office plain paper copier and office-copier stickyback film. Copier appliques let you keep your originals intact. You don't have to worry about special ribbons, and changes and corrections are easy *before* copying.

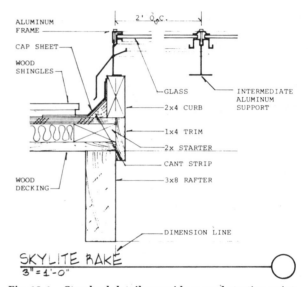

Fig. 10-4.   Standard details provide a good starting point for getting used to typewritten notation. Standards are usually stored on 8½″ × 11″ sheets, so a standard office typewriter can be used.

(Courtesy of Terry Schilling and John Arnold.)

10.8 SCATTERED NOTATION: ARCHITECTURAL AND ENGINEERING PLANS, BUILDING SECTIONS AND ELEVATIONS

Block notation, as we've seen, is fairly easy and straightforward. That's where the efficiency of typing is most obvious. Potential efficiency is more questionable when notes are short and spread all over a working drawing sheet. By the time rough notes are written for guidance, the words typed, and positioning and alignment completed, it seems it would be faster to hand-letter the notes. And there's that famous technical problem: How do you get a big drawing into a little typewriter?

Several procedures for typing on floor plans, site plans, and other "spread-out" drawings are described in this section. I'll open with the method I recommend, the "strip-on" method. It's best suited to small- and medium-sized projects. Here's how it works:

First, assume the typing will be done on an IBM Correcting Selectric II with standard correcting ribbon and lift-off tape. The typing element is Orator, Manifold, Letter Gothic, or other suitably dense, sans serif–type style that will reproduce well. I'm also assuming this is a standard translucent drawing and diazo printing job. Using this typewriter and these elements puts aside problems of special ribbons, corrections, reproducibility of type, etc.

Second, the job has been planned to consolidate the lettering process; that is, most lettering will be done at one time. This is practical with small- and medium-sized jobs, but generally not with larger projects.

Along the way, gather notes that will go onto the final drawing. Use nonphoto blue pencil for such notes on the tracings. Use check prints for additional notes. These "scribble notes" have to show the location of final notes as well as their content. If old job prints have notes that will apply to the current job, they should be marked accordingly as a third reference.

Type the notes onto a thin, stickyback, polyester applique. If you're typing on a standard 8½″ × 11″ applique sheet, divide the sheet into two or more columns as suited to the average

length of the notes. Then just type the notes, line by line, down the applique sheet.

For convenience, position the notes on the applique in approximately the same sequence they'll follow on the drawing: left to right, top to bottom.

A two-column applique sheet will yield about 120 one-line notes. That's plenty for a typical floor plan of a medium-sized building. Generally speaking, that will be more than ample for a site plan or for framing, electrical, and mechanical plans, and far more than enough for any exterior elevation, building cross section, or interior elevation sheets.

Now, the question is: What do you do with the list of notes? Do you cut them out and stick them on the drawing? The answer is yes. You have to follow a special procedure, which is described in the next paragraphs. But first, let me assure you: Typing, cutting out, and adhering even relatively small notes is still faster than hand lettering. It gets even faster when you do certain kinds of buildings over and over.

You'll need to develop finesse for dealing with small pieces of applique film. Stickyback film, for one thing, is really *sticky*. It's difficult to pull the applique from its carrying sheet without an edge to grab hold of. That's why most such products have a narrow, nonadhesive portion running down one side of the applique sheet. That's the "grab strip."

After typing strips of notes on an applique, you have to "preseparate" the applique from its carrier sheet. This means gently pulling the entire applique off the carrier and very lightly sticking it back on again. Then, when note strips are cut out, they'll be fairly easy to pull away from the carrier sheet material. Do the preseparation shortly before you cut out the note strips. Cut the note strips off the carrier just prior to adhering them to the drawing. You'll need a grid or other guideline to get the typed note strips straight on the drawings.

That's basically it. Type notes, cut them out, and stick them on the drawing. It works remarkably well—better than I can convey here. Now here are some qualifications and options:

1. Applique strips will leave ghosts or shadows on later diazo prints if the applique material is too thick or the adhesive isn't completely clear. Select products and test samples for typability and printability.

2. You'll gain an enormous long-term savings when you reuse notes from job to job. They

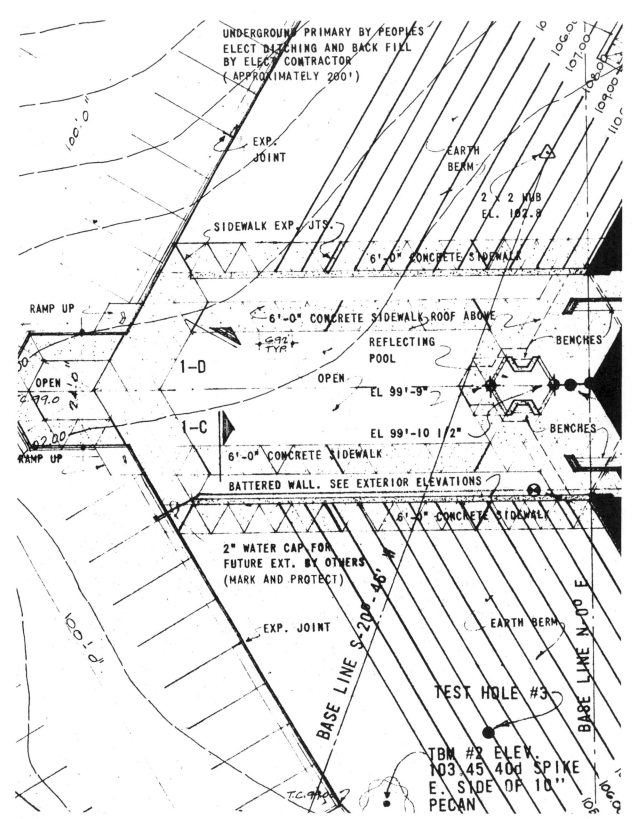

Fig. 10-5. Typewritten notation directly on a site-plan drawing using an open-ended carriage typewriter.

(Ray James-Glen Childers, Architects and Assocs., Inc.)

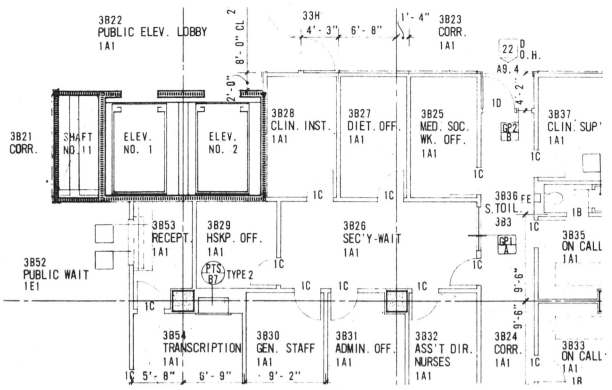

Fig. 10-6. An example of typewritten notation using an open-ended carriage typewriter directly on a floor sheet plan.

(Guidelines.)

will be reusable if you specialize in any particular building type. In this case, standard lines of notes are typed on plain bond paper. The bond is copied with a plain paper copier and imaged onto the applique film. The copy—not the original—is cut, peeled, and adhered to the tracing.

3. Don't apply the strips of stickyback applique if much drafting remains to be done on a drawing. The strips will tend to snag drawing instruments, and the edges are very likely to collect dirt.

4. You can separate "strip-on" notes from the original drawing by applying them instead to a clear polyester overlay sheet. Set the sheet atop the floor plan (or whatever), make four registration marks to assure accurate repositioning later, and apply the notes on the overlay. The two can be printed together later, either in the rotary diazo-print machine (with some slight loss in accuracy of registration) or on a vacuum frame at the print shop. The vacuum-frame print can be a wash-off polyester intermediate print or a "diazo Mylar" from which future prints will be made. This overlay method cancels out some

of the problems inherent in combining appliques with a drawing that's still in process.

THE FOLD METHOD

One method of using a small typewriter for typing notes on a large drawing is rarely thought of. When it is thought of, it's usually immediately dismissed as impractical. The method consists of folding the tracings into strips narrow enough to fit a standard typewriter. The idea appalls most drafting staff; it goes completely against their grain. They'll offer plenty of reasons why it won't work: "The fold creases will show in the prints." "The tracings would get ink-smeared in the typewriter." "The sheets would slip." And so on.

Those are pretty good sounding reasons, and true if you're not careful. Some architects use the "fold method," and it works fine if certain care is taken. For one thing, the problem of compatibility of type, ribbon, and drawing medium has to be worked out.

Drafting media are restricted. Polyester won't work, for example, and some heavier vellums and tracing papers comparable to Clearprint

127

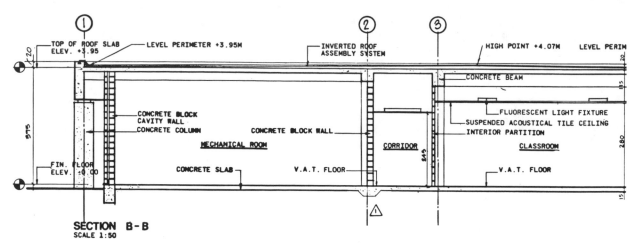

Fig. 10-7. Typewritten notation directly on a cross-sectional drawing of a building.
(Guidelines.)

1010 show crease marks readily. Besides the straight crease line, the heavier papers make visible horizontal "cracks" in paper fiber along a fold. Lighter tracing paper comparable to Clearprint 1000H is less likely to show crease and crack marks.

Half the secret in making this work is the multiple-copy control lever and the paper-release lever on the typewriter. The multiple-copy lever controls the position of the roller (platen) to allow thicker work into the machine. The paper-release lever releases the grip of the roller on the paper. When that grip is released, only the hand and/or the little rollers on the front crossbar hold the paper in place.

By releasing the grip of the roller on the paper, the lightweight folds aren't pressed into sharp, fiber-damaging creases. Experiment with plain typing paper to see some of the latitude that's possible.

The other half of the secret is to avoid a hard crease on the drawing when doing the folding. You fold lightly, with a rounded rather than a sharp turn of the paper. The multiple-copy control lever and the paper-release lever are open all the way to keep the fold from becoming a crease. The noncreased folds won't show up or will show extremely faintly when the tracing is printed later.

This method has been used with very old manual typewriters. One architect found a used manual Remington with a 24" carriage. His drawings were usually 36" or 42" wide. Either size fits the old typewriter with one fold.

A wide carriage can be used to simplify things even further. There's often a natural boundary

line on a drawing sheet that makes a good folding place. For example, a floor plan may take up to 26" on the left-hand side of a tracing, and a block of notes and schedules may take a 10" strip down the right-hand side. A border line separates the note and schedule strip from the plan side, and that's where the sheet is folded.

THE SLICE METHOD

The "slice method" is even more controversial than folding. Far worse than folding, in many people's eyes, would be cutting the plans into strips to fit a typewriter. But there are times when it's practical.

A drawing that will be photoreproduced rather than diazo-printed can be sliced for typing and later spliced together with no problem. It's often done to expedite index sheets, schedule sheets, and the like.

The slice method works well with overlay drafting, too. Typing is done on sections of polyester film that are punched for pin registration with their matched line drawings. Drawing is on one sheet, and notation is on strips of overlay. Overlays and base sheets are later combined into single, reproducible prints, either photographically or by overlay printing on a vacuum frame.

An overlay strip works extremely well with some kinds of drawings. Notes are often done as coherent "lists" straight down one or more parts of a plan, elevation, cross section, etc. Sometimes only one or two note strips will include all notation required for the drawing. Such a strip might be typed on paper and photocopied onto clear acetate or polyester. The clear lettering strip is overlayed and printed with the drawing to make an intermediate transparency that combines the drawing and lettering.

10.9 TYPING FOR COMPOSITE AND OVERLAY DRAFTING

Much of this book deals with the ways of overcoming the problems that come with traditional drafting methods and materials. The standard working drawing tracing, for example, has to be translucent so that light can shine through the sheet and expose diazo reproductions in the print machine. This restriction has excluded architectural and engineering drafting staff from the timesaving paste-up, strip-in, and photographic methods used by all other graphic artists.

Traditionally, we had to worry about translucency and diazo reproducibility. When making a correction, the error had to be removed from the sheet rather than just covered over. When thinking about typewriting on drawings, we had to consider drawing sheet sizes, because we couldn't just type on a piece of paper and stick it onto the drawing. Choices of ribbons, appliques, typewriters, and so on, were all limited to what was compatible with the characteristics of the particular drafting medium *and* its translucency.

With opaque composite drafting, on the other hand, virtually anything goes.

A composite working drawing sheet is assembled rather than drawn. Portions of diazo prints, drawings, tapes, photocopies, press-on and self-adhesive appliques, and so on, are assembled on a work sheet. The work sheet is later photographed rather than run through a diazo machine. The photoimage is projected back onto photosensitive drafting media. The blowback is an intermediate or "second-original" transparency from which diazo prints are made.

This offers immediate advantages as far as typing goes. For example:

1. You type on small sheets or portions of drawings rather than on the full-size work sheet. So fitting drawing size and typical typewriter carriage size is no longer a problem.
2. You can use correction fluid or tape for small changes or retype on self-adhesive label sheets for changes of larger blocks of notation.

Overlay drafting uses photoreproduction too, but the work is still mainly done on translucent tracings. This limits the typing possibilities.

Overlay is also called "registration" or "pin-registration" drafting. It separates elements that are traditionally combined on a single drawing. It separates them during the production phase, but keeps everything aligned (in register) until they're photographically combined onto single sheets later. The system has many advantages in terms of controlled coordination between architect and consultants and in terms of expediting job changes with minimal redrawing.

Architectural floor plans exclude the lettering, restricting it to overlay sheets. The reason is that the same floor plans are used as underlays for consultants' drawings, and those plans do not show the architectural notation.

An overlay lettering sheet can be typed directly on matte-surface polyester—full size if you have an open- or large-carriage machine. To assure correct positioning of the notes, use a marked-up print as underlay for the typing sheet.

If you're using a standard-size typewriter, you can still transfer typing to full-size sheets by using a cut and strip method. First, mark up the underlay print, then cut the print, along with the matte polyester overlay, into vertical strips that will fit the typewriter. Notes are typed as shown on the marked-up print. Later, the overlay strips are photocombined as a washoff reproducible notation overlay. This in turn is combined with the original underlay drawing to make a final reproducible complete with notation.

There are more tips applicable to composite and overlay drafting with typewriting in Section 10.8.

10.10 KEYNOTING

Some advanced production techniques are exotic, some are plain and simple. One of the simple ones is called "keynoting." Keynoting means listing notes by number on a drawing rather than repeatedly writing them out. It's common practice in industrial engineering. An item is drawn and then surrounded by numbers with arrows pointing to various parts. The numbers are keyed to identifying notes or to a parts list typed at one side of the sheet.

Keynoting won't work with some architectural drawings. It would delay take-offs and bidding. But it *does* work for many common elements in architectural working drawings, and where it does, you can gain significant time savings.

The time savings come in two ways: (1) Keynoting facilitates typewriting of notes with standard office typewriters. (2) *A list of keynotes for standard kinds of drawings is usable over and over again.*

Here are examples of how keynoting is done:

1. Photodrawings. Photodrafting is most often used for rehabs, adaptive reuse, etc. Photos of the existing structure are shown, and all the various demolitions, repairs, and additions are so noted. There's tremendous repetition in this kind of notation. A photo detail sheet for one restoration job had notes such as "remove loose paint," "remove curb," and so on, lettered 20 to 30 times each. Overall there were relatively few different notes, but there were many places they had to be applied. That's the kind of situation that's made for keynoting.

2. Detail sheets. Related strings of details of stairs, millwork, flashing, and so on, are likely to include many repeat notes. Easy-to-read detail sheets can be made that have all notes combined in one numbered list. The notes are on the same sheet with the keyed drawings. They're printed with a large typewriter letter style—such as IBM's Orator—for maximum readability. The key reference numbers should also be large and distinct.

3. Building cross sections and exterior elevations. Some offices that specialize in certain

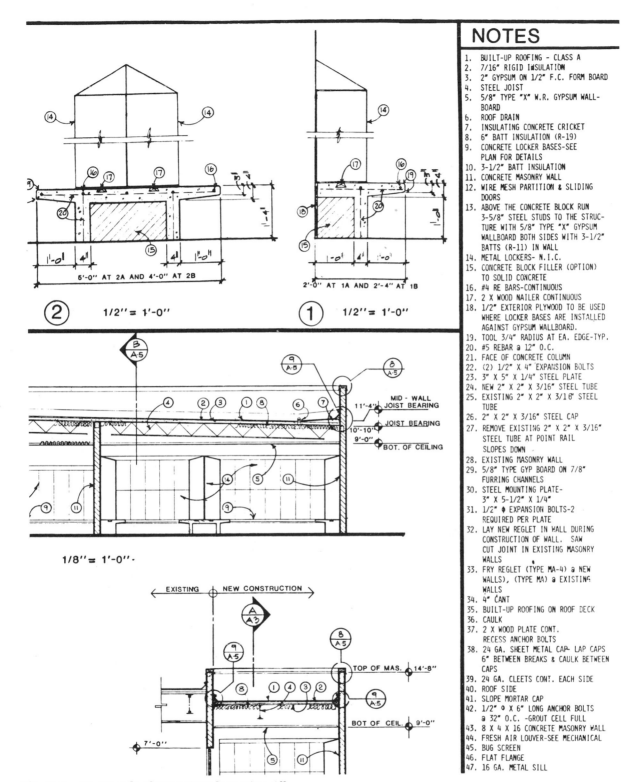

1. BUILT-UP ROOFING - CLASS A
2. 7/16" RIGID INSULATION
3. 2" GYPSUM ON 1/2" F.C. FORM BOARD
4. STEEL JOIST
5. 5/8" TYPE "X" W.R. GYPSUM WALL-BOARD
6. ROOF DRAIN
7. INSULATING CONCRETE CRICKET
8. 6" BATT INSULATION (R-19)
9. CONCRETE LOCKER BASES-SEE PLAN FOR DETAILS
10. 3-1/2" BATT INSULATION
11. CONCRETE MASONRY WALL
12. WIRE MESH PARTITION & SLIDING DOORS
13. ABOVE THE CONCRETE BLOCK RUN 3-5/8" STEEL STUDS TO THE STRUC-TURE WITH 5/8" TYPE "X" GYPSUM WALLBOARD BOTH SIDES WITH 3-1/2" BATTS (R-11) IN WALL
14. METAL LOCKERS- N.I.C.
15. CONCRETE BLOCK FILLER (OPTION) TO SOLID CONCRETE
16. #4 RE BARS-CONTINUOUS
17. 2 X WOOD NAILER CONTINUOUS
18. 1/2" EXTERIOR PLYWOOD TO BE USED WHERE LOCKER BASES ARE INSTALLED AGAINST GYPSUM WALLBOARD.
19. TOOL 3/4" RADIUS AT EA. EDGE-TYP.
20. #5 REBAR a 12" O.C.
21. FACE OF CONCRETE COLUMN
22. (2) 1/2" X 4" EXPANSION BOLTS
23. 3" X 5" X 1/4" STEEL PLATE
24. NEW 2" X 2" X 3/16" STEEL TUBE
25. EXISTING 2" X 2" X 3/16" STEEL TUBE
26. 2" X 2" X 3/16" STEEL CAP
27. REMOVE EXISTING 2" X 2" X 3/16" STEEL TUBE AT POINT RAIL SLOPES DOWN
28. EXISTING MASONRY WALL
29. 5/8" TYPE GYP BOARD ON 7/8" FURRING CHANNELS
30. STEEL MOUNTING PLATE- 3" X 5-1/2" X 1/4"
31. 1/2" ⌀ EXPANSION BOLTS-2 REQUIRED PER PLATE
32. LAY NEW REGLET IN WALL DURING CONSTRUCTION OF WALL. SAW CUT JOINT IN EXISTING MASONRY WALLS
33. FRY REGLET (TYPE MA-4) a NEW WALLS), (TYPE MA) a EXISTING WALLS
34. 4" CANT
35. BUILT-UP ROOFING ON ROOF DECK
36. CAULK
37. 2 X WOOD PLATE CONT. RECESS ANCHOR BOLTS
38. 24 GA. SHEET METAL CAP- LAP CAPS 6" BETWEEN BREAKS & CAULK BETWEEN CAPS
39. 24 GA. CLEETS CONT. EACH SIDE
40. ROOF SIDE
41. SLOPE MORTAR CAP
42. 1/2" ⌀ X 6" LONG ANCHOR BOLTS a 32" O.C. -GROUT CELL FULL
43. 8 X 4 X 16 CONCRETE MASONRY WALL
44. FRESH AIR LOUVER-SEE MECHANICAL
45. BUG SCREEN
46. FLAT FLANGE
47. 16 GA. METAL SILL

Fig. 10-8. An example of typewritten keynoting. All construction notes are provided in the "notes" column and numbered for reference to bubbles on the construction drawing.

(Michael and Kemper Goodwin, Ltd.)

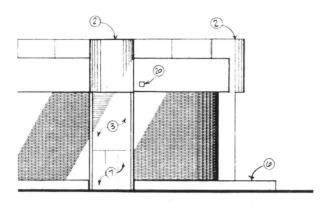

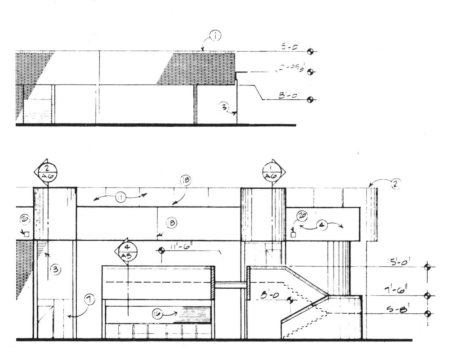

Fig. 10-9. A portion of an exterior elevation drawing utilizing typewritten keynotes. This drawing also utilizes pattern stickyback film to indicate the brickwork.

(Michael and Kemper Goodwin, Ltd.)

NOTES

1. SOLDIER COURSE WITH EXTRUDED ALUMINUM TEE, SEE DETAILS 5,6/A1
2. CAST-IN-PLACE CONCRETE, TYP.
3. 7/8" PROFILE CORRUGATED METAL FASCIA (LAPPED SEAL)
4. CEMENT PLASTER FASCIA ON LATH & METAL STUDS.
5. 8 X 4 X 16 CONCRETE MASONRY UNIT WALL
6. CAST-IN-PLACE CONCRETE PLANTER WALL
7. GALVANIZED METAL PANEL, SEE DETAIL 10/A8
8. WINDOW TYPE "F", SEE SHEET A10
9. DRINKING FOUTAIN/CUSPIDOR, SEE PLUMBING
10. FIELD APPLIED VINYL
11. MECHANICAL SCREEN, CEMENT PLASTER ON LATH & METAL STUDS, SEE DETAIL 5/A7
12. CAST-IN-PLACE CONCRETE BEYOND, TYP.
13. LINE OF EXISTING BUILDING
14. MASONRY CONTROL JOINT, SEE DETAILS 4/A1
15. EXPOSED & INSULATED DUCTS TO RECEIVE PAINT FINISH, SEE MECHANICAL
16. ALUMINUM COUNTER SHUTTER
17. ALUMINUM GRATING, SEE DETAIL 32,34/A10
18. METAL EXPANDED WING TYPE EXPANSION JOINT
19. TECTUM PANELS, FOR SIZES, QUANTITIES & LOCATIONS, SEE SHEET A2. FOR CONSTRUCTION OF PANELS, SEE DETAIL 1,4/A9
20. SPEAKER -SEE DETAIL 1/E3

building types discover that the notes on such drawings are pretty much the same from job to job. They've typed up the common notes and printed them (on the office copier) onto thin polyester appliques. They adhere the copier appliques to the drawing sheet.

On smaller jobs, keynotes are typed on thin acetate applique and are placed directly beside exterior elevations and building cross sections. Identification arrows are drawn from notation to the noted parts of the drawing, without using intervening key reference numbers. Small-building floor plans, site plans, and foundation and framing plans have all been successfully notated this way.

Larger jobs have been keynoted throughout very effectively. In one case, a large master list of general notes was typed with a clean IBM Selectric Manifold typeface. The master was photographically enlarged to nearly double size. (Carbon-ribbon typing can be so enlarged with virtually no loss in sharpness.) Then the keynotes were *offset*-printed on the *backside* of the print paper on which the final job was to be diazo-printed. This way, the general notes and keynotes took up no space on drawing sheets, yet were always at hand for quick reference on the adjacent back side of each drawing print. Here is a related timesaver for users of working drawings: You can have your typewritten drawing index, abbreviations, symbols, and nomenclature list offset-printed on the back side of working drawing sheets. Then people don't have to refer to the index and/or symbol sheet every time they need to look up such data.

Here are steps I recommend for establishing and testing a keynoting system:

____ Target some drawing types as prime candidates for use of keynoting. Likeliest prospects are: "site plans," "roof plans," "building cross sections," and "exterior elevations." These drawing types have limited amounts of notation, and the notes tend to be the same for most building types.

____ Compile an assortment of the drawing types cited above, and have a typist make lists of the notes common to the same kind of drawings. Also ask for a count on the number of times the notes appear on the various drawings.

____ Review the listed notes and excerpt those that are the most common repeats. Prepare

a general note to inform contractors of the intent of keynoting, and show a schedule of keynotes with numbers beside each note, explaining that they will appear in a column along the top, right-hand edge of the working drawing sheet.

____ Keynote schedules should be filed and indexed just like standard details or standard schedule forms. List changes made from job to job so the master keynote schedule for each drawing type can be refined through further experience. Plan on adding long, repeating notes unique to any project onto the keynote schedule. Short, one-time-only notes should be applied on the drawing itself where they would normally go.

____ *Don't start standard keynotes, standard detail notation, schedules, or working drawing typing in general until you've established uniform nomenclature, abbreviations, and type style as office standards.*

____ Create an itemized checklist of components of the various basic working drawing sheets. This checklist, besides serving as an action checklist in planning and completing drawings, could be elaborated on as a master notation checklist for extensive use of keynoting. That is, as a drawing is to be completed in notation, the master note list could be edited for all notes to be included on the drawing—either in schedule form or in the drawing proper. Notes to be used could be identified and called out by number during checking, instead of being written out by hand.

10.11 SYNTHESIS

Typing has been and is a problem when it is "force-fit" into traditional drafting procedures. Typing on large sheets of tracing paper for later diazo printing entails complications—sometimes more complications than people can or should contend with.

The solution is to go all out with reprographic systems. Typing integrates fine when you're using other systems; then it is the old ways such as hand lettering that cause complications.

A major aspect of the new way of doing things is what I call the "horizontal assembly" (composite drafting). If you think in terms of creating comparatively small components of drawings and assembling them later as large composites on a carrying sheet, *then* maybe it's possible that you don't have to worry about typing on large sheets. You type on small sheets instead, which are later combined into larger sheets.

The sequence of small-sheet module to larger sheets isn't practical on broad-scope drawings such as large floor plans, but those are the drawings that aren't most practical for typing anyway because they use mainly short and scattered notes and dimensions that are more convenient to apply by hand lettering or appliques.

The method of assembling standard details described in Chapter 9 is an example of creating large drawing sheets out of units of small drawings. Since those basic units are 8½" × 11" or divisions thereof, it's easy to type their notation with a standard typewriter.

Similarly, it's easy to design schedules as divisions or multiples of 8½" × 11". Then you can design schedules for typing in small-unit form. They can be put together at whatever final size is desired on the full-size working drawing carrying sheets.

The same idea applies to drawing indexes, general notes, keynote strips, legends, charts, maps, tables, etc. Those are small units to be assembled on a larger drawing. As small units they don't require a special typewriter. In many cases the same applies to wall sections, partial elevations, building unit plans, etc.

I advocate getting into typewritten notation gradually. First clear up the graphic standards and get everything organized and consistent in terms of abbreviations and nomenclature. Then, when getting into applique drafting, you'll start using materials such as office-copier appliques that later can be very handy in getting full use of the typewriter.

Once you get a graphics center established, and start training a production assistant, you can then get a typewriter in the drafting room just for drafting purposes. You'll have a place for it, materials to use with it, and a person who can use it.

As you revise or initiate your standard and reference detail bank, you'll want to achieve a consistency in line work, format, and lettering. The consistency and clarity of typewriting is, of course, unbeatable. With a detail bank underway, that's especially the time to get into typewriting. The procedures of typing standard and reference details are the same as for typing any portion of drawings—but you are working with smaller units. There's less risk, less pressure, and it's just easier to learn the new rules of coordinated drafting and typing by working with smaller units such as standard details to start with.

That shows how the typing relates to the steps that precede it. As for the steps that follow, typing proves compatible with photodrawing, especially when using keynoting. It matches up perfectly with the whole concept of horizontal assembly, which is basic to composite drafting, and it will augment the time savings of composite drafting.

Once you get a good typing system going, general production will speed up. That will give you some latitude for shifting into more elaborate production systems. As with other basic steps, it will save time and money in itself and help get people used to new equipment and systems without swamping them. Finally, besides being a good follow-through on the more basic techniques and systems I've described so far, a good typing system will expedite the more complex systems to come.

10.12 EXERCISES

Obtain some past sets of working drawings, and review them as follows:

1. Examine the notes used in the index sheet, site plan, floor plans, and so forth. What notes repeat from drawing to drawing? What notes are likely to repeat from project to project? Create some options for how to best salvage and reuse those repeat notes.

2. Look at notation on the most heavily drawn and notated drawings. Which notes are repeated many times on the same drawing sheet? Which would be good bets for standardization or keynoting?

3. Look at drawing titles, room names, drawing component titles—items such as floor plan scale, detail, wall section, corridor, office, stairs, etc. What titles do you see repeated many times on a single drawing? How many are repeated from drawing to drawing and from job to job?

4. What smaller units on working drawing sheets could have been created as separate units and composited onto the larger sheet? Which of those smaller units could have had their notation typed in a standard-size office typewriter?

5. How would you create a filing and retrieval system for reusing titles and notes that are frequently repeated?

PHOTODRAFTING

11.1 WHAT IS PHOTODRAFTING?

I did a lot of renovation and adaptive reuse projects in San Francisco. The procedure was always the same:

1. Take clipboard, measuring tape, flashlight, and go measure the old building.
2. Return to the office with sketched plan and elevation measurements and "draw them up." (That meant literally redrawing the building.)
3. Go back and get the dimensions missed the first time around.
4. Go back again and figure out why some part of the drawing wasn't coming out right.

At some point we started taking instant-developing photographs to give the designer something more definite to work with. The thought occurred to us: Why not use the pictures to show the rooms instead of plan and elevation drawings? They'd be a lot clearer. The reason was that there was no way to get photographs onto the drawings. And besides, since this firm used blueprints, photos would come out looking like negatives anyway.

Years later an architect called me from Iowa and said: "You know what I just did? I just finished a 4-hour drafting job in about 10 minutes."

He was doing a remodeling of a pharmacy; it was a minor job, maybe half a day's work. He took instant-developing photos of the pharmacy interior and exterior, then copied the photos on his office photocopy machine onto clear film. He taped the clear film copies onto a tracing, and made a sepia print. Then he did his notes and graphic instructions on the sepia—which took about 10 minutes—and the job was set to go.

He was clearly excited when he called and said: "Why didn't somebody tell me about this years ago?"

Since he did this as a rush job, I asked him whether he'd go back to the old methods if and when he had a larger project or more time and money to spend. He seemed a bit taken aback and possibly offended by my question. After a pause he replied: "In the 1930s I was raised on a farm where we pulled water out of a cistern well a dozen times a day for washing and drinking. I went to the bathroom in a packing-crate outhouse 50 yards from the house where I froze in the winter and was smothered in flies in the summer. A person would be an idiot to willingly go back into the Dark Ages. As far as I'm concerned, measuring and drawing instead of taking photographs is the Dark Ages, flies and all."

A renovation project that would normally take 80 to 150 person-hours per detail sheet took 24 hours per sheet on a restoration project as reported by Cynthia Phifer of the Princeton office of Geddes Brecher Qualls Cunningham. She and other architects and engineers who use photo-techniques say the timesaving range is anywhere from 40 to 90%, depending on the job. And, they add, the photodrawings clarify, simplify, and speed up construction.

There's no question about clarifying construction. Most draftspeople were educated in the strict top view, front view, side view, rear view tradition of orthographic projection. An example is an orthographic drawing reputedly in the Smithsonian that shows top, side, and front views of a cannonball. In reality, anything is much easier to understand via a real, live, three-dimensional photo image.

And there is no question about cutting time and cost, either, unless, of course, the designers and/or draftspeople elect to use the slowest and most expensive photo methods possible. The data in this chapter explain how to get any quality results you desire—at maximum convenience and lowest cost.

Let's clarify what we mean by "photodrafting" or "photodrawing." At one time, the words were used to represent practically anything done with a camera, such as in photo restoration and paste-up drafting (composite drafting, the subject of Chapter 12). Now the word refers mainly to one type of photoassisted design and drafting: the photography of job conditions, such as a building site or an existing building. Conditions are photographed and the photoimages are transferred to drafting media.

After photoimages are transferred to a drafting medium, the images can be eradicated, altered, and/or augmented with new drawings, dimensions, and construction notes. A completed photodrawing is normally treated as any other original tracing.

Here are some further examples of the uses of photodrawings:

Aerial photo companies will provide halftone photos of building sites on drafting polyester at any scale you specify. Architects and engineers use such photodrawings to draw site planning, site clearing and demolition, civil engineering, etc. Some architects and engineers photographically combine the image of the site survey with the aerial photo. The survey and aerial photo composite shows contours and boundaries, with the image of the actual existing roads, buildings, rock outcrops, trees, etc. (Please note that such images should be screened so as to be subdued reference background for construction drawings and notes. If printed at full visual strength, an aerial site photo might conflict with the drawn information.)

Some offices enhance their specs with photos so there's no mistaking the materials, products, and models they want.
Some offices include photos of light, plumbing, landscaping, and other fixtures in schedules. Furniture may also be photospecified.
Well-made building models have been photographed as the basis for working drawing roof plans and exterior elevations.
A few offices compile files of standard reference details based on actual construction photos. Similarly, material surfaces, textures, joints, and patterns on all kinds of materials are shown directly by photo rather than by drawing and specification.

Photos are widely used as designer aids and as adjuncts to presentation drawings (as when showing site features around a building). Real-life features are sometimes "rendered" photographically by introducing a screen pattern that breaks up the photoimage to look like ink drawing.

People who could use photodrafting may shy away from it. They have notions that it requires expertise in photo-taking, expensive equipment, and elaborate darkroom and processing facilities. This is not so at all.

As for expertise in picture-taking, the newer cameras are a breeze for anyone to operate. Any photo shop has plenty of concise pamphlets on all aspects of photography, developing, printing, etc. There are only a few technical points to learn for creating photos for photodrafting, and this chapter covers them.

11.2 OVERVIEW

Here's an overall description of the photodrafting process, step by step and in general terms:

1. Suppose you're doing restoration and adaptive reuse of an old building. The first step is to take overall measurements and a comprehensive photograph survey. Photograph interior walls, details of stairs, ceilings, coves, columns, cabinet work, floors, etc. Do a series of all exterior elevation views, along with details of windows, doors, cornices, soffits, steps, parapets, curbs, etc. The general rule is: If there's likely to be some work needed in a particular place, photograph it. It's easy to sort out the unnecessary photos later.

2. Have the film developed and printed directly on "contact sheets." Each sheet will have strips of small photoimages that have been transferred one to one from the exposed rolls of film. Any photo service will do this for you, or you can do it yourself with a simple darkroom setup.

   Circle the photos you want enlarged. Some you'll see immediately as usable; others you'll want blown up for further review and consideration. (Rough "review" enlargements can be made quickly on cheap photo paper.)

3. Draw a schematic plan of the building according to the first rough measurements. Show where previous photos were taken and where additional photos are required. You may need to draw schematic exterior elevation views and interior elevations to clarify what additional detail photos you'll need.

4. As you select photos, decide on their sizes and positions on the drawing sheets. Decide on retouch work, tone changes, cropping, etc. (These items are explained later on in this chapter.)

5. At this juncture, you have some choices as to how to prepare the work for photoreproduction. For example:
   a. You might make a complete finished paste-up of the working drawing sheet that can be photographed "as is" and transferred to drawing media.
   b. You might do a full-sized layout that shows how the final sheet will look but

leave the assembly of the sheet to the repro people.
   c. You might do a small-scale layout made from the contact prints.
   d. You might just compile a folder filled with some photos, negatives, and written instructions. (Consult with your photoreproduction people *before* you prepare work for them, or you're liable to have some unpleasant surprises.)

6. Send the photos, layout, and instructions off to be transformed into a photodrawing "master." That's the sheet (or sheets) you'll be drawing on later. It's like any other working drawing tracing, except it's light-sensitive to begin with in order to retain photoimages.

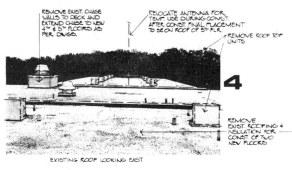

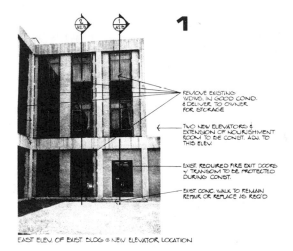

Fig. 11-1. Photodrafting. The most common use of photodrafting is to show alterations to existing construction. It is far faster than measuring existing conditions and drawing them from scratch.

(Gresham and Smith, Architects.)

7. The photoreproduction people take your photos, etc., and transform them into a photodrawing master by one of several methods. For instance:

a. If you provide a complete, finished paste-up, it may be photographed onto a large (8½ × 11) film negative. The negative is touched up as required and then projected—much as a photographic slide would be—onto the light-sensitive drafting medium. The shop uses a "blowback" or "projection camera." Or a finished paste-up might be reproduced on a full-sized negative. Then the negative is pressed against the light-sensitive drafting medium in a contact vacuum frame and exposed to light. The exposed, sensitized drafting medium is processed in an automatic photodeveloper and is ready for drawing.

NOTE: *Photos on a finished paste-up that's combined with line drawing may have to be halftone-screened **before** being pasted up. There is more on that in a later section.*

b. Finished working drawing paste-ups are a rarity. Usually you would provide the repro shop with original photos and/or negatives, plus layout and instructions. The shop might then make appropriate halftone negatives to required size and compose them within holes cut in a carrying sheet. (This is called "stripping.") The photonegative paste-up is then exposed onto the sensitized drafting medium. A second exposure might be made to get the image of sheet border and title block onto the new master photodrawing.

c. Another method is to project light through various negatives one by one and expose the light-sensitive drafting medium master in steps.

d. There are other variations. You'll want to shop out the options. If you have a vacuum frame or flatbed printer of your own, as many offices do now, you'll probably go for some form of contact printing rather than blowback.

8. When the photodrawing comes back to you, you complete the work as with any other working drawing sheet. Detail views are referenced and titled as drawn details would be. Elevation views are titled (with approximate scale) and referenced to a key plan.

11.3 TAKING PHOTOS

Technical competence with a camera is just a matter of following the manual that comes with it. There are, however, some special rules in photography for working drawings. Here they are:

You'll want moderately high contrast prints with a minimum of shadow and highlights. So try for flat lighting in interior shots. It's better to make outdoor shots on bright, overcast days. On the other hand, if you're photographing a scene that includes a lot of detail, such as a batch of piping in a furred crawl space, then higher contrast is desirable to emphasize the detail.

When in doubt on lighting or exposures, "bracket" your photos. That means to do one at likeliest exposure, one at lower exposure, and one at higher exposure. It just takes a couple of extra seconds and is low-cost insurance for getting a usable photo.

Bring a tripod and cable release, especially for interior shots in dim lighting. You'll be using a longer exposure, and you'll want to minimize camera movement.

Generally speaking, you'll do best with head-on, flat-wall views of buildings and building components. Keep the lens parallel to the subject instead of at an off-angle. You'll need a wide-angle lens for most interior shots.

Include a scale mark or measuring stick in the picture. That means a surveyor's rod, a yardstick, chalk marks on a wall, anything to show the sizes of the elements being photographed.

When relevant, show the date and name the subject in the photo. A small chalkboard with the data marked on it will suffice. Some photosupply companies sell camera attachments that date photos as you take them.

Make a map or plan showing the camera location and viewpoint of each photo you take. Later use this to key the photos on a drawing sheet to building plans, site plan, etc.

Don't hesitate to take lots of pictures. The film and the contact prints for review are inexpensive. And, many prints that aren't usable in working drawings will still be valuable for reference and for the job record.

11.4 CAMERAS AND FILM

You don't need special photo equipment; any 35mm film camera will do the job. Cameras of the instant, small, 120-film type aren't suitable. There are cameras that are larger than 35mm film size. These are best of all, but they're expensive. If you happen to have a larger camera, that's good, especially if you'll be dealing with extra-large photo prints. But, as we say, the basic 35mm camera is fine for most purposes.

The single lens reflex (SLR) type of 35mm camera is completely accurate, since you focus right through the lens that exposes the film. That way, you don't miss something around the edges that should be in the photo.

The "automatic" or "semiautomatic" SLRs are a great convenience. The light meter is built in, and your various exposure and lens settings pretty much take care of themselves.

A wide-angle lens is a must. For exterior details, you may need a telephoto lens. A *perspective correction* (PC) lens *isn't* essential in most cases. The PC is a lens that adjusts for the perspective distortion you'll get when photographing a tall building from the ground. Nikon and Canon make PC lenses, and, new or used, they're priced at hundreds of dollars.

All the major brand 35mm SLR cameras are good. Some of the more expensive ones include power drives for action photography. That's irrelevant for architectural photography, of course. Budget between $200 and $300 for a good 35mm camera and from $50 to $200 for each additional wide-angle or telephoto lens.

Features to look for are: bayonet mount for lenses rather than the slower screw mounts, self-timer, clear and bright viewfinder image, light weight, quietness of operation, shock resistance and general ruggedness, and easy handling. We favor the Olympus OM-1 (listed at $400 with 50mm F/1.8 lens, but available at $230 and less). The Minolta SR-T series has comparable qualities: quietness, bayonet mount, etc. Nikons and Nikkormats are long-standing favorites of professional photographers, with their wide range of "system" accessories. The Nikkormat FT-2 is in the quality and price range we're dealing with here, as is the Canon AE-1 and Asahi Pentax KX. (We've listed some camera brands just as a starting guide for the novice. There are other perfectly comparable cameras.)

We've given most attention to the 35mm SLR cameras because they're most widely used. They're versatile and good for travel and architectural slides—for general architectural use as well as for photodrafting.

Larger cameras, called "medium-format," use larger film (220) and give the best-quality prints. There are more special black-and-white films made in 220 than 35mm. Some come with optional Polaroid film packs. Another advantage of some larger cameras is that you can change a film magazine in midroll to match changed photo conditions.

Medium-format or 2¼-format cameras come as single-lens and twin-lens reflex. Leading names are Mamiya/Sekor, Rollei, Hasselblad, and Bronica. Price ranges are about double that of the SLR cameras. Biggest of all are the "press" or "view" cameras. These are boxy affairs with accordion lens extenders; and they use large sheet film.

If you're buying a new camera, do *not* buy at a local camera store, unless it's also a discount camera store. List prices are often twice as high as discount prices, and small stores will often charge the limit. That can mean a hundred or a couple of hundred dollars you don't need to spend. Check the large discount store ads in the popular photography magazines. They have good buys and are reliable stores to deal with, even at long distance.

You won't be using the color-slide film you may be used to. Most photodrafting photography is done on the following Kodak (or comparable) black-and-white 35mm films:

Tri-X Pan film, ASA 400, 20 and 36 exposure rolls.
Plus-X Pan Professional film, ASA 125, 20 and 36 exposures.
Panatomic-X film, ASA 32, 20 and 36 exposures.

Kodak's Tri-X Pan film is high-speed, for dimly lighted interior shots. Even though high-speed, you'll need a tripod or other camera support for long exposures in dark conditions. (Another film, not used too often, is even faster. Its grain is coarse, and it's made for getting shots in dim conditions in the shortest exposure times. It's Kodak's 2475 Recording film, ASA 1000, 36-exposure rolls.)

The Kodak Plus-X Pan film is for average lighting conditions. It has a fine grain for good enlargement capacity.

Kodak Panatomic-X film is for well-lit conditions where you want maximum sharpness and greatest enlargement capacity. It's especially well suited for exterior shots where you want to pick up lots of detail.

If you do use a large "view" or "press" camera, the recommended films are: Kodak Super Panchro-Press Film 6146, Type B; Plus-X Pan Professional Film 4147 (Estar Thick Base); and the Royal Pan Film 4141 (Estar Thick Base).

If using GAF or other films, just check specifications for qualities comparable to the Kodak products cited here.

11.5 HOW TO PLAN AND LAY OUT THE PHOTODRAFTING SHEET

A drawing "plan" and a drawing "layout" are two different things. The plan can be a rough minisketch or diagrammatic outline. It's for your own guidance at first and later develops into an instruction guide for others. It may help to do a plan before photos are taken, for example, to guide the photographer. It'll tell what views are needed and from what viewpoints. The plan will usually be revised after prints of the photos are in hand.

A rough plan is all you need for a simple photodrawing. It will name the few photos involved and show their sizes and positions on the final sheet. Diagrammatic scale or precision isn't important, as long as the intent is clear.

More complex photodrawings require a true-to-scale or full-size layout. A complete layout shows everything in proper size and location on a true-to-size format sheet. Photos may be in sketch form, or they may be paper or cardboard cutouts labeled with identifying notation and taped to the layout sheet. If preferred, mock-up photos may be made inexpensively to desired size as photostats or office-copier prints.

To add another complication in terminology: A "layout" is *not* a "paste-up." The word "paste-up" designates a sheet that has the whole works assembled and pasted on it in finished form. In graphic terminology, a paste-up (also called a "mechanical") is "camera-ready"—it's the finished product just prior to being photographed in final form.

The steps, then, are: (1) sketch plan, (2) layout, and (3) paste-up. Any step might be excluded, depending on your circumstances. A sketch might serve as plan *and* layout, for example, and there may be no paste-up. For more details, see Section 11.6, which deals with the photoreproduction shop.

After you receive your first photographs on a project, you'll have to make five general kinds of decisions: final *sizes* of the printed photoimages on the drawing; *intensity* of images; *cropping* or proportioning of photos; and *sequence* and *positioning* of images on the final sheet.

Sequence and positioning are pretty much self-evident. Any series of views around a site

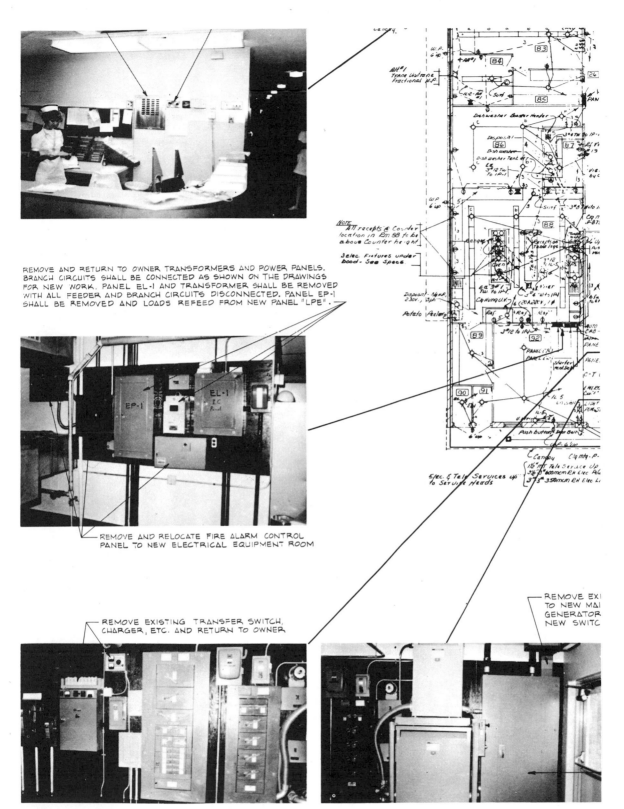

REMOVE AND RETURN TO OWNER TRANSFORMERS AND POWER PANELS. BRANCH CIRCUITS SHALL BE CONNECTED AS SHOWN ON THE DRAWINGS FOR NEW WORK. PANEL EL-1 AND TRANSFORMER SHALL BE REMOVED WITH ALL FEEDER AND BRANCH CIRCUITS DISCONNECTED. PANEL EP-1 SHALL BE REMOVED AND LOADS REFEED FROM NEW PANEL "LPE".

REMOVE AND RELOCATE FIRE ALARM CONTROL PANEL TO NEW ELECTRICAL EQUIPMENT ROOM

REMOVE EXISTING TRANSFER SWITCH, CHARGER, ETC. AND RETURN TO OWNER

Fig. 11-2. A portion of a photodrawing showing electrical work alterations. Photos are connected by arrows to the areas of work on the plan. The original was offset-printed with new construction and new construction notation shown in color.

(Mini-Max.)

or around and in a building should follow an obvious logical progression.

There's one danger in positioning: spacing may be too close. Allow ample space between photos for notes, dimensions, symbols, titles, and additional drawing. Some people don't allow enough space; then notation and other elements have to be drawn on photoimage areas. Lettering and dimensions on gray photo background may be unreadable, especially in later diazo prints made from the reproducible.

Use two L-shaped pieces of cardboard to help judge if and where photos should be cropped. "Cropping" means trimming or cutting away unneeded portions of a photo. It often goes along with enlarging; a portion of a photo is selected and then specified to be blown up to a certain size. This process is called "scaling."

Chances are you shouldn't do your own trimming. Unless you're doing a finished paste-up, don't cut pictures to size yourself—the graphics photographer may need the border area. Just draw tick marks to show the area to be cropped, along with a note of instruction.

You'll save time and trouble by making a well-considered estimate of the size of the original photo prints. If they come out at the same size, they'll be on the drawings; nothing further need be done in that regard. Otherwise, it's a little tricky.

One thing that makes size change tricky is the way ratios of height to width change when you alter a photo's size. If a 3″ × 5″ photo is enlarged so the height is 4″, then you'll need to know what happens to the width. An inch added to the height does *not* add an inch to the width—an easy but false assumption. Instead, it adds 1¾″ to the width.

Wide, horizontal photos increase significantly in width with minor increases in height. Similarly, if you make a slight increase in the width of a tall, narrow photo, you'll have a major increase in height.

Be sure to use proportioning tools or calculators for dealing with photo size changes. Many graphic supply stores carry Formatt Company's simple and relatively low-cost Computagrid. There are other devices—rotary slide rules, etc.—ranging in price from $2 to $20.

You can use smaller photos than you might imagine. A 3″ × 4″ photo is sufficient for relatively close views of planned demolition, repair, and alteration. If you print an exterior elevation view, the building "scale" shouldn't be much less than ⅛″ to the foot. (The word "scale" is used loosely here; photodrawings aren't usually made to any precise scale.)

At an approximate ⅛″ scale, a 16′-wide wall would measure about 2″. A floor-to-ceiling height of 8′ would be 1″ high.

NOTE: *Take advantage of cheap photocopies when playing around with a layout. Office-copier reproductions won't be first-class, but they'll do for planning and guidance purposes. Use an enlarging and reducing copier such as Xerox 1860 or 840. If you don't have immediate access to such a copier, a quick-print or other nearby repro shop can probably provide inexpensive copies at various sizes.*

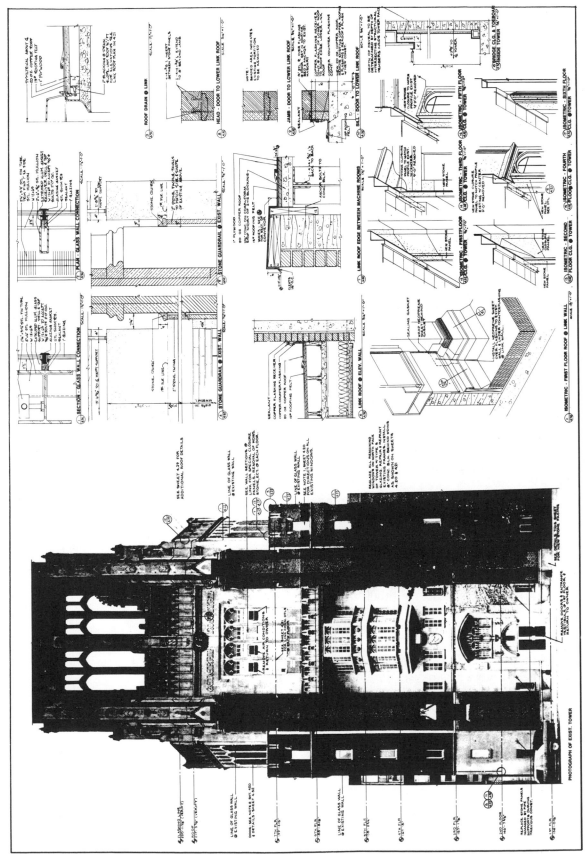

Fig. 11-3. Photodrafting. Restoration and repair drawings are shown in direct relationship to actual existing conditions. (Hansen Lind Meyer.)

145

11.6 DEALING WITH PHOTOREPRODUCTION SHOPS

Here are some important pointers for dealing with the photorepro people:

1. Number or otherwise label all photos for identification, but don't write on the back of a photo with hard pencil or ball point pen. A hard writing instrument may read through a photo and ruin it. If instructions or identification are written on the back of a photo, they should be in felt tip or soft pencil.

2. Use a formal system providing explicit instructions for enlargements, cropping, touchups, etc. Detailed, full-size layouts of your photodrawing are ideal. With or without a comprehensive layout, it's good to work with a checklist to ensure that all points in your instructions are covered. Some shops provide a checklist with their repro order form.

   If you don't provide a complete layout, a good alternate is to send a *double* set of photos. Specific instructions are written on one set of photos. The other set is clean and ready to be photographed according to instructions.

3. When practical, ask for proofs of the final photodrawings before they're reproduced on drafting media. A "proof" is an inexpensive print made by contact from the graphic photographer's negative or from a paste-up. It's just for checking purposes and doesn't need to be full size. Examine the proof for errors and oversights. *Especially watch for photographs that have been reversed and/or mismatched with their titles.*

4. Along with your instructions, include the note that photos, negatives, and other material that you provide are to be returned to you.

5. If final working drawings will be blueprinted for any reason, be sure the photos are printed as *negatives* on the reproducible. The reason is that blueprints are themselves negatives. A *positive* print on a reproducible would come out *negative* in a final blueprint.

6. Should your photoimages be printed on the front or back of reproducible drafting media? If you'll be drawing atop the photos without major erasures or eradications, it's advisable to have the images on the back side of the sheet. This is called "reverse read." If you're making major eradications on the photoimages, it may be more convenient to have them printed on the front or top side of the medium. That's called "right read." In general, reverse read is more desirable. One reason is that photoimages on the back of a sheet will make direct surface contact with diazoprint paper and will print somewhat more sharply.

7. Polyester film is your best bet for intermediate reproducible drafting media. You *can* use paper sepia transparencies, and erasable sepias are especially convenient. But the polyester is best. Polyester is the strong plastic film most people call by its DuPont trade name of Mylar. There are different brands, and therefore different names, for light-sensitive polyester with matte surface that can be made into a photodrawing. It's generally best to specify that the film be "moist-erasable" for greatest ease in making changes in the photoimages.

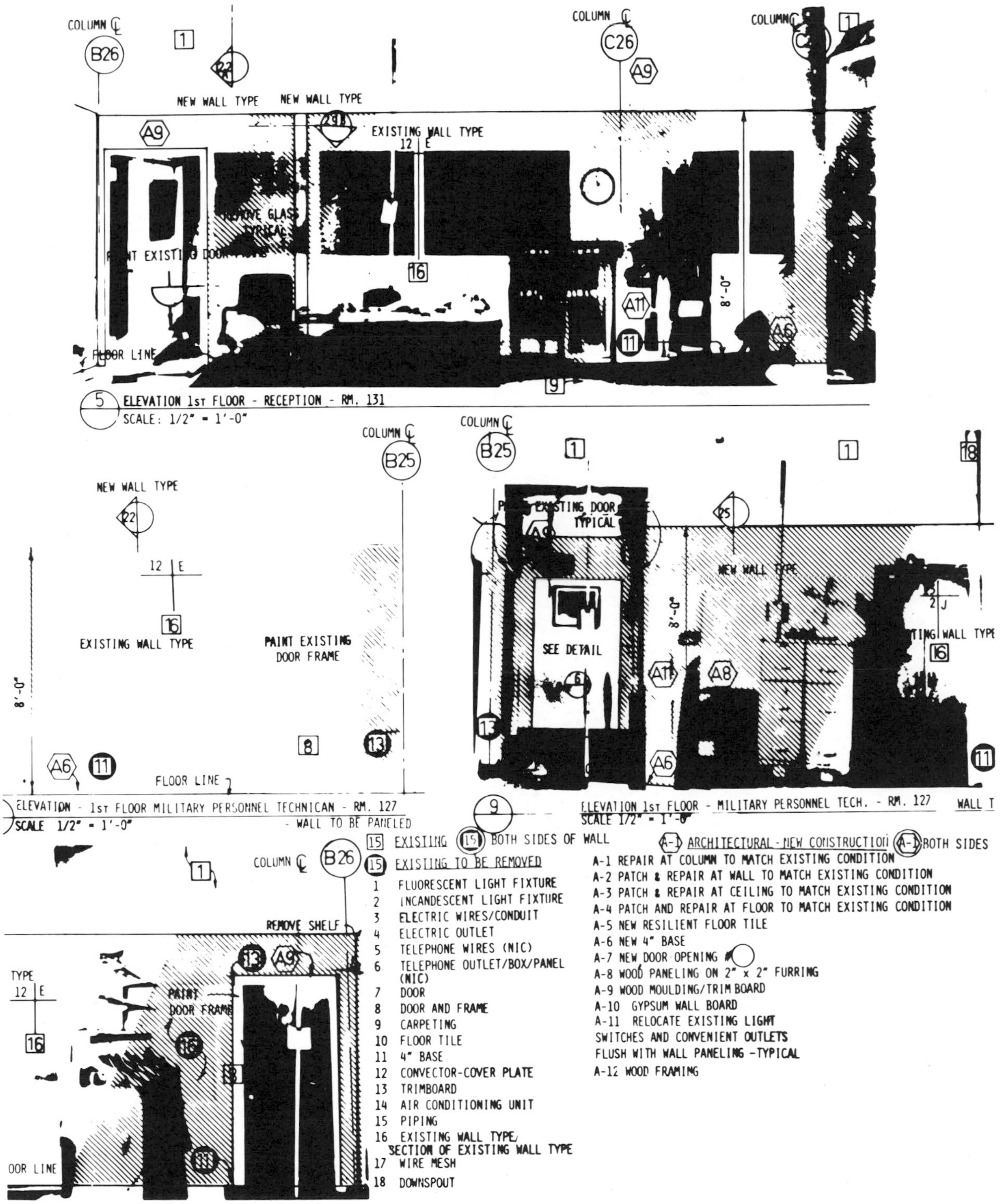
COLUMN ℄
B26
NEW WALL TYPE
NEW WALL TYPE
EXISTING WALL TYPE
COLUMN ℄
C26
A9
FLOOR LINE
ELEVATION 1st FLOOR - RECEPTION - RM. 131
SCALE: 1/2" = 1'-0"
COLUMN ℄
B25
NEW WALL TYPE
EXISTING WALL TYPE
PAINT EXISTING DOOR FRAME
FLOOR LINE
ELEVATION - 1st FLOOR MILITARY PERSONNEL TECHNICAN - RM. 127
SCALE 1/2" = 1'-0"
- WALL TO BE PANELED
EXISTING DOOR TYPICAL
SEE DETAIL
ELEVATION 1st FLOOR - MILITARY PERSONNEL TECH. - RM. 127
SCALE 1/2" = 1'-0"
REMOVE SHELF
PAINT DOOR FRAME
15 EXISTING 15 BOTH SIDES OF WALL
15 EXISTING TO BE REMOVED
1 FLUORESCENT LIGHT FIXTURE
2 INCANDESCENT LIGHT FIXTURE
3 ELECTRIC WIRES/CONDUIT
4 ELECTRIC OUTLET
5 TELEPHONE WIRES (NIC)
6 TELEPHONE OUTLET/BOX/PANEL (NIC)
7 DOOR
8 DOOR AND FRAME
9 CARPETING
10 FLOOR TILE
11 4" BASE
12 CONVECTOR-COVER PLATE
13 TRIMBOARD
14 AIR CONDITIONING UNIT
15 PIPING
16 EXISTING WALL TYPE/ SECTION OF EXISTING WALL TYPE
17 WIRE MESH
18 DOWNSPOUT
A-1 ARCHITECTURAL - NEW CONSTRUCTION A-1 BOTH SIDES
A-1 REPAIR AT COLUMN TO MATCH EXISTING CONDITION
A-2 PATCH & REPAIR AT WALL TO MATCH EXISTING CONDITION
A-3 PATCH & REPAIR AT CEILING TO MATCH EXISTING CONDITION
A-4 PATCH AND REPAIR AT FLOOR TO MATCH EXISTING CONDITION
A-5 NEW RESILIENT FLOOR TILE
A-6 NEW 4" BASE
A-7 NEW DOOR OPENING
A-8 WOOD PANELING ON 2" x 2" FURRING
A-9 WOOD MOULDING/TRIM BOARD
A-10 GYPSUM WALL BOARD
A-11 RELOCATE EXISTING LIGHT SWITCHES AND CONVENIENT OUTLETS FLUSH WITH WALL PANELING -TYPICAL
A-12 WOOD FRAMING

Fig. 11-4. A combination of photodrafting, applique drafting, typewritten notation, and keynoting. (Mini-Max.)

CONSTRUCTION CHARACTERISTICS

Construction: A specular alzak ellipsoidal reflector from 16 gauge aluminum is combined with a minimum round aperture one-piece baffle/trim and encapsulated and potted (brick style) "B" ballast integrally mounted to a combination sound deadening — heat sink 20 gauge reinforced steel pan. (Pan is first phosphatized then finished with baked acrylic enamel for lasting protection). The ballast is easily removed by simply loosening wing nuts on its special unitized mounting plate and sliding through luminaire opening.

Electrical: As standard, socket is mogul base in 100W, 175W, and 250W, mercury vapor and 175W metal halide units. Available with 120 volt or 277 volt encapsulated and potted (brick style) ballast as standard (mercury vapor constant wattage autotransformer high power factor type or metal halide lead-peaked autotransformer high power type). Other voltages available as options. All units suitable for use with 75°C rated supply wire (Lamps by others.)

Automatic auxiliary incandescent lighting: Incandescent lighting during start up period of the H.I.D. mercury vapor or metal halide lamps is available as an option. For further information, contact your Perfeclite representative.

U.L. listed and labeled for wet locations.

Minimum elliptical alzak baffle (MQMEA): This specular alzak baffle increases the low brightness spread of light.

CONSTRUCTION: Rigid and uniform die-formed housing with sufficient knockouts provided for convenient mounting. Housing forms continuous wireway. Reflector covers on 6' and 8' units fabricated in two sections for maximum ease of installation and maintenance and are attached by means of a spring catch which provides a positive locking device. Socket mounting plates designed for snap-in installation in die-cut slots in housing. Combination end plate couplers lock channels together to form a continuous wireway.

FINISH: All metal parts treated with a protective phosphate bonderizing coating applied in a 5-stage process prior to baked white enamel with minimum 89% reflectivity.

ELECTRICAL: Ballasts Class P, CBM/ETL, U.L. approved. Sockets, pedestal type, rotating lock bi-pin or spring loaded single pin.

TYPE "F"	KEYSTONE #C240-277 2 - F40 CWRS LAMPS
TYPE "F1"	KEYSTONE #C230-277 2 - F30 CWRS LAMPS
TYPE "F2"	KEYSTONE #C230-6-277 2 - F30 CWRS LAMPS
TYPE "F4"	KEYSTONE #C240-277-4WGA 2 - F40 CWRS LAMPS

TYPE "G"	PERFECLITE #MQMEA9 - M-100/277/TW 1 - 100 WATT MERCURY VAPOR LAMP
TYPE "G1"	PERFECLITE #MQMEA9-M-100/277/TW-QEL 1 - 100 WATT MERCURY VAPOR LAMP 1 - 150 WATT QUARTZ LAMP
TYPE "G2"	PERFECLITE #MQMEA9-M-100/277/TW/WHITE 30° SLOPE ADAPTOR 1 - 100 WATT MERCURY VAPOR LAMP
TYPE "G3"	PERFECLITE #MQMEA9-M-100/277/TW-QEL/WHITE 30° SLOPE ADAPTOR 1 - 100 WATT MERCURY VAPOR LAMP 1 - 150 WATT QUARTZ LAMP

10.4-7 FIXTURE F DETAIL
NO SCALE

10.4-8 FIXTURE G DETAIL
NO SCALE

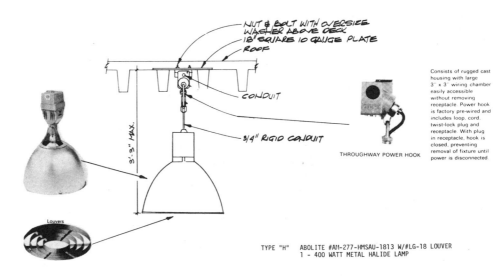

NUT & BOLT WITH OVERSIZE WASHER ABOVE DECK

18' SQUARE 10 GAUGE PLATE

ROOF

CONDUIT

3/4" RIGID CONDUIT

3'-3" MAX.

Louvers

Consists of rugged cast housing with large 3" x 3" wiring chamber easily accessible without removing receptacle. Power hook is factory pre-wired and includes loop, cord, twist-lock plug and receptacle. With plug in receptacle, hook is closed, preventing removal of fixture until power is disconnected.

THROUGHWAY POWER HOOK

TYPE "H"   ABOLITE #AM-277-HMSAU-1813 W/#LG-18 LOUVER
1 - 400 WATT METAL HALIDE LAMP

10.4-12 FIXTURE H DETAIL
NO SCALE

Fig. 11-5. Photodrafting used to show exact fixtures specified.

(Jarvis Putty Jarvis.)

11.7 IN-HOUSE PHOTODRAFTING

For greatest flexibility in preparing photodrawings you can create an in-house system. This will permit you to add or subtract photos in the course of a project, and make the changes you need as you need them. This is a great value during renovation projects where job conditions and design decisions are subject to change.

There are two options: positive transparency paste-ups and office-copier photodrawings. Positive transparencies are like regular photo prints except that instead of being processed on opaque photo paper they're processed on transparent film. Some offices tape up transparencies on the back side of a carrying sheet and add new drawing and notation on the front side. If final job prints will be diazo-printed rather than offset-printed, you won't need to use halftone screen.

The office-copier option is becoming increasingly popular as plain paper copiers become more versatile. You can photocopy directly onto thin, matte polyester stickybacks and apply the stickybacks to paper or polyester drafting media. Saga, Stanpat, Xerox, Kroy, and other companies make stickybacks for office copiers.

Some plain paper copiers will copy adequately clearly on plain, clear polyester film, on 1000H tracing paper, or on polyester with a drafting tooth on it. This allows you to create your own positive transparencies directly from regular photo prints. They're convenient because you can tape them down, lift them up, and move them around with minimal fuss. The stickybacks are sometimes a problem in that regard.

The copier photos on stickyback or nonstickyback film won't be first rate. With some copiers they're completely unsatisfactory. But with many copiers you'll get *adequate* quality to convey the information.

If you create a carrying sheet with taped-on transparencies of your photos, you can make a reproducible or job prints in-house on your regular diazo machine. Just be careful to tape only the top corners of the transparencies relative to the direction in which the carrying sheet will go through the print machine. And, of course, use clear tape. You may have to experiment with this to learn how to eliminate printing the tape along with the photos.

11.8 SYNTHESIS

Photodrafting is a combination of two kinds of economy and clarification in working drawings. First, it's an example of the reuse of existing data. Second, it's the introduction of specialized, nondrafting equipment and processes—"new tools"—to expedite something that used to be done laboriously by hand.

Photodrafting can be introduced almost any time, but choices in photodrafting systems must be consistent with other choices. For example, using office-copier photos will have a bearing on your choice of copiers. That in turn will influence your choice of transfer method and media: copying on stickybacks, copying on tracing paper for paste-ups, or copying on clear film for tape-on translucent composites. Those choices will affect and be affected by other decisions: whether you'll use typewritten notes, keynoting, photos in standard details, and so on.

Photodrafting is at the center of all the techniques and systems that comprise Systems Drafting. If yours is the kind of design practice that will benefit greatly from photodrafting, then give very serious consideration to designing your systems around the photodrafting technique you finally choose.

COMPOSITE DRAFTING

12.1 INTRODUCTION

I first saw "composite drafting" done on a large scale in 1960, when I was working for a New York housing specialist. We were rushing out a public housing project, working two shifts. There was overtime galore, and it was a big crisis.

The job captain made a tough decision. Instead of having us redraw items from previous jobs, he had us cut them out and paste them up on carrier sheets. Instead of drawing and redrawing an apartment unit all over a floor plan page, we drew one, made diazo black-line copies, and pasted them up. Instead of redrawing senior draftspeople's yellow, flimsy, sketch paper drawings on 1000H, we just taped them down as they were.

We assembled door schedules by paste-ups. We copped details right off old reference prints—cut them out instead of tracing them. We even pulled prints of stairs, public rest rooms, laundries, elevators, and parking off old prints and stuck them down on the new job. It was amazing. The job was done on time, it was as good as any other job, and the office came out ahead despite the overtime crisis.

The paste-ups were all photocopied onto translucent intermediate print media, from which final bids sets were printed. When the sets went out to bid, the job captain echoed what almost everyone seemed to feel: "I hope we never have to do that again." And as far as I know, they never did.

12.2 ASSEMBLY RATHER THAN DRAWING

With composite drafting, you actually *assemble*, rather than *draw*, a large final working drawing sheet. This is how newspaper and magazine graphic departments, ad agencies, and book publishers do it. They gather a mixture of components—original drawings, photos, appliques, typeset copy, and so on—and paste them up for photoreproduction.

Visiting a graphics studio is always a revelation for an architect or engineer. At the studio they do essentially the same thing designers and draftspersons do, but with a far greater variety of resources, tools, and techniques. It becomes painfully clear how limiting it is to make drawings on translucent tracing paper.

Terminology can get confusing. A final "drawing" may have no original drawing on it at all. It may be a composite of photocopies, diazo prints, and typing. We'll call the final combination of composited elements plus their carrying sheet a "work sheet composite." If the work sheet composite has been printed on a reproducible medium such as a photo washoff or a diazo sepia, we'll call it a composite reproducible. (A "reproducible" is a translucent print that can be run through a diazo machine to generate new prints as if it were an original tracing. That's why reproducible prints are often called "second originals.")

It's easier to grasp composite drafting if you think of it as "horizontal separation and assembly." Visualize creating your final composite from various sheets from various sources and pulling them together *horizontally* on the drafting board. "Overlay drafting," as we'll see, mainly deals with "vertical separation and assembly." With overlay drafting, you separate the information on base sheets and overlay sheets, in layers, *vertically*. We'll see the advantages of doing that later on.

As I said in Chapter 1, the essence of Systems Drafting is *reuse of existing elements*. No matter how unique the building design is or how original the detailing, no one invents a whole new system of titles, notes, schedules, and so on, or whole new construction systems for every new project. And within the job's drawings, there are repeats from discipline to discipline, from drawing sheet to drawing sheet, and within individual drawing sheets.

With composite drafting, repeat information is saved and reused in what proves to be a very convenient way. That is its primary value. And, be assured, there are *plenty* of repeat components in *any* job.

Some repeat components don't *look* like repeat components. That's because they appear in different forms and sizes. A common example is the ⅛" and ¼" floor plans that might appear in the same set of drawings. The floor plans are the same, but they are different in size. Some repeat components have one kind of information on one sheet, another kind on another. The larger-scale floor plans, for example, are likely to have more notation and symbols.

The structural drawings may have a structural concrete detail showing the reinforcing. The same detail appears in architectural drawings but only shows the dimensions of the exterior configuration. It's still a repeat of the same basic drawing. Some repeat components are basically the same but different in location. Or they may be inverted, flip-flopped, or emphasized in one drawing and lightly shown as background in another.

Not only is reuse of existing information the main value to be gained from composite drafting, it's also the main value common to overlay drafting, applique drafting, and photodrafting. All the systems are actually variations of the composite idea.

While reuse is a primary value, using the composite system provides secondary values as well. Composite drafting's main secondary value, in terms of time and cost savings, is that changes are much easier to handle. Instead of erasing a detail from a drawing, you physically pick it up and move it. To modify a portion of a plan, cut the portion out and place a modified piece in. Doing it this way is cleaner and much faster than erasing and redrawing. Composite drafting provides an additional secondary value in that several people can simultaneously put together one "drawing."

We'll get into specific techniques and uses of composite drafting shortly. First an important distinction must be made between "opaque original composite" and "translucent original composite."

An "opaque original composite" can be made up from just about anything: diazo prints, office-copier prints, cutouts from catalogs, etc. Changes can be handled by adhering a new portion right over the old. Opaque original composites are recreated as translucent intermediate prints later on by photographic (rather than diazo) methods. That is, they're reproduced with the process or blowback camera onto photographically sensitive drafting material rather than the diazo intermediate material.

Basically, graphics artists who do magazine and newspaper layouts use opaque paste-up. The paste-ups are assembled on thin cardboard, with no intent of ever making a diazo print. Remember, diazo printing is the basic print system of the architectural and engineering professions. It depends on shining light through a translucent or transparent original sheet and transferring the drawing image from the original onto the light-sensitive, ammonia-developed, diazo paper or plastic film.

With ready access to a blowback camera, the opaque paste-up approach may be most convenient. Without such access, you might decide to assemble your composite originals from translucent or transparent components. That way you can recreate the composite sheets as reproducibles by means of diazo printing or vacuum frame contact printing.

Since translucent paste-up is a nonphoto technique, its main advantage lies in liberation from the repro shop for that kind of reproduction, and much lower repro cost.

12.3 BASIC COMPOSITE TECHNIQUE NUMBER 1: OPAQUE PASTE-UP FROM OLD PRINTS

Imagine you have a large project that incorporates door details and a door schedule, a project similar to a job you've recently completed. Following is the classic procedure for reusing the existing details.

1. Make good, high-contrast, diazo black-line prints of the original tracings.
2. Lay down a blank sheet of exposed print paper (or other suitable carrier sheet) and sketch out, with no-print blue pencil, some alignment and location lines.
3. Cut out the reusable original black-line print elements and tape or rubber-cement them down onto the carrying sheet. (In this case you could use rubber cement, repositionable spray adhesive, double-sided tape, or mending tape.)
4. Add title block, borders, and newly drawn additions.
5. Send the composited sheet to the photorepro shop. They'll make a negative, either full size (the expensive way) or 8½″ × 11″ (the less expensive way). Then they'll make a copy on drafting medium from the negative.
6. Treat the reproducible on drafting medium as an original tracing; add to it or subtract from it, as with any other tracing.

It's that simple. I chose that example because it's simple and clearly illustrates the essentials of the composite technique.

12.4 BASIC COMPOSITE TECHNIQUE NUMBER 2: REPROGRAPHIC PASTE-UP—DESIGN DRAWING TO WORKING DRAWING

The second technique is a little more complex. It illustrates one aspect of the design production technique that Ned Abrams has taught hundreds of architects in his California office. The example was created by a participating architect during one of Ned's training sessions. Here's what happened, as originally reported in the February 1977 issue of *The Guidelines Letter*:

1. The architect sketched a final design for a typical hospital patient room at ⅛″ scale. The sketch was enlarged with an A.B. Dick Design Master (Model 150 Platemaker) to double size, ¼″ scale. The enlargement served as underlay for a finish-drawn plan of the typical unit.
2. The finish unit plan was "drawn" with black tape. (Tape drawing goes very fast, even faster when more than one person gets into the act. But taping and cutting techniques require a little practice before going full steam.) Walls were done with tape; door swings and other single-line details were drawn with ink.
3. The ¼″-scale finish unit plan was photoreduced back to ⅛″ scale. The reduced-size plan was then copied in quantity.
4. Multiple prints of the room were cut out and assembled on a work sheet as an overall paste-up of the complete building. Special rooms, stairs, etc., were added—some as tape drawing, some as paste-up. Stairs were cut out of prints from another building. Lettering and titles were done as printout on transparent tape with a Kroy Company lettering machine.
5. The completed ⅛″-scale building plan was photoreduced to ⅟₂₀″ scale to match the site-survey scale. Plan and site survey would later be photographically combined as a finish site plan. A same-size reproduction of the ⅛″ building plan was made for finish-up as a presentation drawing.

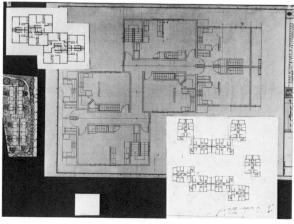

(a)

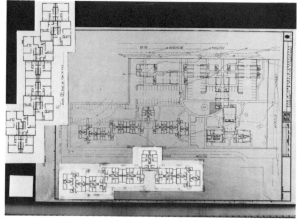

(b)

Fig. 12-1. (*a*) An example of photoreduction and multiple copy to create composite drawing floor plans. ¼"-scale plans of apartment units are drawn (gray center portion). These are reduced and combined with flip-flop plans of the same unit (upper left). Units are photoreduced further, copied in multiples, and combined into building floor plans (lower right). These in turn are pasted up as site plans (far left). (*b*) The plans in further combination and different scales.

(Courtesy of Ned Abrams, Design Production Techniques, Inc.)

That was the transition from sketch to finish unit, building, and site plans. The repros—enlarged, reduced, and in quantities—eliminate most of the hand drawing. Tape and applique lettering all fit together and augment the time savings. The process, using the same basic drawings, would continue into working drawing production. Revisions of the presentation drawings are easy to make. It's just a matter of paste-up and further photocopying.

12.5 BASIC COMPOSITE TECHNIQUE NUMBER 3: MAKING FURTHER USE OF PHOTOREDUCTION IN MULTIUNIT BUILDINGS SUCH AS HOSPITALS, HOTELS, MOTELS, AND HOUSING

The reprographic paste-up technique just cited requires the use of a copier that can reproduce drawings at reduced or enlarged size. In Ned Abrams' case, the reduction and enlargement capacity is provided by an in-house, A.B. Dick Design Master. It could also be photographically done by most any photoreproduction shop.

The previous example illustrates two dominant time and money savings. First, repeat apartment units don't have to be redrawn over and over, as they would be in most offices. You draw them once and then photocopy them in multiples for assembly into buildings. The second savings comes when the design starter drawings (in this case, larger-scale ones) are directly transposed into smaller-scale drawings.

This basic composite technique is a four-part process:

1. Start with large-scale plans (¼" scale) of the units (apartments in this example).
2. Make reverse ("flip-flop") reproductions of reverse-plan apartment units.
3. Make half-size copies of the units. That means the scale will go from ¼" to the foot to ⅛" to the foot. Cut out and assemble the ⅛"-scale units into the overall building plans.
4. Follow through and carry the process further after assembling the building plans at ⅛" scale. That is, make half-size copies of the plans to assemble on a ¹⁄₁₆"-scale site plan.

Here's a further, 12-step breakdown of the process, using a one-to-one size photocopier to make the basic photocopies and a reduction copier. Assume a modest-sized housing development, one- and two-story, multiunit dwelling units, with reverses of the basic plans. The detailed floor plans for each unit will be at ¼" scale. Construction plans for each building will be at

⅛″ scale, as will structural and mechanical plans. The site plan, as noted above, will be at ¹⁄₁₆″ scale. Here are the 12 steps:

1. Draw the standard unit plans at ¼″ scale on small sheets of tracing paper. Show doors, windows, stairs, and fixtures. Don't include room names, notes, or dimensions yet. Use tape or ink for maximum darkness of wall poche. Make line work dark and crisp for good photoreproduction.

2. Next make a large number of reduced-size (⅛″ scale) copies of the unit plans to assemble into building plans.

3. Cut out the ⅛″-scale copies of the dwelling units, and assemble them into overall building plans. Use clear tape or spray-on, remountable glue to secure the unit plans to the work sheet.

4. When the building configurations are completed, and before adding dimensioning and detailed notation, make 50% reductions of the ⅛″ ground floor plans to make ¹⁄₁₆″-scale plans. These ¹⁄₁₆″ building plans will be assembled on the site-plan work sheet.

5. Cut out, position, and adhere the ¹⁄₁₆″-scale ground floor plans onto the site plan.

6. Return to the ⅛″ floor plans. Add dimensions, titles, and notation necessary to bring the plans to the degree of completion required for structural drawings.

7. Have the photorepro shop make screened (50%, 133-line) reproducibles of the ⅛″-scale plans to be used for structural drawings. Have them made either on erasable drafting media or on washoff polyester—emulsion on back, matte surface on the front.

8. Do structural drawings on the screened reproducibles. Later you'll do the foundation plan on the image of a ground floor plan. You'll also draw roof framing on a screened second floor plan. You may also make an extra shadow print of each second floor for the base drawings for the architectural roof plans.

NOTE: *This aspect of the composite system is practical only if there will be virtually no changes in the plans. If there are changes, you'll be required to change the background reproducibles and redraw plan elements in dot pattern to match the screening. If changes are anticipated, use the overlay drafting system described in the next chapter.*

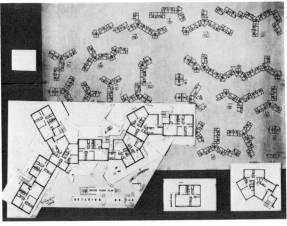

(a)

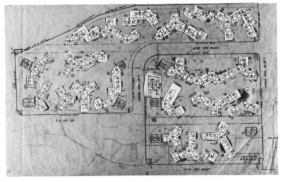

(b)

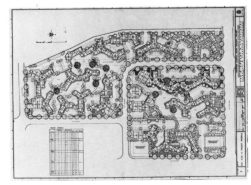

(c)

Fig. 12-2. (*a*) Basic apartment units (lower right) are "drawn" with graphic tape and ink, copied, and taped together as a building plan (left). (*b*) The building plans are photoreduced and (*c*) copied to create the site-plan paste-up.

(Courtesy of Ned Abrams, Design Production Techniques, Inc.)

9. Make additional shadow print reproducibles if separate plumbing, heating, air conditioning, and/or electrical plans will be drawn.

10. Complete all architectural construction data on the ⅛″-scale plan work sheets.

11. Add room titles to the ¼″-scale floor plans. Make prints for the client's marketing brochures and for the interior consultant. If interior designers want to work with ½″-scale plans, have the photorepro shop make blow-ups.

12. Finish up the architectural data on the ¼″-scale unit plans. Assemble the plans on a work sheet, add titles for each plan, and put them aside until it's time to make the final reproducibles.

12.6 BASIC COMPOSITE TECHNIQUE NUMBER 4: REPROGRAPHIC BACKGROUND DRAWING FOR MULTISTORY BUILDINGS

The following steps are based on a technique introduced at Gruzen & Partners in New York. The example is based on a moderate-height (12-story) administration building. I *don't* recommend adopting this procedure until you've reviewed the values of overlay drafting. I recommend it for only the simplest types of projects, where the engineering work is mainly done in-house and where no major plan revisions are likely to occur along the way. Here are the steps:

1. Finalize the structural grid with the engineer, and draw it in ink on a polyester drafting medium. Include letter and number coordinates, north arrow, and other data that will appear on all architectural and consultants' floor plans. Include sheet border and title block.

2. Determine how many architectural floor plan sheets will be included in the set. In this example there'll be a basement level, ground floor, mezzanine balcony level, typical floor, and the penthouse. That's five reproducibles you'll need for the architectural plans. The structural engineer will also need reproducibles to rough out framing plans.

3. Make architectural and structural reproducibles of the structural grid sheet. They can be made by vacuum-frame contact printing, since there's no change in size. Prints can be on washoff polyester (emulsion on back, matte surface on front) or on diazo media.

4. Lay out the basement and ground floor plans on the reproducible structural grid sheets. Show exterior walls and openings, interior walls, chases, elevator shafts, stairs, toilet rooms, fire hose cabinets, and drinking fountains.

5. In this example the mezzanine and typical office floor plans have exterior wall configurations that differ from the ground floor plan. Draw the new configurations. Continue the stairs, shafts, and so on, as on the lower-

level plans. Draw walls and partitions that delineate corridors and other major spatial divisions.

6. Start the penthouse plan. At this point don't include interior dimensions, architectural notation, room titles, symbols, detail keys, etc., on any plans. Develop the plans only to the point where they'll be usable as base working drawing sheets by the structural, electrical, and mechanical consultants.

7. Make a reproducible of the basement plan. Pass this reproducible on to the structural engineer, to develop the foundation plan.

8. Bring other floor plans up to the point that shows fire hose cabinets, electrical panels, transformer rooms, door swings, and plumbing fixtures.

9. Make polyester reproducibles of the ground floor plan, mezzanine, and penthouse. Make them screened shadow prints (50% screen, 133-line, emulsion on back side, matte on front surface). Make four copies of each plan, and send them to the consultants to develop their heating, air conditioning, plumbing, electrical supply, and lighting plans.

10. Complete the typical office floor plan as in Step 8, and add exterior dimensions. Don't include interior dimensions, room titles, symbols, etc. Include *only* those items that are typical and repeated from floor to floor.

11. Make a screened reproducible of the typical floor, and send it to the mechanical consultant to develop the typical floor riser diagram. At the same time make solid-line reproducibles of the typical floor. These will be base sheets for nontypical levels. In this example, only four floor plans differ from the typical, so a total of five reproducibles are made.

12. Finish the partitions and doors that are unique to the nontypical levels. Make screened prints of the nontypical levels, then send them to the consultants. Make solid-line repros as needed for the telephone company, interior designers, tenants, etc.

13. Finish all architectural floor plans with interior dimensions, room names and numbers, symbols, detail keys, special notation, etc.

12.7 ELABORATIONS ON COMPOSITE DRAFTING IN ARCHITECTURAL DRAWING

SITE PLANS

The traditional method of preparing a site plan sheet has always been tedious and clumsy. The first step usually involves redrawing the original survey. You'll often see someone tape an old, beat-up surveyor's print to a window, tape a tracing over that, and then painstakingly copy off the boundary lines and contours.

Sometimes a site survey is copied several times by hand. For example, a site plan may be drawn for the preliminary design drawings and redrawn again for working drawings. Then it may be redrawn on other sheets for a landscaping plan, a drainage plan, special site-work plans, and various engineers' site plans.

Reprographic systems make it possible to avoid tracing or redrawing the survey. With photoreproduction the surveyor's drawing can be changed to any scale. You can eliminate extraneous data, marks, wrinkles, sloppy drafting, etc., and end up with a good, basic, architectural work sheet. Here's what to do:

1. Start with an uncreased print of the survey. Better yet, if possible, get a washoff or erasable reproducible from the client or surveyor. A good print in the right scale can be used "as is" for the site-plan work sheet. Unwanted data on the print can be taken out on the board or removed during the photorepro process. If all you've got is a tattered and wrinkled survey print, the photorepro shop can probably salvage it by masking and retouching it. This is called "drawing restoration." Most repro shops are experienced in such work.

2. To change the scale of the original survey, have a blowback photoreproduction made to the desired size on washoff polyester. Unwanted data and marks can be masked out during this process, according to your instructions. One way or another, the result should be a cleaned up survey ready to develop into the architectural site plan.

3. Next tape cutout copies of the ground floor plans in position on the site-plan work sheet. **157**

SYSTEMS DRAFTING

It's often desirable to use the ground floor plans of the building on the site plan rather than to show a roof plan or a blocked-in building outline. It makes it *much* easier for the architect and consultants to lay out walkways, landscaping, electrical work, plumbing, drainage, etc.

4. After the floor plans are completed on the work sheet, draw in new contours, roads, utilities, dimensions, etc. At the proper, predetermined stop point, make new reproducibles of the site plan to send to the landscape consultant and, as needed, to civil, electrical, and mechanical engineers. If the plans have a lot of architectural data on them, it may aid clarity to have consultants' drawings done on screened prints. In that case, order 50%, 133-line, screened reproducibles—emulsion on the back side, matte surface on the front.

If your work sheet is a reproducible, there are ways to avoid having a final reproducible made by the photorepro shop. This can save some money. The trick is to print on clear film any floor plans or other items that will be adhered to the work sheet. The final work sheet becomes a transparency paste-up. This means final reproducibles can be made from the work sheet on the diazo machine (with care) or by vacuum-frame contact print.

Photoreproducing the final reproducibles can save even more time. Then you can really cut loose and use every kind of applique on the work sheet. Since the sheet is opaque and you're not limited by the transparency requirements of diazo printing, you can use tapes, press-on letters and symbols, paste-ups of typewritten notes, cutouts from other prints, and so on. Large-area revisions can be made without erasing; glue paper or self-adhesive label paper over the revision area, and redraw over that.

Photographs taken during site visits can be added. Tape the photos (with clear mending tape) next to the site plan, and include a keying system with arrows. This shows major site features as they really are—a big help in many cases.

To make a vicinity map, cut one out of a road map or a United States geodetic survey map. Mask out unwanted data, mark the site location, and add title, notes, and north arrow. Adhere to the site-plan work sheet.

12.8 REFLECTED CEILING PLANS

This procedure has multiple uses. Apply it to paving patterns, computer floor grids, and construction module grids as well as ceiling patterns. Structural engineers can use it for reflected plans of any kind of repetitive framing. The idea is always the same: draw a little, print a lot, then cut and paste. Here are the steps:

1. Develop the floor plan to the stop point, where there's enough—but not too much—data for the reflected ceiling plan.
2. Run a plain diazo print or a reproducible of each floor plan. These will be worksheets for assembling the ceiling plan.
3. Prepare ceiling grid material. If possible, use ready-made, printed, black-line grid paper (or polyester) from a drafting supply outlet. Or draw a portion of the grid with ink on 8½″ × 11″ tracing paper. Run off a stack of copies adequate to cover the floor plan. (A fast, low-cost option is to have a quick-print shop make offset copies of the grid sheet.)
4. Take floor plan worksheets and grid sheets to a light table. Lay out the printed grid sheets over the floor plans. Cut the grids to fit various rooms. Adhere them to the plans.
5. Add miscellaneous ceiling plan data and notes onto the worksheet.
6. Have two solid-line, washoff reproducibles (reverse-read) made of each plan. File one set of the ceiling plan reproducibles for later finish-up as architectural sheets, and send the duplicates to your electrical consultant.

You can avoid the expense of photorepro on the final reproducibles by making an entirely translucent paste-up worksheet. Have the floor plan work sheets printed on polyester. Print the ceiling grid pattern on clear polyester. Tape the transparent grid material onto the worksheet and have the final reproducibles made by diazo (with care, tape grids at top edge only) or by vacuum-frame contact printing.

12.9 EXTERIOR ELEVATIONS

Some kinds of exterior elevations are a natural for composite drafting, and some clearly are not. High-rises are very good, of course. So are blocks of repeat-facade townhouses or long buildings with repetitive bays and/or fenestration. Here is the process, step by step:

1. If the building is mainly horizontal, draw one typical bay or facade unit. If the building is tall, decide whether to draw a typical vertical band of fenestration or a typical floor-to-floor horizontal band. (Read the section on building cross sections. You may be able to use the same unit drawing for exterior elevations and cross sections, and that will affect your choice of starting unit.)
2. Run exact-size copies (background-free diazos or office-copier reproductions) of facade units. Cut them out right at their border lines and/or match the lines.
3. Lightly draw the ground, floor, roof, and vertical boundary lines of the building on a worksheet.
4. Assemble and adhere the cutout units onto the worksheet. Add touch-up drawing, special elements, notes, and dimensions. If your worksheet is for a design drawing, hold off on the notes and dimensions until later.
5. Send the completed worksheet to the photorepro shop to make a washoff reproducible (emulsion on the back, matte on the front, as usual).

A building may not be highly repetitive in terms of bays or curtain wall but still include many repeat individual units, such as windows of a certain size, ornament, railings, etc. In such a case you might adapt the procedure for interior elevations described in the next section.

If one or more exterior views of the building are alike, just do one paste-up of the repeat view and instruct the photorepro shop to make a duplicate image and place it, as directed, on the final reproducible. Do the same with reverse facades (such as townhouse units) or with one-half of a large, symmetrical facade.

12.10 INTERIOR ELEVATIONS

Composite drafting is very useful for interior elevations when you're including large numbers of repeat elements such as doors, cabinets, shelving, chalkboards, etc. But if the interior elevation drawings are fairly "empty," you'll be better off with standard drafting procedures. If you want to go the composite route, here are the steps:

1. Draw a long strip of typical walls. Show floor line, base, wainscot, ceiling line—whatever will be horizontally typical in most of the interior elevation views. Add lightweight height lines for standard openings and wall-mounted equipment.
2. Run clear, shadow-free, diazo copies of the wall strip. Run the strip the long way through the machine to avoid stretching that would distort the heights.
3. Mount the printed wall strips across a worksheet in typical interior elevation format.
4. Scale off the wall lengths for various rooms, and draw left- and right-hand borders for each wall segment on the mounted wall strips.
5. Draw samples of repeated elements on 8½" × 11" tracing paper. Common repeat elements are doors, windows, counters, benches, cabinets, chalkboards, pin boards, drinking fountains, fire hose cabinets, railings, etc.
6. Make copies of the repeat elements on the diazo machine or office copier. Have them cut out and placed in some convenient holder, such as a compartmentalized plastic tray.
7. Scale off and mark the locations of repeat elements on the walls. Adhere the cutouts onto the wall strips.
8. Add room numbers and names, dimensions, notes, special fixtures, and materials indications. Since you're working with an opaque worksheet, you can use any kind of paste-up or applique.
9. Have the photorepro shop make a washoff reproducible of the worksheet (emulsion on the back and matte surface on the front). Moist erase the leftover, extraneous wall strip boundary and height lines on the reproducible.

12.11 BUILDING CROSS SECTIONS

Composite drafting procedures for building cross sections may be identical to those for exterior elevations. For example:

If the building is long and consists of repeat bays, draw just one typical bay. Make copies and assemble on a worksheet.

If the building is multistory, draw a typical floor-to-floor section across the building. Make copies and assemble.

If there are a substantial number of repeat elements, and if they are complex enough that cutting out and adhering copies is faster than repeat drawing, follow the procedure for interior elevations described in the previous section.

If engineering drawings will include building cross sections, provide consultants with reproducibles of your sections before finishing up the strictly architectural data.

One option is to draw cross sections directly over shadow prints of the exterior elevations. Select two exterior elevations, one for the longitudinal section and one for the lateral cross section.

Have the photorepro shop copy the elevations onto washoff polyester drafting medium using 50%, 133-line screen. Send the exterior elevations out for this screened reproduction before showing notes, symbols, and other data that are not relevant to the cross-section drawing.

Reverse-print the exterior views you've selected to use as screened background for section drawings. That is, print them in a flopover view so fenestration and other openings in the exterior wall are seen as they would be from inside the building looking out.

Finally, draw the cross-sectional data (such as left and right exterior wall sections, interior walls, slabs, ceiling, etc.) in solid line on the screened shadow print reproducible.

When considering this option, watch your time and cost comparisons. If the building is simple, plain old hand drafting will most likely be the economical way to go.

12.12 THROUGH-WALL CONSTRUCTION SECTIONS

Working drawings of low-rise buildings often include a series of sections to show exterior wall construction. One drawing shows typical wall construction, from foundation to parapet. Other drawings show variations in the typical section (door and window openings, cantilevered balconies, etc.). Following is the photorepro way to avoid repeat drawing of the typical wall section in a wall-section series:

1. Draw the typical wall section. [Drawing the section at twice its final working drawing size allows fast freehand drafting (described in the section on construction details).]
2. Draw notes, dimensions, and title on a separate strip sheet that can be set beside the typical wall section.
3. Decide how many wall sections are needed to show all variations on wall construction.
4. Instruct the photorepro shop to reproduce the typical section on a washoff reproducible: make one solid-line print on the left of the sheet along with the notes and dimensions strip, then a series of screened shadow print images of the same section without the notes and dimensions. Sketch a mock-up to show the photorepro people the exact positioning of the section on the final reproducible. If the original has been drawn double size, order a 50% reduction in the section images. (Screening should be 50%, 133-line; the reproducible should be washoff polyester—emulsion on the back, matte on the front—or it can be erasable vellum. Screen for final size; don't photoreduce the screened image.)
5. Draw the variations of construction in solid line over the shadow print images. Add titles and special notes and dimensions.

One option is to order a batch of screened copies of the original wall-section drawing. Tape the solid-line original and the screened copies on a worksheet. Draw in the variations, add notes, and so on, and have the completed worksheet photoreproduced on washoff drafting medium.

A graphic arts or offset printing shop may be able to do small screened copies faster than your regular photorepro shop.

12.13 CONSTRUCTION DETAILS

Most offices have used paste-up details at one time or another. The old, standard procedures are pretty self-evident. However, new techniques have evolved in recent years that are not as self-evident.

One such new technique is freehand detailing, which has worked very well for many offices. Senior drafting staff sketch original details on no-print, blue-line grid paper—usually 8½″ × 11″ sheets. They sketch at double size; that is, if the final detail is to be at ½″ scale, they sketch at 1″ scale. The detail sketches are later assembled on a large worksheet, and the sheet is photoreduced to half size—the size of the final working drawing sheet.

Photoreduction smooths out the freehand irregularities. The final printed details look as good as tool-drafted drawings. Of course, the original freehand drawing shouldn't be *too* sketchy (take care in scaling and line quality). But freehand work still goes considerably faster than standard drafting.

The big time and cost savings come from the fact that details are drawn only once, rather than drawn roughly and then redrawn.

When details are reused from old jobs, they are still often traced directly onto the new working drawing sheet. This is clearly wasteful, but if only a couple of items are involved, it's less fussy to do it this way than to bother with elaborate photorepro methods. There are other options, however.

With some stickyback polyester appliques, details can be "lifted" from old prints or tracings. Some applique products are designed to work with the office copier; some are diazo products. Your drafting supply outlet should have both types.

Most office copiers cause some size distortion, but that may be irrelevant, depending on the drawing. And there may be background problems, especially with the diazo polyester applique sheets. But many offices find this manageable.

One way of reducing shadow background caused by the use of appliques is to mount the stickybacks on a clear film worksheet and do an extra-long diazo exposure of the final reproducible to burn out the shadowing.

Another way to deal with background shadowing is to design the detail drawing sheet with wide, black borders between the individual detail sections. The wide borders mask out the edges of the appliques and add overall uniformity, even when backgrounding varies somewhat from detail to detail.

Applique products have been much improved in recent years, and it's worth experimenting to find out the best ways to put them to work.

Use light-sensitive acetate or polyester film as a nonphotographic paste-up medium. Transfer details from old tracings onto small sheets of the clear plastic. Assemble and tape the clear sheets onto a tracing or polyester working drawing worksheet. Since the worksheet is translucent

and the tape-on units are transparent, there's minimal background effect. Make the final composite reproducible either by diazo or by vacuum-frame contact printing.

Manufacturers' catalogs and detail books are often a good source of details. However, most design professionals balk at using photocopies of such details directly on drawings. They prefer to hand-copy or trace them. One reason is that the drawing quality and lettering of the commercially printed copy will not match other parts of the working drawings.

A compromise some offices use is to photostat the ready-made drawings only, without the typeset notes. Notes and dimensions are added by hand or typewriter in a style consistent with the rest of the drawings.

Fig. 12-3. Composite drafting. (a) The carrying sheet with taped-on details is photographed, and (b) the image is blown back onto photowashoff drafting film. (Courtesy of Jack Wally, Opti-Copy, Inc.)

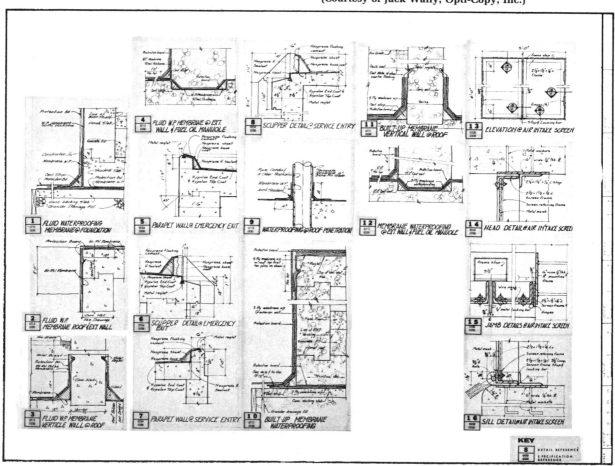

(a)

12.14 SCHEDULES

If you haven't reviewed and standardized your door, window, color, finish, hardware, and other schedules, now's the time. Go over the schedules used on previous jobs. Get hold of the schedule formats used by other offices. Ask people to bring in suggestions for new and better formats. Then design the best standard schedule forms to use on your future jobs.

Design the schedules in modular form. Forms and portions of forms should be narrow enough to fit the office typewriter. Determine what titles and notes apply to all work and which portions of the standard forms should remain blank.

Draw up the schedule forms. Reproduce them on transparent polyester film as permanent reproducible copies. Then, on your next job, follow these steps:

1. Do a mock-up worksheet. Note where drawings, if any, are to be pasted in. Print diazos of the schedule forms and adhere them to the mock-up.

2. Write the new notations on the schedules. These notes will be typewritten later from this copy, so they should be written quickly but legibly.

3. Make copies of the schedules on erasable diazo vellum. Give the vellum blanks and the notated mock-up sheet to the typist to transfer handwritten notes onto the schedules.

4. Decide whether to proceed with a new opaque worksheet to be photoreproduced, or with a transparency worksheet to be contact- or diazo-printed onto the final reproducible.

5. If the worksheet will be translucent, make film diazos of drawings and typewritten forms. Assemble and tape them onto a clear film worksheet. Make the final reproducible on the diazo machine or vacuum-contact print machine.

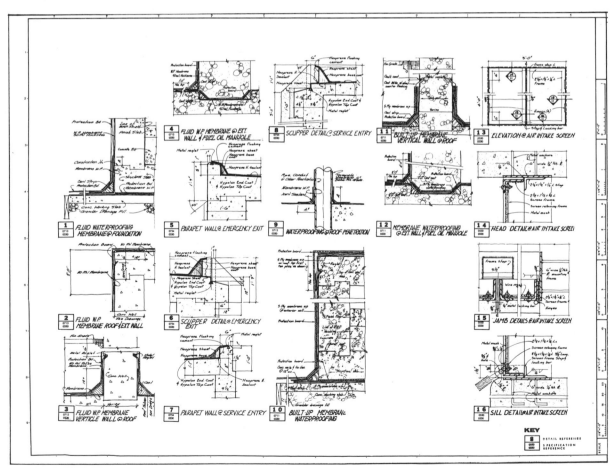

(b)

12.15 MAKING COMPOSITE DRAFTING WORK

Planning your jobs is everything with composite drafting. It requires sketching out the entire working drawing set, knowing what's what, and knowing where everything goes in the drawings. You have to plan the "stop points" at which time a sheet will go to a flatbed or to a repro shop, to make reproducibles for consultants. You have to know what information should be on the sheets at each stop point and what information has to be left off. These things have to be written down, and the staff has to know them. *There can be no secrets.* Everyone has to know the plan and how their work fits in the plan.

Keep the staff to a minimum on any job. Two or three drafting people can do the work of six with this system. If too many people are on the job, "work" will be invented to keep them busy. That means a reversion from composite drafting to traditional methods.

Plan back-up work in advance. Drawings will often be out to the print shop or photorepro shop, sometimes for days. Have plenty of auxiliary work on hand for the down times.

When expecting a large number of changes during the working drawing phase, consider using a combination of composite drafting and overlay drafting. Overlay drafting is especially effective for dealing with the problem of excessive revisions during a job.

When dealing with unfamiliar procedures, play around with them on evenings and weekends. The time pressures of the workday discourage experimentation. If problems arise while you're under pressure, it's too easy to revert to familiar drafting methods.

Drop in on your local photoreproduction shop. Take a look at the process camera, vacuum-frame contact printer, developers, and other equipment that will be doing your work. *Seeing what they do will provide understanding and control over the system that no amount of reading can give.*

Compare prices and turnaround times for various services. If there's more than one photoreproduction facility in your area, you're lucky. Prices will vary widely on the same type of job,

depending on the methods and equipment used by a shop. To reduce turnaround time to a minimum, find out the best times to bring in work.

Visit local offset printing, quick-print, and graphic arts shops. Check out their prices and services. Small shops can often rush out work while you wait at lower cost than the large photorepro companies that are geared for massive jobs. Later I deal with some of the variations of photo and printing work that go with this system.

Being no longer subject to the restraints of drawing with lead or ink on translucent drafting media will bring changes in your perception of the production process. You'll start thinking in terms of *graphic communication* rather than in terms of drawing. This will tend to open a flood of ideas for new ways to do things in the office. Welcome the flood, but keep in mind that most new ideas won't work. Experiment, but keep it systematic and coordinated so it doesn't distract from getting the work out.

Drafting staff might get a little carried away with paste-up drafting and start photocopying every little item. Some will carry the virtue of fastidiousness too far with precise cutouts, ultraneat (and slow) paste-up methods, and the highest price photoreproduction methods and media. Supervision has to be very close at hand when composite drafting is introduced.

The technique of composite drafting is much faster than the work pace that drafting staff members are accustomed to. Usually they plan their work time to match major divisions in the workday and work week. For example, a drafting technician may plan a small drafting task to fill in the time until the next break or until lunch. An afternoon task is paced to carry through to quitting time. Larger assignments are welcomed because they can be carried through to the end of Friday. Although composite work goes much faster, some people will hang on to old scheduling habits and drag out the assignments to fill in large blocks of time.

Supervisors also have a problem with the faster pace. Those who like to hand out assignments and then not be bothered for a while will not like the faster, jumpy production. People move rapidly from task to task; drawings come and go quickly. There's heavy traffic from drafting board to light table to print machines to the photorepro shop. Planning, updating, and coordinating are unusually demanding. It's *easy* to lose control of a job.

Take advantage of the fact that two or three people can work on the same paste-up worksheet at the same time. Such cooperative division of labor results in a gain of efficiency. It's fun for the participants—energy levels go up. It's especially effective for moving rush jobs along.

You'll often have to decide whether tracing or drawing some item is cheaper than photoreproducing it. A good rule of thumb is to determine whether a task will take 3 or more hours to do by hand. If it will, it should probably go to the photorepro shop. For more precision, keep up-to-date price lists of various repro media and services at hand. When estimating time for hand-drafting tasks, keep in mind that real hourly costs are considerably higher than a straight hourly wage.

Ink drawing may be needed to finish up polyester sheets that have been started as photoreproductions. The photo process prints dark, ink-like lines that often won't match up with plain lead drawing.

When doing cutouts and paste-ups, don't wad up unused prints and discard them. Keep unused material on the side in flat scrap piles. You'll invariably discover that some items that were tossed out should have been saved.

Don't surprise your consultants with a sudden switch to composite drafting. Go over the system with them in advance. Explain how coordination will be improved and, since you'll be supplying some of the drawing they would otherwise have to do, how their work flow will be improved. Have consultants help make a checklist to show how far an architectural drawing should go before it's usable as a base sheet for their work. Work with the structural engineer to develop a list of architectural details that can be photocopied and used in the structural drawings. (Details that are often redrawn by engineers include concrete spandrels, concrete stairs, wall sections with framing details, etc.) Note at what point of completion a detail should be pulled to be copied for the engineer.

Go to smaller sheet sizes, especially on smaller jobs. Consult with your photorepro shop on this. Any time two sheets can be reproduced simultaneously on a large reproducible, money will be saved. A slight change in drawing size could drastically cut your final photorepro bills.

Ask the photorepro shop for a price break on "hold" work, similar to what is done for third-class mail. If some of your items aren't rushed and can be put aside at the shop until their slow periods, the shop should allow your office a markdown.

Ask the photorepro and offset printing shops what their markups are on supplies. Ordering your own materials may save 10% on their cost. Photorepro shops are least likely to do this, but offset printers usually will. To save money, send a maximum amount of similar work at any one time (especially during their off hours).

While doing everything to keep reproduction costs down, be sure the client agrees to pay for the work. It's a legitimate reimbursable expense. The client will gain more work in less time and will *save* money by paying the higher-than-normal reproduction costs.

When drawings are to be reduced to half size, watch your lettering sizes. Drafting staff often overlook the need to keep lettering large to compensate for the final photoreduction. This rule applies to symbols, material indications, keys, etc.

Progress prints for the client and office check prints may be a problem. When working on a half-completed paste-up sheet, it's obviously uneconomical to have a photoreproducible made just to run off a diazo check print. Most times the reproducible phase has already been reached when interim prints are called for. If not, have photocopy reductions made on an engineering drawing copier. If the original worksheet is large, partial prints can be made and spliced together. The scale will be off, but the data will be adequate for checking purposes.

There may be some confusion about getting sheet border lines and title blocks onto the final reproducibles. There are two main options: (1) If the worksheet is to be reproduced at the same size, preprint the worksheet as a tracing which includes borders and title block; (2) if the graphic data on the worksheet is to be photoreproduced at a different size, order a "double burn." The image of the border and title block is recorded on a negative and blown back onto the reproducible along with the graphic data.

Here is one final point: Composite drafting is as useful for designers as it is for production staff. Convey the system to your design staff and work with them to find special applications to speed up design drawings. *This is very important: Persuade designers to produce work that will be reusable by the production people.* For example, when a final preliminary floor plan is created, have the rendering done on a reproduction and save the outline original as a starter for the working drawing plan.

12.16 SYNTHESIS

The compelling thing about composite drafting is that it solves so many problems that arise when you use other advanced techniques.

All the techniques are problem solvers, but, almost invariably, they introduce some snag or inconvenience of their own. Applique drafting, for example, is a fabulous timesaver. It can also be an incredible nuisance. The stick-on elements are easily damaged, they catch dust, and they're often hard to remove when you have to make revisions. And even the best of the stickyback film products still often leave a background haze when printed via diazo.

When you introduce applique elements as *composite* elements, most of the problems evaporate. Instead of fussing to lay down a stickyback sheet, get the bubbles and wrinkles out, and print the sheet at slow enough speed to eliminate the background haze, you just lay down a nonstickyback sheet and secure it with a couple of small pieces of clear tape. Later, if you want to remove the sheet, you just pick it up. This is far simpler than working with stickyback products.

This "lay it down and pick it up" simplicity of composite drafting helps solve complexities and problems in all phases of Systems Drafting. In photodrafting, for example, you just lay photos down, pick them up, move them around. Or, if using typewritten notation, you assemble, position, and lay down notes with the ease of setting a dinner table. A large assembly sheet of standard details is much easier to handle using taped-on composites rather than stickybacks.

Not that stickybacks aren't also useful, especially in combination with composite techniques. There are repetitive small elements such as symbols, walls, titles, that are clearly better stored and more conveniently applied by means of dry transfer or stickyback. This all becomes obvious enough as you refine your system.

Once you're into composite drafting, all the subsystems—techniques, materials, and equipment—truly start to click into place. For example, ink drafting will give you better reproductions to use for paste-ups. Simplified and correctly sized drafting elements will help keep the drawings crisp, uncrowded, and readable. A modular drawing sheet design plus a grid underlayment will expedite composition and alignment of paste-up elements. Your graphics center, with light table, storage systems, and the right tools, paves the way for successful composite work.

So we see a meshing of techniques: composite drafting eliminates or reduces many problems of the subsystems. And the subsystems are the foundation of successful composite drafting.

In the same way, all the integrations that make up composite drafting pave the way for successful overlay drafting. It's true that overlay has been done without use of composite techniques, but it's more successful in combination with composite. Overlay comes easier, it's augmented and enhanced, when treated as part of a still larger five-stage system that combines overlay and composite.

Finally, just as composite drafting expedites overlay, overlay does the same for composite. You'll see how all that comes together in the next two chapters.

12.17 EXERCISES

1. Review a past set of working drawings and list your answers to the following questions:
    a. What elements that were drawn on large original sheets could have been drawn separately, on smaller sheets, and assembled later as a final drawing?
    b. What elements that were drawn could have been created by various applique and composite techniques such as typewritten notes for paste-up, reprinted elements from design development drawings, and so on?
    c. What plan drawings or portions of plans could have been created by making units—such as repeat suites, apartments, offices, building wings, etc.—and reprographically reproducing them instead of redrawing them?
    d. What other items in cross sections, exterior elevations, or interior elevations could have been created by making copies of repeat elements and adhering them to a carrying sheet?
2. Review some past design development and presentation drawings and list answers to the following questions:
    a. How could you create such a drawing using *nothing but the following*: appliques such as tapes for walls; dry transfer for simple elements such as fixtures, symbols, and furnishings; texture and pattern films; diazo or office-copier reproductions of repeat floor plan and other elements?
    b. What elements were redrawn at different sizes that could have been photoreduced or photoenlarged instead?
3. Review your entire design development drawing process and answer the following:
    a. At what point could you start substituting appliques and paste-ups for sketch drawing?
    b. What portions of design development drawings are redrawn repeatedly to study various options and refinements?

13

BASICS OF
OVERLAY DRAFTING

13.1 INTRODUCTION

"Well, here's an exercise in futility." That's what I first said when told about overlay drafting. I didn't understand it. Once I did, it seemed silly and pointless. Why draw a floor plan—just the walls, windows, and doors—and then lay another drawing over that and do notes, titles, and dimensions? Why have consultants work on overlay sheets instead of directly on reproducible background prints of the architectural plans?

My spot checks of a couple of overlay jobs in action didn't reassure me at all: drawings coming and going all over the place; a big storage hassle; confused draftspeople duplicating information on base and overlay sheets; repro costs going through the roof; too much staff down time during printings; and plenty of staff complaints to boot. "What a mess," I thought. "Who needs this?"

The "mess," as it turned out, got the jobs done faster, better, and at lower cost than traditional nonoverlay methods could have. But the real clincher was the unexpected multiple advantages that emerged. The coordination between architect and consultants was much improved—as was coordination between consultants.

The biggest improvement is that overlay has made job revisions infinitely easier to manage and far less time-consuming than normal.

The best things about overlay are not at all apparent at first. For one thing, it *looks* far more complicated than it is. Overlay pertains mainly to *one* portion of a set of drawings—usually just plans. Also, much of that plan creation process should be completed during final design devel-

opment. So the process doesn't permeate a whole project, and much of it should be ready to go when production starts.

What's more, *most* base sheet and overlay sheet combinations are just that: *one* base and *one* overlay. The more complex combinations are a rarity. The basic drafting operation is easy to master with very little instruction.

A final irony is that most of the benefits and the basic simplicity of overlay were discovered by accident. Overlay was originally a means to an ambitious end: multicolor offset-printed working drawings. To get color printing, you have to use base and overlay separations. In the process, the simplicity and an incredible variety of special advantages and uses came to light. The benefits will emerge for you, too. Just learn the rules, plan the work in detail, and get a handle on the printing processes. It all comes together in this chapter and the next.

13.2 HOW AND WHY IT WORKS

After 20, possibly 30, years of off-and-on stabs by architects and engineers, overlay is catching on. The potential advantages have always been there, but it was too much fuss to go after them. Now there are simplifications. There's a new "pin-bar" registration. Reproduction materials and processes are much improved, and cheaper.

Overlay may be catching on, but the inevitable question from the novice and skeptic is: Why? What is it and what good is it? Overlay is an exotic way to do things. You work with two or more sheets of drawings, one on top of the other, just to end up with a single final sheet. It seems like you're taking a detour instead of a shortcut.

To grasp the essence of the system and its potential advantages, let's follow the thought processes of a project architect planning out a new project. The project has some typical problems, and we'll see how overlay can be used to deal with them.

First of all, the project is multistory, and there will be lots of floor plans in the architectural, structural, mechanical, plumbing, and electrical drawings. The architect doesn't want the consulting engineers to draw the floor plans themselves, but wants to control those drawings, and decides to provide background floor plans for the engineers to work on.

The common way of providing floor plans to consulting engineers is to give them reproducible prints on drafting media. Those are second originals like sepia prints on vellum or sepia or black-line prints on polyester.

That "common" way of doing it may be an advance over letting engineers redraw the architectural background plans. But it has its flaws. These will become evident in a moment.

The architect has another desire: to improve readability of the drawings by "fading out" the architectural background plans to let the engineers' work stand out vividly. One way is to print the architectural plans with a 50% screen, as a dotted image that will appear gray, similar to "halftone." Then the architectural background comes out as a "shadow print" and the consulting engineers' work is printed in solid line. It's a graphic improvement—a clarifier.

If the architect provides regular hard-line reproducible prints for the consultants to draw on, there's no way to get a screened shadow print of the architectural background.

A solution is to print the reproducibles that will go to the consultants in screened "shadow print" image to begin with. Then the consultants would draw over the gray architectural plans in hard-line and the final prints would come out in shadow print and hard-line combination.

Is this a good solution? No. It is a nice try, but it creates a hazard. There will be revisions in the plans along the way. That means drafting staff will erase or eradicate portions of the screened line work. Then they'll draw plan revisions with little ink dots to try to match the existing screened line work.

The architect realizes another aspect of the same problem. *Any* plan revisions would mean lots of erasing and redrawing in the architect's and consultants' drafting rooms, even without screened architectural plans. The project at hand is a high-rise, and one change in the perimeter wall might have to be made dozens, even hundreds of times, on all the plan sheets that show that wall. The problem exists no matter who does the architectural background drawings. The architect would love to avoid all those duplicate, hand-drawn revisions.

It's clear by now that there is one technique that will cover *all* the architect's problems and considerations: overlay drafting.

An overlay job plan soon emerges that achieves the architect's initial goals and throws in a few bonus benefits to boot. Here's how it works:

1. The plans to be drawn in final design development will be separated into base sheets and overlay sheets. Base sheets will show the walls and any other data that would also be on the architectural working drawing plan sheets. Design development overlays will show the rendered portions, textures, special titles, etc., that pertain only to design development or presentation drawings. (The designer will lay the completed base sheet on the drafting board and place the overlay atop it for completing the drawing. Later they can be put back into registration for printing. A single combined print will come out which has both the base sheet and the overlay sheet images merged on one surface.)

2. In working drawings, the architectural floor plan base sheet from design development will be elaborated on up to the point necessary for use by the consulting engineers. Structural walls will be shown for the struc-

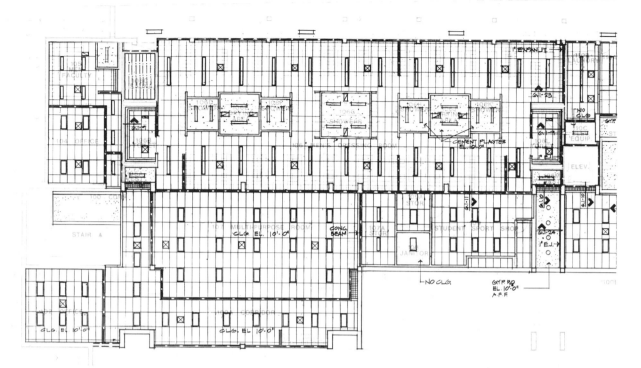

Fig. 13-1. Offset-printed screened shadow print floor plan with solid-line reflected ceiling plan. The solid-line reflected ceiling plan was created as an overlay. Later, the base sheet image was screened and both base and overlay images were combined on a single offset printing plate.

(Jarvis Putty Jarvis.)

tural engineer's drawings, for example, but movable partitions will not. Architectural notes, door and detail symbols, etc., will not be included on these base sheets.

3. The specifically architectural information on plans will be drawn on overlay sheets laid atop the architectural base sheets.
4. The specifically engineering information on plans will be drawn on overlay sheets in the same manner as above.
5. For check printing and progress printing, base and overlay sheets will be printed together as one. For example, the base sheet of the ground floor plan of the building will be combined in printing with the architectural overlay for the architectural portion of the drawings; and with the electrical, plumbing, and HVAC overlays for their respective portions of the drawing set.

We pause now for some clarification. What are the base sheets that architectural and consulting drafting staff use? The *original* base sheet floor plan is that which is drawn or pasted up by the

architect's draftsperson. The base sheet is reprinted in the exact same size on a stable plastic film—polyester sepia line or black line. These are reproducible prints, but they're not being used for that purpose at this point. They're just clear film reproductions—usually hard-line, not erasable, and usually without drafting matte surface on either side. They're only for reference for people drawing overlay sheets and are not to be revised or used as originals at all. They're called "throwaways," and that's just what they are—used and thrown away.

What's gained from that overlay job plan? What purpose is served by drawing base and overlay sheets separately and later merging them in a printing process? Remember the architect's goals:

1. The architect wanted to provide architectural plans to consultants instead of consultants redrawing them themselves, both as an economy in time and money and as a means of gaining tighter job control.
2. The architect favored using screened "shadow" prints of the architectural data on **171**

the consultants' prints for greater graphic clarity in the final prints.

3. The architect wanted to avoid the problem of drafting staff having to make revisions on dozens and dozens of plan sheets every time there was a modification in the building design.

All these are achieved rather handily using the overlay system. Here's how:

1. Architectural base data that show only what consultants need can be printed and distributed to consultants' drafting staff inexpensively. It's there for direct reference right on their drafting boards, and they have no need to do any but engineering drawing. That takes care of the first goal.

2. Since the architectural base sheet is physically separate from the overlays, the printer can introduce a screen that "grays" the architectural background while printing consultants' work in solid line work. That handles the second goal.

NOTE: *Although screening could be introduced in check-print and progress-print phases, it adds an unnecessary expense. The screening process for shadow background prints is usually saved for the very final printing of bid and construction sets.*

3. The final goal, reducing the erasing and redrafting of plan revisions on a multitude of plans, is achieved readily because there's only *one* original floor plan base sheet to contend with. The polyester prints of the original base sheet are not erased or drawn upon. If there's a revision of the ground floor plan perimeter wall, for example, it really only has to be drawn on that particular architectural base sheet. The consultants have to be notified of the change, but they don't have to draw it. They only have to modify whatever portion of their work is actually affected by the architectural change.

The vast reduction in "revision drafting" applies also to the architectural staff. Here's how:

The building in question is multistory. The perimeter wall and core design is consistent through all floors, as is the structural grid. But the interior wall types and sizes vary from floor to floor: some are fixed, and others relocatable. Architectural staff can draw the individual floor

plans as interiors only on overlays atop base sheets that show perimeter walls, core, and structural grid. Thus, if and when there are changes in the perimeter and core, they don't have to be made on all the architectural floor plan sheets—only on the original base sheet. Again, only one drawing has to be changed instead of dozens. More important, the draftspeople don't have to draw that perimeter wall, core, and structural grid over and over and over again on every single architectural floor plan sheet, which is the real economic justification for providing throwaway polyester prints of the base sheet. Anyone who's labored through a project of this type will appreciate the extraordinary time and cost savings of this change in procedure.

There are other uses and other advantages to overlay. They will become clear further on in this and the next chapter.

There are also limitations. Overlay has been used successfully on small projects, even houses. It's also worked out badly for many projects. The rules for choosing what projects to use overlay on will become clear later in the text.

People who first use overlay and composite drafting sometimes lose sight of important differences in the systems: how they relate and how they don't relate. That leads to confusion in job planning, and the technical language in the drafting and print rooms becomes cloudy. The next section will clarify overlay technology and terminology.

13.3 TOOLS, MATERIALS, AND EQUIPMENT

The symbol $\oplus$ is called a "target," "gunsight," or "registration mark." Graphic artists and printers use such marks as guides to align two or more sheets that are laid over one another. Once a sheet and an overlay have been aligned with targets, they can be put back in registration any time after being separated.

Hand-drawn or press-on targets are adequate for simple overlay jobs on very small sheets. Larger architectural and engineering work requires a more reliable and convenient method of alignment. The appropriate drafting medium is polyester film. Polyester, popularly known by the DuPont trade name of Mylar, is strong and stable. Polyester base sheets and overlays won't shrink or expand relative to one another as will sheets of tracing paper or diazo-print paper.

For overlay drafting, the polyester sheets are punched with seven holes along the top trim margin space. Holes rather than targets provide the alignment. The hole punching has to be precise and requires a special puncher made for this purpose. Your photoreproduction shop will most likely do punching.

Punched base sheets and overlays are aligned by means of a "pin bar," also called a "registration bar." The pin bar is a stainless steel strip with seven protruding nubs that snugly fit the prepunched holes in the polyester sheets. Pin bars are taped at the top edge of drafting boards. Alignment of all base sheets and overlays is guaranteed by the matching of prepunched holes and the pin bar. Identical pin bars are used by the consultants for aligning their drawings. And a matching pin bar is used at the repro shop in mounting sheets for photo work.

At intervals during a job, you'll need check prints that combine base sheets and overlays. Precise registration is *not* critical for these prints.

Base sheets and overlays can be run together through a regular rotary diazo machine. The registration of images on the diazo print will be slightly off. But the prints will be adequate for most checking purposes. Some offices tape base sheet and overlays at their top edge to run combination prints. Other offices use a simpler method. They connect the sheets with a few small rubber pins that fit the prepunched holes.

Perfect registration is required for the final prints, and this requires more sophisticated equipment than the diazo machine. One device is the "contact printer," "vacuum frame," or "flatbed printer." The contact printer is a printing machine that presses the base sheet, overlays, and diazo-print or photoprint medium together—all flat—and exposes the sensitized medium to light. The principle of light exposure is the same as for a diazo machine, but it's done on a flat bed instead of moving rollers. Most often the prints will be diazo (ammonia developed), and the light source should then be mainly ultraviolet.

Vacuum frames use powered suction to keep sheets tightly pressed together. Inexpensive diazo prints and reproducibles, as well as more expensive photographic washoff polyesters, can be made on the vacuum frame. Many offices that are well into overlay drafting have chosen to purchase or lease such printers. You get higher-quality check prints and progress prints with flatbed printers (better than you get with diazo machines), and they vastly reduce the waiting time for all one-to-one photoreproduction work. Please note that if you expose diazo material on a vacuum frame, you'll need to use a separate ammonia developer to develop the image. If you expose photo media, you'll need a washoff photo processor.

Besides diazo and vacuum frame, the third main method for combining base sheets and overlays is photographic. The tool is the "process camera," also called "blowback camera" or "camera projector." The camera will photograph a drawing onto an $8\frac{1}{2}'' \times 11''$ negative. Once processed, the negative is used to project the photographed image back out onto light-sensitive paper or polyester.

The blowback camera is also used in composite drafting as well as overlay drafting because it lets you change the scale of drawings without redrawing. For example, $\frac{1}{4}''$-scale detailed floor plans can be photoreduced to $\frac{1}{8}''$-scale overall construction plans. The $\frac{1}{8}''$-scale plans can be photoreduced further for, say, a $\frac{1}{32}''$-scale site plan.

The blowback camera serves a different function in overlay drafting. Negatives are made of the base sheet and each overlay. The negative images are then blown back onto a light-sensitive medium as a multiple exposure. The multiple exposure, also called "burn and double burn," is the final working drawing image. You can expose any number of base and overlay images onto one sheet in this fashion.

173

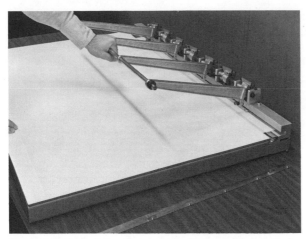

Fig. 13-2.   A pin bar and a seven-hole pin-register punch. The punch makes holes in the drafting polyester and the diazo and washoff polyesters to match the size and spacing of the pins on the registration pin bar.

(DuPont Photo Systems.)

A blowback camera is more time-consuming and expensive to use than a flatbed printer. Some repro shops have used the photoblowback method when the contact-print method would do as good a job at much lower cost. The vacuum frame will usually work fine for all one-to-one size reproductions of translucent originals. The blowback camera is appropriate when there are changes in the size of the image or when the original work sheet is an opaque paste-up.

"Screened" prints are an integral part of the overlay system. "Screened" prints, also called "shadow" prints, "ghost image," and "subordinate image," are made by inserting a literal screen, called a "tint," when making or projecting a negative image. The screen blocks off a percentage of the line work so the print comes out lighter, made up of a series of tiny dashed lines. Screens come in many sizes to block out whatever percentage of image is desired. Architects and engineers most commonly use the 50%, 133-line screen.

A print of a consultant's drawing is much clearer when consultants' work is printed in solid line over a screened background print of the architectural base sheet.

One caution is: Screening should not be done until the final assembly and photoreproduction of the working drawing set. If screened base sheets are made during an intermediate stage and then photoreduced, the shadow image may wash out. Also, hand-drawn revisions will not match up with screen printing.

The variations in polyester drafting and pho-

toreproduction media can be confusing. The most commonly used polyester drafting media come in thicknesses of from 0.002 to 0.007" (2 to 7 mil) with a matte tooth finish for drafting on one or both sides. Generally a lighter-weight polyester (4 or 5 mil) with matte on *one* side is best for overlay drafting work. When using more than one overlay at a time, excessive thickness and too many layers of matte surface will obscure the view. Thick polyester with double-sided matte also interferes with flatbed printing.

When drafting or checking multiple overlay images, it's best to work on a drafting light table. Before starting to use overlay, it's best to purchase or build one or more light tables.

Besides the plain polyester drafting media, there are light-sensitive polyester media with emulsion on matte or nonmatte sides. Choices include "fixed line," "erasable," or "washoff" emulsion. Washoff, also called "moist-erasable," is, just as its name implies, erasable with moisture. It's the most convenient material for dealing with revisions of the photoexposed image.

As noted above, the matte surface for drafting may be on one or both sides. Or there may be no matte. If a polyester transparency is to be used as a base sheet, it should be on clear nonmatte polyester—called a "clear," a "sepia Mylar," a "slick," or a "throwaway." The nonmatte "slicks"

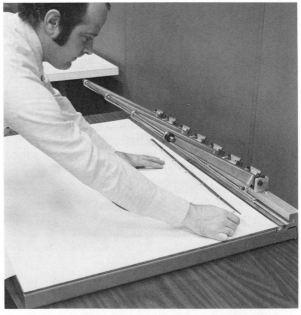

Fig. 13-3.   A punched sheet of drafting polyester and a pin bar on the pin-register punch. Slight deviations can occur, so it is desirable to obtain all the punched media at one time from the same punch.

(DuPont Photo Systems.)

can't be drawn on or erased. This prevents unauthorized revisions and clearly identifies them as base sheets.

Diazo polyester is a good, low-cost alternative to regular photosensitive material. When making base sheets of a floor plan to send to consultants, for example, polyester diazos made on a vacuum frame are as usable as the more expensive photoemulsion washoff material.

13.4 DESIGN DEVELOPMENT DRAWINGS

Design drawings and working drawings have traditionally been treated as two separate worlds. Designers lay out floor plans, site plans, exterior elevations, and cross sections. Later, if the job goes through, these items are all redone in working drawing format.

Many offices have rejected the old system. They've introduced changes in procedure that permit them to convert final design drawings directly into working drawings. Overlay drafting is a big help in this kind of conversion.

The office of Hansen Lind Meyer reports impressive results in recycling design drawings. In one early experiment, they attained 20% completion of architectural working drawings in the process of doing the design development. At the same time, data for mechanical and electrical drawings were 21% completed.

An intermediate step must be introduced to make design drawings usable as working drawings. This is not an increase in the work; it's a reduction in work. Some design staff will consider it extra work and will balk at doing it.

The intermediate step is the drawing of base sheets. Your floor plan base sheet, for example, might show all walls and partitions but exclude titles, notation, and materials indications. Derive the base sheet floor plan from final schematic drawings, just as with an ordinary presentation drawing floor plan.

The base sheets are jumping-off points. A base sheet will be the background for a rendered presentation drawing, and, later, the background for a working drawing.

The base sheets are working drawing size and drawn at working drawing scale. The rendered presentation drawings are done on prints of the base sheets. The prints can be transparency or opaque, enlarged or reduced—whatever you want.

All the presentation style lettering, color, texture, poche, entourage, and so on, go on the prints. If there are revisions in the design, the changes are made on the original base sheets. If and when there's a green light on working drawings, the base sheets are printed onto polyester drafting media and you're off and running.

Subdivide base sheets and overlays for presentation drawings, just as for working drawings. For example, a base sheet can have an overall exterior-view outline of a building and different overlays can show optional refinements of the exterior design. Or an outline site plan can be the base sheet for several overlays showing variations in building siting and landscaping.

For greatest convenience and economy, keep your presentation drawings at the same scale and at a similar sheet size as the working drawings. Designers may resist this, but it's worth fighting for.

NOTE: *Use a "format sheet" rather than drawing a sheet border and title block on the base sheets. One format sheet with border and title block suited to presentation drawings will be reprographically combined with those prints. And another format sheet in working drawing style will later become a part of all working drawing reproducibles.*

13.5 THE ARCHITECT'S BASE SHEETS AND OVERLAYS

The ins and outs of the overlay technique are almost self-evident for the consultants. Typically, they use an architectural drawing as a base sheet and draw the work of special trades over that. It's basically no different than traditional practice.

Architectural applications of the system are more complex and sophisticated. While a consultant's drawing may involve a base sheet and one or two overlays, an architectural drawing may ultimately be made up of three or more different overlays. The following list illustrates various types of architectural sheets:

1. There is the "format sheet." This consists of sheet border and title block. It also has trim margin and may include tick marks to show 8½" × 11" or other divisions of the sheet. Some offices include general notes regarding ownership of drawings and other items on all drawings; they can be done once on the format sheet. An overall small-scale key plan may be included. The image of the format sheet appears on all final architectural and *consultants'* prints.

2. Another fairly common sheet is the "template sheet." This is an ink drawing of the structural grid or construction module. It includes the grid reference numbers and letters, north arrow, cross-section arrows, scale, general notes, and other items that repeat on all floor plan drawings. It might include a title "floor plan" positioned so that the particular floor level number can be added in later on each appropriate overlay.

3. Then there are the base sheets. A multistory floor plan base sheet shows construction of the exterior wall at a typical floor level. If the core elements (elevators, stairs, toilet rooms, utility spaces, etc.) are constant from floor to floor, they are also on the base sheet. Sometimes the structural grid or module grid is drawn on this sheet rather than on a separate template sheet. You'll need to weigh the advantages and disadvantages of doing a whole separate template sheet. For example, if there are a number of floor levels with different

perimeter wall configurations, it may pay to do a template sheet to avoid redrawing the grid for each unique floor plan base sheet. If there are only a couple of instances where the grid would have to be drawn on base sheets, it would then pay to have both drawings on one sheet and *not* have a separate template sheet done.

4. Interior partition plans are done as overlays on the exterior wall floor plan base sheet. Each nontypical floor level is drawn with all partitions, doors, built-ins (built-ins may be on a separate "fixtures and fittings" overlay), furred spaces, fire hose cabinets, drinking fountains, etc. Dimensions, symbols, and notations are not included on these overlays; they're done as separate overlays. And, of course, no exterior wall construction or structural grids are drawn since they are on the base and template sheets.

5. Interior dimensions, symbols, and notations may be done as one or two separate overlays for each floor level, or they might be done directly on the interior partition overlay. It all depends on the circumstances. For example, if your floor plan base sheets are *not* to have architectural dimensions and notes on them, such data should be on overlay. That way the consultant's base sheet plans can be printed without extraneous and/or unwanted data. (Keep in mind that an architectural floor plan base sheet and partition overlay may be combined into a new print that becomes a base sheet for the consultant's further overlay work.)

   If it's okay for some purely architectural data to show as background on the consultant's base sheets (and it often is), there's no need to overdo the overlays. Some offices have overdone overlays in their initial experiments. For example, some people do dimensions on one overlay and space identification and notes on another. Such overlays inevitably contain overlaps and data conflicts which only appear later when they're merged.

6. Fixtures and fittings are another good prospect for an overlay sheet. Equipment, cabinets, furnishings, and so on, are often obscured on working drawings. And sometimes the line work of built-ins is confused with the drawing of building construction. Such confusion can be avoided by doing fixtures, equipment, and furnishings as an overlay

item. The final print can show fixtures, and so on, in solid line on a screened floor plan background.

NOTE: *Your electrical consultant may need composites of fixtures and fittings plus building floor plans as base sheets for electrical plan overlays.*

The following sequence shows architectural base sheets and overlays. These would precede the base sheets and consultant's overlays shown in the next sequence.
(DuPont Photo Systems.)

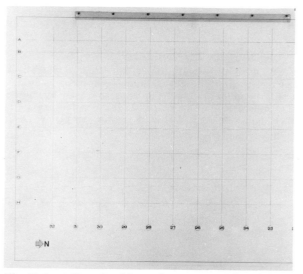

Fig. 13-4. A "template" base sheet—structural module and drawing format. It will be used as a reference base for architectural draftspersons working on different floor plans of the building. Later the image of grid and format will be combined with the various overlay floor plan images for check printing and final job printing.
(DuPont Photo Systems.)

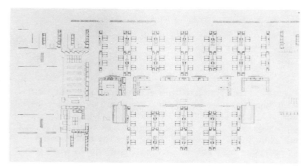

Fig. 13-5. A furnishings and fixtures overlay sheet without the partitions and walls base sheet.
(DuPont Photo Systems.)

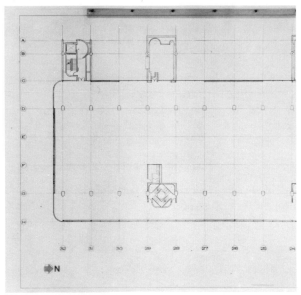

Fig. 13-6. Exterior walls, stairs, and columns—data common to all floors of the building—are drawn as an overlay atop the grid and template base sheet. (Sometimes it is preferable to avoid a separate grid template base sheet and draw the grid directly on this floor plan.)

(DuPont Photo Systems.)

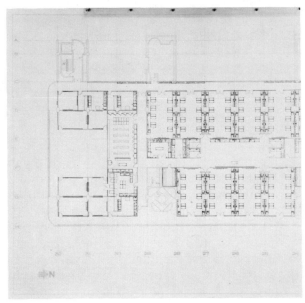

Fig. 13-8. Furnishings and fixtures are drawn on an overlay sheet atop a partition plan base sheet.

(DuPont Photo Systems.)

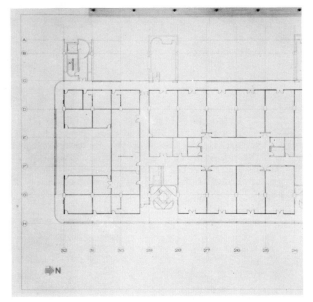

Fig. 13-7. Interior partition arrangements for different floor levels are drawn as overlays atop the exterior wall and grid base sheet. Note that such overlays are drawn atop polyester prints of the original base sheet drawing, not atop the original itself. Later these will be printed as polyester base sheets for the consultants to work with.

(DuPont Photo Systems.)

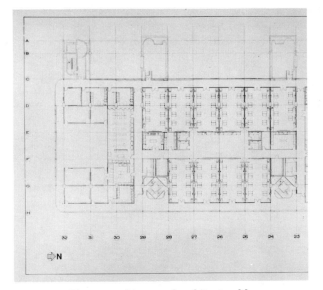

Fig. 13-9. The merged image of architectural base template and overlays. Still another overlay will be done for strictly architectural titles, notation, symbols, and dimensions.

(DuPont Photo Systems.)

13.6 THE CONSULTANTS' DRAWINGS

Following are the basic steps of coordination between architect and consultant:

1. The architect does a drawing with as much data on it as the consultant needs for background reference.
2. The architect has an exact-size duplicate of the background reference drawing made on prepunched, polyester print media. This print is the *base sheet* for the consultant's overlay. A one-to-one reproduction made with a contact printer on diazo polyester is the least expensive means of getting an exact-size stable base sheet. The consultant's base

sheet can most likely be clear, that is, without a matte surface, and printed in fixed line. This prevents the consultant's staff from making unauthorized erasures and/or drawings on the architectural work. If some flexibility is desired and some revision capacity by the consultant is OK, the base sheet can be erasable with matte surface.

3. The consultant's draftsperson receives the base sheet and attaches it to a pin-bar sheet holder at the drafting table. A fresh sheet of polyester drafting medium is laid over the base sheet.
4. The consultant draws (framing, electrical, plumbing, HVAC—whatever) on the overlay sheet. This will often be a multistep process. A preliminary layout may be started over a preliminary base sheet and then refined as the architect provides more finished drawings. Sometimes the consultant will do a

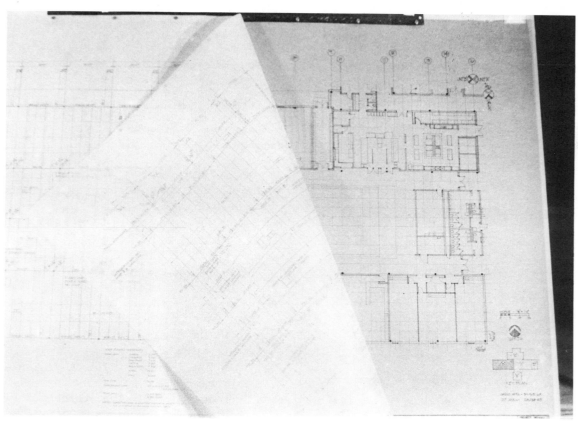

Fig. 13-10.   Overlay drafting. The architectural background information is on a sepia diazo polyester "slick" on the pin bar and drafting board. The consultant's overlay is drawn on a separate sheet overlayed atop the base sheet. Later the images of base sheet and overlay sheet will be merged on a single reproducible sheet for check prints and job prints.
(Guidelines.)

rough layout on sketch tracing paper over a diazo print of the architectural drawing and transpose this onto the polyester sheet later as the data firm up.

5. When the architect makes major revisions, a new base sheet is sent to the consultant. A diazo print also goes along showing the revised areas marked in red circles. This shows the consultant exactly where to alter the overlay sheet. (Occasionally a red-marked print would be extraneous. Use only when needed for clarity.) A memo and sketch are often adequate to describe minor changes without sending out a whole new base sheet. Sometimes, however, there are borderline cases when a memo and sketch are not enough and a whole new base sheet would be too much. Send a portion of the print as an amendment to slip under the base sheet. (Sometimes no decision will be exactly right. This is one of

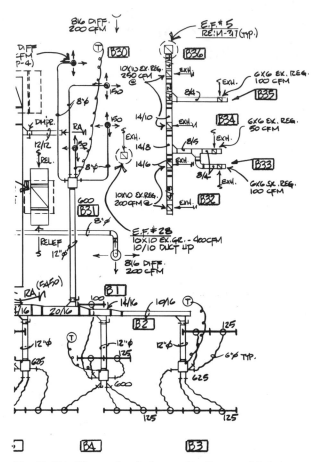

Fig. 13-12.   The mechanical consultant's completed overlay. It was drawn atop a polyester print of the architectural base sheet.

(Mini-Max.)

the frustrating aspects of the system. You'll have to make allowances for errors of judgment in this area.)

6. Periodically, the architect will call for progress prints from the consultant. The consultant can provide informal prints, such as plain diazo paper base sheet and overlay sheet combinations. As noted before, regular diazo prints of base sheets and overlays will be slightly out of register. Flatbed vacuum-frame prints are fairly inexpensive and will be in register.

7. The architect studies the overlays atop the architectural base sheets. Then they're viewed in combination with the overlays of other consultants. This examination of overlays is the surest way to catch conflicts, such as plumbing access blocked by ductwork, structural framing that interferes with waste lines, etc.

Some offices order special combination prints of consultants' work. These are overlaid combi-

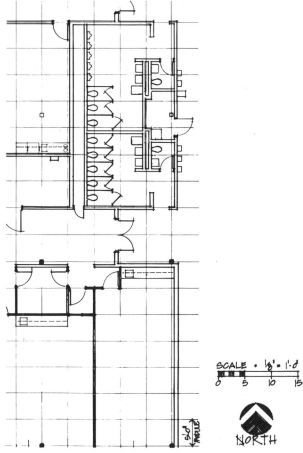

Fig. 13-11.   Architectural background data on a base sheet. Only the information required for consultants is shown. (Room identification is usually included but is shown on an overlay in this case.)

(Mini-Max.)

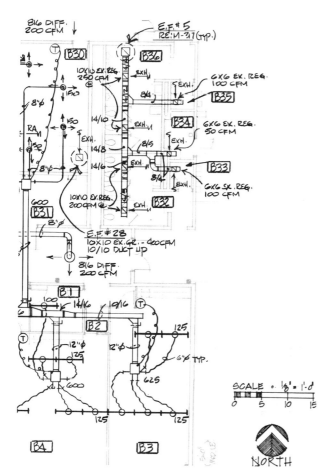

Fig. 13-13. A diazo print of the mechanical overlay shown on the adjacent page now merged with a screened image of the architectural base sheet. This is approximately what the consultant's draftsperson saw when drawing the overlay atop the architectural base sheet, except that the base sheet image was not yet screened.

(Mini-Max.)

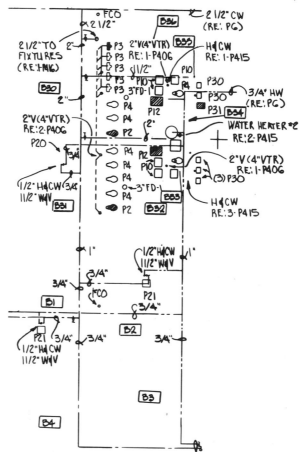

Fig. 13-14. The plumbing consultant's overlay. Just as polyester prints of the architectural base sheet went to the mechanical consultant, they were also provided to drafting staff for structural, electrical, and plumbing consultants. Again, note that the overlay looks meaningless without reference to the architectural background.

(Mini-Max.)

nations of the work of various trades that are normally not shown on the same drawing. For example, such a print might show a screened architectural floor plan base sheet, the reflected ceiling plan, ceiling electrical and lighting, ceiling communications conduit and fixtures, sprinkler system, ceiling fire blocking and soundproofing, and ceiling ductwork and diffusers.

Another useful combination print shows floor plan, slab reinforcement, and framing, plus risers and runs for plumbing, HVAC, electrical, and communications work.

The mixture of all those items on single prints is extremely helpful for checking for omissions and conflicts. They're also very handy as job-site coordination drawings and should be included with the final working drawings as reference prints.

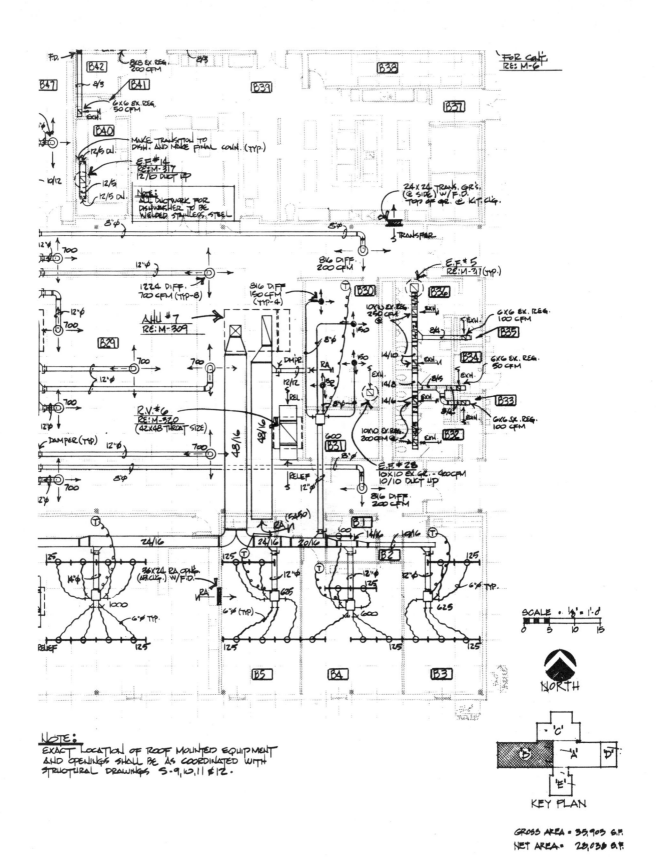

Fig. 13-15. A full-size print of the screened architectural background and the solid-line mechanical consultant's drawing.

(Mini-Max.)

182

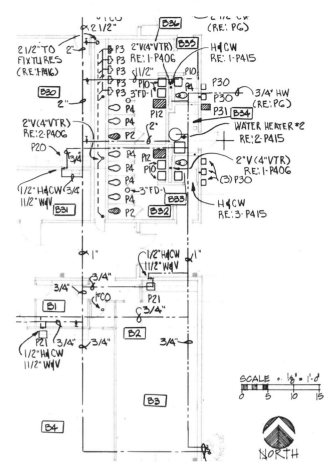

Fig. 13-16. The image of the architectural plan is screened and merged with the hard-line image of the plumbing work as shown in this final, reduced-size diazo working drawing print.

(Mini-Max.)

13.7 SYNTHESIS

Just as composite drafting consists of "horizontal" separation and assembly of graphic information, overlay drafting is a system of "vertical" separation and assembly. Why is the separation aspect necessary, and why call them horizontal and vertical?

First, constant or repeat data have to be separated out and stored, or put on hold, in some manner in order to be reusable. Otherwise, variable or nonrepeat data will be mixed in and the constant data won't be directly reusable. Nonrepeat data will have to be erased or cut out, or the repeat data will have to be redrawn instead of reprographically reproduced and reused. That's why *separation* is so important.

The "assembly" idea is basic to the whole system. Repeat information should be physically pulled from storage and physically put together rather than copied or redrawn by hand.

The horizontal aspect of composite drafting and applique drafting is pretty clear. Diverse elements from various sources are pulled together onto a carrying sheet, more or less literally *horizontally*.

The vertical aspect is more sophisticated but relies on the same principle. You store the constants, the repeats, on base sheets and create the variables, the nonrepeat data, on overlays.

Notice some other differences and special relationships between composite and overlay drafting:

Composite drafting can be used for virtually any kind of drawing: detail sheets, sections, elevations, plans of all kinds. But overlay drafting pertains almost exclusively to plans. Therefore, in a basic way, composite precedes overlay. You'll probably create and assemble plan drawing base sheets with composite elements and appliques and then use a reproducible of the composite for the final base.

Both composite and applique techniques can be profitably used on overlay drawings. When an overlay consists of special line work and commonly repeated symbols—as might occur in electrical drawings—then that overlay can be done as a composite atop the reference base sheet.

That's when the main systems of Systems Drafting really start to merge. You use composite and applique drafting to create your base sheets and overlays, and you start getting maximum value of both systems simultaneously.

183

13.8 EXERCISES

If you're new to overlay, you can enlarge your grasp of the idea by systematically working from the simple to the complex. These exercises have practical on-the-job as well as training value:

1. Plan portions of an overlay job by actually drawing base sheets and overlays (very sketchily, just to indicate basic content) on very transparent tracing paper or polyester. You can also sketch on completely transparent acetate or polyester and use felt-tip markers like those used to draw on transparencies for overhead projectors. If you want to do a complete job mock-up, refer to the job-planning steps outlined in the next chapter. Even a partial mock-up will demonstrate the techniques you'll need for controlling a full-size job.

2. Mock up an overlay project for your next design development presentation drawing phase. Design your presentation drawings for maximum reusability as construction drawings. Plan on doing plans, elevations, sections, and so on, as hard line without titles and notes. Titles, room identification, and so on, can be reserved for overlays. All presentation drawing entourage—shading, shadows, textures, landscaping, trees, people, cars—will be done on overlay.

3. Consider how to combine composite drafting and overlay drafting in design development drawings and, later, when doing production drawings. Original base sheets can be reproducibles made from composited elements, *and* many overlay sheets can also be the products of applique and composite drafting. Review what kinds of composites and appliques could be done on overlays by structural, mechanical, and electrical consultants.

PLANNING AND MANAGING COMPOSITE AND OVERLAY DRAFTING

14.1 INTRODUCTION

"We tried overlay. Drawings were all over the place. Printing bills were out of sight. It was a madhouse. We'll never, never do it again."

That was the office manager of a well-known design firm. They had introduced overlay drafting on a large project for Middle East clients. Apparently the project was right and they had set up for the job properly, but results, as noted, were poor.

I wanted to learn why they had so many problems and visited the project architect who managed the job. I said I'd heard there were a lot of bugs in the project and asked him to fill me in on it.

"Bugs?" he said. "Who told you that? I don't see how it could have been smoother. We didn't save much money, but we were ahead of schedule all the way through. I can hardly wait to do another one."

Clearly, there was a communications gap. Why did the office manager say the job was a mess and the person directly responsible say it was terrific?

I went back to the office manager. No, he hadn't reviewed all the costs yet. Yes, the job came in on time but seemingly in spite of itself. There had been complaints, angry ones, from staff about inconveniences of the new technique. Printing bills were definitely exorbitant. The production staff were out of work for hours at a time during interim printings. Maybe the job wasn't all that bad, but it sure *looked* chaotic from a distance.

It was just a typical overlay job after all. Nothing earthshaking in time and cost savings and no big losses either. It didn't live up to high hopes and expectations, and thus seemed less successful than it really was. There were the usual management kinks the first time through, and that looked bad.

The communications gap in that office was a long-standing problem. It became magnified by the higher intensity and faster pace of overlay drafting. That firm is squared away on it now, but they had to go back and do a little housecleaning in terms of management-level communications systems. And, the second time around on overlay, they did some detailed advance planning. Planning is, in effect, a dress rehearsal. Problems that will emerge later on the job come to the surface during the planning process and are taken care of then instead of during the rush of full-scale work.

14.2 JOB PLANNING WITH MINI–WORKING DRAWINGS

"We are hired in the first place because no one in his right mind would try to put a building together without plans. Yet some architects think they can improvise their way through something as complex as a set of working drawings by the seat of their pants. Good plans require their own planning."

Those were the words of a drafting room manager in 1968. They're 100% relevant today and will remain 100% relevant 20 years from now. If you want good drawings, you've got to plan them out in miniature.

A mini–working drawing set is a literal, booklet-sized mock-up of the final set of working drawings. You include every drawing and drawing number and show—sketchily or in detail—the contents of each drawing.

The usual size of mini–working drawing mock-up sheets or job-planning sheets is 8½" × 11". Some offices prefer 8½" × 14" (legal size) or larger to allow extra space for job-planning notes, checklists, time and cost budgets, etc.

The actual "minidrawing" is normally done on a grid with a border that's one-fourth the dimensions of the final full-size drawing. If the final drawings are to be done on 24" × 36" sheets, the dimensions of the minidrawing would be 6" × 9". If the final drawing sheet size is 30" × 42", the mock-up size is 7½" × 10½".

Miniature working drawing sets are great for any kind of project, but they are mandatory when you get into systems. They'll cut the redundancies and errors, simplify coordination and supervision, reduce errors and omissions, and help keep the job on schedule.

Unfortunately, many project leaders who do miniature mock-ups don't share them with the staff. They keep them hidden in a drawer and miss out on a valuable supervision tool. Staff always like to have a miniature reference set that lets them know where they are in a job, what they'll be doing next, and where their work fits in with all the other work.

Following are the steps for laying out a mini-working drawing set. They are divided into three stages: (1) the steps that apply to any kind of project; (2) the steps to add when planning for composite drafting; and (3) the steps and considerations to add when doing overlay drafting.

PART 1: BASIC STEPS OF PLANNING A SET OF WORKING DRAWINGS

1. Start a preliminary list of final drawing sheets with a sublist of the content of those sheets. For example, "site plan" might include sub-items such as "test-boring plan," "vicinity map," "site-work symbols and abbreviations," and "site-work details."

2. Consult previous sets of working drawings to review the types, sizes, and numbers of drawings and the contents of those drawings. Modify the preliminary job list accordingly as you go along.

3. Organize your list of drawings into a drawing index as would appear on the "contents" or "index" sheet of the final set. Decide on the kind of section or division system to use (see Chapter 3 for suggestions). Number the drawings as they would be numbered in the final set.

4. Coordinate the drawing list with your time and cost limitations. Budget the set of drawings according to the time and money that will actually be available. If you have a time and cost data bank, you'll naturally refer to that data to estimate time and cost for each kind of drawing sheet.

5. Review the drawing list with others in the office and with consultants. (If the project is fairly small, you won't bother with such review.)

6. Complete the drawing list with the intent of creating a master list useful on future jobs. Similarly, you'll plan the working drawing sheets with an eye toward creating a master miniplan that can also be adapted in future job planning.

7. Prepare a design for the miniature working drawing mock-up sheets. Include border sizes, tick marks to represent your working drawing sheet module or design (normally multiples and divisions of 8½" × 11"), a grid for guidance in sketching, and additional title block information for whatever scheduling, delegation, or other data you want to include.

8. Sketch the entire job on the mini–working drawing sheets. Avoid being overly detailed

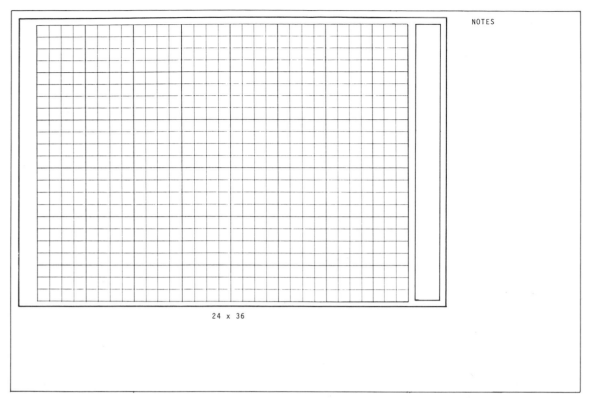

24 x 36

Fig. 14-1. A half-size reduction of a typical working drawing layout sheet (the original sheet is 8½″ × 14″). It has space to represent a 24″ × 36″ working drawing sheet at one-fourth scale plus job planning and instruction notes.

(Guidelines.)

(some people draw mock-ups in such detail they could be sent out to bid). You only need to sketch an outline and name the content of each major element on each drawing sheet. A set of details can be noted as a block rather than sketched in individually.

9. Note on the mock-up sheets the architectural drafting stop points when background or base-sheet prints should be sent to the consultants.

10. Send prints of the mock-up out for review by others who'll be on the job, including consultants. Then finalize and date the miniset.

PART 2: PLANNING THE WORKING DRAWING MOCK-UP FOR COMPOSITE DRAFTING

Plan on making maximum use of composite drafting techniques to expedite the creation of the working drawing mock-ups. Use some suitable abbreviation, symbol, or color to indicate reusable elements in the drawings—items that can be reproduced either at the same size or at

different sizes and assembled on drawing sheets rather than hand-drawn. Watch for the following:

1. Elements that are reusable from drawing sheet to drawing sheet at the same size, such as architectural plans used in consultants' drawings or the basic site plan as used in various grading, irrigation, demolition, and other site plans.

2. Elements reusable from drawing sheet to drawing sheet at different sizes, such as construction floor plans that appear in larger scale as unit plans and possibly in smaller scale on site plans.

3. Elements that might be used as is or with modifications from "outside" sources, such as surveyors' drawings, site photographs, elements from previous jobs, and elements from reference sources such as trade manuals and manufacturers' catalogs.

4. Elements that might be used as is or modified from in-house storage such as standard details; standard notation or keynotes; standard

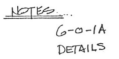

NOTES
6-0-1A
DETAILS

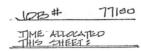

JOB # 77100
TIME ALLOCATED THIS SHEET:

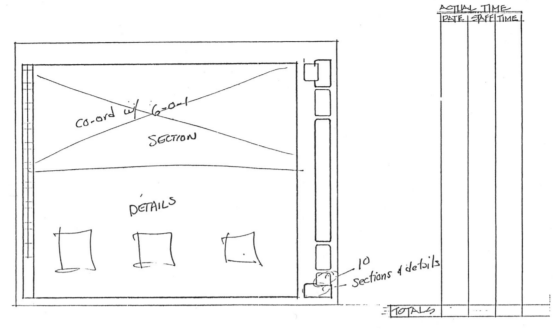

ACTUAL TIME
RATE | STAFF | TIME

Co-ord w/ 6-0-1
SECTION

DETAILS

10
sections & details

TOTALS

MINI-SHEET 18 x 24

NOTES - B4

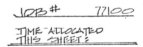

JOB # 77100
TIME ALLOCATED THIS SHEET:

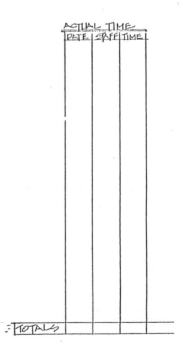

ACTUAL TIME
RATE | STAFF | TIME

TOTALS

MINI-SHEET 18 x 24

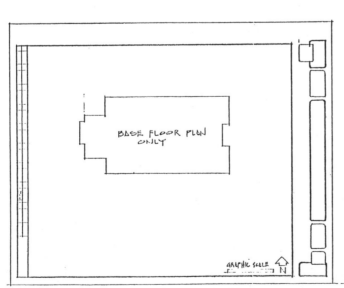

BASE FLOOR PLAN ONLY

GRAPHIC SCALE
N

Fig. 14-2. Planning sheets for sketching working drawing layout.

(Octagon Associates.)

fixture heights sheets to substitute for interior elevation drawings; standard symbol, nomenclature, and abbreviations lists; and standard schedule forms.

5. Elements stored as appliques such as north symbols, drawing and spatial identifications, detail and section symbols, walls and partitions in graphic tape form, texture and pattern sheets, and fixtures, furnishings, and equipment sheets.

6. Notation that can be assembled as appliques, typewritten on overlays, or typed on the drawing sheets.

7. If proceeding to overlay drafting, note what items could be assembled as composites and/or appliques on overlay sheets. (Base sheets used by drafting staff will be reproducible polyester prints of drafted and/or composited elements.)

NOTE: *Consider applying this entire composite planning and review process to the design and planning of the design development drawings, both to maximize use of ready-made and repeat elements and to maximize reusability of design drawings as production drawings.*

PART 3: PLANNING THE WORKING DRAWING MOCK-UP FOR OVERLAY DRAFTING

Start with a complete drawing index and mock-up of what the final set of drawings is to be. That means proceeding through Parts 1 and 2 of this process. Then continue as follows:

1. Examine the final mock-up for constants and variables. (This will pertain to plans and possibly building elevations and cross sections that might be used by consultants.)

2. Sort out the architectural base sheets and overlays in terms of constants and variables. For example, the architectural plans might be divided according to perimeter walls, and structural grid and core as constants for base sheets. The interior partitions at different floor levels might be variables to be created on overlay sheets. Strictly architectural notation, dimensions, detail keys, and so on, will be considered variables for overlay treatment, as would specialized plans (e.g., furniture plans for guidance of electrical work).

3. Sketch architectural base sheets and note what overlays they'll be used with. Sketch

the overlays, preferably on highly transparent tracing paper, or on clear acetate or polyester.

4. Sketch further separations of the overlays that will be prepared by consultants. Note which base sheets they will be combined with during drafting and during printing.

5. Apply base and overlay code numbers to mock-up sheets just as they'll be used on the final real sheets. See the sections on traffic control later in this chapter.

6. Prepare a drawing guide. This is a list of your base sheets, with their respective code numbers and description of content. If some base sheets are combined with overlays to make new composited base sheets, make a separate list of those. And finish with a list of overlay sheets and their code numbers and contents.

7. If the project is small enough, make extra-small minisheets on 3″ × 5″ cards and create a wall chart or storyboard that lays out all the divisions of the job, including individual base sheets and overlay sheets. A wall chart or storyboard is especially useful to staff to show them where their work fits in—a difficult thing to judge sometimes during an overlay job.

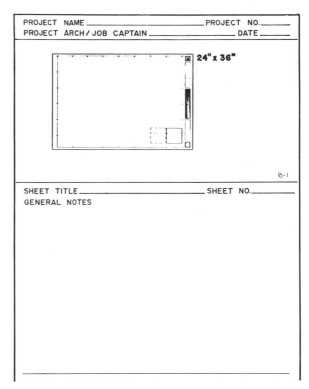

Fig. 14-3. **Another version of a working drawing job-planning mock-up sheet.**
(Hansen Lind Meyer.)

The final result is a portion of the working drawing mock-up that is now done in literal base sheet and overlay miniatures. This planning process will catch virtually all the problems and complexities that might come up in the real job and resolve them in advance. It is also an excellent training and guidance tool for staff.

NOTE: *Consider applying this overlay planning technique to design development drawings. Plan out stop points and base sheets for plans, exterior elevations, sections, and so forth, and sketch overlays for final design development and/or presentation drawings. As with planning design development for composite drafting, this will help ensure maximum economy in preparing design and presentation drawings and will help maximize reusability of design development drawings as working drawings.*

14.3 STOP POINTS FOR BASE SHEETS IN OVERLAY DRAFTING

It's not always self-evident which information is "constant" and should go on a base sheet, and which is "variable" and therefore the subject of overlay sheets. With some minor elements it's just a matter of individual preference. With other elements it's pretty much universally established.

The questions arise, for example: "Which drawings get the title block and border?" "Which drawings, base or overlay, get the sheet titles and final drawing numbers?"

You have to think it through to grasp the principle. Once the principle is understood, the individual decisions take care of themselves. That's part of the function of job planning with mock-ups: It's an educational process for understanding overlay as well as a management tool.

When considering title blocks and borders, for example, most firms simplify things ultimately by just eliminating the border entirely. In that case they also have to provide drafting-board underlayment guides—drawn perhaps on the gridded drafting surface—that show the limits for drawing. Without some visual limits, draftspeople will run over the margin. (There will be a margin limit, whether there are actual line borders on the final sheets or not.)

Whether or not borders are used, what sheets get title blocks (and/or borders), titles, and final sheet numbers? The rule is that the unique information—the variables—is identified with final drawing titles. A structural overlay sheet, for example, might be identified as Structural Framing Plan, S-1, and identified as such right on the overlay itself. An electrical overlay, a plumbing plan, and so on, are titled the same way whenever that unique overlay is to be used only once and not in combination with other overlays.

The reason is clear when you consider the alternative. If, on a base sheet, the architectural background used for structural, electrical, *and* plumbing were to be titled "structural," the title would be useful only for printing with a structural overlay and would have to be removed and changed for use with the electrical and plumbing overlays. The sheet titles and numbers are variables, hence subjects for overlays.

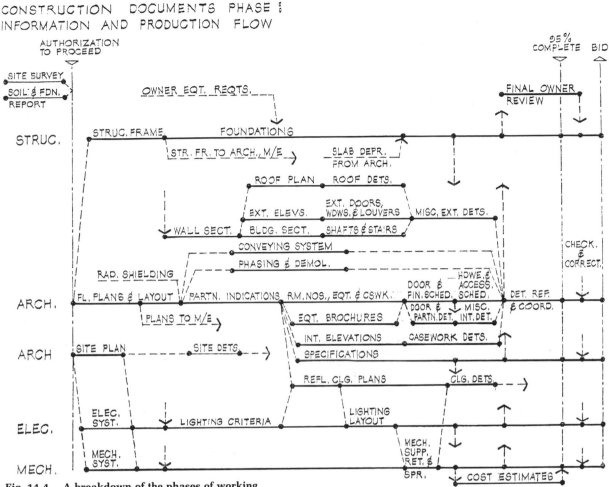

Fig. 14-4. A breakdown of the phases of working drawings for a typical hospital project.

(Spencer Jue, Design Logic.)

Sheet titles and numbers may be unique, but the basic title block is not. It appears in basically the same form on every final drawing. Therefore, it's a constant and the subject for base sheets. That can be handled in one of two ways:

1. The title blocks can be applied as stickybacks onto the base sheet originals with specifics such as sheet title and number left blank. Later, when the image of a base sheet and an overlay sheet are merged in the final overlay composite, the title block and title block data will merge as one image.
2. The title block (and border if one is used) can be created just once on one single base sheet. That will be combined later with all base and overlay composites.

Applying the "constants and variables" principle, it's fairly clear when to stop a drawing as a base sheet and continue it, in varying forms,

as overlays. It's also a matter of need. For example, if you're doing a presentation drawing site plan, you'll stop short of applying the foliage, textures, shadows, and so on, since those are variables for overlay.

Similarly, when thinking ahead for the base sheet information the structural consultant will need, you'll stop short with the exterior walls, structural grid, core (stairs, elevators, service shafts), and major and minor structural elements. Nonstructural partitions, room names, door swings, and architectural notes, symbols, and dimensions won't be on structural drawings, so those are done on an architectural overlay.

There are differing opinions as to whether the structural grid should be drawn once, as a base sheet for multiple uses, or whether it's just as well to draw it separately on each architectural base sheet. It really depends on how many times it would have to be drawn if it's *not* made up as

191

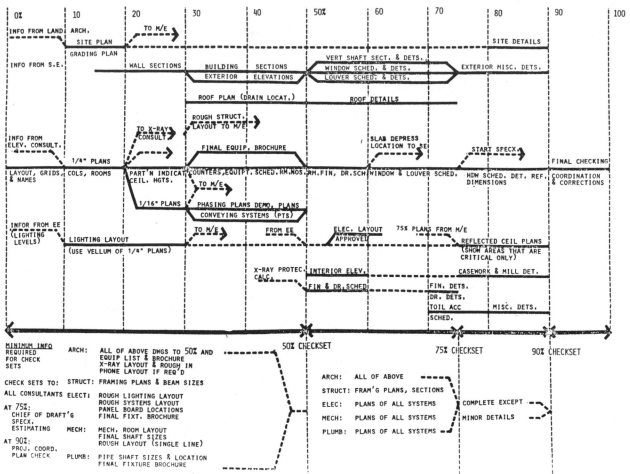

Fig. 14-5. Another example of a working drawing schedule. This one is broken down in 10% completion phases.

a separate base. (A structural grid sheet is usually called a "template sheet.") If there are a large number of differing floor plan base sheets that use the same grid, it will be economical to make it up as a separate base. Otherwise, it's more convenient to have it as an integral part of the floor plan base sheets. Often the question is academic because the architectural working drawing floor plans are continued directly from design development plans which already have the grid included.

The stop point of base sheets to be used for electrical, plumbing, and mechanical drawings goes somewhat beyond what's needed for structural overlays. Generally, such base sheets should stop short of including strictly architectural dimensions, notes, and detail symbols. What's needed mainly are: grid, exterior and interior walls and partitions, room names and numbers, door swings, built-in fixtures and equipment, and changes in floor and ceiling levels.

In particular, base sheets for plumbing con-

sultants should show all relevant fixtures, drinking fountains, floor drains, fire hose cabinets, chases, access panels, and openings in slabs and walls, as well as ceiling plans and data for sprinkler locations.

Electrical consultants will often need reflected ceiling grid and/or plan, relevant built-ins and fixtures, electrical panel locations, electrical closets, vaults, chases, and openings in slabs in walls.

Naturally, much of the above special data will be worked out through interchange with and among the various consultants. Major items of coordination include: floor elevations, slab depressions, raised floors, and curbs with the structural consultant; mechanical openings through slabs and walls plus access with the mechanical consultant; slab slopes, penetrations, slab elevations with the plumbing consultant; and electrical room ventilation, structural slabs, banks, pits, trenches, and special bases with the electrical consultant.

Specific stop points should be worked out and time schedules coordinated with and among all consultants. Many consulting engineers will provide checklists that show the architects exactly what they need and don't need for their reference background or base sheets.

14.4 TRAFFIC CONTROL OF ARCHITECTURAL BASE SHEETS AND OVERLAYS

There are two main trouble spots with architectural base sheets and overlays. They can be avoided by: (1) Stopping the base sheets at the *right moment*, as described in Section 14.3, and (2) preventing people from drawing overlay information on base sheets and putting base sheet data on overlays.

Remember the principle of "constants and variables." The constants within a particular situation are the base sheet information; the variables go on the overlays.

In the case of architectural plans, there's constant construction data that form the background for finished architectural, structural, electrical, plumbing, and HVAC drawings. Those constants are, in the main, the perimeter wall construction, the structural grid, the planning module (if any), and the unvarying core elements (stairs, elevators, chases, mechanical spaces, etc.).

The architectural variables that go on overlays atop a base sheet include: architectural notes, equipment, interior partitions, doors, door and window symbols, detail bubbles, dimensions, and finish schedule keys.

A simple architectural base sheet and overlay combination might just be two parts: base sheet of exterior and interior wall construction and overlay sheet of architectural notes, dimensions, keys, etc.

For larger projects a further breakdown is likely. It may happen that some consultants' base sheets should show different architectural background information. For example, the structural drawings may not require any interior partitions, room identifications, door swings, or equipment locations, but the electrical drawings do. So the architectural background stops with minimal data on Base Sheet S-1 for structural. The architectural background is more comprehensive on base sheets for the electrical consultant and has to include more than is included for structural drawings but not as much as the complete architectural drawings.

In such a job, architectural data are divided into one constant base sheet and two overlays. The base sheet has the exterior walls, grid, and core as needed background for *all* plan

193

drawings. The architectural overlays are divided. One has data such as partitions, door swings, room identifications, and equipment locations, as necessary, for electrical and lighting. The other continues with strictly architectural notes, dimensions, schedule, and detail references.

In later printings, the architectural floor plans will be combinations of the base sheet, the overlay for electrical background, and the overlay for final architectural data—a three-way combination. The structural plans will be the architectural base sheet plus the structural overlay. The electrical plans will be the architectural base sheet plus an added architectural overlay and the final electrical overlay.

Note that the base sheets that will be provided the electrical consultants are a *combination* of a base sheet and overlay printed together as a new, second stage, base sheet. These are called "combination base sheets."

There's no easy way to make this aspect of overlay drafting crystal clear the first time through. It's tough enough getting used to base sheets and overlays, then we start combining base sheets and overlays to make new base sheets! It can be nerve wracking.

It should be clear enough from the foregoing that there will be some confusion if too much or too little information is provided on the base sheets sent to the consultants. That's the first trouble spot.

The second trouble spot noted was that people mix information on base sheets and overlays. This happens often and must be prevented; if it gets out of hand, it will destroy the whole system.

It's important to understand why mixing data is such a threat. At the moment it's done, it will often seem like a convenience or, under tight time pressure, a necessity. There's always a "good" reason for doing it. Let's identify the circumstances in which this happens, and the consequences.

Consider the base sheet and the divided architectural overlays we were just describing. The draftsperson is plugging away and was properly alerted as to when to quit work on the first base sheet. So far so good. Now the first layer of overlay goes on, and he or she draws the partitions, doors, room identifications, and equipment. There is still no problem.

Suddenly there's a break in the routine. The client needs prints showing architectural data in a hurry. Word comes down to get on it and make the drawings look more finished. Right at that

moment it seems easier just to add in some of the architectural data right on the overlay that's on the drafting board, rather than start a whole new sheet.

Some overlay "2" data go onto the overlay "1" sheet, the overlay and base sheets are combined for printing, and the job goes on.

The draftsperson just described has been doing the overlay atop a polyester print of the original architectural base sheet. Meanwhile, someone else has that original base sheet, and in the same rush to get some finished-looking prints to the client is adding overlay information on the base sheet. That draftsperson is adding finish wall construction dimensions around the perimeter, wall section and building section reference bubbles, and window schedule symbols. There's no compelling reason to do these on the base sheet; it's just that the reasons not to aren't clear and, at the moment, it seems easier.

The result is that architectural dimensions and wall section and window symbols are on the original base sheet, which confuses use of that sheet as background for consultants' work. Similar information is on an overlay, and when the original base sheet and overlay are later combined for printing, redundant lettering and notes will overlay and overlap one another and be unreadable. Someone will have to go over one or more of the sheets and sort out the mixed data, that is, take some off one sheet and add it to the other. Much of the economy of doing overlay will be lost in the process.

Sometimes drafting staff have had to make their own decisions without understanding the overall picture. Orders may come down from the top to get something done, but the immediate supervisor isn't available to assign the work according to the job plan. Then several drafting staff may duplicate or contradict each other's work on several overlays simultaneously. If that goes too far, it will be impossible to sort out the mixed data economically and the job will have to revert to traditional procedure.

If you keep in mind that base sheets retain the *constants*, that is, the data that are common and shared by a number of the final prints, and the overlays have the *variables*, that is, the data that are unique to final prints, it should be clear that the final drawing numbers have to go on the unique overlays. That leaves base sheets and sub-overlays without final drawing numbers. They, along with overlays, have to have special markings on them to identify the following:

1. Job
2. Type of sheet: base sheet, overlay sheet, or base and overlay combination
3. Base or overlay code number
4. Drawing progress record (a small grid with spaces to note date, initials of draftsperson, and hours spent in each work period on the drawing)

The job identification, sheet type, and code numbers can be sketched on informally with a non-photo blue pencil. The identification will keep the job sheets properly filed and, most important, avoid laying the base sheets in reverse on the drafting board by mistake.

Base sheets have the above-noted identifying and control information, and so do the overlays. The overlays have, in addition, the final drawing sheet number in position, where it will merge with the title block sheet number slot.

There are several aids for controlling storage of architectural base sheets and overlays. One is the "vertical file." There are variations, but the common aspect is that the vertical file stores the polyester base sheets and overlays vertically and provides easy random access. That means you can open the file and pull what you need immediately, without shuffling through sheets.

Similarly, you can replace a sheet—right in its correct sequential position—just as easily as placing it out of sequence. (On larger jobs it also helps to have someone available part-time just to keep track of all the sheets and keep the files updated and organized. This saves lots of time for high-priced drafting staff.)

The most popular vertical storage method as of this writing includes a "hanging strip" which goes on the binding margin of the sheets. This has space for job identification and other identifying code data to keep the sheets clearly differentiated.

Speaking of differentiation, both architectural and consulting staff need to be aware of the difference between original base sheets or combination base sheets and the background prints of base sheets. Most of what are called "base sheets," the sheets that go on the drafting boards under the overlays, are actually prints rather than the original drawings. These are one-to-one same-size reproductions and are called "slicks" (because they're usually not supposed to have a draftable surface). They're also called "throwaways." After they're used as reference base sheets, they're tossed out. (Final printing will merge the original overlays with the original base sheets.)

To clarify that difference, we'll call the base sheet prints that are used as reference for drafting staff "reference base sheets." Original composited or drawn base sheets we'll call just that, "original base sheets."

Another aid for controlling architectural base sheets and overlays is the wall-chart storyboard. Some offices do a miniature version of their working drawing mock-up set—just little cards on a wallboard. It's all laid out: base sheets and overlays in a large matrix with identifying labels and schedule deadlines. People in the firm can see vividly where the individual drawings they're working on actually fit within the total context of the job. Some firms augment this kind of a job storyboard by adding red dots or gold stars when sheets are finished. This gives people a sense of progress in what otherwise can be a confusing and frustrating process.

Here is a final note for this section: Planning and supervision have to be unusually thorough in this kind of work. It's brisk in pace, and there are lots of forks in the road. They come up fast, so you have to have most of your decisions made in advance of need.

14.5 TRAFFIC CONTROL OF CONSULTANTS' BASE SHEETS AND OVERLAYS

At *Guidelines* we always take a moderate approach to controversial subjects. Logic and common sense are the great persuaders, after all. With that in mind, it doesn't strain moderation to point out that having engineers' drafting staff trace or redraw architectural plans for their background drawings is just plain raving lunacy. Of course there are reasons for it, but it's still lunacy.

It's a mixed picture. Some consultants are dead set against overlay and refuse to do it. Others love it and complain that the architects they deal with are stick-in-the-muds. Some hear rumors that architects want to cut fees in exchange for doing much of their drafting for them. Such rumors cause violent resistance. Others jump at the chance to eliminate the indefensible waste of time and money of traditional procedures.

Eventually all consultants will come into a new alignment and will be able, if not 100% willing, to handle overlay jobs. But it will remain the architects' responsibility to avoid major blunders and to keep drafting and printing costs under control.

The first rule to assure economy and coherence in consultants' work is, naturally enough, planning. It's not a bad idea to share the preliminary indexing and mocking up of the whole job with consultants. When the planning is completed, consultants should have their copies for their in-house supervisory control of the process.

There may be a training session required for consultants' staff. They need to "walk through" the process. It will help for them to see previously completed base sheets and overlays and grasp how others have done it before they confront them on their own drafting boards.

If consultants aren't used to polyester drafting, they'll need some instruction (see Chapter 5). If consultants' drafting staff don't letter large and clear, they will need some instruction in that. That will be the toughest new rule to enforce.

Some problems can be prevented by not allowing the consultants' drafting staff to have a choice. For example, the base sheet prints that the architect provides *should, in most instances, be clear, nonmatte surface, film reproducibles that are not erasable and not draftable.*

If the architectural backgrounds aren't erasable and draftable, there will be no problem about architects' control. No architectural changes will be made within the consultants' drafting rooms.

Providing nonerasable, nondraftable slicks to the engineers is an excellent safety measure. (Many readers will ignore the advice, to their later regret.) It raises an obvious question: If consultants can't change the base sheets in their possession, how are such changes made? There will be revisions along the way in architectural work. There will be updated prints from the architect, and consultants' staffs will be scrambling around to sort the relevant from the irrelevant revisions. This is the same as always, but with a difference. In the past (and today too in some sad instances) architects would submit updated architectural prints of plans *and not show what changes had been made since the last set was sent.* The architects maintained that it was the consultants' responsibility to discover the changes and incorporate them. Thus did we have many undiscovered changes, conflicts and wildly strange interferences such as light fixtures inside of warm-air ducts, and plumbing stub-ups for rooms that no longer existed.

Even if an architectural office exhibits a degree of sophistication and cooperation so that it will actually show where revisions occur on updated prints, there's still an improvement possible with overlay.

No one wants to replace the original slicks unless absolutely necessary. If there are very many and very severe changes in the architectural plans, there may be no sensible alternative but to reprint the slicks and replace the old ones. But that really should be the exception.

Most architectural changes are likely to be slight: a shift in a partition, a change in some wall construction, or an enlargement of a mechanical space. Most of these revisions can be handled just by indications on updated check prints. If the change is a little more substantial—and this admittedly gets "iffy" in judgment—then the change can be indicated by a printed partial-plan segment (blue-line diazo print or an office-copier print). Multiples of the plan segment, or directions to make copies, can be sent over, and the segments can be distributed to drafting staff to slip underneath their base sheets.

Make your terminology about base sheets clear because there's room for mix-ups. For example, you'll most likely want to use sepia reproducibles as the slick throwaway base sheets. The sepia reproducibles are desirable because of the color contrast—they clearly designate themselves as the architectural bases. But, although they're "reproducibles," that's not their primary role, especially in final printings. They *can* be used as reproducibles but for check-printing purposes only. The draftsperson can pull the overlay tracing and the base sheet, tape them at the top so that they remain in register, and make a diazo print.

Diazo prints run this way in the rotary printer will be a little out of register. If run on a flatbed, they can be linked with a pin bar, matched one-to-one when exposed to light, and should be in perfect registration.

Many offices have used rubber pins to link the sheets together in register in intermediate printings in the regular diazo printers. Others say a little tape on the top edge does just as good a job and does it more conveniently.

Who pays the added cost of these sepia base sheets? In general, and this is likely to become the rule, the architect charges the consultant some reasonable price for the bases. The architect can compute drafting time on tracing the architectural backgrounds and offer to split that cost. At the same time the architect may have to refuse to pay for such drafting by the consultant except for straight hourly wages.

Another way, a clever cost saver devised by an Arizona architect, is this: Ask the consultant to bid on doing his or her drawings including the whole drafting operation in the traditional approach. Ask for an alternate bid just for doing preliminary design and calculations, and then check-printing the architect's drawings of engineering work. In other words, the consultant would do normal basic engineering, but the architect would provide the drafting staff. Architects often make out very well doing engineering drafting, especially with Systems Drafting.

Here are a couple of further pointers on control of consultants' base sheets and overlays:

When base sheets are replaced, insist that all be returned to the architect. That helps prevent discards from creeping back onto the drafting board and misleading drafting staff with obsolete information.

The final printing will feature consultants' information as hard-line drawing on a screened architectural shadow print background. The screening does not have to be done for interim submittal prints or check prints, nor should one expect to find screened polyester sepia prints on the drafting boards as base sheets. This will be obvious to many readers, but the confusion has arisen often enough that it's worth a warning.

14.6 TRAFFIC CONTROL OF INTERMEDIATE PRINTING: CHECK PRINTS AND PROGRESS PRINTS

In-between time submittals of prints are a bother under the best of circumstances. Some drafting has to be rushed before printing and, during printing, you may as well send the drafting team home. It's down time, pure and simple.

The bother is compounded with overlay drafting. There are more sheets to assemble, and the printing process is more complex and time-consuming. This is a nuisance, but this section will deal with ways to keep the nuisance to a minimum.

The first goal in making a set of diazo check or progress prints is to get a complete set of reproducibles. With composite and overlay drafted sheets, you don't make prints directly from the originals. Most readers will perceive this by now and know that in Systems Drafting most check prints, bidding prints, and construction prints are all made from reproducibles rather than original drawings. It's a departure from tradition, not a radical departure, but enough to cause confusion.

How do you get the reproducibles? Therein lies the first opportunity for blunder. There are simple ways, and there are complicated ways. The challenge is to find the simplest way that will match the circumstances at hand. One way which is definitely *not* the simplest is photoblowback.

True enough, some brochures from the reprographic industry will show people sending all work to the repro shop at the drop of a hat. Want a check print? Sure. Send the base sheets and overlays down to the shop. They'll photograph them onto 8½" × 11" negatives (or full-size negatives at some shops), then blow the images back onto photo washoff reproducible media and make your prints for you. What's wrong with that? Nothing, except that it's the most costly way to go. "You want the best quality, don't you?" asks the repro manager. There's no arguing that photoblowback will give you the finest quality. The question is, do you want first-rate prints for plain old check printing? In most cases, ab-

solutely not. Not when it's four to ten times more expensive and takes twice as long.

Here are your other options. Choose the one that matches the circumstances:

1. Expose the base and overlay combinations to photo washoff media in a vacuum-frame contact printer at the repro shop. This will normally be somewhat less expensive than photoblowback. Because of even less expensive alternate methods, this one is becoming obsolete.

2. Expose base and overlay sheet combinations to diazo-reproducible media in a vacuum-frame contact printer. This is the far likelier method. Diazo media are less expensive materials and less expensive to handle than photographic media. The repro shop can do this, or you can do it in-house with a flatbed printer. Since you can use the pin bar right on the contact printer and since the operation is flat (nonmoving), you'll get perfect one-to-one size fidelity and should expect perfect registration.

3. If prints don't have to be exact, just run the combination base sheets and overlays—taped at their top edge—together through the rotary diazo machine. They'll be slightly out of register and a bit fuzzy. If you're only doing a few prints, you can skip making a reproducible and, as an exception to the general rule, just run final reference prints directly from the originals.

If you need quick check prints of translucent paste-up sheets, you can run them by just laying a thin, clear polyester film over the paste-up carrying sheet and run the works through the rotary diazo printer. You can make a diazo reproducible that way for more extensive printing or, for a few diazo paper prints, just rerun the covered and protected original. The clear film cover will keep the taped-on units in place. Make sure that units are not taped on the carrying sheet in such a way as to pop up under the pressure of the diazo rollers. Top taping is the general rule for elements on a carrying sheet.

That kind of rough printing of composited paste-ups and appliques will probably allow various ghost shadows, tape marks, and so on, to show through on the prints. That's no problem for checking. Final prints at the end of the job will be given a longer exposure to burn out such marks. Incidentally, in making sepia reproducible polyester prints, some ghosting that appears on the reproducible will not print through on the later diazo paper prints.

Those are your main options in making interim prints: camera photo, contact photo, contact diazo, and regular diazo, in descending order of cost and trouble.

Now, we will discuss some of those related problems, like down time for the drafting staff.

Unless your repro shop is close by and in need of work, you'll probably do interim printings much faster in-house. In that case you can put print-room personnel on overtime to handle the peak loads; that is you can have them do the interim printings after hours or, if it's a large batch, over a weekend. Generally, that's been the most convenient solution to the problem of staff down time.

Many consulting engineers have in-house flatbed exposure units of their own now and can do check prints of their work for you without drastically disrupting their staff. Since most consultants' work will be overlays over constant base sheets, it's mainly a matter of placing one base sheet on a pin bar on the flatbed contact printer and laying one overlay after another on the base for each reproducible print. Then the originals go back to the drafting boards as the reproducibles go off for reprinting of diazo paper prints. Again, if only one or two sets of check prints are needed, the reproducible can be dispensed with and the paper diazos can be made directly on the flatbed.

Refinements such as screened shadow print background of architectural data aren't necessary in check printing, but you can approximate the effect if you like. That just requires stacking overlays and base sheet in sequence away from the print medium on the flatbed exposing unit. The sheet furthest away from the print will be most subdued in the final printing. Or, if there's only one overlay and there won't be any noticeable subduing effect from accumulated overlays, you can add in a sheet of thin tracing paper or a matte polyester between the overlay and the architectural base sheet. That will subdue the image of the base sheet on the final print—ghost it out so the consultants' overlay data will stand out in hard-line contrast.

The main question remaining is: How do you instruct printing personnel as to which overlays are printed with which base sheets? And how do you make it comparatively foolproof?

The main tools of printing control are:

Matrix charts. (Sometimes these are made as print order forms.)
Miniature mock-ups that show the relationships of bases and overlays.
Print control "boxes" as stickers or preprinted grids on base and overlay sheets. (These take some study to grasp but, once grasped, are an effective control device.)

These are all also used to control printing final bid and construction sets of drawings, so we'll review them in the next section of this chapter.

14.7 TRAFFIC CONTROL OF FINAL PRINTING

The first tool of printing control is the "print matrix." This is a chart that lists the base sheets and overlays and shows their printing relationships. It can be wall size or 8½″ × 11″. It will show what base sheets will be screened, and how much. If the job will be "half-size" offset-printed and/or color-printed, it will include indications for those instructions too.

A commonly used print matrix lists the final drawings—the combined image that will be on the reproducibles—along one side of the chart. These include final drawing sheet numbers, and they're grouped by divisions and/or according to the architectural, structural, plumbing, mechanical, and electrical disciplines.

Across the top of the matrix is a list of base sheets and overlays; these are listed by title and by base or overlay code number. There will be points of intersection—marked by checks, dots, circles—spotted below each final drawing title. These show the base and overlay sheets that will be combined to make up that final reproducible sheet.

This kind of matrix can be confusing at first because it doesn't work in quite the way most people expect. A normal expectation is that the matrix would list base sheets along one column and overlays along the other. Then the intersection points would be the final combinations—the final sheets. This is not so. This matrix mixes bases and overlays in one column, so the way you identify what units are combined in final printing is to look for *all* those included in a single row next to the final drawing sheet title. The illustrated matrix will make this clear.

Other matrix constructions are possible, of course. The sample shown here illustrates the basic principle. Adapt it any way you like.

When you're planning a job, you start with index and base sheet and overlay breakdown lists as described earlier in this chapter. As the lists firm up and the mock-up is completed, you'll have the basic data you need to make the matrix.

The matrix can be used as a drafting guide, but it's usually used to guide printing processes. So it might not be necessary to do one until you're into the job awhile. However, most planners will do one at the outset to budget final printing costs. This is especially valuable if the economics of going overlay are in doubt. It will

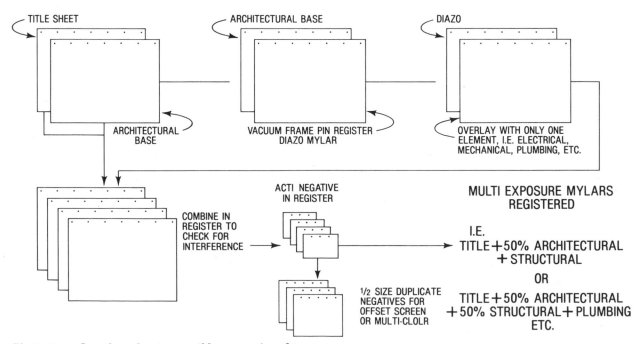

Fig. 14-6. A flow chart showing possible sequencing of overlay drawing and printing.

(San Francisco Blue Print Service Co. and Mini-Max.)

show you how many reproducibles you have to make. It will also show how many negatives and blowbacks you need if you go that route in the final printing.

The matrix is a good general guide as to what goes with what in printing overlays. As a backup, many firms use a "control box" or sticker system which visually double-checks whether the base and overlay sheet combinations are correct.

SHEET TITLE	NUMBER	BORDER	COVER SIGN	COVER BASE	B-2	B-4	B-4-A	B-8	B-01	B-02A	B-02B	B-0-3
COVER SHEET			/	30								
GEN. SITE PLAN	2											
GRADING PLAN	3							30				30
PLUMBING PLOT P.	4							30				30
LANDSCAPE IRRIG.	5							30				30
FLOOR PLAN	6					50				30		
DIMENSION FLOOR P.	7									30		
FIRST FLOOR FRM.	8				30							
ROOF PLAN	9				30							
SECTION/DETAILS	10											
REF. CLG. PLAN	11				30							
PLUMBG PLAN	12				30							
H.V.A.C SECTION	13											
LIGHT'G PLAN	14				30	30				30		
POWER PLAN	15				30	30				30		

Fig. 14-7. A somewhat different version of the overlay drafting printing matrix. The *30* and *50* in the chart refer to the percentage of screening of base sheets.

(Octagon Associates.)

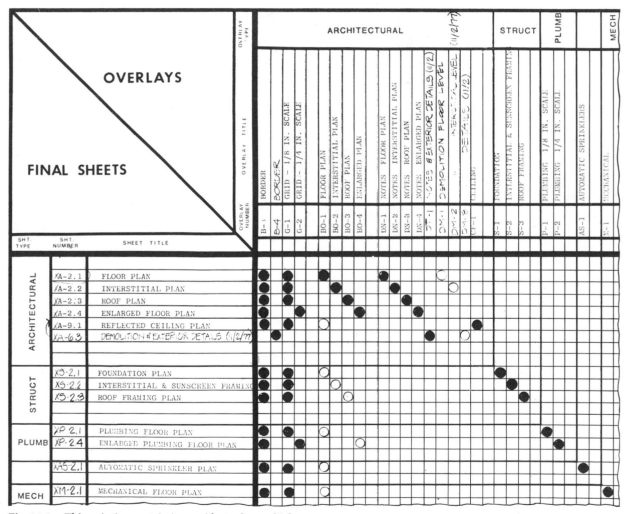

Fig. 14-8. This printing matrix is a guide to show which base sheets and overlays are combined for interim and/ or final printing.

(Mini-Max.)

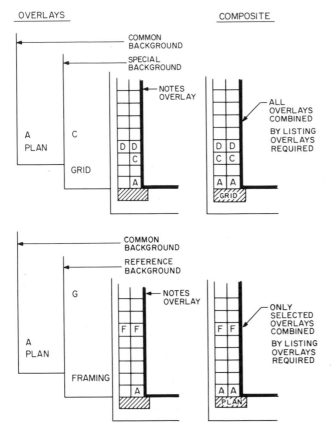

Fig. 14-9. Another kind of printing guide that shows when the correct base and overlay sheets have been combined for a final print.

14.8 EXTENDED USES AND ADVANTAGES OF SYSTEMS DRAFTING

When planning for composite and overlay drafting, plan especially to exploit the extended uses and advantages of both systems. Most of these extended uses and advantages come from two aspects of composite and overlay:

1. The originals are composites of ink drawing, printed applique, or done as dense-line diazo copies or photo copies. This opaque line work is suitable to photographic reproduction and multigeneration reproduction. Graphite drawing on paper is *not* best suited for photoreproduction or multigeneration reproduction.

2. Both composite and overlay drafting technology make it very convenient to sort out, separate, and relocate graphic information for special uses.

Here are special advantages and new applications that now come easily:

You don't have to start from scratch to create solid-line graphics suitable for reproduction when making submittals for awards programs, newspaper publicity, or entries in the professional journals. "Camera-ready" graphics are already prepared and ready for reuse.

Special project brochures for client presentations are comparatively easy to produce, directly from design development drawings. New additions to regular office brochures are easier, as are any real estate and/or tenant brochures you might create for a completed project.

It's not nearly as much a sacrifice in time and cost to enter competitions. The design process is greatly speeded with repro techniques because elements are "moved around" instead of erased and redrawn, and repetitive elements are drawn only once. Instead of having to be redrawn, final "schematics" can be made to be directly usable for presentation drawings.

Normal design processes are speeded up, as cited above, allowing more time for testing options and for checking through the validity of initial design assumptions and decisions.

When there are options such as possible variations in plans, site work, and/or exterior elevations, they're most conveniently handled as base sheets and overlays. This expedites the creative process by avoiding redrawing of constant "base" data. It also simplifies the presentation process when options have to be reviewed with clients or agencies.

Base sheet and overlay techniques expedite the creation of furniture or equipment plans. Furniture and equipment can be assembled as composites or appliques on transparent overlays. That leaves the original plans clean and ready for revisions and transformation into working drawings. Later, the same, albeit modified, furniture overlays can be used to guide the electrical consultant in locating fixtures and to show the phone company where to locate its equipment. The client will also use such layouts in purchasing and positioning the actual furnishings.

Overlay can expedite building renovations and restorations. If old drawings or prints of original construction are available, clean them up and print them on polyester as new base sheets. Then do new construction and alterations on overlays. Later you can combine the images of base and overlays in contrasting tones or colors. Incidentally, even if existing construction has to be measured and drawn from scratch, it's still advantageous to do "measure" drawings of existing conditions as base sheets and to do all new work on overlays. It's advantageous because existing work doesn't have to be drawn once for design development and redrawn for production drawings. Additionally, it eliminates the need to erase existing work or take extra effort to differentiate new work from previous work. Differentiation is taken care of in the printing process, which will show new work in hard line and existing work as screened "shadow print."

You can create special prints for regulatory or special interest agencies, emphasizing the portions of work they're most concerned with. Fire inspector checkers, for example, can work on prints in which all work is screened and subdued except for the corridors, fire exits, building zones, fire-wall construction, and so on, that they're particularly interested in.

Special "reference prints" expedite checking and coordination among consultants. Besides being able to lay translucent polyester base and overlay sheets in many combinations to find interferences, you can also make diazo prints for the same purpose. Using techniques described in Section 14.6, you can print combinations of structural, mechanical, and plumbing plans—some screened, some not—to identify potential conflicts.

"Reference prints" also help the bidders and greatly aid coordination among building trades. A reference print of just the electrical overlay, for example, makes it easy to pick out and count switches, outlets, and fixtures. Take-offs of just plumbing or mechanical plans, equipment, etc., are all comparatively easier when a quantity surveyor has access to prints of just the overlay drawings.

Reference prints such as those used to help consultants avoid interferences have the same function with subcontractors. A New York City architectural firm introduced this idea some time ago and says they've cut way back on job-site conflicts and union jurisdiction problems by using what they call "reference coordination drawings."

Many shop drawings can be done on copies of base sheets. That lets fabricators' drafting staffs avoid some drawing, which, in turn, helps avoid errors of translation and keeps things moving along.

Overlay drafting simplifies making "as-built" drawings. First, during construction, deviations from the original drawings are noted on check prints. Later, the deviations are recorded on base sheets and/or overlay reproducibles.

A new concept emerges: "living documents" for clients. Some clients require more drawing after construction than for the initial project. This is the case for buildings subject to continuous changes after construction: new offices, laboratory alterations, etc. These entail attendant changes in electrical and mechanical systems. That kind of work is tedious and error-prone when done by traditional drafting methods. But composite and overlay techniques simplify it: Existing conditions are on base sheets; design and as-builts of alterations are done on overlays. These new kinds of composite and overlay drawings of ongoing as-builts and building changes are called "living documents." The capability of providing living documents is a strong marketing point for certain types of clients who face major ongoing building alterations.

You can ease the way for expansions of or additions to a project. If a client decides to add another floor to the building, or a wing, or duplicate a building elsewhere on a site, it's often a windfall for the designer. The windfall is augmented with composite and overlay because redrawing of any previous elements, or removal and change of details and titles, is simplified. You can prepare new documents for the new situation with virtually no drafting, erasing, or eradicating. It can be done just by shifting composite elements or recombining bases and overlays.

A related convenience is that overlay drafting simplifies foreign language translations for overseas work. In one case original base sheets were drawn without notation, overlays were done in English, another notation overlay was translated into Korean for the contractor, and still another was done in Arabic for the client.

Special after-job graphics are easy, such as building floor plans for elevator lobbies and orientation maps for a multibuilding site. These graphics, normally redrawn from scratch, can be lifted directly from hard-line architectural base sheets for photoreduction and color printing.

14.9 SYNTHESIS

These chapter closings are titled ''synthesis'' because they're designed to pull things together and remind you of how the content of a major chapter relates to the content of preceding and subsequent chapters.

The Synthesis sections are also reminders of the basic pattern of this book: *the five stages of transition to Systems Drafting.*

We're now just about at stage 5. That's where all the subsystems come together as modular parts of the big system we call Systems Drafting.

Synthesis—integration—has been the name of the game all the way through this text. Every item is introduced in the same sequence that you would ideally use in office practice. Of course, all offices are in a mixed situation, and most will run ahead with one technique and hold back on others somewhat out of phase with what we might see as most logical. This doesn't matter, so long as *in general* the materials, equipment, and techniques are integrated and are introduced so as to augment and enhance one another. The more you do this, the more you make subsequent steps easier and ensure that each subsequent step adds to the value of your previous ones.

We've covered the basic integrations, such as simplifying the graphics to make photo reprographics more readable and easier to do. And we've seen how to integrate standard details, typewriting, appliques, ink, polyester, and so forth.

We also covered some of the larger integrations, such as creating a continuum of design development via construction drawings throughout the life of a new building, in the form of living documents. We showed how management reforms are essential to systems and how systems add new demands, and rewards, to management.

We haven't dealt with financial management. There are many other sources, including *The Guidelines Letter,* to keep you up to date on that. For now, let's just say that financial management and Systems Drafting can and should support and augment one another in any design firm.

The final integration goes well beyond office practice. All the techniques and systems have value only as means to an end. The end is well-designed environments: buildings that support, nurture, and enrich human existence. People are desperate for logic and beauty. Good and great environments provide reminders and stimulation of these positive values. I'm convinced that we'll be seeing more of such environments, thanks partly to the integrative techniques described in this book.

14.10 EXERCISES

1. Prepare a standard, reusable, mini–working drawing mock-up suitable for future use on a building type you're likely to do often. Follow these steps:
   a. Start a plan for the standard mock-up by making a preliminary master list of the types of drawings that are normally done for the building type you've chosen. (This can be a very general list that would apply to most building types, if you prefer.)
   b. On your preliminary drawing list, note the elements that would normally go onto the drawings you've listed.
   c. Plan how you could make maximum use of composite and overlay drafting in preparing the final standard mini-working drawing mock-up. For example, could you prepare schematic elements labeled "details," "schedules," "plan," "wall sections," etc., that could be copied in quantity and taped onto master mock-up sheets? List, and try, other Systems Drafting methods that would expedite the mock-up job-planning process.

2. Do a mini-working drawing mock-up of your next final design development drawings. Because not many drawings will be involved, you may prefer to sketch this out on a single sheet that shows the relationship of all the final drawings. Make a checklist of all elements in final design or presentation drawings that could be done using typing, appliques, photodrafting, and composite drafting. Make a checklist of all the elements that could be created using overlay drafting.

3. In reference to the preceding checklists, create a list of graphic elements that are likely to be reused in various future design development or presentation drawings. What titles could be filed as standards? What rendering entourage could be filed for later reuse?

4. Review the relationship of office financial management to Systems Drafting. Are fees charged in a manner that encourages efficiency and the use of new equipment and techniques? Does your contract provide properly for the higher reimbursable expenses that occur when using reprographic systems?

15

"HALF-SIZE," OFFSET, AND MULTICOLOR PRINTING

15.1 WHY "HALF SIZE" HASN'T WORKED

Offices have attempted to print working drawings at half their normal sheet size, from 34″ × 44″ to 17″ × 22″, for example. Many retreated when clients, building departments, and/or contractors rejected the small size.

The intent was good: Half-size prints are far more convenient on the job, and less expensive to print. But, in the case of the rejects, there was one fundamental problem: The original drawings were not drawn properly for half-size reduction. For example, most drafting lettering is too small to begin with. When you reduce that by half, you have lettering that is "twice" too small and totally unreadable. (See Section 3.3 for correct drafting and lettering standards.)

The secret to it is this: Half-size final prints are actually *full size*. You're just preparing originals that are *double size* to get your final full-size result. If you work from that standpoint—of doing double-size drawings if you're going to photoreduce to half size—you'll create the oversized lettering (⅛″ high minimum), patterns, symbols, dimensions, arrowheads, and so on, that you need for final readability. And, if the final size is the "real" size, then the scale you indicate on your originals should be the scale of the final drawing people will be reading.

Here are some selling points, some important advantages of half-size working drawings, to consider:

1. They're convenient to handle and read, much more so than traditional, tabletop-size drawings.

2. They're economical to mail or ship. This advantage is doubled when sets are offset-printed on both sides of each sheet, like a book. If the original drawing sheet is 24″ × 36″ and halved to 12″ × 18″, and if the original number of individual sheets is halved from, say, 100 to 50, by printing each sheet back to back, there are obvious substantial savings in handling costs.

3. They're inexpensive to print. Diazo printing is cheaper at half size, since such work is usually charged by the square foot. In large quantities, you can print multicolor with offset at lower cost than plain, full-size, single-color diazo.

4. Smaller, lower-cost working drawing sets permit the distribution of full sets to subcontractors. Subs are often stuck with portions of drawings that pertain directly to their trades. This prevents them from gaining an overview and causes worry about unexpected contingencies. Bids are reportedly lower from subs who get complete sets of drawings.

5. Small-size drawing sets are like construction handbooks. Since they're convenient and readily available, they're widely used by tradespeople on the job site, thus speeding up the construction process.

Here's a final thought on half size. Just because the first half-size prints were made from photoreductions of full-size originals doesn't mean that everyone has to follow along doing the same two-step process. Some offices that are sold on the smaller drawing sizes have had a "bright-flash" revelation: If the final prints will be reduced size, *why not just draw the originals that size to begin with?*

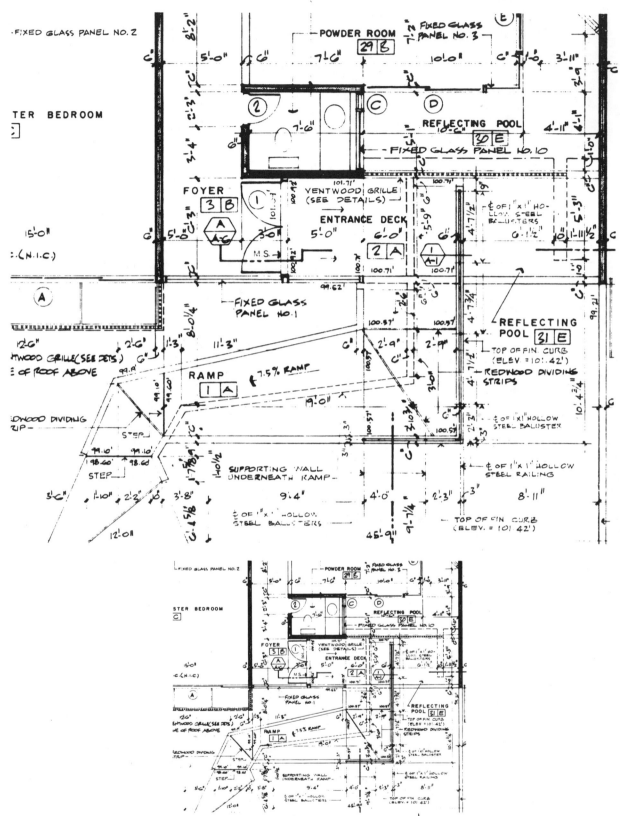

Fig. 15-1. When lettering is not made consistent and large, it becomes virtually unreadable in half-size reduction.

(Guidelines.)

15.2 THE "OFFSET" OPTION

Most printing in the world is done by offset. This book is offset-printed, for example, as are the magazines you read and your daily newspaper. You can use the same printing process for your working drawings.

Working drawing offset is economical in larger print quantities. The general rule is that if you're printing 100 or more sets of drawings, the offset-printing cost will be about the same as regular diazo printing. Even multicolor is competitive with diazo at that quantity. But there may be a time delay that makes color printing impractical. The cost and time situation varies considerably from shop to shop and community to community. You will have to check out your local situation.

The following is a list of the main advantages of offset and multicolor printing of working drawings. If these look good to you, read on for more data on how it all works.

1. Clarity is the most obvious advantage. Crisp blacks on white background, contrasting with gray "shadow" printing, create very readable contrasts. Red, blue, and green lines showing the work of various trades provide clear delineation of graphic data. Similarly, if dimension lines and notation are done in color, then the notes stand out vividly and there is no confusing the dimension lines with construction lines.

2. Offset prints don't fade as diazo prints do. They're more readable to begin with, and they stay that way. Offset prints come out at exact size. You don't get the scale-distorting paper stretch common to the diazo-print process.

3. Offset printing can lead to major changes in the way you organize production documents. For example, *you can print on both sides of a sheet.* Working drawings become booklike, with left- and right-hand pages. One leading office prints each primary sheet, such as floor plan, on the right-hand page. Then supporting data, such as schedules, details and notes, that go with that plan are beside it on the left-hand page. Matching up left- and right-hand sheets solves a problem that comes up with small-size drawings: It helps assure there's enough space for all the data.

4. Back-to-back printing raises another opportunity. Many architects have wanted to print specifications on the drawing sheets, each section with the appropriate drawing or drawings. But there's been a space problem. The formerly blank "backs" of sheets provide more than enough added space. These specifications are usually typed on standard 8½" × 11" sheets and pasted up to full working drawing sheet size. Photographs of fixtures and products can also be included with the paste-ups of specs and schedules.

5. Working drawings can be offset-printed on colored paper. Black printing on yellow paper improves readability, for example, because of the vivid contrast. Consultants' drawings can be differentiated by being printed on different hues of paper. Colored sets of drawings attract attention, and this has been used to gain a little speedier checking by regulatory agencies. (A good basic paper for offset printing is white "60 pound book." You can also offset-print onto tracing paper as a means of making archival copies that can be reproduced later on diazo.)

6. Multicolor working drawings look great. They put ordinary prints to shame in terms of quality appearance. They look better than some offices' glossy brochures.

To gain full advantage of black and white or multicolor offset printing, you have to use overlay drafting. If you're already using overlay, it's a short step to go to offset.

Before describing the offset process, let's clear up a possible misunderstanding. To get multicolor separations, you do *not* have to draw originals in color. More experienced people will find that cautionary note laughable, but it's a pretty common notion.

To clarify it all, here's a rundown on the offset process: If you've printed an office brochure, you undoubtedly used offset. Offset starts with photography of original drawings or paste-ups. Photonegatives are used to transfer the images onto light-sensitive printing plates—usually thin sheets of aluminum. The printing plate is mounted on a large roller on the offset printing press. When printing, the exposed image on the plate picks up ink and passes it to a rotating rubber mat. The mat, with its inked image from the plate, presses the ink onto each sheet of paper that passes through the machine.

The image is said to "off set" from plate to paper, hence the term "offset." Other words that basically mean the same as offset are "multilith" and "multigraph."

The overlays used in overlay drafting are essential to multicolor offset printing. For example, suppose you want to show site electrical work in blue on a screened-background architectural site plan. Two plates will be made: one of the site plan and another of the electrical consultant's site-plan overlay drawing. The site-plan plate is printed first, and the sheets are put aside to dry. Later, the remaining black ink in the press is removed and replaced with blue ink. The electrical overlay plate is mounted, and the site-plan prints are run through the printing machine again. Any number of such "overprints" can be made in any number of colors.

Registration of the printing is everything. The printer has to match up the plates precisely to assure perfect alignment of the multiple-color images. Slight shifts during the printing process can knock the images out of registration. You've seen this occasionally in color newspaper or magazine ads.

Offset printing adds another facet to the job-planning process. If you're not experienced with offset printing, it's probably best to stick to black and white the first time through. And take your time shopping for a good offset printer: There are wide spreads in both cost and quality.

You'll have to instruct your printer about color overlays with the matrix or "sticker" described in the last chapter. You won't be concerned about such instructions during interim printings, so it's no great new complexity to add to the job-planning and management process.

For further details on photoprocesses, plate making, screening, and other information on offset, see Chapter 16 and the Glossary.

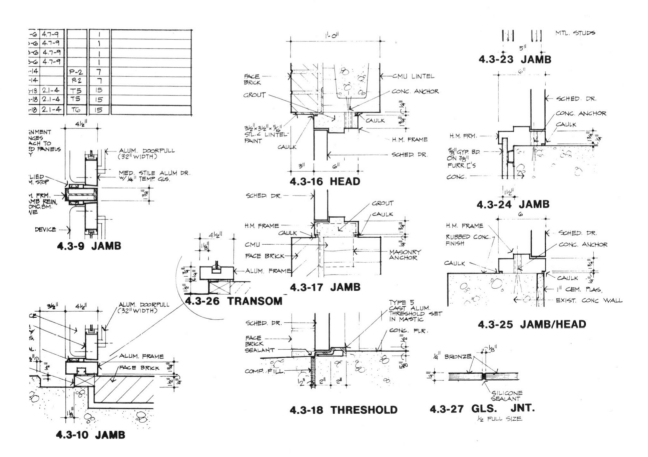

Fig. 15-2. Diazo prints tend to gray out. This sample working drawing shows the sharp black and white contrast that is possible with offset printing.

(Jarvis Putty Jarvis.)

ESSENTIALS
OF REPROGRAPHICS

16.1 GETTING THE MOST FROM A REPRO SHOP

In my lectures and workshops I emphasize the values of creating an in-house reprographic setup. Some people in the repro industry resent that and feel that I'm encouraging architects and engineers to bypass professional repro services. The truth is, I'm encouraging both use of in-house facilities *and* greater use of outside repro services. The more offices use systems, the more they will need a diversity of repro services that they never even considered using before.

Here's something we published in *The Guidelines Letter* in 1976. It illuminates some of the differences between the limited tracing paper and diazo printing sequence and the new reprographic approach:

"Professional graphic artists wouldn't dream of fooling around the way drafting employees are compelled to. When they revise a layout, they don't erase and redraw; they paste new data over the old. If an element is repeated, they photograph it, print it larger, smaller, reversed—modified in any way they want. But they don't redraw it.

"Working drawing production procedures are drastically limited by the requirements of drawing for diazo printing. The medium is limited, has to be translucent. Drawing materials are limited to those compatible with the printing process. Potentially timesaving appliques or paste-ups require excessive care and often print badly anyway.

"When the architect starts thinking in terms of opaque drafting media, photocopying and offset printing, a new world of flexibility and timesaving opportunities starts to open up."

The term "Systems Drafting" is something of a misnomer, since we're trying to get rid of "drafting." Similarly, the word "blueprinter" is obsolete. But we'll probably keep using it for years after the last blueprint is ever printed.

A substitute term for blueprinter is "reprographic specialist." With their extensive involvement in implementing Systems Drafting and the other varied services repro shops now offer, "specialist" is a pretty fair description.

Their new, higher professional status hasn't made repro specialists any more popular among architects and engineers. The main things I hear when the subject comes up are items about how some repro shop insisted on using photoblowback instead of the less expensive contact printing method of making base sheets, or about the shop that refused to sell an architect a reproducible polyester material in order to block the architect from doing in-house work, or about the costs, turnaround time, and confusion over printing instructions.

I've seen it both ways. I know architects and engineers who dump mountains of work on repro shops with no warning and then demand an impossible deadline. I've seen original paste-up combinations of onionskin paper with 6-H lead drawing adjacent to a blurred photocopy print with some inked-in notes—an absolute horror—and the designer demands a presentation quality reproduction. And I've seen some incompetent and/or dishonest print shop managers.

211

The rules are simple for getting the best repro work. Know enough about repro processes to give clear instructions and to know whether the shop is working honestly and competently for you or not; and treat the repro shop manager as a consultant. Visit the repro shop or shops you use. Have staff visit them on noontime tours. Ask the manager for tips on the best ways to prepare work for reproduction. Work out the best times to send in your work, and make appointments as soon as you know when a job will be ready. If the shop can store some of your prints and if it's convenient for them, arrange to preprint completed portions of a job instead of waiting until the last minute and unloading everything you have at once.

You aren't limited to blueprint companies. Some architects and engineers hire small newspaper printing companies for repro work. Many large industrial engineering firms have complete in-house facilities that take in outside work. Graphic art studios, letter shops, and quick-print offset printing or platemaking shops may have facilities that will do the kind of repro work described in this chapter.

If you don't have a shop lined up for such work, take the opportunity to visit a few. Lunchtime tours of facilities, and comparison of services and prices, can be a real eye-opener. Ask for samples of work. Beware of sloppy-looking shops.

You may not be able to find photorepro services listed in the yellow pages under names used in this text. If so, check listings under the headings "lithographers" and "lithographic negatives and plates." A "litho" shop is an offset printing shop. Offset printing or platemaking shops often have the vacuum frame needed for making contact prints and will also often have a graphics or process camera. Sometimes they will have a blowback camera and a large developing machine that will handle working drawing–size prints.

16.2 HOW DIAZO WORKS

The basic common repro system known to all design professionals is diazo printing. Other words used for diazo are "ozalid" and "white print." These refer to light-sensitive print paper which is developed by exposure to ammonia fumes. The varieties of diazo-print paper—black line, brown line, blue line, etc.—are well known. Diazo polyester and acetate films are also available and are a boon to Systems Drafting.

New nonammonia print processes similar to diazo have been developed, but, as of this writing, they haven't achieved adequate quality in their reproducible films to be usable in Systems Drafting.

Most people in design and drafting use the diazo process, and most offices have at least a small version of the print machine and ammonia developer for in-house printing.

The following illustrates how diazo works: To make a diazo print, you place an original translucent drawing against light-sensitive diazo paper and run the combined sheets through the diazo machine. The machine shines ultraviolet light through the tracing. The exposure to light "burns off" the light-sensitive emulsion of the diazo paper *except* where there's line work or shading. Where the light is blocked by drawing on the tracing, the emulsion remains on the diazo material. After exposure to light, the sensitized diazo paper is developed by exposure to ammonia fumes, and the emulsion that hasn't been "burned off" by ultraviolet light turns dark. The terms "black line," "brown line," "blue line," and so on, refer to the diazo-print color options.

The diazo-print machine you're most likely used to is the rotary type. That is, the original tracing and print paper combination is inserted through rollers or rotating drums that grab the sheets and press them around a long light tube to expose the print paper. The sheets roll in, the sheets roll out, and the diazo paper is routed through some further rollers that expose it to the ammonia fume tank.

That's basically it. There are volumes of data available on all aspects of diazo technology if you want to get into it. But these essentials are all you really need to know for now to use diazo in Systems Drafting.

16.3 REPROGRAPHIC POLYESTERS

There are three main kinds of polyester (Mylar) that you will be dealing with: drafting, diazo, and photosensitive. The drafting media were described in detail in Chapter 5.

The diazo and photosensitive polyesters are like the drafting polyester in terms of base material and thicknesses (0.002 to .007"—2 to 7 mil—is the commonly used thickness range). The diazo and photosensitive polyester films have light-sensitive emulsions, and they may or may not have a drafting matte surface on one or both sides. Those that have no drafting surface are called "clear film" or "slicks."

The most widely used diazo polyesters are sepia line, which reproduces best when reprinting to make further diazo prints, and black line. Although the sepia line prints better, the black line tends to look sharper—like ink drafting. The nonmatte-surface sepia polyesters (popularly called "sepia Mylars") are also called "clear brown lines," "throwaways," and, as noted above, "slicks."

You'll have a choice of diazo emulsions: nonerasable fixed line, emulsions removable with an eradicator, and moist-erasable. All have their uses. You'll likely provide nonerasable line throwaways as base sheets for consultants when doing overlay drafting. That way there can be no unauthorized revisions to the base sheet data. But for most reproducibles for general Systems Drafting uses, you'll probably select moist-erasable film with matte on one side.

The key word in all this is "reproducible." A reproducible is a translucent or transparent clear film print of an original drawing, paste-up, photo, or overlay and base sheet combination. It's called reproducible because you can use it as a "second original" and run diazo prints from it. Many blueprint shops routinely make a reproducible of a regular tracing paper drawing before running prints if they believe the original might be damaged by the print process. Other words used for reproducible, besides "second original," are "intermediate print" and "transparency."

The paper diazo "sepia," also sometimes called "ozalid sepia," is a common old-style type of reproducible. The older sepia reproducibles required a two-step eradication process when making revisions and were not pleasant to use. Newer products are erasable—a great improvement. Generally, you'll be getting away from the paper sepia, despite its improvements, in favor of durable polyester.

The photosensitive polyester is commonly called photo "washoff." The photo line work of a washoff print is water-soluble and is moist-erasable. That means that you can erase with a moistened cotton-tipped stick or a wet soft eraser. New erasers are appearing on the market that contain a built-in erasing fluid. Large areas of photo washoff polyester print can be erased with a solution of 15% bleach mixed with 85% water.

Whereas the diazo products, especially the sepia polyesters, have a limited life if exposed to light, the photo washoff is essentially permanent. That's why it's so often selected as the final, archival quality, reproducible material for extensive composite or overlay drafting jobs.

The photosensitive polyester can be exposed either by projection with a blowback camera, as described in a later section of this chapter, or through direct one-to-one contact printing. The contact printing method is generally most economical and is described in the next section.

16.4 DIAZO FLATBED PRINTERS AND PLATE-MAKER CONTACT VACUUM FRAMES

A special type of diazo-print machine is the flatbed contact printer. With the flatbed, you lay the translucent original with the print paper or film onto a bed of glass or plastic, cover it with a weighted or vacuum-sealed lid (rather like putting the lid down on a waffle maker), turn on the light, and expose the sensitized diazo material. The light goes off after a preset period; you pull the original and the print, and you develop the print in an ammonia developer. For developing, use the developer portion of the standard rotary diazo/developer combination machine.

Since the original and the diazo copy material are pressed together flat, without movement around a cylindrical light tube, the reproduction is exactly one to one in size. There's no stretching, nothing to get out of phase. This comes in handy when you get into overlay drafting. It's especially useful with some kinds of composite drafting.

Some repro people have led architects and engineers down the garden path by insisting on doing camera work when it wasn't necessary. For example, if you need a same-size reproducible of a tracing, and there's no other reason to go to photography, the reproducible should be made by direct one-to-one contact printing.

"Contact" printing is like flatbed diazo printing. The difference is that normally a reprographics shop would use a "vacuum frame" for contact printing. And, traditionally, a special photosensitive film rather than diazo film would be used as the print medium. The main difference between a contact vacuum frame and a flatbed diazo printer is in the intensity and type of light source. The professional vacuum frames use very high-intensity light, usually from a point source. The flatbeds use a bank of fluorescent or ultraviolet light tubes to spread and diffuse the light. The point source light of the standard "vacuum frame" is fine for its normal use, which is exposing light-sensitive printing plates to a negative. But the high-intensity light tends to create a hot spot at the center and hazy fade-out around the edges when used with diazo products.

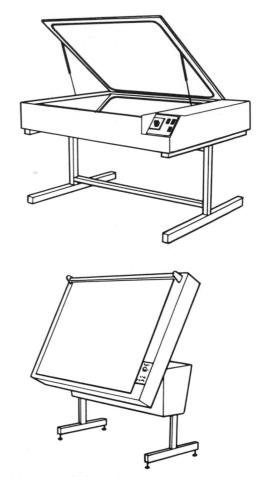

Fig. 16-1. Two flatbed printers.
(Design-Mates, Inc. and Charles Causey.)

Fig. 16-2. A vacuum-frame contact printer or plate maker now widely used as a flatbed printer for overlay and composite drawing.
(nuArc Co., Inc.)

As of this writing, flatbed technology—particularly as developed for composite and overlay drafting—is still very young. Some equipment that has been sold has not been reliable. Some manufacturers have appeared and disappeared rather suddenly.

A flatbed unit is essential for making best use of the systems described in this book; so tread cautiously when shopping for and testing such equipment. Until the technology is more reliable, consider renting rather than purchasing. If you lease a machine, insist on return privilege if it doesn't perform as reliably as promised.

We'll include a listing of the latest sources of flatbed units and vacuum frames in our updated *Reprographic Resources Guide*. See Resources at the end of this book.

16.5 REPROGRAPHIC PHOTOGRAPHY

A visit to a well-equipped reprographic shop can be intimidating. There may be a camera as big as a small truck; large photodeveloping machines, sinks, and dryers; immense copy-holding vacuum frames; and arc lights and unidentifiable auxiliary equipment of all sorts.

Despite the impressive scale, not much happens in a heavy-duty repro shop that's different from when you send your snapshots to a corner photo service. When you take a snapshot, you expose a light-sensitive negative film to light. In the first stage of processing, the exposed image is fixed onto the negative film. After that the negative image is mounted as a slide in a projector called an enlarger, and projected for a split second onto light-sensitive photographic paper. Then the image on the exposed photo paper is developed and fixed permanently with chemical solutions. The paper is dried, and there's your photo.

Repro shops do the same things a photo service does—but on a larger scale. They'll take a picture of your drawing. That makes an exposed negative which they use to make a "blowback" photo print. The difference, besides size, is that your final print won't be made on photographic paper; it will be on light-sensitive photo washoff polyester film. Usually this will be a polyester film with a drafting surface.

This is the washoff polyester material described in Section 16.3. The image is water-soluble and moist-erasable. That is, you're supposed to use a soft wet eraser when making changes in the image. It's called washoff not because you can wash or moist-erase the image, but because of a washing procedure used during the photoprocessing.

The photoblowback system has several common applications: You might have an old diazo print, with no original tracing, and need to get the print image onto translucent drafting material. Photoblowback can do an adequate job in many cases. It can intensify, or fill in, some faded or spotty lines from the original print.

Or you might have an opaque paste-up sheet with patchy cutouts and tape all over it. The repro shop can photograph the paste-up and paint out the tape marks and other flaws with opaquing fluid on the negative. Then the shop can create a clean, translucent, new second original to run diazo prints from or to continue drawing on. This is the basic original technique for composite drafting.

Or you might have a dirty, wrinkled, and torn tracing or diazo print to be reconstructed. The photoblowback process, combined with touchup of the negative, can usually create an acceptable new second original.

Those are some of the common past uses of photoreproduction of drawings. Shortly we'll name some newer, more important uses. First, here are a few pointers that you should know:

As mentioned before, some repro shops tend to do photo work when contact printing would do the job and do it at lower cost. Once you understand the processes involved, you'll be able to decide on the best and most economical repro methods to use in any particular circumstance. There's a wide range of equipment and repro services available. Some shops have older cameras which tend to fuzz the image around the perimeters of a large print.

Some repro shops make full-size negatives. That is, their negatives will match the size of the drawings you have photographed. This can be expensive. Generally you'll seek repro shops that have up-to-date process cameras capable of making

$8\frac{1}{2}'' \times 11''$ negatives. This size is proving very practical and economical for most drawing photorepro work. In some cases, it isn't more expensive to use full-size negatives. A lot depends on what the repro shop is used to. Some shops have obsolete equipment, but it's all paid for, and they can fudge around a bit to compensate and still charge competitive repro prices.

Smaller negatives, such as $8'' \times 10''$, are generally considered a little too constricting. Some repro shops are equipped to make microfilm using 35mm or 105mm negatives. Those are OK for some purposes, especially as a means of storing smaller engineering drawings. But they're not good enough for clear photoblowback of large drawings.

The cameras used at the repro shop are called "process" or "blowback" cameras. Not all process cameras have the blowback capability. "Blowback," as described, means it acts like a slide projector or photo enlarger and can "blow" the image of a negative back out onto light-sensitive media.

The process of making a blowback goes like this:

1. The original drawing or paste-up is mounted onto a vertical copyboard and photographed. The original may be opaque, in which case all the lighting will be set up for optimum reflective reproduction. If the original is translucent, some back lighting may be used to help intensify the image. The copyboard surface is glass to permit back lighting.

2. After the negative is processed, the image of the original drawing is blown back. This requires a sheet of photosensitive paper or polyester mounted on the copyboard. It's just a direct reverse operation from the original picture-taking process.

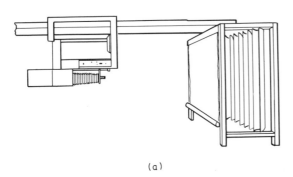

(a)

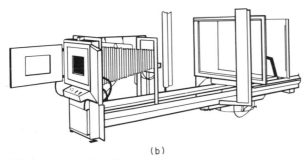

(b)

Fig. 16-3. Two blowbacks or "camera projectors" (*a*) with overhead track and copyboard, (*b*) with floor-mounted track and copyboard.

(Opti-Copy, Inc. and Acti Products, Inc.)

Just as a darkroom enlarger can alter a photoimage size, so the blowback camera can give you an enlargement or reduction of your original drawing.

In architectural and engineering work, most reductions are straight half size: $\frac{1}{4}''$ unit plans are reduced to $\frac{1}{8}''$ scale, large freehand detail drawings are reduced by half to sharpen up the line work, etc. If you're going to print a job at half size, the blowback camera would create half-sized reproducibles for diazo printing or blow the reduced image onto light-sensitive printing plates for offset printing.

Screened shadow prints are most often made with a blowback camera. A screened reproducible is made by introducing a literal screen of lines printed on clear plastic (called a "tint") over the negative in the process camera. A 50% screen, for example, has enough lines to block out half the image.

As described earlier in this book, a popular use of screened prints is to provide subdued background information on a drawing, allowing other data to stand out in solid-line contrast. A structural framing plan might be drawn directly on a reproducible which has a screened image of the building walls and partitions. An electrical plan might be drawn on a screened image of the architectural floor plan and/or reflected ceiling plan.

The use of screened background reproducibles for consultants' drafting is *not* recommended in most cases. It's OK if no changes will occur in the background information. But if and when changes do occur, it's very difficult to make corrections that aren't glaring in the screened background drawing. For most jobs, it's much better to use base sheets and overlays and reserve the screening of base sheet information for the final printing process.

People often confuse a "tint" or line screen with the "halftone" screen that's used in making photographs for offset printing. Halftones are like tints, but they allow all gradations in printing from white to black by means of dots instead of lines. The most commonly used line screen for

making shadow prints is 50%, 133-line. That means half the image is screened out and there are 133 lines to an inch.

Other words used to refer to screened prints are "ghost image," "phantom image," "gray-line background," and "subordinate image."

The blowback camera can do other tricks besides enlargement and reduction, and screening. It can produce double, triple, or more exposures on one print. For example, you might have three drawing sheets: one with floor plan, one with title block and drawing border, and one with floor plan furniture layout. Each sheet can be photographed onto an 8½″ × 11″ negative. Then each negative can be blown back onto a shared sheet of light-sensitive drafting film. This kind of blowback is called "multiple exposure" or "burn and double burn." It's just like the "double exposure" of our "snapshot" days except that the images are "ganged up" on the final print instead of on a single negative.

The polyester used with the blowback camera has a photographic emulsion rather than the ammonia-developed diazo emulsion. Kodak and DuPont are well known as producers of such polyester photo products, and other manufacturers are coming up with competitive photo-sensitive drafting films.

In the earlier days of overlay drafting systems, repro shops tended to do an excessive amount of camera work. They would use the blowback camera to make overlay and base sheet composites for interim printings, for example. In some

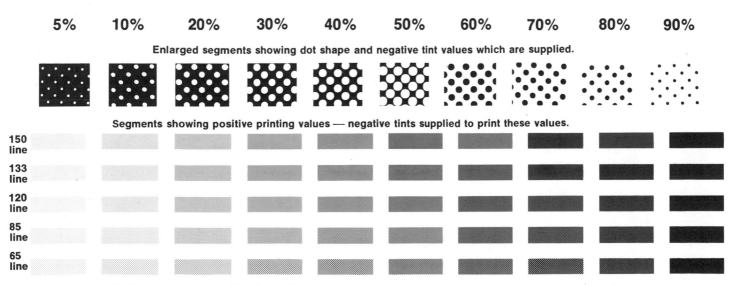

Fig. 16-4. Tints available to create screened background "shadow prints."

(R. W. Borrowdale Co.)

cases they used camera techniques and blowback to create base sheet reproducibles for the consultants' drafting staffs. This was inordinately expensive and time-consuming.

Photoblowback work should be reserved for the final printing—if it's used at all. If you're not going to half-size offset printing, you may not need to use blowback at all. Your "slicks" for base sheets, and composite reproducibles for interim and final printings, are most economically made on a flatbed or vacuum-frame exposing unit rather than by blowback.

How about acquiring an in-house camera? Some design firms have done this and swear by it. Camera designs have been simplified in recent years, bringing the price down to just a few thousand dollars for some units. The investment also includes processing units, darkroom-type storage facilities, and someone to watch over the operation.

The cameras are useful for much more than creating final half-size reproducibles or offset printing plates. As noted, they're handy for screening background drawings in final printing and for enlargements and reductions. In addition, they'll give you very sharp reproductions of any element you want reproduced—from fixtures in catalogs to photographs to repeat elements in plans and elevations for composite drafting.

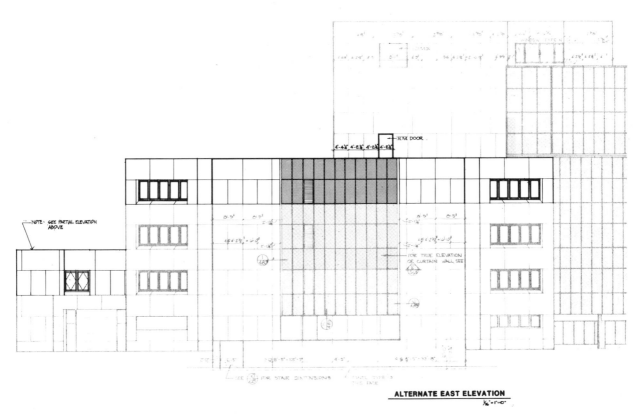

ALTERNATE EAST ELEVATION

Fig. 16-5.   Screened shadow printing is combined with solid-line printing to show clearly the extent of a possible alternate construction.

(Hansen Lind Meyer.)

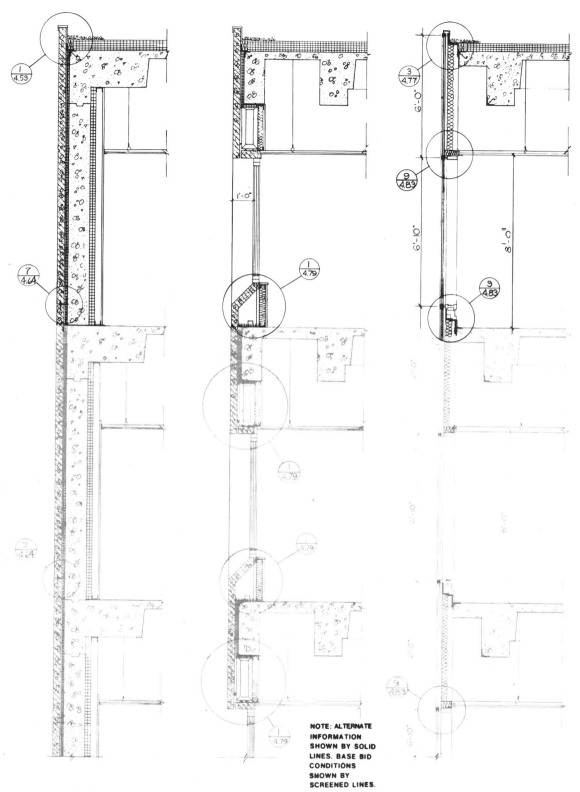

NOTE: ALTERNATE
INFORMATION
SHOWN BY SOLID
LINES. BASE BID
CONDITIONS
SHOWN BY
SCREENED LINES.

Fig. 16-6. Screened shadow printing with solid-line printing in wall sections to show alternate construction. Base bid conditions are shown by the screened lines as noted on the drawing.

(Hansen Lind Meyer.)

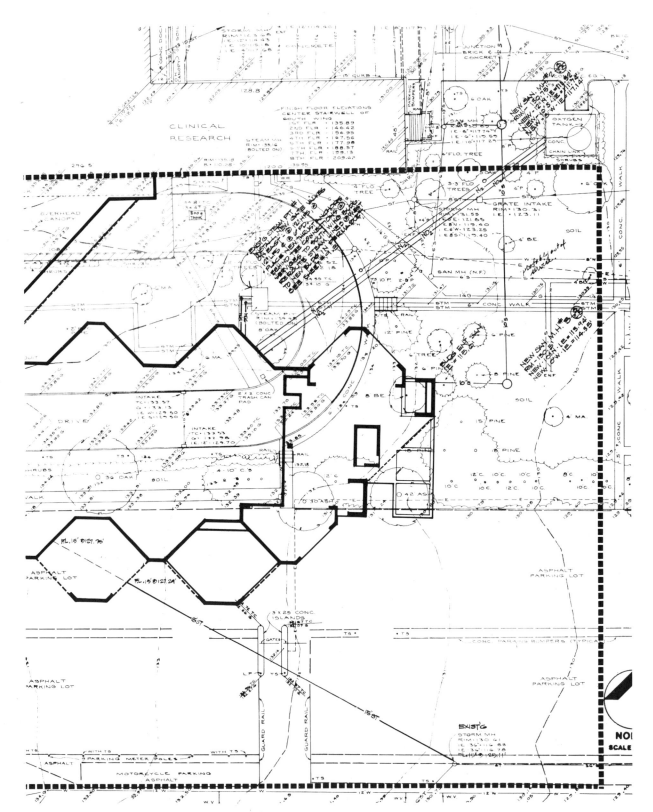

Fig. 16-7. A portion of one of a series of site plans showing work of different trades and construction alternates. The work is drawn with graphic tape and ink as an overlay and printed in solid line over a screened shadow print of the site survey. The site utilities alternate work was done on another overlay and printed in red in the final offset-printed working drawing sheet.

220 (Hansen Lind Meyer.)

17

AUTOMATED DRAFTING

17.1 PAVING THE WAY

Why bother with Systems Drafting when the whole business will eventually be computerized and automated anyhow? This is a good question. It often comes up during my workshops, and it expresses a very legitimate concern. Of course the whole business will be automated, as will everything else in life, fairly soon, and, in my view, the sooner the better.

So why invest in composite and overlay drafting when the Super 8 Power Blast Model ZZX-'84 may be coming over the horizon to take over all our drafting chores? There are two reasons. First, while waiting for your high-powered machine, you'll gain all the quality control, design enhancement, and time and cost advantages described in this book. Those advantages are considerable, even in the short run, and they will help you afford the start-up costs of the computer. Second, you'll have to master virtually all the techniques outlined in this text in order to use your computer properly. Those who plunge into computer drafting without the "five stages" kind of preparation are likely to bungle the automation process badly.

I know some readers have apprehensions about computers. There's a widespread notion that they really are thinking machines that will displace the need for human consciousness, just as they're displacing a large amount of human drudgery.

Let's clear that up. There's nothing conscious or even mysterious about computers. They are just devices for storing and retrieving symbols. The symbols represent data—locations, quantities, and other attributes—just as words in this book do. The main difference is that the words are printed, fixed on the pages of this book. Imagine that you could pick up these letters, words, and sentences and move them around in new combinations. That's what a computer lets you do.

Most often, computers function solely as a book or a file—a place of input, storage, and retrieval. Information goes in. Take your airline reservation, for example. It becomes visible when it is called up by the ticket agent when you arrive at the airport counter to buy your ticket. And it's altered or removed from the file as directed.

Computers can also sort information and simulate decision making. The standard routine is: "If such and such, then do this and that." All the sorting, routing, and manipulating is channeled and directed by previous design, just as fluids in a piping system.

Storage and retrieval are at the heart of computer functioning just as they are at the heart of Systems Drafting. That's why I say that all the stages of Systems Drafting are also stages of preparation for computerization.

It would be absurd, for example, to store notes and titles and have them printed out on a computer plotter too small to be readable; or to store in a computer detail drawings that haven't been coordinated, checked by experienced construction people, and set up in graphic format that's consistent with other detail drawings; or to have the computer produce drawings that have all the flaws and inconsistencies of hand-drawn documents. Absurd, but it will happen to those offices that don't get their whole production system coordinated and semiautomated before the computer comes along.

As for composite and overlay drafting, they're not only compatible with computer drafting operations, they *are* computer drafting. They happen to be *the* way and the only way computer drafting can work. You'll see why that is so further on in this chapter.

17.2 HOW SOON?

How long until we automate? Prospects are unclear as this is being written. There was a spurt of enthusiasm, a flurry of computer graphics activity in the 1960s. Many of us thought we'd be well along by the early 1970s. That was premature. Now we're on a "second phase" of development; some of the dreams of many years back are coming true. But start-up and operating costs are still too high for 90% of design practitioners.

As of now, there's widespread use of computer graphics in industrial engineering offices and in drafting specialties such as map making, piping design and drafting, highway planning, etc. Linear drafting with a limited range of symbols—as in wiring and circuit diagrams, mechanical ductwork, and structural frames—is all being done successfully by computer drafting.*

Architectural drafting is tougher. There's an immense array of special shapes, titles, and symbols to work with. So, to date, the architectural drafting installations are few in number, and costly.

Currently an installation adequate for architectural and architectural-related engineering drafting costs roughly $400,000 for hardware plus an equal amount of software, start-up, and related costs. ("Software" means the programming to make the computer do its job; "hardware" means the actual computer and computer graphics equipment.)

Leasing and operating costs are unimportant *if* the computer creates an adequate improvement in productivity and *if* you have a staff and workload large enough to keep the equipment and operations consistently busy. That's the tripper for most firms right now—work volume.

Two things have to happen to make computerized drafting widely available. First, naturally, the costs have to come down. Second, time sharing has to become available for smaller firms that cannot support a full-time computer operation. A reasonable guess, as of 1979, is that low-cost equipment and time sharing will be available

*Productivity ratios right now are approximately 6 to 1 when comparing a computer drafting station with a traditional drafting station for linear schematic types of drafting. Architectural firms estimate a 3 to 1 productivity ratio for their work. It's the ratios and the dollars they represent that will ultimately determine when an office can cost-justify the computer investment.

and cost-effective for all but the smallest firms within 7 years.

It may also happen that further advances in circuitry design and manufacture will permit use of minicomputers complete with package programs at lower cost than time sharing. As I say, it's all kind of indefinite right now, but one way or another it should be affordable by most firms by 1986.

Something else will happen simultaneously with the growth in computerized drafting. Other computer services that a design firm needs will become part of the package. That will include:

1. *Text editing and automatic typing.* You'll store specifications, proposal text, form letters, stock paragraphs, and standard drawing notation as part of the word-processing part of your setup. A fair number of architectural and engineering firms already have text editors or word processors. Some text editors and word processors are linked with office computers, and some are not. Eventually they will all be computer-linked.

2. *Financial management and accounting programs.* Before long *all* design firms will keep close track of time and costs, categorize them logically, and feed the data for computer analysis. Analysis will let principals know how they're doing, where upcoming problems are developing, and what they should be doing in the future to ensure their financial health. Marvelous, exciting work has been done in this seemingly dull and dreary area. Some financial analysis programs are already available at low cost for use with so-called personal computers or minicomputers.

3. *Spatial allocation programming for building design and planning.* Programs exist that lay out the most economical relationships of spaces within a building according to standards established by client and designer. Plan options are machine-drawn as schematic diagrams, which can then be reworked and refined by hand.

4. *Engineering calculations.* These are a natural, long-standing use of the computer and, with computerized drafting, can be integrated with schematic designs of cut and fill, structural, mechanical, electrical, and plumbing work.

5. *Materials and cost estimating.* Computers can count fixtures and measure linear and square footage of all materials and assemblies (such as fire walls), compare with current prices, and keep a running tally of construction costs.

6. *Project person-hours, scheduling, and budget.* The whole production process, as it's being completed, can be monitored in time and costs both off and on computer equipment.

These multiple uses are among the circumstances that conspire to get computerization into the drafting rooms. Even if a firm had no desire to automate its drafting, it would still get the computer because of the combination of low cost and multiple benefits. Then with the equipment on hand, its's a small step to tack on the drafting hardware. It would be pointless not to, like buying and expensive stereo system without including a turntable or tape deck.

One major computer application is "computer-aided design" (CAD). This is still a high-cost function, but its potential is fantastic. CAD means being able to sketch, draw, and test the implications of a drawing directly on a cathode ray tube (CRT). A CRT is like a TV screen, and through what is called "interactive graphics," you can draw and manipulate drawn elements on the screen with a "light pencil."

When you sketch an object on a screen in plan and elevation, the computer can straighten out your line work. Then, if you ask, it will show you isometric views or perspective views. There are programs that will walk you through a space, showing perspective views in sequence as you proceed. There are elaborate programs that will display your objects in solid planes, shades, shadows, color, and as viewed in motion inside or out and from any vantage point.

Eventually, as laser and holographic industries get things together, you should be able to "draw" in three-dimensional, full-color holograms with the aid of a computer console. You'll go much further than that ultimately, but I'll save that for the last chapter.

The initials CAD are sometimes used for "computer-aided drafting." This causes confusion. It's preferable to label the drafting aspect as AD for "automated drafting."

The foregoing gives a fair idea of where we are. Now we'll take a closer look at what automated drafting actually consists of and how you'll put it to work as part of Systems Drafting.

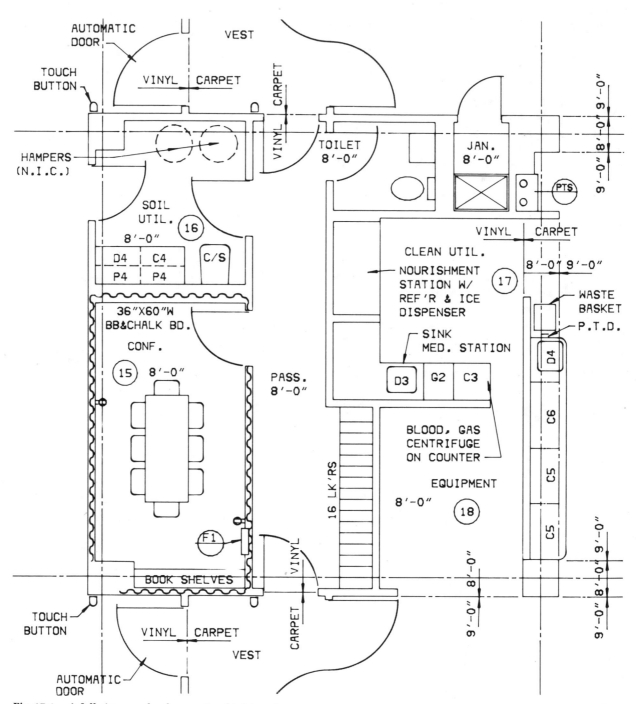

Fig. 17-1. A full-size sample of computer drafting of an architectural floor plan.

(Courtesy of Spencer Jue, Stone Marraccini & Patterson.)

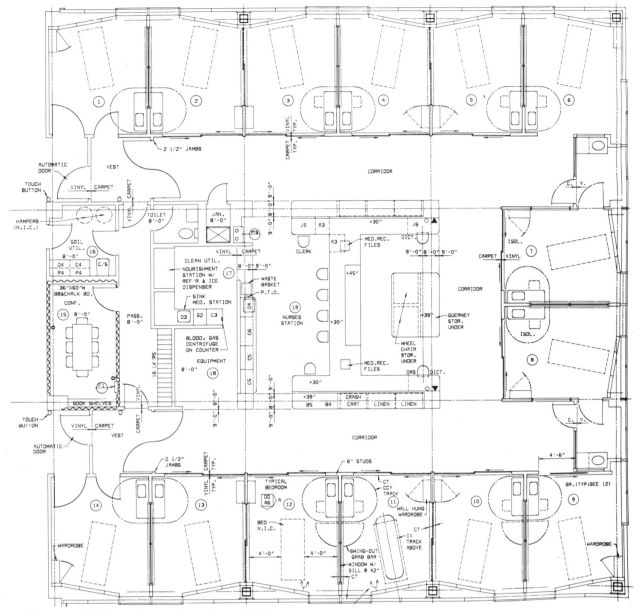

Fig. 17-2.   Half-size reduction from the partial floor plan shown in Fig. 17-1.

(Courtesy of Spencer Jue, Stone Marraccini & Patterson.)

17.3 HOW DO YOU WORK IT?

The stages and steps we've followed throughout this book all lead to automated drafting and computer-aided design. Here's why: Everything described—the management reforms, the graphic housecleaning, the simplifications, the new techniques, materials, and equipment—all have one overriding purpose: *to facilitate the storage, manipulation, and retrieval of repeat information.*

That's mainly what Systems Drafting is all about: storing material for adaptation and reuse. This book describes filing systems, standardization systems, and appliques, photocopying, and diazo systems. Their whole purpose is convenient storage and retrieval. Composite drafting, whether opaque or translucent, deals with storage and retrieval of repeat data. The essence of overlay drafting is again the storage and retrieval of repeat data. As I said earlier, storage, manipulation, and retrieval are at the heart of it all and, not so coincidentally, are also at the heart of computer functioning.

Automated drafting accomplishes storage, manipulation, and retrieval of graphic images. The only substantial difference is that it stores the images electronically instead of physically or photographically.

It all starts with a sketch, just as any drawing you do now. The sketch is translated into electronic impulses, stored as such, and, when retrieved, comes back out as a drawing on paper or polyester. *Final* bid and construction printing for a project will most likely be by diazo or offset printing, just as it is now. And, as users of automated drafting have discovered, most preliminary work and much final finish-up work will be done at drafting stations using all the present normal techniques of traditional drafting and Systems Drafting.

How do you get a sketch or any graphic image into the computer memory? The popular device for inputting graphic images is called a "digitizer." Other methods may replace this later on, but digitizers are very popular now. A digitizer is also called a "coordinatograph," which precisely describes what it does: it establishes coordinates. It translates a line into numbers—numbers representing coordinates at one end of a line and numbers representing the location of the other end. A computer can't see; it can only record positions by coordinates of a grid. By recording positions, it can translate sizes, locations, shapes, and so on, from an image to an electronic impulse and back to a graphic image.

Two main parts of the digitizer are the "digitizing board" and the "cursor." The board is similar to a vertical drafting board. The cursor is just an aiming device, something like a magnifying glass with cross hairs or a bull's-eye reticle. By setting the cross hairs at a point on a sketch and punching a button, you locate that point in computer memory. Move it to another point and punch again, and you've located two ends of a line.

Cursors are often attached to a track similar to a vertical drafting machine. If you are copying a standard detail to go into computer memory, for example, you would "trace" the end points of lines on the original drawing with the cursor.

You can also input graphic images directly on a CRT, or by straight numeric input. The cursor is reliable and convenient, however, and most likely will become a self-propelled tool. Later versions may run across a digitizing board tracing line work automatically.

Digitizing gets the graphic information into the computer memory. How do you get it out? The CRT is a way to get immediate output of stored memory. The image is broadcast to the screen and you can play with it directly (interactive graphics). Other modes of output are ink drafting with an automatic drafting device—either flatbed plotter or drum plotter. Just as the names indicate, they involve a flat drawing surface or a rotating drum. There's a variation used now that moves the platform that holds the drawing sheet and moves the ink pen simultaneously for very fast drafting output. For intermediate checking output, you can get electrostatic prints. Drawings or printed output from a computer are called "hard copy" to differentiate them from the transitory CRT image.

The guts of a computer system is its "central processing unit" (CPU). The CPU includes memory, which may be on magnetic tape or disks, plus storage of instructions of what to do with memory. Instructions are called the "program" or "software."

Interactive instructions are handled with a "menu keyboard." In the context of CAD or AD, "menu" means an array of symbols, titles, figures, and so on, that are stored whole for quick retrieval. A menu might include a catalog of things like arrowheads, door swings, detail key bubbles, electrical symbols, textures, patterns,

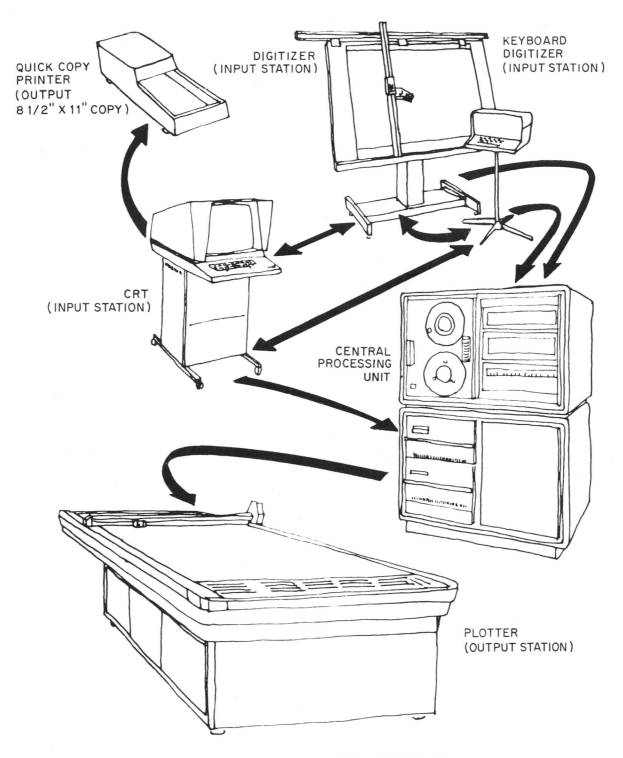

QUICK COPY
PRINTER
(OUTPUT
8 1/2" X 11" COPY)

DIGITIZER
(INPUT STATION)

KEYBOARD
DIGITIZER
(INPUT STATION)

CRT
(INPUT STATION)

CENTRAL
PROCESSING
UNIT

PLOTTER
(OUTPUT STATION)

COMPUTER GRAPHICS SYSTEM HARDWARE

Fig. 17-3.   Computer graphics system hardware.
(Courtesy of Spencer Jue, Stone Marraccini & Patterson.)

plumbing fixtures, and equipment—items that are very similar to the kinds of graphic elements often stored as appliques. A menu may also include sets of instruction for the computer operator. This is the more common use of the term.

Menu elements might be stored as "addresses." If you wanted to get an item onto the CRT screen, for example, you would punch in an index code that would call up the element you wanted to see.

Another version of a menu is a tablet covered with a grid work of squares. Each square has a symbol, rather like keys of a calculator, and by touching the symbol with an "editing pen" stylus, you call up the image you're after. Sometimes such a menu tablet or keyboard is called an "input surface."

The instructional part of a menu is called a "command menu." It will contain instructions such as "copy," "show front and right," "delete," "enlarge/reduce," "rotate," "use solid line," and "mirror image."

There's your set of tools: a way to store images, a way to call them up,* ways to manipulate them, a surface to monitor manipulation, and a way to get hard copy anywhere along the way. Most improvements in automated drafting will be in simplification and an increase in the ways you can manipulate images on the CRT.

Recent improvements, for example, allow you to manipulate small elements within larger ones directly on the screen and to overlay a virtually limitless number of elements from different parts of memory.

*Other ways of manipulating images include a "screen cursor" you apply to the CRT and a "light pen" with which you erase, move, or otherwise create and alter images directly on the CRT screen.

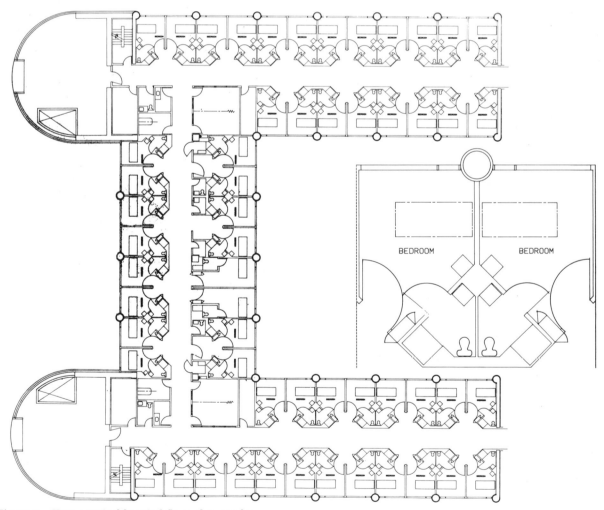

Fig. 17-4. How a typical hospital floor plan can be drawn and assembled with automated drafting.

228   (Courtesy of Spencer Jue, Stone Marraccini & Patterson.)

Here's a sequence to show how you might create a hospital floor plan via interactive graphic CAD and AD:

1. Create the basic patient room plan. This can be composed as a hand-drawn sketch that's digitized into computer memory or "drawn" by manipulating lines and shapes on the CRT screen.

2. Once the patient room plan is composed, duplicate it in "flip-flop" as an adjacent patient room would be. Flip-flop duplication is automatic upon command to the computer.

Then splice the original and the flip-flop as a single two-room suite (normally with shared bathroom).

3. Replicate the pair of rooms as many times as needed to complete a room string down one side of the hospital corridor.

4. Instruct the computer to make a mirror image of the string of rooms and reproduce it opposite the first string, as an opposite row of rooms adjacent to the same corridor.

5. Take the hospital wing with the double-loaded corridor just created and replicate it as another wing of the building.

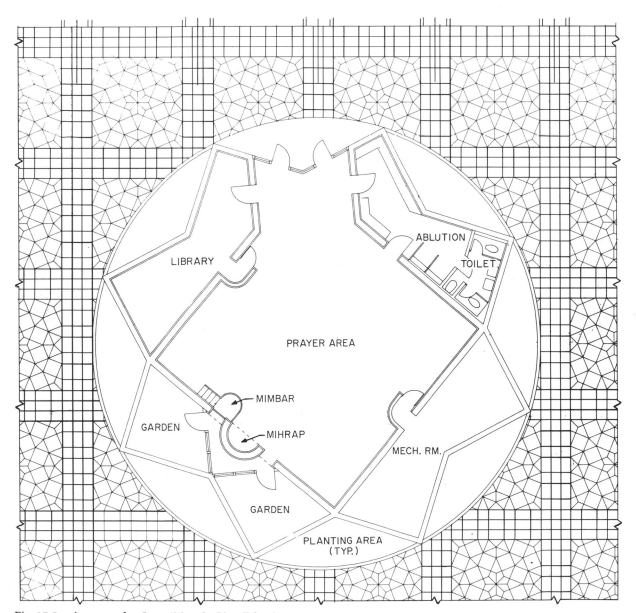

Fig. 17-5.   An example of repetitive drafting (Islamic paving in this case) that is handled expeditiously with automated drafting.

(Courtesy of Spencer Jue, Stone Marraccini & Patterson.)

6. Complete the overall building floor plan by calling up stairs, elevators, and other standard plan units from memory. Add in composed nurses' stations, and mechanical and other support spaces. The basic floor plan design is completed, and room titles can be added.

7. Make hard copies of the plan for study and revision, and as base sheets for consultants.

8. After revisions and refinements, the basic plan can be made into a working drawing by adding dimensions, detail notes, room and finish schedule, door symbols, etc. These can be done as an electronic "overlay" to keep constant and variable data properly separated.

The whole sequence just described is identical to the first-phase composite drafting and later overlay drafting phases of Systems Drafting. It's just that you are using the computer instead of copiers, cameras, or diazo machines.

Although hard copy of final drawings is now limited to electrostatic copies, similar to those from an office copier, or line drawings from an ink plotter, there's a change in the wind.

Some inventive people are working out systems of getting hard copy directly onto microfilm or larger-size photonegatives. This would allow direct translation, at the end of a job, to photoblowback reproducibles for final printing, or to offset printing plates.

That's largely where we are and where we're heading in AD, CAD, and interactive graphics. By no means will that be the endpoint. Environmental design and the tools for creating it are going to change beyond recognition in the generation ahead. You'll find some provocative suggestions on that in the next chapter.

18

BEYOND
STAGE FIVE

Let me correct a misunderstanding: I and others who advocate and teach Systems Drafting are not out to eliminate hand drawing. On the contrary, I for one would like to see more time given to it. What we want to eliminate is not drawing but old-time pencil pushing: hand *drafting*.

Drawing is an *originating* process: a creative, aesthetic, and problem-solving process. Drafting is a copying process, as mechanical as the word "copying" implies. People will object that there is some creativity, some aesthetics, and a fair amount of problem solving in drafting processes. That's true. But the *dominant* aspect of drafting is still plain old copying. The last thing any employer wants is a drafting room staffed with creators and aesthetes.

For now at least, hand drawing is the fastest way to create original problem-solving sketches and basic designs. The copying, elaboration, and refinement are best done with the tools and materials of Systems Drafting.

Drawing is often described as a communications tool, but it goes beyond that. Its primary value is really as a problem-solving tool. You can create graphic "models" of shapes and structures and test them out in different configurations and relationships. You can chart the movement and relationships of processes, things, and people through time and space and see, in miniature, just how things are going to work—or not work.

Part of the creative process is speculation: What if . . . ? You can *speculate* with pencil on paper just as wildly as you want. That's a stimulating process that refines and elaborates, creates and recreates.

So drawing, in its formative aspect, remains indispensable. If sketching can be done economically and effectively on a CRT or any other device other than paper, so much the better. Draw-

ing and sketching remain, drafting goes. Then we alter and augment the sketching and drawing process with Systems Drafting.

As of this writing, most design offices use some aspect of Systems Drafting. But very few—certainly less than 1%—know how to utilize all aspects.

From this modest beginning, the profession will undergo a radical turnaround. Over the next 5 years, most design offices will become knowledgeable and experienced in all major aspects of Systems. Eventually, most will become what we call "Stage-5" offices.

Stage-5 offices don't use every technique on every single project. They just know how to pick and choose: this technique for this project, that procedure for that one. Most important, all the varied techniques, materials, equipment, and procedures they use fit and work well together.

What do design offices gain from the changeover to systems and the progression to stage 5? Here are some of the gains:

1. Beyond a doubt, there is greatly enhanced control over design and construction quality. For Systems to work, a job has to be planned in greater detail and monitored more severely than has been traditionally common. That in itself will cut problems and improve quality control.

2. There is more time available and greater necessity for studying out the design phase of a project before plunging into the production phase. That has a decided beneficial effect on both design and construction quality.

3. There is less time and complication between conception and execution of a project. That means fewer glitches in communications, fewer misunderstandings, less boredom, and

far less chance of error. A tightly-knit staff of skilled personnel can push through the work directly instead of trying to herd along a small army of inexperienced draftspeople.

4. Since graphic data is prepared for storage, retrieval, and reuse, it gets more study and follow-through attention than used to be practical. In one large firm, for example, standard details reflect only the very best, most proven of quality construction standards. The details are monitored by a committee of construction-wise experts in the firm, and anyone's modifications to standard details have to be reviewed by that committee.

5. Besides design and quality enhancement, the systems are supposed to save time and money. That's what attracts most design offices into trying them. As of now, the small number of offices that could be called Stage-5 offices generally report overall time and/or cost savings of from 30 to 40% compared to traditional methods.

Some offices report substantial savings with just partial systemization: 10 to 20% overall savings by using typewritten notation; 10 to 20% by using freehand drafting; a dramatic savings of 10 to 1 over old methods when using photodrafting for remodelings, preservation, adaptive reuse, etc.

The following is a set of time and cost figures compiled from the March 1979 issue of our newsletter, *The Guidelines Letter*:

"It took an average of 10.8 work hours per drawing for a custom condominium project," says Ronald Fash of Rapp Fash Sundin Inc. of Galveston, Texas. The 24″ × 36″ drawings would take from 30 to 40 hours using traditional methods, according to Mr. Fash.

"Slightly over 17 hours per drawing were required for a recent $6.5 million multischool project," reports Michael Goodwin of Michael and Kemper Goodwin, Ltd., Tempe, Arizona. Architectural drawings were completed by one project architect and a drafting assistant. The main timesavers include intensive production planning, typewriting and keynoting of *all* notation, plus applique and photocomposite techniques.

"45 architectural drawings for a medical facility were finished in 900 work hours—less than 20 hours per sheet," reports Michael Lengyel at Ronald T. Aday Inc. in Pasadena, California. Michael estimates normal drafting time without using systems would have been a typical 35 to 40 hours per sheet.

"We're getting an overall savings now of 30 to 40% over old systems," says Barry Rowe of Page-Werner and Partners in Great Falls, Montana.

"Around 38% savings," says Ed Powers of Gresham and Smith in Nashville. Besides extensive use of composite and overlay drafting, they've created a comprehensive detail file. With the file they can produce composite detail sheets in about 20 hours for institutional buildings for which detail sheets used to require 100 hours of research and drafting.

A 1978 General Services Administration cost comparison study* suggests an even greater savings. A Value Management study of alternate methods to produce drawings for a $2.5 million alterations and restoration job concludes that traditional drafting and materials would cost $34,320, paste-up drafting would cost $15,190, and overlay drafting would cost $13,226. (The latter includes $2,754 in materials and repro costs as opposed to $120 materials and printing costs for the traditional methods.)

Some firms tell us they've made no major reductions in project time. But they do much more work within traditional time frames— more design, more refinements, more detail studies, etc. Many firms now achieve both— more work and in faster time. The owner of one medium-size firm, using paste-up and overlay techniques, can now produce four complete 24″ × 30″ presentation drawings in 3 hours. He says the graphic techniques, plus tight financial management, have more than tripled their annual profit margin.

Inevitably, word gets around about these extraordinary time and cost savings. Today's more advanced design offices find they become willing or unwilling hosts to a steady stream of callers and visitors, people who've heard "wild stories" and want to see what's going on for themselves. As of now, the word has gotten around so much that the trend to changeover is irreversible.

*GSA Value Management Workbook, Study No. V-R10-6-77.

While the changeover may be irreversible, it isn't necessarily smooth. Most architects and engineers will dip into Systems Drafting, get burned a little by inadequate planning or experience, draw back for a while, and then dip in a little more later on. Eventually, they gain thorough understanding and control of the processes, and they're hooked henceforth.

That process will accelerate in the years ahead for several reasons. Architects and engineers who would really rather not bother at all are becoming convinced they have to change just to keep up. They'll put their heads down and bang their way through, problems or no problems, until they have adequate grasp to use Systems Drafting effectively. They'll be helped in the process by new tools, materials, equipment, and improvements in the repro shops.

What improvements can we expect in the near future? Most will be based on the rather glaring needs, the main hitches people run into now when they try to systematize their working drawing production. Here's what to expect (possibly already realized by the time some of you read this book):

1. Office copiers will provide exact one-to-one size reproductions, very dense black images, size reduction capabilities, and the capability to copy directly onto tracing papers, stickybacks, and clear transparent films. Some copiers already have some of these features. None have all, but before long copier makers will perceive the need and come across with machines that have all the qualities required by architects and engineers.

2. Stickyback and dry-transfer appliques will be produced in a greater variety of architectural and engineering designs. Stickybacks will become increasingly transparent, so there'll be less ghosting or shadow on diazo prints. And they'll have improved adhesive so they'll remain repositionable—not adhered for eternity as some are now. Wall construction, in particular, will become available in dry-transfer patterns as well as tapes, and these may prove faster and more economical than the graphic tapes.

3. There'll be better reproducible materials, particularly in the realm of sepia polyester films. They'll have better matte drafting surface (when they have matte), be more easily moist-erasable, and will retain their image and clarity without fading out or fogging up. Where such products now are only usable as throwaway intermediates, they'll become permanent for archival storage. Permanency will save a clumsy final step in going to permanent photographic material, as many offices find they have to do now.

4. There'll be simpler, cheaper blowback cameras and processors for in-house use. Many offices that go to Stage 5 establish their own camera and processing rooms. As this market enlarges, manufacturers will produce more of the smaller special cameras for exposing and blowing back 8½″ × 11″ negatives.

5. There'll be more sharing of technical information within the design professions. Some of the pioneers in Systems Drafting have met regularly over the years to trade information with like-minded colleagues. This will become more widespread. Standard details will become widely available, as will standard notations, improved standard forms, production manuals, and overlay drafting control charts. These will be refined products of many firms' experiences and, whether used as is or revised, they'll save immense wasted trial-and-error time. It's very likely that a volunteer organization will spring up to sponsor meetings and share information on a more formal basis. This has already happened for professionals dealing with marketing (The Society for Marketing of Professional Services), those concerned especially with financial management (The Professional Services Business Management Association), and spec writers (The Construction Specifications Institute).

All these changes are already in the works, and the predictions are simple extensions of what's already well underway.

How about beyond the next few years? What can be expected in design offices in 8 to 10 years? 20 years?

Computerization, of course, will be the next big integrative step, combined with very large-scale use of photoprocesses in-house and, probably, almost universal use of offset printing in color for working drawings.

The firms already at Stage 5 are usually the ones most eager to extend what they've done, to install their own offset printing facilities, and to get into computer-aided design and automated drafting. Some will be inventing extremely divergent approaches to construction documents. Here are some likely possibilities:

1. Some firms will start photographing their design models, adding notes and dimensions, and using them in working drawings. As of this writing, one firm that uses modeling extensively in design processes is preparing to use specially screened model photos both for presentation and working drawings. The screening is to "soften" some details that make models look like models instead of the real thing.

2. Some offices will make increasing use of construction photographs to complete their standard detail files. As photos become more conveniently transferable to drawings, people come up with an endless array of ideas for using them. They're already proving handy for conveying items that are especially hard to communicate verbally or by drawing, such as stonework or the textures desired in finished concrete. It's possible to photograph a corner of typical roofing flashing on a parapet and show more about the construction with the click of a shutter than a draftsperson could in hours of drawing sections and isometrics.

3. We'll see hybrid drawings that substitute a new kind of descriptive notation for much of the drawing—something halfway between a drawing and a specification. This has already been done at HOK in St. Louis.

4. Some firms who produce drawings and have them photoreduced for half-size printing will ask themselves: "Why not draw them at the smaller size to begin with?" Some firms have done this for years. Others will take the seemingly opposite approach: "Since it's easy to photoreduce, why not draw original studies much larger to get all the bugs out?"

5. Inevitably, some architects and engineers will question whether drawings are needed at all and will find other means to do the job.

Along with all this, there will be major changes in the structure of the profession. If current trends continue, for example, there'll either be an end to professional licensing or enough exceptions will be made that it won't matter one way or another. There are strong arguments that licensing is exclusionist in intent and in practice and a means of preserving a forced monopoly privilege. There's evidence that we're losing a large amount of creative talent because of it. Why, it's asked, should a creative person put up with years of mediocre professional schools, plus years pushing pencils for registered architects, to become eligible to take exams to finally produce some buildings? It's easier to become an artist or a filmmaker than to struggle with all the obstacles that have been erected to the design practice. Admittedly, there's a need for an accrediting system, but it can be privately administered.

Clients are grown-up people. They manage more people, more money, and more major decisions than most architects will ever see. They're capable of deciding for themselves who should produce their buildings. These are some of the arguments being heard today regarding limits on professional entry. And the arguments are becoming more insistent.

I'll add a personal note regarding the future of licensing. I'm a registered architect. I'm dedicated 100% to this profession; it's virtually all I think about and work at for 16 hours a day. I naturally have friendships and acquaintances with a very large number of designers, drafting people, architects, and engineers. When they talk to me privately and personally about such matters as licensing, they *don't* talk about protecting aesthetic quality or "the public health and welfare." That's for the press and the public. They talk about trying to keep people out of the profession to keep fees up and to keep the competition down. With that sort of foundation, I don't believe licensing can survive any serious long-term challenge.

Privatization of professional accreditation could have a major impact on how design services are delivered. We'll look at some in a moment, but first there's another major professional change to consider: elimination of building codes.

Here's a report on proposals to eliminate codes from the May 1979 issue of our publication, *The Guidelines Letter*:

"Get rid of the building codes," says the National Commission on Neighborhoods' final report to the White House. The Commission questions whether code enforcement provides any net benefit for public health and safety. The report says that besides failing to achieve intended benefits, "evidence is extensive and convincing (that) the code system frustrates and inflates the cost of construction and rehabilitation."

A HUD Task Force on Housing Costs said much the same thing in 1978, blaming regulation for disproportionate rises in building costs. The National Commission on Urban Problems drew the same conclusion back in 1968. This year the Council on Wage and Price Stability plans to urge local government to cut back on costly regulations.

There's a way to cut through it all, suggests the National Commission on Neighborhoods. The Commission points to the French system, which virtually eliminates all the problems created by the U.S. system. Except for fire safety in public access buildings, France has quality construction without government building codes or agencies.

The French solution is based on strict civil liability requirements. To protect themselves, French builders buy warranty insurance. Insurance and financing companies use private inspection companies to check compliance with good building practice.

The National Commission on Neighborhoods says the private system cuts out major problems. Labor unions cannot impose make-work laws. Neither can commercial interests stop would-be competitors by outlawing new products or materials. Complex building components can be mass-produced and distributed nationally without being blocked by an army of independent jurisdictions with contradictory rules. Private codes are flexible and allow building innovation; building standards aren't rigid, capricious or contradictory—a major source of extortion demands by U.S. city public employees.

What happens if and when the nation eliminates legally enforced licensing and prescriptive building codes? One unquestionable result, and the one relevant to the subject of this book, is that such changes will bring new blood and new ideas into the profession. We can expect a surge of experimentation and innovation: new building systems, new design methodologies, new problem-solving methods, and, in general, more release of creative and intellectual energies. That means an expansion and enlargement of new production methods.

Looking ahead 20 years, we can foresee a loosening up of the profession and of society in general. There are fascinating, well-established trends in science that will enlarge the picture considerably too. For example, biologists are looking forward to with varying degrees of excitement and fear—the understanding and *control* of genetic processes. That has immense implications, and among them is the concept, already well studied, of biological or "living" buildings. How does one "design" an environment that grows? Or that has even some limited degree of consciousness? That is going to require design at the level of the seed, as it were, and some very sophisticated methodologies to do the task.

Architectural design methodologies in the universities, such as at the University of California in Berkeley, are already well into problems that once would have been considered strictly epistemological. They're dealing with the nature of consciousness and our techniques for perceiving and thinking about reality. They're drawn into subjects of mental functioning because the potential scope and depth of design practice is becoming so vast. New tools and new creative techniques are needed to deal with the emerging problems.

As the problem-solving tools become more sophisticated, so will the range of services that can be offered by design professionals. We'll see architects and engineers who will consult on everything from new methods of learning, to computer design, to the creation of private management of government. Those are easy predictions because they're already starting to happen. We can only expect more extreme diversifications in the future.

Another major change, already in the works is an explosion of concern over issues of aesthetics. After years of a mixture of comparative indifference and confusion, there's extreme seriousness about achieving beauty in buildings. The profession will be welcoming artists once again. And, thanks to the extreme proliferation of new design tools and Systems Drafting and other tools to follow, those artists' powers should be vastly greater than ever before.

A little further on, for example, with computer power magnified, we'll all have "magic drafting boards." We'll draw with our fingers; interact with design programs; create large screen images to play with; transmit them by phone line; pull full-color hard copy at any point of design we want; have access to virtually all the design and construction information there is in the world. We'll be able to do all that in anywhere from 5 to 20 years, subject to general political and economic stability.

Further down the line things get even livelier, with genetic manipulation, design of ocean and space habitats, high tech autonomous environments, and so on. Somewhere along the way, there will be a team-up of the computer and laser technology. This can help us create living, three-dimensional design and construction documents right on a site. Do you want to create a surface or a form? Here it is in three-dimensional full-color holographic image right before your eyes. Do you need some design refinement? You'll be able to walk through a full-size holographic image of an environment and make all revisions you need based on the full-scale experience of the final result.

Ultimately, we'll see a marvelous integration of the designing and building process. Living buildings is one option. Another one being explored by futurist-oriented architects is based on polymer technology. Some plastic catalysts are light-sensitive and, like photographic emulsions, they'll harden when exposed to light. So, we'll design an environment, display a full-scale holographic image of it, and spray light-sensitive hardening chemicals through the image. The spray will solidify like a three-dimensional "real-life" photograph. It will be the real thing—first designed with computer assistance, refined as a hologram, and then, a solid structure made from light. In those days we'll be making dreams real—literally.

Until a welcomed future makes this book obsolete, I'll encourage inquiries from readers as to the latest sources of data on Systems Drafting and all its related technologies and implications. As announced elsewhere in the text, there are so many changes and advances in this field every year that we'll have to provide a separate annual supplement to keep readers up to date.

If you come up with something new, no matter how seemingly far out or how minor, that we can share with our readers in the future, please drop me a note about it: Box 456, Orinda, CA 94563.

I sincerely hope you'll gain all the values that are available from the ideas in this book.

Best of luck to you, and to *your* System.

GLOSSARY

Acetate Base Transparent cellulose acetate support for film emulsion.

Acetate Reproducible Acetate-base diazo film.

Actinic Light Radiation causing chemical change, such as light reacting with photographic emulsion to activate or harden it.

Activator A solution that makes a developing agent work, such as in activator-type washoff film.

Agitation Moving photographic material in solution so processing solution uniformly covers entire film.

Ammonia Developing agent in the diazo printing process.

Anamorphic Effect Foreshortening or elongation of photographic image.

Angstrom Measurement unit for a wavelength of light, ultraviolet energy, and other radiation.

Angular Coverage Area defined by circle of illumination of lens.

Aperture Opening in lens that admits light. Indicated by "f number."

Aperture Card Electronic data processing card with window for placing microfilm frames.

Applique Graphic material to be adhered to another material such as a decal, pressure-sensitive label, dry-transfer letters or symbols, tape, and stickyback films.

Applique Drafting Use of tapes, films, dry transfer, etc., to transfer symbols, patterns, letters, titles, and drawing images to a drawing sheet.

Archival Quality Ability to resist deterioration for a specific long period of time.

Autopositive Photo paper or polyester that reproduces as direct positive when exposed on a contact printer.

Background Shading or "ghosting" in the nonimage part of a reproduction.

Background Drawing or Print A reference drawing or print with information provided by an architect as base information for a consulting engineer. A building floor plan printed on a reproducible for an engineer's draftsperson to continue drawing on would be a background print.

Base Glass, paper, polyester, plastic, or cellulose acetate base for film emulsion.

Base Sheet Drawing drafted for registration purposes containing information that remains constant during project development.

Bleaching Chemically changing developed silver images to silver halide to remove or reduce photographic images.

Bleed Offset printing where print appears to continue "off" the edges of the page; done by trimming edges.

Blocking Out Opaquing a negative to eliminate superfluous background details.

Blowback Projecting an image from a negative through a projection camera onto light-sensitive material such as washoff drafting film.

Blowback Camera Reprographic camera that exposes large (usually 8½" × 11" negatives) and can project a negative's image back out onto photosensitive media such as washoff polyester. For enlarging, reducing, and/or screening.

Blowup Photographic enlargement.

Blue-Line Print Reproduction with blue lines on white paper background; usually a diazo print.

Blue, Nonreproducing Light blue ink or pencil that does not photograph or reproduce in diazo printing. Also called nonphoto blue.

Blueprint Reproduction with white lines on a blue background (negative image) made from an original or a positive intermediate. Largely obsolete due to diazo printing.

Call-Out Window Drawing areas with instructions or dimensions on specific items.

Carbon Arc Reprographic light source produced by passing an electrical arc between carbon terminals. Color temperature variable by including metal additives in the carbon. Largely obsolete.

Card-to-Card Printing Card-mounted microfilm duplicated by contact printing.

Carrier Sheet A sheet of paper, plastic film, or thin cardboard upon which appliques or elements of composite drawing are assembled.

Clean Room Room constructed with high-efficiency filters to remove dust from incoming air.

Clean Work Station Enclosed work area kept dust-free by a stream of filtered air.

Clearing Removal of undeveloped silver halide during fixing of photographs.

Collating Assembling sheets into correct numerical order.

Color Separation Photographic separation of primary colors from color originals into separate printing plates. In graphic art, the technique consists of drawing each color on separate clear film overlays.

Composite Drafting   Assembly of graphic information on a carrying sheet as opposed to hand drawing. Similar to the creation of paste-ups or mechanicals in the graphic arts.

Composite, Overlay   Projection or printing of several kinds of information from different disciplines on one finished sheet. Done by combining overlay drawings with a common base drawing.

Contact Positive   Print made by placing reproduction material in contact with original or intermediate of same size.

Contact Print   Same as "Contact Positive."

Contact Printer   A device, like the vacuum frame, for exposing light sensitive media in direct one-to-one contact with original or reproducible copy. Used both for translucent composite drafting and for compositing base and overlay sheets into one print in overlay drafting. Also called "flatbed" and "exposure unit."

Continuous Tone   Photographic or diazo-printed image with gradations of tone from black through white. (Black-and-white image with no gradation is called "line image.")

Copy   In the graphic arts, copy refers to the original work that is to be reproduced. A paste-up mounted to be photographed would be called the "copy."

Copyboard   A horizontal or vertical panel (usually glass) for holding copy flat while it is being photographed.

Copyboard Illumination   Arrangement of lights to properly illuminate copy being photographed.

Copy Camera   Camera adapted for enlarging, reducing, or screening color separations of photographs for printing reproduction.

Copy Negative   Negative used as an intermediate to produce prints.

Cropping   Marking photographs or illustrations to indicate boundaries of the reproduction. Trimming or cutting away unwanted portions of a photo before reproduction.

Definition   Sharpness of photographic images.

Densitometer   Electronic or visual instrument that measures density of photographic image.

Density, Background   Opacity of the nonimage part of a photograph.

Design Development   Project phases ranging from project programming through schematics and refinement and elaboration studies, to final preliminary or presentation drawings, to working drawings.

Developer   Chemical solution that darkens silver halide that has been exposed to light to black metallic silver, thus producing an image.

Developing Tank   Hard rubber, stainless steel, or plastic tank for developing photographic materials. Sometimes an integral part of processing machine.

Developing Time   Time it takes to develop a negative or print to the desired density. Depends on material and developer type, and temperature of developing solution.

Diazo   Reproduction method using paper coated with light-sensitive diazo compound. The paper is developed with ammonia vapor after exposure, resulting in a positive, solid-line azo dye image.

Dimensional Stability   Ability of materials to withstand changes in size due to temperature, aging, relative humidity, and/or processing.

Direct-Image Film   Film that will retain same polarity as the original material with conventional processing.

Direct Positive   Image on paper or film made directly from exposure without a negative.

Drawdown   Behavior of vacuum in printing frame that makes the original and reproduction material come in close contact during exposure.

Drop-Out   Portions of originals that do not reproduce.

Drying   Removing water from processed photo material.

Dry Silver Film   Nongelatin silver film developed by applying heat.

Dummy   A mock-up or rough layout in working drawings of how the printed job is to appear. Information may simply be sketched in.

Emulsion   Coating of light-sensitive chemicals that create a latent image upon exposure to light.

Enlargement   Optical projection to increase the size of an original from microfilm or negatives.

Enlargement Printer   Instrument that projects, develops, and fixes an enlarged image from microfilm onto suitable material.

Enlarger   Instrument for making enlarged prints from photographic negatives.

Eradicator   Chemical solution that removes image areas from photographic reproductions or diazo prints.

Exposure Time   Length of time required to expose photographic material to light in order to get an image on film, paper, or plate.

Exposure Unit   See "Contact Printer."

Film   Transparent plastic coated with light-sensitive emulsion.

Film Speed   Degree of sensitivity of emulsion to light. Indicated by the ASA number: a higher number indicates more sensitive film.

Filter   Colored glass or gelatin sheets that alter the color quality of exposing light.

Finishing   Retouching, spotting, or coloring photographs.

Fixed-Line Film   Film reproducible requiring a chemical eradicator for removal of photographic lines.

Fixer   Chemical solution that performs fixing (see below).

Fixing   Chemical removal of unexposed silver salts from developed film to prevent further action of light on the film.

Fixing Tank   Container that holds fixing solution.

Flatbed Printer   See "Contact Printer."

Floating Lid   Lid that floats on surface of processing solution in tank to minimize oxidation of chemicals by the atmosphere.

Flow Camera   Instrument that moves photographs, documents, and so on, in conjunction with the film for continuous photographic reproduction.

Fluorescent Light   Primarily a mercury vapor lamp with a coating of phosphor which emits light when reacting with ultraviolet light from the mercury discharge.

Fog   Density in nonimage portion of a photo.

Format   Arrangement of information on drawings.

Frame A single image in a strip of film.

Freehand Drafting Drafting without straightedge tools or with minimal use of tools. Used most often for construction details. Frequently done in combination with photoreduction so that original, freehand-sketched drawings end up looking tool-drafted in the reduced-sized image.

Gelatin The substance in which light-sensitive salts are suspended in photographic emulsions.

Generation Each consecutive stage in photographic or diazo reproduction from original copy.

Ghost Low-density image or background tone on a reproduction. Unwanted image remaining after erasure or eradication.

Ground-Glass Screen Finely ground glass in camera for focusing on the image.

Half-Size Prints Working drawing sheets that are one-half what might be considered normal size, such as 12″ × 18″ instead of 24″ × 36″. Most offset-printed working drawings are reduced-size for convenience in printing.

Halftone Printing with dots to break up a photoimage into gradations from white to black. Halftone screens are used for photographs with continuous tones. Line screens or tints are used for line work or strictly black and white, nontonal work such as working drawings.

Horizontal Enlarger Enlarger that projects image horizontally rather than vertically, often for making larger enlargements and photomurals.

Hypo Fixer solution used to remove unexposed silver halides from silver emulsion film. Ammonium or sodium thiosulfate.

Intermediate Transparent or translucent reproduction that can in turn be used to make reproductions. Also called reproducible, second original.

Internegative Negative used as an intermediate stage in photographic reproduction.

Interpositive Positive used as an intermediate stage in photographic reproduction.

Keynoting The use of a list of numbered identification notes beside a drawing that refers to numbers keyed to different parts of the drawing. It's a method of avoiding hand-lettered notation, since the block of keynotes can conveniently be typewritten.

Lamp Refers to the lighting used in a reprographic studio to illuminate the front and/or back of original copy that's mounted on the copyboard or vacuum frame. Different lamps emphasize different portions of the spectrum. See Carbon Arc, Mercury Vapor Lamp, Metal Halide Lamp, Pulsed Xenon Lamp, and Tungsten/Quartz Lamp.

Lateral Reversal (Mirror Image) Image reversed left to right.

Latitude Range of exposure and processing conditions over which photographic materials still produce acceptable images.

Letterpress Printing process where the ink-bearing area is raised above the nonprinting area.

Light Integrator Adjusts reprographic light exposures to compensate for changes in light intensities caused by line-voltage fluctuations and other varying conditions.

Line Refers to straight black-and-white reprographic work without gradation of tone.

Line Material High-contrast photographic material used in reproducing drawings, prints, etc.

Lithography Printing process from a plane surface based on mutual repulsion of water and grease.

Lofting Process of producing full-size templates of complex sectional cuts of aircraft, automobile, or ship parts.

Mask Film transparency made by contact from a negative or positive to reduce or increase contrast or change color reproduction. A rectangular opening in a sheet of opaque material to cover edges of a negative or projected image to create a clear border. Prevents actinic light on copy.

Master Original copy for reproduction.

Matte A "tooth" or low-gloss surface on plastic film for drafting in pencil or ink.

Mechanical The graphic arts term for paste-up. Camera-ready copy assembled on a carrying sheet or board.

Mercury Vapor Lamp Ionizes mercury in a quartz envelope to produce a bluish green light. Most energy is in the blue, violet, and ultraviolet region. Efficient for exposing blue-sensitive emulsions and diazo materials.

Metal Halide Lamp A mercury lamp with metal halide additives. It is flexible in use and allows relatively short exposure times. One type is specifically for diazo exposures.

Microfiche A 3″ × 5″ or 4″ × 6″ sheet of microfilm with a group of photo images.

Microfilm Film for miniaturized photo storage of drawings and documents (16mm, 35mm, 70mm, 105mm).

Microfilm Reader Type of projector that enlarges microfilm negatives to a readable size.

Moist-Erasable Film A polyester film reproducible that can be erased with a moistened eraser.

Monitor In photography, to check the activity of a processing solution using control strips and standard references.

Mosaic Aerial photographs arranged to represent the total terrain.

Multiple Exposure Two or more exposures made by either contact or projection.

Mylar DuPont's registered trade name for polyester film.

Negative Dark and light reversal of an original image.

Negative Processing Processing negatives manually or with a machine.

Nonreproducible Visible images not reproduced in photo, diazo, or blueprint processes, usually blue in color, such as grid lines.

Offset The most common mass-printing system. Photonegatives transfer the original image onto light-sensitive, thin printing plates. A printing plate, mounted on a rotating cylinder, transfers the inked image to paper or film as it passes through the printing press. Offset, also called multilith, litho, or multigraph, provides the cleanest and sharpest working drawing prints possible. Multicolor printing is achieved through offset by repassing sheets through the printing press with different printing plates and different colored inks.

Opaque Nontransparent material that blocks out areas in a reproduction process so that actinic light cannot penetrate.

Orthochromatic Sensitive to ultraviolet light and all colors except red.

Overlay Drafting A method of retaining repeat information common to two or more drawings on a printed base sheet instead of redrawing it. Information that's unique to a drawing is prepared on overlay sheets. Later, images from base and overlay sheets are merged and printed on new "overlay and base composite" sheets. The most common use of overlay is the printing of basic floor plan construction information on base sheets which are used as underlays by consultants when drawing their particularized structural, electrical, and plumbing information. Also called registration drafting and pin-registration drafting.

Panchromatic Sensitive to all visible colors and ultraviolet radiation.

Paste-Up An assembly of graphics—drawing, text, photo, etc.—adhered to a carrying sheet. In graphic arts, a paste-up prepared as final copy to be photographed is called a mechanical. Paste-up is basic to composite drafting, but specific techniques in doing design drawing or working drawing composites are quite different from those used by graphic artists.

Photodrafting Techniques for getting literal photographic images onto drafting media for reference or for modifications. The word formerly was used as a general name for all reprographic techniques.

Photogrammetry Making maps using photographic techniques.

Photopolymer Chemical compound whose properties react to light.

Photoreproduction Use of photographic techniques to copy information.

Photostat Inexpensive technique for getting enlarged, reduced, or same-size photocopies made directly as positive prints on special paper.

Pica Printing measurement; about ⅙″.

Pin Bar Bar with brass pins that holds sheets of film in registration.

Planetary Camera Microfilm camera in which the document being photographed and the film are stationary during the exposure.

Plate Metal, plastic, or paper sheet bearing a fixed inked-in image to be reproduced on another material, usually paper, by offset printing.

Plotter Computerized drafting device. In photogrammetry, a device used to draw contour maps.

Polyester Plastic film sheets, durable and dimensionally stable, used for drafting and reproduction media. Commonly called by its DuPont trade name Mylar. Polyester sheets are available with matte surface for drafting, as clear transparent sheets, as photosensitive material (with and without matte surfaces), and as diazo-print material (with and without matte surfaces).

Positive Photographic or diazo reproductions with light and dark areas the same as originals.

Print-Back Direct-reading print from reverse-reading intermediate.

Printed Circuit Electrical wiring board photographically created.

Printing Speed Feet per minute rate of exposure of reproduction materials.

Process Camera The large negative camera used for reprographic photography. Also called a copy camera and, when able to project images back to light-sensitive media, called a blowback or projector camera.

Processing Series of steps consisting of developing, fixing, washing, and drying to make latent images visible. Most repro processing is done with automatic equipment.

Projector Camera See "Blowback Camera", "Copy Camera."

Proof A test print of text and/or graphics as it is to look in final printing. Proofs are made before printing for a final check for corrections or revisions.

Pulsed Xenon Lamp A vacuum-frame light with high and constant-color temperature and a spectral output similar to sunlight. Relatively low blue and ultraviolet output.

Reader Projection device for viewing microfilm images.

Reader Printer Microfilm viewer that can produce hard copies of selected frames.

Reflex Printing Contact printing of opaque originals.

Reflex Reproduction Technique and photographic material for making same-size positive prints on a contact printer from opaque instead of translucent originals.

Registration Bar Same as Pin Bar.

Registration Marks Marks to guide correct alignment of base and overlay sheets.

Reproducible Photo or diazo translucent vellum or polyester print that can be reproduced via diazo to make another print. Also called second original, intermediate, or transparency.

Reprographics The whole range of graphic work that can be done through photographic and other reproduction methods to replace hand graphics and drafting. Most of what used to be called blueprinting shops are now called reprographic services.

Resolution Measure of sharpness of image, expressed as the number of lines per millimeter visible.

Restoration Photographic repair of damaged drawings to make new reproducibles.

Reverse Printing in which type or illustrations appear as white on black.

Reverse Reading Lateral reversal where images are transposed left to right.

Right Reading Image that can be read from emulsion side.

Roll-to-Roll Printer Machine that produces duplicates of microfilm by contact printing.

Rotary Camera Microfilm camera that photographs documents while they're in motion.

Rubylith Red light–safe stripping film. It photographs as black and is used as a mask to allow color to be added to particular areas.

Rule Line.

Scale The range of gray densities in a specified range of exposures.

Scaling Selecting a portion of a photograph to be changed to a specified size.

Scissors Drafting Same as paste-up or composite drafting. Also refers to cutting out unwanted portions of a drawing to create a "window" for fitting in a new portion of drawing.

Screened Print In Systems Drafting, a final print that shows background or reference information in subdued image by breaking line work into small dot patterns. Also called shadow print, ghost, subordinate, or phantom image.

Scribe Film Opaque coating on a drafting medium that allows lines to be cut with a stylus.

Second Original Direct-reading intermediate print to replace original drawing. Same as reproducible.

Sepia Brown-like diazo reproducible on vellum or plastic film. Sepia reproducibles are preferred over black-line reproducibles because the sepia line is opaque to ultraviolet light and prints better in the diazo process.

Shadow Print A grayed or subordinated background image. Same as screened print.

Silver Film Film coated with silver halide emulsion.

Silver Halide Compound of silver and a halogen (chlorine, bromine, iodine, fluorine) that is light-sensitive.

Slick A smooth surface clear film transparency.

Sodium Thiosulfate Hypo, the primary element in photo-fixing baths. (Another agent is ammonium thiosulfate.)

Spectral Sensitivity Response of photographic emulsions to electromagnetic wavelengths.

Spotting Removing spots from prints or negatives.

Stabilization Processing Quick processing method where silver halides remaining in the material after development are not removed, but converted to stable compounds.

Static Electrical charges due to friction when film is handled in a dry atmosphere. Humidity above 40% alleviates problem. Light from static creates marks on the film or photo paper.

Step and Repeat Camera Microfilm camera that photographs separate images on an area of film according to a fixed pattern, such as rows or columns.

Stickyback Thin acetate or polyester film with adhesive on one surface.

Still Development Technique in which film is agitated for only the first 15 seconds of developing time to produce fine lines.

Stop Bath Rinse bath that stops development.

Stripping Cutting and placing a negative in a mask or combining it with another negative.

Sulfurized Image Brown stain on photographic film as a result of improper fixing.

Systems Drafting The reduction or elimination of hand drawing in the creation of construction documents. Includes use of appliques, typewritten notation, keynoting, freehand drafting, and composite and overlay drafting.

Tint A dot pattern that reproduces as one tone. Screen that creates subordinate image on photoreproductions.

Tint Screen Use of equal-sized dots in place of solid lines to reduce intensity of line weights. The greater the percentage (10%–100%), the more dense the line, with 100% a solid line. Usual line-per-inch rulings are 85, 120, 133, 150.

Tooth Surface on plastic film for drafting, a matte.

Transilluminated Backlighting of the copyboard so light shines through the copy to be photographed instead of just being reflected from it.

Translucent Admits diffused light.

Transmission Percent of light that passes through a medium.

Transparency Color or monochrome photographic positive print on transparent film.

Tungsten/Quartz Lamps Used for copyboard illumination, mainly black-and-white work, and for small vacuum frames for film contact printing. Low ultraviolet output makes this light impractical for plate or diazo work.

Turnaround Time. Period of time it takes to process an original drawing through reproduction and back to the drafting table.

Vacuum Back Suction device that holds film in a process camera.

Vacuum Board Copyboard that holds material in place by suction.

Vacuum Frame Suction device to press copy and reproduction material tightly together. Sometimes the word is used to mean the same as flatbed printer, exposure unit, or contact printer.

Vellum Translucent paper used for original drawings and as a base for sepia diazo reproducibles.

Vertical Copy Camera Copy camera with horizontal copyboard device where either the camera or board travels vertically.

View Camera Large-format camera, usually mounted on a tripod, for commercial photography.

Washing Tank Tank for washing residual processing chemicals from photographic materials.

Washoff Photosensitive emulsion that hardens upon exposure to light and subsequent chemical development. In processing, the unexposed and unhardened areas are washed off. The final image is moist-erasable.

White Print See "Diazo."

Working Drawings The plans, elevations, sections, details, schedules, and notes that tell bidders and contractors how to put construction together. Drawings usually show identities, sizes, shapes, and locations. Exact names of products and characteristics of materials are reserved for written specifications.

Wrong Reading See Reverse Reading

Xenon One of several rare gases having high luminous efficiency. Used in gas discharge lamps.

Xerography Technique of copying images through an electrically charged latent image made visible with powders.

Xerox 1860 Copier with six printing selections that enables the making of reductions in several reduction percentages.

Zipatone Graphic patterns on thin transparent sticky back films.

RESOURCES

**Important Notice on
Update Information on Systems Drafting**

New developments in the field of Systems Drafting require a continuous update on sources of information and products. We're offering an annual supplement on the latest sources to keep readers up to date. To receive the current supplement, please send $2.00 per copy to: *Reprographic Resources Guide,* Guidelines, Box 456, Orinda, CA 94563.

INDEX